T0140680

The Past Web

Daniel Gomes • Elena Demidova • Jane Winters •
Thomas Risse

Editors

The Past Web

Exploring Web Archives

 Springer

Editors
Daniel Gomes
Fundação para a Ciência e a Tecnologia
Lisbon, Portugal

Elena Demidova
Data Science & Intelligent Systems
Computer Science Institute
University of Bonn
Bonn, Germany

L3S Research Center
Leibniz University Hannover
Hannover, Germany

Jane Winters
School of Advanced Study
University of London
London, UK

Thomas Risse
University Library J. C. Senckenberg
Goethe University Frankfurt
Frankfurt am Main, Germany

ISBN 978-3-030-63293-9   ISBN 978-3-030-63291-5   (eBook)
https://doi.org/10.1007/978-3-030-63291-5

This Springer imprint is published by the registered company Springer Nature Switzerland AG.
The registered company address is: Gewerbestrasse 11, 6330 Cham, Switzerland

This book is dedicated to Vitalino Gomes who taught me that the value of a Man is in his Integrity.
—*Daniel Gomes*

Foreword: Web Archiving Comes of Age

Many people do not know that the Web is being archived, not to mention that such work has been ongoing for 25 years. This book exemplifies the growing maturity of web archiving, arguing for consideration of the Web, and the burgeoning collections of web archives, as foundational sources of cultural memory. At the same time, it claims that web archiving is peculiar, given that the new medium is exceptional. It thereby exposes an interesting tension, arising from the institutionalisation and domestication of new media. Web archiving is becoming enfolded into the traditions of archival culture, yet it seeks to maintain itself as a novel digital culture.

Is the Web losing its content forever, and how to consider the value of that loss? Among the points of departure in answering that question, as Daniela Major and Daniel Gomes take up, is to consider that the Web is by far the largest information source to date, and like other media that came before it, such as film, the losses of the earliest material but also more recent contributions are significant. Another way to consider the question is through a term like "link rot" that captures how webs of surfable writing and references decay as sites are updated, disappear or are replaced by hosting companies' placeholder pages. Although much website visiting these days is habitual or via search, with link decay, one can no longer "surf" the Web as hypertext when appreciable percentages of its documents have become unlinked. Rather than only rot, here the study of what one could call "web maintenance" becomes of interest. Web archives perform that humble task.

Web archives have "curatorial effects", as Paul Koerbin points out in his discussion of the Australian national web archive. One manner of thinking through curatorial effects would be to consider how some institutions see and subsequently demarcate the Web for archiving. It also introduces inevitable discussions of bias, together with efforts to redress or defend them. For the original Internet Archive project, the Web was always cyberspace, and the collection strategy was to preserve "everything". The goal would be to enable its eventual users to "time travel" and "surf the Web as it was". For the Australian national library (and other national archiving institutions), the Web is rather a national space, often demarcated by the top-level country domain, .AU in this case. The effect is to preserve a national Web, and consider it part of "national documentary heritage". In their Trove system to access the content, by default one searches the historical Web next to historical newspapers, magazines, etc., thereby demonstrating how the Web is made a part of Australian documentary heritage, rather than, say, a global village or Tower of Babel, as early Web or "new media" ideology had it.

A less obvious curatorial effect that is mentioned is how national web archives, as more archive than Web, are not indexed by (commercial) search engines, thereby (among other things) showing sensitivity to copyright and privacy concerns. Here, it is worthwhile to recall that web content has long been considered not just ephemeral but also long-lasting. It seems like a contradiction, but it is not when taking into account both archival policies and rights written into European legislation. The EU's "right to be forgotten" and its implementation by Google's (regional) web search remind us of how content may abide despite certain individuals' desire for it to vanish. Similarly, archives may have content some would prefer to no longer exist, but more than a simple Google search is required to find it. On a related note, the Australian system also "push[es] possible offensive content down the results rankings".

Web archiving is rather technical. When one searches for academic articles on the subject matter, the majority is technical rather than theoretical or historical, such as accounts of the fruits of their use, though that is changing. One particularly interesting development, reported by Elena Demidova and Thomas Risse, is that crawlers, deployed to date to scrape and archive the Web, are now being employed inside web archives themselves to make sub-collections. There is also continued work on how to simultaneously crawl or search multiple web archives, one of which is known as the Memento interoperability protocol. Technically and substantively, it is a remarkable breakthrough for scholars and others to be able to create at will sub-collections of websites from multiple archival sources, be they for events (and cross-cultural comparison of their impact), as is discussed, or other memorable materials. It also opens up the prospects of viewing web archives not as just media to be "accessed" by users but as data for scientific computing, as Helge Holzmann and Wolfgang Nejdl remind us.

Questions of the (creative) use of web archives as well as how to address their under-utilisation have been long-standing themes in web archiving theory, as have rejoinders concerning how well their study is coming along. Here, anew, are some robust demonstrations of how to work creatively with web archives, such as recreating a web sphere from a particular period of time, as Peter Webster demonstrates, undertaking a full-scale, longitudinal study of the development of a national Web (Janne Nielsen's contribution) and tracing version histories (and thus biographies) of apps from web archives (Anne Helmond and Fernando van der Vlist's contribution). Having observed a maturing of web archive studies, Anat Ben-David argues that its scholarship should not become complacent, "normal science" but continue to remain in its "revolutionary" phase, to put it in terms deployed by the philosopher of science, Thomas Kuhn. To that end, she calls for continued, critical deconstruction work, e.g., on why one URL and not another has been archived and the historiographical effects on the record of one's inclusion and another's exclusion, a point also raised in the chapter by Saskia Huc-Hepher and Naomi Wells.

Finally, two signs of a maturing field are the discussions of nearly 25 years of web archiving practice as well as calls, made by Niels Brügger and others, for a stable web archiving research infrastructure—one that still can support such innovative tools under construction as those reported here including timeline-makers, throwback browser environments and big data analytics.

There is also a specificity to web archives that, to the pioneering Julien Masanès, cannot be retrofitted to exist easily within existing cultural memory and heritage institutions, in a way reintroducing the exceptionalism of "new media". There is also an argument to be made about the constraints and redundancies of multiple national libraries web archiving up to the border of the one next door. The big thinking with which the volume concludes—"the future of the past Web"—ranges from the services that archives could provide to supporting open access to web-archived material, perhaps adjoining web archives to the open access movement. It concludes, though, as it began with a call to recognise the weighty importance of online information, how a changing Web is affecting the capacity to archive it and the need for sustained institutional growth. Rather than established, web archives still exhibit fragility and require care. The book demonstrates the worthiness of providing it.

Media Studies, University of Amsterdam   Richard Rogers
Amsterdam, The Netherlands

Preface

Before the digital era, societies were organised based on the assumption of information scarcity. Consulting printed publications, such as books, frequently required long and expensive journeys, and they were unreachable to most of the world's population. The Internet radically changed this societal paradigm as most information produced worldwide became accessible at the distance of one click. Humanity shifted from a paradigm of information scarcity to information abundance (or even overload). However, a new problem arose: memory scarcity. Just as a common belief that "everything is online" was becoming widespread, it became hard to access information published in the recent past.

Never before in the history of humankind has so much information been produced, so much information been so widely available and so much information been irreparably lost forever. However, the aforementioned observation may no longer be valid as you are reading this book: a premise of science is that scientific knowledge must be verifiable and updated if necessary. Therefore, we invite you to conduct the following experiment: try to find information about an event of your interest published today. Then, try to access information about similar events published 1, 10 and 20 years ago. Did you have any trouble? If so, this book was written for you.

In the early 2000s, Julien Masanès organised the first web archiving meetings named the International Web Archiving Workshops. At the time we were just a handful of people, mostly librarians who knew about the importance of preserving the information being published online but did not know how to go about doing it, and computer geeks who, despite their technical skills, did not know why it was necessary. The use cases for web archives were mostly speculative and poorly documented. About two decades later the situation has changed. There are web archiving initiatives spread all over the world, with all kinds of users and sound scientific studies that have relied on web archives as their primary source of data. Web archiving activities have engaged social scientists, computer scientists, IT professionals, librarians and historians. The web archiving community is widespread.

This book aims to promote web archives as broadly accessible research infrastructures to citizens, scholars and scientists. It aims to provide an initial context for newcomers to web archiving and, at the same time, share inspiring examples of the innovative use of web archives with experts in the field. The level of technical complexity may vary across the parts of this book, as some will provide overviews while others will include more detailed information for specialists.

Our motivation to write this book was to provide an answer to the question: "I am new to web archiving, where do I start?" Start by reading this book. This is a real need felt by web archiving institutions when they have to train and integrate new team members or provide an introduction about their activities to external partners. Note that despite its manifest relevance in the digital era, web archiving is not currently taught as a dedicated course in any university of the world. We believe that one reason for this failure to address web archives in teaching and training is that there are no adequate books published to support professors who would like to introduce web archiving into their disciplines. This book aims to fill this gap and become an initial reference point for students and professionals from all areas of knowledge to introduce the subject of exploring online history through web archives. This book introduces available services provided by web archiving activities and shares inspiring examples of their usage in research or societal contexts. Its content is potentially interesting to a broad range of research areas such as digital humanities, social sciences, history, media studies and information or computer science.

We aimed to move away from the idea of a "book for web archivists". It is broadly targeted at all web users who have an interest in the past. We hope that this book will become broadly used and will contribute to raising awareness about the importance of preserving and exploring humanity's digital heritage. It provides practical information about web archives, offers inspiring examples for web archivists and raises new challenges, but primarily shares everything that has been done in recent years using the existing access methods to explore information from the past preserved by web archives. The web archiving community must continue to disseminate knowledge and practice until web preservation becomes a common awareness.

Book Structure

In the following chapters, we will highlight some web archiving initiatives and services available to explore the past Web.

Part I promotes the importance of web archives to preserve our collective memory in the digital era and address the problem of web ephemera.

Part II focuses on different strategies for selecting web content to be preserved and on the media types that different web archives host. It provides an overview of efforts to address the preservation of World Wide Web content but also to create smaller-scale but high-quality collections targeted at social media or audiovisual content.

Part III presents examples of initiatives to improve access to archived web information so that its knowledge may be explored and unfolded for humankind. It provides an overview of access mechanisms for web archives designed to be used by humans or automatically accessed by machines.

Part IV focuses on presenting research use cases for web archives. Researchers value historical information as a necessary source of knowledge for their work, and they also use the Web as a primary source of information and means of communication. However, studying information published online many years ago is still an exceptional research method among scientists. This part discusses how to engage more researchers in using web archives and presents inspiring research studies performed through the exploration of web archives.

Part V focuses on demonstrating that web archives should become crucial infrastructures for modern connected societies. It makes the case for developing web archives for research purposes and presents several inspiring examples of added-value services built on web archives.

Part VI presents final reflections on the evolution of the Web and the sustainability of web archiving activities and the potential innovative use cases that may arise from processing and analysing large sets of historical web data. It debates the requirements and challenges for web archives so that they may assume the responsibility of becoming societal infrastructures that enable the preservation of memory.

Lisbon, Portugal   Daniel Gomes
Hannover, Germany   Elena Demidova
London, UK   Jane Winters
Frankfurt am Main, Germany   Thomas Risse

Acknowledgments

The Arquivo.pt web archive assumed the responsibility of preserving the content of the web links cited in this book so that these references may prevail valid over time. Thus, any broken link you may find cited in this book can be recovered from www.arquivo.pt. The YAKE! Keyword Extractor (http://yake.inesctec.pt/) was applied to help generate the Index of this book.

Contents

Part VI   A Look into the Future

Part I
The Era of Information Abundance and Memory Scarcity

Daniel Gomes

For thousands of years, information was a scarce commodity. In the fifteenth century, the printing press invented by Gutenberg hastened the widespread production and consumption of information in written format. The subsequent creation of libraries and archives enabled the aggregation and preservation of this documentation of human knowledge for current and future generations. However, for most humans, information remained a scarce commodity until the twentieth century because it was inaccessible. The majority of the human population could not read or travel to reach the locations where the required knowledge, documented through print, could be accessed. Imagine the feasibility of an American farmer in the nineteenth century traveling to European libraries to learn about the most suitable plants to grow. The Internet radically changed this paradigm. All kinds of information became accessible at the distance of one click, touch, or spoken question. Even the human cognitive and educational limitations that posed barriers to knowledge dissemination were overcome by using multiple and complementary communication modes based on audio, visual, written, or automatically translated media. People who cannot read, cannot travel, or cannot understand a foreign language can still access information in some sort of understandable and accessible format. Access to information no longer seems to be a barrier to attaining knowledge. "Every two days, we create as much information as we did from the dawn of civilization up until 2003" was stated by the former CEO of Google Eric Schmidt in 2010. Within a single generation, humanity has evolved from a situation of information scarcity to information abundance or even overload. However, how long will this vast and ever-growing amount of information remain accessible? In 2004, Ntoulas et al. observed that within a year, 80% of webpages changed their content or disappeared (Ntoulas, 2004). Most of this information is irreplaceable because it was exclusively published online. Digital resources published on the

D. Gomes
Fundação para a Ciência e a Tecnologia, Lisbon, Portugal
e-mail: daniel.gomes@fccn.pt

Web are extremely ephemeral. This study focused on web pages in 2004, but in the 2010s, information began to be widely disseminated by other digital means, such as social media platforms, which tend to be even more transient. History has taught that societies without memory collapse. We must look into the past to foresee the future so that we do not persist in repeating the same errors committed by previous generations. Knowledge must be built incrementally. However, humanity has never before produced so much information, never before has information been so widely accessible, and never before has so much information been irreparably lost. We live in the era of information abundance but memory scarcity. Besides losing important scientific and historical information, web transience means that most citizens are losing their personal reminders of the past. Consider, for instance, that every day people take photos and share them directly and exclusively on the Web without having the slightest concern for their preservation. As a consequence, many people will find it difficult in the future to show portraits of their families or photos of holidays long past.

Within merely a few decades, most information consumed by humankind has become born-digital and disseminated digitally mainly through the Web. But in the midst of this fast-paced revolution, somehow we are forgetting to preserve the information that we generate. The answers to most questions that arise in your everyday life are now answerable with one click:

- What are the main policies of your country's political parties?
- What are the main outputs of your most interesting project?
- Which are today's top news?

Now, try to answer the same questions above but shift them to just 10 years ago:

- What were the main proposals of your country's political parties 10 years ago?
- What were the main outputs of the project you worked on 10 years ago?
- Which were the top news 10 years ago?

What about 20 years ago? 30 years ago? Can you still find your answers with one click? Every current piece of information will inevitably become part of the past. What will happen to societies heavily dependent on online information that do not keep the record of their past? One may argue that the rise of a new communication medium is not a new problem and humanity has been able to address this issue in the past. The preservation of movies, for instance, was also disregarded in the early days of the Lumière brothers, and even in the decades afterward. The difference is that societies did not exclusively rely on movies to communicate. Modern societies in developed countries have come to rely almost exclusively on online information to perform most everyday tasks, such as disseminating news, providing education, trading products or managing multinational corporations and governments. But there is no way back; humankind has entered the digital era. The use of the Internet will continue to grow and become widespread within all aspects of society. The tremendously fast-paced penetration and widespread adoption of the Web, along with the change that it has driven, obliges us to move faster to tackle the preservation of the information disseminated through this communication medium than we did for cinema. Otherwise, we will become amnesiac societies. As historian George Santayana noted, "Those who cannot remember the past are condemned to repeat it."

This part introduces the problem of web ephemera to help readers understand the pressing need for web archiving initiatives that enable long-term access to web publications, especially those who are newcomers to web archiving and presents a brief history of web archiving by highlighting its main milestones for archiving different kinds of media and publications.

Reference

Ntoulas A, Cho J, Olston C (2004) What's new on the web?: the evolution of the web from a search engine perspective. In: WWW '04: Proceedings of the 13th international World Wide Web conference, New York, May 2004 https://dl.acm.org/doi/proceedings/10.1145/1013367

The Problem of Web Ephemera

Daniela Major

Abstract This chapter introduces the problem of web-data transience and its impact on modern societies.

Initial studies of the transience of online information presented general figures that demonstrated the prevalence of this problem on the Web (Douglis et al. 1997). In the early days of the Web, the main problem was one of link rot that degraded navigation across webpages. At that time, the information available on the Web was findable mainly through browsing across directories that listed URLs grouped by subject. Web users then had to browse pages by following links across them. There were no large-scale search engines or worldwide social networks of interconnected users who contribute with millions of content recommendations per second. The problem of Web ephemerality extended to science in a concerning way, as citations of scientific publications increasingly began to cite online resources (Zittrain et al. 2013). The Web has come to be used to publish important scientific information that complements published literature (e.g. datasets, documentation or software), but a few years after publication, the cited online information commonly disappears, causing a permanent loss of unique and valuable scientific information. This jeopardises the scientific value of official publications because the experiments described can no longer be reproduced and the secondary literature referenced can no longer be reread. In 2018, we can no longer address the Web as a homogeneous communication media. Link rot among citations to web resources varies because today the Web hosts very heterogeneous types of publications, from personal blogs to official governmental websites (Gomes and Silva 2006). However, the ephemerality of citations to web resources is prevalent across all types of printed and digital publications.

D. Major (✉)
School of Advanced Study, University of London, London, UK
e-mail: daniela.major@sas.ac.uk

© Springer Nature Switzerland AG 2021
D. Gomes et al. (eds.), *The Past Web*,
https://doi.org/10.1007/978-3-030-63291-5_1

1   Why Does Information Disappear from the Web?

In the early 1990s, when the World Wide Web was beginning to expand, an American technology entrepreneur, David Bohnett, founded a blogging and social communications platform named Geocities. It gave users the ability to create and publish online their own content. This content was organised by neighbourhoods, which were sections of the website dedicated to various themes. For example, the neighbourhood Athens was dedicated to writing, art and education. The Hollywood neighbourhood was focused on entertainment. Within each of these neighbourhoods, users could post text and images on personalised webpages or in the forums (Milligan 2019, p. 346). In 1999, Yahoo! bought Geocities. The changes that it introduced did not please users. It "scrapped the neighborhood structure", which was a hallmark of Geocities as it established a sense of community linked by shared interests and hobbies, and instead implemented username-based URLs (Milligan 2017). Yahoo! additionally enacted new copyright rules which allowed it to claim full ownership of all content posted by Geocities users (Napoli 1999). Although that measure was reversed, users started to leave the website. In 2001, Yahoo! introduced paid services that were meant to improve upon the existing Geocities experience. These included "storage, domain names [and] data transfer". Members who wanted to use Geocities for free would be able to do so, but they would be subjected to advertising (Schiffman 2001). As a result, users started to leave Geocities for other platforms. The user base decreased to the point that in 2009 the technological giant decided to close Geocities. This could well have resulted in the loss of all content produced had it not been for the intervention of a team of web archivists.

Another popular example is Quizilla, a website that allowed users to post their own quizzes and which was taken down in 2014. In the same year, Orkut, a social network owned by Google, was closed down, although Google kept a public archive. Posterous, a blogging platform bought by Twitter in 2012, was shut down in the following year (Holt 2013). The website AbsolutePunk, which by 2008 had more than 500,000 members and provided "one of the largest alternative music zines on the web", was closed down in 2016 (Kafka 2008). Other websites similarly closed down over the course of the past decade include Diplomacy Monitor, which tracked diplomatic and international affairs; *Feed Magazine*, one of the earliest online publications (Manjoo 2001); and Wiser.org a "kind of wikipedia of green and social justice groups" (Grover 2007).

The closure of websites commonly results in the loss of content. Flickr, recently bought by the photo-hosting service SmugMug, announced that free user accounts would be "limited to 1000 pictures on the photo sharing site, instead of the free 1 TB of storage that was previously offered". Users were notified to download any surplus images by February 2019, at which point "free accounts that are still over the limit will have their content actively deleted until they're back under 1000" (Gartenberg 2018).

There are, therefore, several explanations for the disappearance of content on the Web. Some changes occur when the companies that host services wish to make them more profitable; or conversely, such services may be taken down when it emerges that the models are not profitable after all. These decisions, as we have seen, are rather common and affect all major technological enterprises. However, online content can be produced by any individual with an Internet connection, which means that websites are liable to disappear for all sorts of reasons: lack of funding, as many site managers cannot support the long-term cost of maintenance; technical issues ranging from malfunctions to viruses or malware affecting the website; the server might be down; the URL might have been changed; the website might be undergoing reconstruction, which could result in a broken link, defined as "a web reference that for a variety of reasons will not lead to a valid or correct webpage" (Spinellis 2003). A study of the published material made available through the Digital Library of the ACM and the IEEE Computer Society showed that the half-life of links, that is, the "time required for half of all web citations in a publication to disintegrate" (Sife and Bernard 2013), is just 4 years after publication. This means that 4 years after a study is published, 50% of the links referenced are no longer accessible. In fact, only a year after publication, 20% of the links were no longer accessible, and the decay occurred at a steady rate of 10% in the next 3 years (Spinellis 2003). The disappearance of content online is a serious problem for future historians and for current researchers. If online content is vanishing, then primary sources of information are disappearing. Without them, many fields of research are impaired, such as digital humanities or social sciences. This means that the disappearance of websites referenced in scientific articles, dissertations and other academic work jeopardises the scientific validity of published results because they become irreproducible and unverifiable. One particular study, which examined the top six most-quoted scientific journals in the USA, concluded that between 4.6% and 9.6% of the links quoted ceased to work between 2 and 5 years after publication (Evangelou et al. 2005). Another study, by Alfred S. Sife and Ronald Bernard (2013) at Sokoine University, Tanzania, looked at the decay of web citations in theses and dissertations available at their university. They concluded that out of 1847 citations, a total of 862 were no longer accessible. On the one hand, these results indicate "that even in the most prestigious and visible journals, some scientific information may eventually become unavailable when it is supplied only online" (Evangelou et al. 2005), and on the other, "this lack of persistence of web references implies that the long term availability of online resources cannot be guaranteed" (Spinellis 2003).

Websites may also be closed because of political pressure. In certain parts of the world where free speech is curtailed, websites are often removed by government officials (Barone et al. 2015). Websites may also cease to exist because their original purpose has been rendered useless, for example official political campaign websites whose reason for existence is a specific moment in history which begins and ends at established dates.

2   Web Ephemera Jeopardises Human Knowledge

It is common to claim that once something is online, it is online forever (Fineman 2014). However, this saying is valid mainly for security reasons. It warns people to be careful about their online information as it can easily be stolen for criminal purposes or to damage someone's life or reputation. In fact, numbers show that online content is constantly disappearing. Research concerning a sample of websites demonstrated that 80% of them disappeared after a year (Ntoulas et al. 2004). Other studies suggest that 11% of social content disappears after a year, rising to nearly 30% over 2 years (Barone et al. 2015).

But why is the preservation of the Web so important? First, it is important to preserve data for the sake of keeping accurate historical records. If Donald Trump deletes his Twitter account tomorrow, a significant part of the history of his presidency would be lost. Web preservation also contributes to accountability. Despite President Trump deleting his famous "covfefe" tweet—an incomplete tweet probably published by accident, which initiated considerable online discussion as to its meaning—only a few hours after posting, it had already been archived by the Internet Archive (Trump 2017).

However, it is not only a matter of safeguarding historical heritage. More and more of our professional and personal lives take place online. It was estimated that in 2017 more data would be created "than [in] the previous 5000 years of humanity" (Harris, 2006). Furthermore, by 2013 "a full 90% of all data in the world" had "been generated over the last 2 years" (Dragland 2013). Governmental bodies, politicians, newspapers, television networks, academic journals and businesses all have an online presence. The Web contains company websites with all sorts of pertinent information. Companies such as Amazon or eBay sell their services exclusively online, which means that all of their information, from terms and conditions to shipping rates, is on the Web. Professional photographers keep samples of their work on websites for potential customers to peruse. Web designers keep their portfolios exclusively in an online format. More and more newspapers are reliant on their online editions. In fact, some news venues like BuzzFeed exist only in an online format. Scientific journals such as the *Medieval Review*, the *Journal of the American Association of Pharmaceutical Sciences* or the *Genetics Journal* are exclusively published online.

In 2017, the historian Yuval Noah Harari published the bestseller *Homo Deus— A Brief History of Tomorrow* (Harari 2017). The author explored the fingerprint of thousands of years of human evolution on the contemporary world in order to predict future trends: A conclusion that emerges is that the pace of evolution accelerated exponentially in recent decades. The book is provocative and frequently controversial but throughout Harari bases his discussions on evidence carefully documented through references. However, it is worth noting that 2 years after the publication of *Homo Deus*, 19 of the 125 referenced links were no longer valid (15%).

Over the years, several possible solutions have emerged to deal with these problems. One such is WebCite, a "service run by Professor Gunther Eysenbach at the University of Toronto", which "has been serving as a central repository for caching documents for medical journals and other sources for a number of years". Another proposed solution is Perma.cc, created by "a consortium of dozens of law school libraries, as well as nonprofit entities such as the Internet Archive and Digital Public Library of America". Perma.cc "uses the citation process itself as a solution to link rot. As the author cites the material, the author can provide a link to Perma, and the Perma server will save a copy of the information relevant to the citation" (Zittrain et al. 2013).

However, these solutions are designed to address very specific fields of research, and furthermore, they count on the cooperation of authors, who, in addition to writing and researching, would have to curate the links they are using. The easiest and most viable solution, then, seems to be the use of web archiving initiatives that have accompanied the development and growth of the Web.

References

Barone F, Zeitlyn D, Mayer-Schönberger V (2015) Learning from failure: the case of the disappearing web site. First Monday 20(5). https://firstmonday.org/article/view/5852/4456

Douglis F, Feldmann A Krishnamurthy B, Mogul JC (1997) Rate of change and other metrics: a live study of the world wide web. USENIX Symposium on Internet Technologies and Systems. Available at: https://www.usenix.org/legacy/publications/library/proceedings/usits97/full_papers/duska/duska_html/duska.html

Dragland A (2013) Big data, for better or worse: 90% of world's data generated over last two years. Science Daily. Available at: https://www.sciencedaily.com/releases/2013/05/130522085217.htm. Accessed on 22 May 2020

Evangelou E, Trikalinos TA, Ioannidis JP (2005) Unavailability of online supplementary scientific information from articles published in major journals. FASEB J 19(14):1943–1944

Fineman (2014) What we post online is forever, and we need a reminder, Inc. 24 November. Available at: https://www.inc.com/meredith-fineman/what-we-post-online-is-forever-and-we-need-a-reminder.html

Gartenberg C (2018) Flick will end 1TB of free storage and limit free users to 1,000 photos, The Verge. Available at: https://www.theverge.com/2018/11/1/18051950/flickr-1000-photo-limit-free-accounts-changes-pro-subscription-smugmug. Accessed on 1 November 2020

Gomes D, Silva M (2006) Modelling information persistence on the web. ICWE '06: Proceedings of the 6th international conference on Web engineering. New York: Association for Computing Machinery. Available at: http://citeseerx.ist.psu.edu/viewdoc/download?doi=10.1.1.66.7773&rep=rep1&type=pdf

Grover S (2007) WISER Earth: user created directory of the "Largest Movement On Earth", Tree Hunger. Available at: https://www.treehugger.com/culture/wiser-earth-user-created-directory-of-the-largest-movement-on-earth.html. Accessed on 21 June 2020

Harari YN (2017) Homo Deus: a brief history of tomorrow. Harper Collins, New York

Holt K (2013) Archive Team races to preserve Posterous before it goes dark. Daily Dot. Available at: https://www.dailydot.com/news/archive-team-preserving-posterous/. Accessed on 13 March

Kafka P (2008) Buzz net still buying music sites, adds absolute punk. Business Insider. Available at: https://www.businessinsider.com.au/buzznet-still-buying-music-sites-adds-absolute-punk-2008-5. Accessed on 6 May 2020

Manjoo F (2001) Salon: last one standing. Wired. Available at: https://www.wired.com/2001/06/salon-last-one-standing/?currentPage=all. Accessed on 15 June 2020

Milligan I (2017) Welcome to the web. In: Brugger and Schroeder (eds) The Web as history, pp. 197–215

Milligan I (2019) Exploring web archives in the age of abundance. In: Brügger N, Milligan I (eds) The Sage handbook of web history. SAGE, London

Napoli L (1999) Yahoo angers Geo Cities members with copyright rules. The New York Times. Available at: https://archive.nytimes.com/www.nytimes.com/library/tech/99/07/cyber/articles/01yahoo.html. Accessed on 30 June 2020

Ntoulas A, Cho J, Olston C (2004) What's new on the web?: the evolution of the web from a search engine perspective. In: WWW '04: Proceedings of the 13th international World Wide Web conference, New York, May 2004. https://dl.acm.org/doi/proceedings/10.1145/1013367

Schiffman B (2001) A community that stays together, pays together. Forbes. Available at: https://www.forbes.com/2001/08/28/0828yahoo.html#1e39a72c1da3. Accessed on 28 August

Sife AS, Bernard R (2013) Persistence and decay of web citations used in theses and dissertations available at the Sokoine National Agricultural Library, Tanzania. Int J Educ Devel Inform Commun Technol (IJEDICT) 9(2):85–94

Spinellis D (2003) The decay and failure of web references. Commun ACM:46(1). Available at: https://www2.dmst.aueb.gr/dds/pubs/jrnl/2003-CACM-URLcite/html/urlcite.html

Trump D (2017) Twitter. Available at: https://web.archive.org/web/20170531040626/https:/twitter.com/realDonaldTrump/status/869766994899468288. Accessed on 30 May 2020

Zittrain J, Albert K, Lessig L (2013) Perma: scoping and addressing the problem of link and reference rot in legal citations. Harvard Public Law Working Paper 13(42). https://harvardlawreview.org/2014/03/perma-scoping-and-addressing-the-problem-of-link-and-reference-rot-in-legal-citations/

Web Archives Preserve Our Digital Collective Memory

Daniela Major and Daniel Gomes

Abstract This chapter discusses the importance of web archiving, briefly presents its history from the beginning with the Internet Archive in 1996 and exposes the challenges with archiving certain types of online data.

Contemporary generations have the responsibility of preserving current information for future ones, in the same way that previous generations have contributed their knowledge legacy to us. But is it possible to provide a meaningful description of our current times for future generations that ignores web heritage? Most web authors do not have either the resources nor the awareness to preserve their digital works. The mission of web archives is to provide web authors with the right to be remembered. In 1996, Brewster Kahle initiated the Internet Archive, which aimed to preserve the information on the pages published through a new technology named the World Wide Web. Fortunately, many other initiatives with the same objective followed around the world. Web archives collect and preserve information published online, so that it can be consulted after it is no longer available on its original websites. They contribute to solving numerous everyday problems, for example web users coming across broken links; journalists looking for past information to reference in articles; software engineers searching for technical manuals to fix legacy systems; webmasters recovering past versions of their sites' pages; historians searching for web documents describing past events; or researchers looking for related work published open-access. In general, all the use cases existing for the current Web are applicable to the past Web when we adopt a historical perspective, because all current information used today will one day be part of the past. Use cases such as longitudinal studies of sociological events like political trends or the

D. Major (✉)
School of Advanced Study, University of London, London, UK
e-mail: daniela.major@sas.ac.uk

D. Gomes
Fundação para a Ciência e a Tecnologia, Lisbon, Portugal
e-mail: daniel.gomes@fccn.pt

© Springer Nature Switzerland AG 2021
D. Gomes et al. (eds.), *The Past Web*,
https://doi.org/10.1007/978-3-030-63291-5_2

evolution of media communication come to mind. However, other use cases may not be so obvious. For instance, web archives can contribute to the prevention of terrorist attacks. Terrorists' communications have been shared using the public Web, through special code keywords and nicknames, so that anyone interested in their actions could easily find information. There are people interested in terrorist organisations who are not yet active—they are called *hobbyists*. However, terrorist organisations incrementally incite them to perform more incisive actions. The probability of a hobbyist becoming violent increases with time. A hobbyist with a given nickname active on the Web for several years is potentially more dangerous than a newcomer. If the hobbyist's publications present indications of different geographical locations across time, this could also be an alert indicator. Web platforms evolve but terrorists leave online traces among them over time which can be tracked to measure their level of engagement and dangerousness. This historical analysis can only be performed by security agencies through web archives. Focused web archives for national security or counterterrorism that collect information from the dark Web are important tools to ensure security. Maybe they already exist; or maybe this awareness has not reached security agencies and governments yet.

1   Word Wide Web Archiving

Web archives are crucial for preserving information published on the Web and making it reusable in the future. Since 1996, several web archiving initiatives have been created around the world. In 2020, there were at least 94 web archiving initiatives (Wikipedia 2020). Web archives worldwide host at least 981 billion web pages, which are stored on 29 petabytes of disk space. This volume of data will continue to grow as they acquire information incrementally to build their historical collections documenting the past Web. In 2006, Julien Masanès edited the book *Web Archiving*, which was a major milestone in establishing the preservation of the Web as a scientific and professional field (Masanès 2006). Since 2006, a lot has changed in the world and in the area of web archiving. In the early 2000s, web archiving was an effort pursued mainly by librarians and a few computer scientists. The challenges focused mainly on how to collect information from the Web and store it. During the 2010s, all kinds of professionals became involved in web archiving activities. The web archiving community was widespread and engaged social scientists, data scientists, IT professionals, librarians and historians. In this new decade, collecting and storing web data remains an essential and demanding task, but the main challenges today concern how to provide efficient access so that the stored web data can be effectively preserved. There is no preservation without proper access methods. The professionals that work at cultural heritage organisations do not hold themselves the knowledge contained in the artefacts they preserve (e.g. books, paintings, songs or movies). Their mission has been to grant access to that knowledge so that it can be explored by suitable experts, students or citizens. The breakthrough of the digital era was to enable large-scale and low-cost access to knowledge through the widespread usage of the Web as it became a ubiquitous communication medium.

For the first time, "universal access to all knowledge" became an achievable goal for humankind. Web archives are gatekeepers that safeguard the collective memory of societies in the digital era. However, without providing open and efficient online tools for engaging with web archives, the precious historical artefacts that document the digital era are as inaccessible as books stored in distant monasteries during the Middle Ages. Knowledge exists but nobody can access it. It was with these principles in mind that organisations such as the International Internet Preservation Consortium (IIPC) and the Digital Preservation Coalition (DPC) were created. The IIPC was formally set up in 2003, sponsored by the Bibliothèque nationale de France, and now includes libraries, museums and cultural institutions in an effort to "acquire, preserve and make accessible knowledge and information from the Internet for future generations everywhere" (IIPC 2021, *about* ...). The DPC is a non-profit organisation which allows "members to deliver resilient long-term access to digital content and services, helping them to derive enduring value from digital assets" (Digital Preservation Coalition 2021a, b) and counts as members the British Library, Cambridge University Library, CERN, as well as universities or private companies such as banks.

2 A Brief History of Web Archiving

The first webpage was published on the Internet in 1990, although access to the Internet was only made available to the general public in the following year (World Wide Web Foundation 2021). Five years later, in 1996, the Internet Archive (IA) was founded by Brewster Kahle and Bruce Gilliat. Months earlier, Kahle and Gilliat had also founded Alexa Internet, a for-profit search engine that catalogued the Web and provided data about sites visited to a browser toolbar. Alexa then went into partnership with Microsoft and Netscape, so that it could have a presence in most desktop computers (Masanès 2006). Alexa contributed to the Internet Archive by taking snapshots of webpages and donating them to the IA, which then created collections (Morh et al. 2004). While initially the material archived was not publicly available, as the Internet grew in size and usage, it became clear that the next step was to make the content easily accessible. Consequently, the Wayback Machine service, which the IA had been using since 1996, was made public in 2001. To use the Wayback Machine, users simply insert the URL of a page into a search bar, and then, if the page has been archived, they are able to peruse all the old versions that have been captured along time. However, the crawler utilised to harvest the Web and provide the archived pages, the aforementioned Alexa, did not belong to the IA. It had been bought by Amazon in 1999. The IA needed to develop its own software and techniques to gather web data. Thus, a joint team of computer scientists at the IA and the Nordic national libraries developed the Heritrix software, "an open source, extensible web crawler" (IIPC 2017) whose purpose was to archive "websites and to support multiple different use cases including focused and broad crawling" (Lee et al. 2011). Web crawling is the process by which a software component automatically gathers information from the Web (Manning 2008).

Heritrix made it possible for the IA to enlarge the scope of the material archived, and the software could also be moulded to meet the needs of users. Alexa was mainly dedicated to indexing text, which is and continues to be the most common content on the Internet; it was only with Heritrix that the IA began systematically to archive the images contained in the websites they crawled and archived.

Web archiving may be defined as the process of "gathering up data that has been recorded on the World Wide Web, storing it, ensuring the data is preserved in an archive, and making the collected data available for future research" (Niu 2012). When Yahoo! announced the closure of Geocities in 2009, the IA and groups of independent web archivists such as the Archive Team (Archive Team 2021) worked together to save the site's content. This effort ensured that as early as 2010 a huge file of 652 GB was made available online, encompassing data from the now-defunct Geocities platform (Gilbertson 2010). Much of this content can today be accessed using the Wayback Machine, and it documents an important part of Internet history (Internet Archive 2009).

The concern to archive webpages is relatively new, but awareness is spreading. In 2015, a survey of academics from the social sciences and humanities in New Zealand universities found that 44% of correspondents had "at some point used some of the following international sources of web archives" (the list included the Internet Archive, the Library of Congress Web Archive and the UK Web Archive). Furthermore, a large majority of the correspondents stated they believed that "it is important for New Zealand websites and blogs to be archived", and half of those surveyed answered that the New Zealand Web Archive would be "important for their current research within the next 5 years" (Riley and Crookston 2015).

As of 2016, the indexed Web, that is, those websites indexed by major search engines such as Google and Bing, contained 4.75 billion websites. It is estimated that since 2012, the Web has doubled in size every year. It is further estimated that over 3 billion people use the Web worldwide (Fischer 2020). While it is not possible to archive all of the Web, web archives do manage to gather impressive amounts of information. According to the IA's website, the Web Archive Collection amounts to 330 billion webpages, 20 million books and texts, 4.5 million audio recordings, 4 million videos, 3 million images and 200,000 software programmes (Internet Archive 2021).

3   Archiving Online Social and Multimedia

The sheer variety of the material collected by web archives demonstrates that the Web is a medium that includes multiple content formats—text, images, videos, audio—but these have not been collected equally. A breakthrough came when it became possible to archive moving images, namely videos. Here the Institut national de l'audiovisuel (INA) has assumed a very important role. Established in 1975, INA had a mission to preserve the archives of existing radio and television channels. In 1992, together with the Bibliothèque nationale de France and the Centre national du cinéma et de l'image animée, INA became a legal repository of French audiovisual patrimony. Finally, in 2006, INA also became responsible for archiving a part of the Web. Its work focused on French websites, especially those that concerned web television and radio, radio and television websites, and institutional websites on the subject of communication and audiovisual media. Since 2008, INA has archived social media accounts whose prime medium of communication is video (INA 2021). INA is a very important initiative both for the scope of its content and for how accessible it is to ordinary users. However, it is not the only institution that is concerned with the archiving of moving images from the Web. Coca-Cola, a private corporation, has a web archive which, apart from containing "all Coca-Cola sites and other selected sites associated with Coca Cola", includes "social media and video" (Digital Preservation Coalition 2021a, b).

The development of web archives necessarily has to keep pace with the development of the Web. Many people use the Web, among other things, for social media. In 2018, around 2.62 billion people used social media platforms. In 2020, a global average of 49% of Internet users had some kind of social media presence (Clement 2020). Ever since the 2016 American presidential election, debate has been growing about the influence of social media on current events. It has become clear that social media produces large volumes of relevant information that concerns the general public. But who is archiving this information? The National Archives of the UK has an initiative to archive tweets from official government Twitter accounts, such as those from various governmental departments (National Archives 2021). INA also has incorporated tweets into its web archive, although they are not yet widely available for consultation as it is only possible to access the database from specific locations in France. Although recently abandoned (Bruns 2018), for several years the Library of Congress undertook a very ambitious project to archive all public Twitter data, with help from Twitter itself, which gave the Library of Congress access to its own archive (Stone 2010). With regard to Facebook pages, the IA and other web archives tend to keep a record of those made public. For instance, Donald Trump's Facebook page has been captured nearly every day since 2016 by the IA. Some additional social media is archived by Internet Archive such as the Instagram page of the photographer responsible for Humans of New York[1] or the Tumblr blog of the fiction writer Neil Gaiman.[2]

4   Cloud Web-Archiving and Crowdsourcing

An important, and relatively recent, development in web archiving is that it can be undertaken through cooperation between Internet users and institutions. Archive-It, for instance, is a collaboration between the IA and institutions all over the world,

---

[1] https://www.instagram.com/humansofny/?hl=en

[2] https://neil-gaiman.tumblr.com/

from state and university libraries, national archives and museums to governmental bodies. Archive-It helps these institutions to archive content considered important in exchange for a fee and then creates thematic collections which can be made accessible to everyone. For instance, the Human Rights Documentation Initiative, a collaboration between Archive-It and the University of Texas at Austin, features "fragile websites containing human rights documentation and related content from human rights organizations and advocates across the globe" which can be browsed by topic, geographic area, language or keyword search (Archive-it 2021). Furthermore, it is possible for an independent user to contribute to the archiving of webpages. When a user searches for a URL in the IA and the page cannot be found, the service automatically suggests that the user can add the missing page to the archive, which can be done by simply clicking on a link. In the case of Arquivo.pt., the Portuguese web-archive, users can suggest a website or a list of websites that they consider worth archiving by completing an online form. In 2016, Rhizome, an arts organisation that supports the preservation of new media art, launched Webrecorder, a free tool that allows users to create collections of recorded webpages, which they can then keep for themselves or share with others (Espenschied 2016). Webrecorder saves more than just a screenshot of the page; it saves all the associated links and images that are presented on a given page.

5   Preserving the Web: New Media, Same Problem

The issue of how to preserve new media formats is not novel. It is estimated that about 50% of the movies made before 1950 are irremediably lost; 90% of movies made in the USA before 1929 have completely disappeared (Film Foundation 2021); and 75% of American silent movies have been lost (Ohlheiser 2013). This means that a significant portion of film history has disappeared both because there was insufficient space to archive movies in the studios and because the material used to make the film—nitrate—deteriorated quickly without proper preservation. The cost of such preservation was often deemed too expensive. There were other causes for film destruction. In Europe, the First and Second World Wars contributed to the destruction of film. For instance, Bezhin Meadow, an unfinished movie by Sergei Eisenstein, was destroyed during the bombing of Moscow in the Second World War (Kenez 2001).

However, during the 1930s institutional attempts began to be made to try to preserve film. "Numerous departments for audiovisual media were set up within existing, well-established institutions" such as the Museum of Modern Art Film Library, the British Film Institute, the Cinemathèque Française and the Reichsfilmarchiv. In 1938, all of these came together to found the International Federation of Film Archives (FIAF). Its members were "committed to the rescue, collection, preservation, screening, and promotion of films, which are valued both as works of art and culture and as historical documents" through "the creation of moving image archives in countries which lack them" and the establishment of "a code of ethics for film preservation and practical standards for all areas of film archive work". As of May 2018, FIAF "comprises more than 166 institutions in 75 countries" (FIAF 2021).

Samewise to the archiving of the Web, archiving film was not considered of historical importance for decades. Awareness was slowly raised, and now it is universally believed that film ought to be preserved, not only to be viewed after its release but because of its cultural and social significance. The same can be said about the archiving of the Web, with the added knowledge that the Web is not only a medium of culture but has become an integral part of all aspects of our daily lives.

6 A Future of Open Challenges

Web archiving must keep up with the development of the Web. Video, for example, is currently a frequently used medium of content creation, but the majority of web archiving projects are still "unable to properly download and archive a YouTube video and preserve it for posterity as part of their core crawling activity" (Leetaru 2017). Much of the content that is produced on social media is locked away not only because many accounts are private but because in some cases logins are needed to access the websites. There is no easy solution to this problem, as privacy must be a concern for web archivists. There is also much content that is produced by online services such as Google Maps that are not currently being archived, as well as pages that use JavaScript, which some web archives are still unable to crawl.

In the early days of the Web, it became clear that acquiring and storing online information before it quickly vanished was a challenge. But it was a rather simple challenge in comparison with ensuring the accessibility of the stored web data over time. It is a naive common belief that everything is online, leading to the misleading conclusion that, if it is not online, it does not exist; or even more concerning, that it never happened. The tremendously fast pace at which the Internet has penetrated societies, without the development of proper digital preservation services, may actually have created an online amnesia about recent events. On the other hand, for the first time in the history of humankind, the technology exists to make information published in the past as accessible as the information about the present.

References

Archive Team (2021) Geocities. Archive Team. Available at: https://www.archiveteam.org/index.php?title=GeoCities. Accessed on 29 January 2021

Archive-it (2021) Human rights documentation initiative. Archive-it. Available at: https://archive-it.org/collections/1475. Accessed on 29 January 2021

Bruns A (2018) The library of congress twitter archive: a failure of historic proportions. Medium. Available at: https://medium.com/dmrc-at-large/the-library-of-congress-twitter-archive-a-failure-of-historic-proportions-6dc1c3bc9e2c. Accessed on 2 January 2021

Clement (2020) Number of social network users worldwide from 2010 to 2023. Statista. Available at: https://www.statista.com/statistics/278414/number-of-worldwide-social-network-users/. Accessed on 1 April 2020

Digital Preservation Coalition (2021a) About. Digital Preservation Coalition. Available at: https://www.dpconline.org/about. Accessed on 29 January 2021

Digital Preservation Coalition (2021b) Web-archiving. Digital Preservation Coalition. Available at: https://www.dpconline.org/handbook/content-specific-preservation/web-archiving. Accessed on 29 January 2021

Espenschied D (2016) Rhizome releases first public version of webrecorder. Rhizome. Available at: https://rhizome.org/editorial/2016/aug/09/rhizome-releases-first-public-version-of-webrecorder/. Accessed on 9 August 2020

FIAF-International Federation of Film Archives (2021) FIAF's Mission. FIAF. Availble at: https://www.fiafnet.org/pages/Community/Mission-FIAF.html. Accessed on 29 January 2021

Film Foundation (2021) About us-film preservation. The Film Foundation. Available at: https://web.archive.org/web/20130312021638/http://www.film-foundation.org/common/11004/aboutAboutUs.cfm?clientID=11004&sid=2&ssid=5. Accessed on 29 January 2021

Fischer T (2020) How big is the web? Lifewire. Available at: https://www.lifewire.com/how-big-is-the-web-4065573. Accessed on 15 January 2020

Gilbertson S (2010) Geocities lives on a massive torrent download. Wired. Available at: https://www.wired.com/2010/11/geocities-lives-on-as-massive-torrent-download/. Accessed on 1 November 2020

IIPC-International Internet Preservation Consortium (2017) Tools and Software. Git Hub. Available at: https://github.com/iipc/iipc.github.io/wiki/Tools-and-Software. Accessed on 29 January 2021

IIPC-International Internet Preservation Consortium (2021) About IIPC. Net-Preserve. Available at: http://netpreserve.org/about-us/. Accessed on 29 January 2021

INA (2021) Dépôt légal radio, télé et web. Institut national de l'audiovisuel. Available at: https://institut.ina.fr/institut/statut-missions/depot-legal-radio-tele-et-web. Accessed on 29 January 2021

Internet Archive (2009) Geocities special collection 2009. Internet Archive. Available at: https://archive.org/web/geocities.php. Accessed on 29 January 2021

Internet Archive (2021) About the Internet Archive. Internet Archive. Available at: https://archive.org/about/. Accessed on 29 January 2021

Kenez P (2001) A history of Bezhin meadow. In: LaValley AJ, Scherr BP (eds) Eisenstein at 100: a reconsideration. Rutgers University Press, New Jersey

Lee HB, Nazareno F, Jung SH, Cho WS (2011) A vertical search engine for school information based on Heritrix and Lucene. In: Lee G, Howard D, Ślęzak D (eds) Convergence and hybrid information technology. Springer, Berlin

Leetaru K (2017) Are web archives failing the modern web: video, social media, dynamic pages and the mobile web. Forbes. Available at: https://www.forbes.com/sites/kalevleetaru/2017/02/24/are-web-archives-failing-the-modern-web-video-social-media-dynamic-pages-and-the-mobile-web/#53a22d3845b1. Accessed on 24 February 2020

Manning CD, Raghavan P, Schutze H (2008) Introduction to information retrieval. Cambridge University Press, Cambridge

Masanès J (2006) Web archiving. Springer, New York

Mohr G, Kimpton M, Stack M, Ranitovic I (2004) Introduction to heritrix, an archival quality web crawler. In: Proceedings of the 4th International Web Archiving Workshop IWAW'04

National Archives (2021) Twitter archives. National archives-UK Government. Available at: https://webarchive.nationalarchives.gov.uk/twitter/. Accessed on 29 January 2021

Niu J (2012) An overview of web archiving. D-Lib Mag 18(3–4). Available at: http://www.dlib.org/dlib/march12/niu/03niu1.html

Ohlheiser A (2013) Most of America's silent films are lost forever. The Atlantic. Available at: https://www.theatlantic.com/culture/archive/2013/12/most-americas-silent-films-are-lost-forever/355775/. Accessed on 4 December 2020

Riley H, Crookston M (2015) Use of the NZ web archive: introduction and context. National Library of New Zealand. Available at: https://natlib.govt.nz/librarians/reports-and-research/use-of-the-nz-web-archive/introduction

Stone B (2010) Tweet preservation. Blog Twitter. Available at: https://blog.twitter.com/official/en_us/a/2010/tweet-preservation.html. Accessed on 14 April 2020

Wikimedia Foundation, Inc (2020) List of web archiving initiatives. https://en.wikipedia.org/wiki/List_of_Web_archiving_initiatives, last update on 21 April 2020. Accessed on 28 April 2020

World Wide Web Foundation (2021) History of the Web. Available at: https://webfoundation.org/about/vision/history-of-the-web/. Accessed on 29 January 2021

Part II
Collecting Before It Vanishes

Thomas Risse

The World Wide Web is the largest information space we have. However, this information is very volatile: the typical half-life of content referenced by URLs is just a few years. This trend is even more aggravated in social media, where social networking APIs sometimes only extend to a week's worth of content. Collection, enrichment, curation and preservation are the typical tasks that web archiving organisations have to deal with to build up web archives for future users. The archival task depends on the context of the archiving organisation (e.g. libraries, museums and personal archives). Depending on the collection and archiving goals, different methods and strategies to select web content need to be applied. This part presents different selection and crawling strategies as examples of how to address the various collection target contexts.

National libraries have a long-term strategic focus and mandate to collect and preserve the national documentary heritage. Hence, they developed collection and preservation strategies for web content at an early stage. In the chapter "National Web Archiving in Australia: Representing the Comprehensive", Paul Koerbin from the National Library of Australia gives an overview of the evolution of the Australian web archive programme from its beginnings in 1996 until today.

Since every country has its own history, culture, priorities and structures, Ivy Lee Huey Shin and Shereen Tay from the National Library of Singapore presents in the chapter "Web Archiving in Singapore: The Realities of National Web Archiving" the approach that Singapore is taking. Interesting aspects of the chapter are the involvement of the stakeholders and the general public in the genesis of the legislation and public education on web archiving and legal deposit. A special kind of web application that is very popular today is social media. Billions of users meet virtually on sites like Facebook, Instagram, YouTube or Twitter every day for social interactions. These interactions provide important insights into society. Therefore,

T. Risse
University Library J. C. Senckenberg, Goethe University Frankfurt, Frankfurt am Main, Germany
e-mail: t.risse@ub.uni-frankfurt.de

it is important to preserve them for future generations. In contrast to the classic Web, social media sites do not provide a single view of a page that can be collected. Instead, everything is always in flux. Different ways for archiving social media data are discussed in the chapter "Archiving the Social Media: The Case of Twitter" by Zeynep Pehlivan et al.

Large-scale crawling activities, e.g. by national libraries, typically result in huge and topically broad collections. This makes it difficult for researchers to access relevant event-specific materials and use them in their analytic tasks. Elena Demidova and Thomas Risse discuss different methods for creating event-centric collections from large-scale web archives. A special focus of this chapter is the crawl-based methods that identify relevant documents in and across web archives to create an event-centric collection.

National Web Archiving in Australia: Representing the Comprehensive

Paul Koerbin

It's an impossible task but we started anyway!
(Dr Marie-Louise Ayres, Director-General of the National
Library of Australia, [Easton 2019]).

Abstract National libraries have been at the forefront of web archiving since the activity commenced in the mid-1990s. This effort is built upon and sustained by their long-term strategic focus, curatorial experience and mandate to collect a nation's documentary heritage. Nevertheless, their specific legal remit, resources and strategic priorities will affect the objectives and the outcomes of national web archiving programmes. The National Library of Australia's web archiving programme, being among the earliest established and longest sustained activities, provides a case study on the origin and building of a practical approach to comprehensive national collecting and access.

1 Introduction

In what is now more than a quarter of a century of active collecting and preserving web content, it should be no surprise that national heritage collecting institutions, and more specifically national libraries, have been at the vanguard of web archiving programmes. National web archiving has been a driver for web archiving initiatives because the core function of national libraries is to collect and preserve their national documentary heritage in a manner that usually aims to be comprehensive and consequently inclusive of online publication. Moreover, national libraries have the strategic and operational history and expertise in collecting other published (and unpublished) materials on a national scale. These institutions, especially those supported by legal deposit legislation, are in function and mandate focused on the

P. Koerbin (✉)
National Library of Australia, Parkes Place, Canberra, Australia
e-mail: pkoerbin@nla.gov.au

© Springer Nature Switzerland AG 2021
D. Gomes et al. (eds.), *The Past Web*,
https://doi.org/10.1007/978-3-030-63291-5_3

long-term maintenance and sustainability of their national collections. Web archiving more than any other collecting is an activity dependent upon a commitment to sustainability. Collecting essentially ephemeral and intangible digital artefacts commits the institution to the considerable resource required for digital preservation and access along with the concomitant complexities and uncertainties that require strategic, sustainable policy development and programme management.[1]

Web archiving, approaching 2020, is now a much broader-based activity with a range of collecting and research institutions engaged, many with objectives to serve more narrowly defined and not necessarily national audiences. In 2003, the International Internet Preservation Consortium (IIPC) was established, 7 years after the earliest web archiving programmes began. The IIPC was originally constituted of the national libraries of France, Great Britain, Finland, Iceland, Canada, Denmark, Sweden, Norway and Australia together with the United States Library of Congress, the National Central Library of Florence and the ambitious and visionary Internet Archive (the only non-state organisation). By 2019, the IIPC membership had expanded to include numerous research institutions and academic libraries, yet national libraries still made up around two-thirds (67%) of the member organisations. The newer members of the web archiving community from the research and academic sector add a necessary vitality for innovation, research and development; nevertheless, it remains true that collecting content remains, as Winters (2019, p. 83) states, "with a few exceptions … conducted on a national basis by major national institutions, in keeping with well-established missions to preserve national cultural heritage".

The National Library of Australia (NLA) began its web archiving programme in 1996. The programme, which was given the name PANDORA—originally an initialism for Preserving and Accessing Networked Documentary Resources of Australia[2]—grew out of existing and established library operations, specifically the acquisition and cataloguing of serial publications. The conceptualisation of the Web at that seminal time was largely as a publishing medium and thus readily understood as an extension of existing collecting paradigms. The web archiving programme was based in the collections management and description area of the Library, not the information technology area. This had an important impact on the NLA's approach to web archiving because it meant process and procedure

---

[1]For a monograph-length collection covering a broad range of aspects relating to national domain collecting and preservation, see Brügger and Laursen (2019). That volume includes only passing reference to the National Library of Australia's web archiving activities—one of the earliest established long-maintained web archiving programmes. It is in this context that this chapter therefore focuses specifically on the Australian experience. On business planning for web archives, see Koerbin (2010).

[2]This initialism is no longer promoted and PANDORA is merely used as a branding for the collaborative selective web archiving programme that forms one part of the NLA's broader web archiving strategy. If the designation was formulated today, it would likely read "Digital Online" in place of "Documentary". In retrospect, the use of the term "documentary", linking the resources to be preserved to the NLA's statutory function to comprehensively collect Australia's documentary heritage, rather than to format and medium, is itself instructive.

was the driving factor rather than the development of technologies. Consequently, the first tasks undertaken were to select and catalogue Australian online journal publications. The selective approach operating in the context of general collecting objectives meant that online materials that were also available in print formats were not selected for archiving. This approach presented an understanding of comprehensive not as the collecting of the entire web publishing medium per se, but as web archiving supplementing the established collecting of print publishing and supporting a broader concept of the national collection.[3]

This nascent approach to web archiving engendered a sense that comprehensive collecting, as it was then understood, was possible. The technological and resource challenges were not ignored but they did not drive nor, more importantly, hinder application to take up the task. Even pioneer visionaries such as Brewster Kahle and Peter Lyman, who recognised the Web as a new medium for cultural expression that in its early stages would imitate the forms of existing media, characterised the Web as essentially a cultural *artefact* (Lyman and Kahle 1998). While stressing the need for a technological response at that time, the characterisation was still in terms of documents, publishers and libraries, concepts that national collecting institutions were best equipped to tackle. Since future developments that would change the character of the Web—Web 2.0, social media, interactivity—were, self-evidently, yet to emerge, this was not entirely a naïve perception and the objective of comprehensive collecting not outlandish. Conceptualising the Web in terms of existing publishing media gave impetus to a programme like that at the NLA precisely because it presented as achievable and sustainable within existing institutional infrastructures and resources. Reinforcing this point, the NLA has conducted its web archiving programme of a quarter of a century within its established operating model and without having received any additional resources specifically for the web archiving programme. Thus, there is the critical need to make the activity incremental, operational and directed towards delivering strategic outcomes such as open access.

2 Comprehensive Collecting

While the NLA's web archiving programme (operating as PANDORA) began as a selective approach to collecting web content—and was the only approach adopted by the Library until 2005 when country-level domain harvesting began— it was still conceptually part of a comprehensive collecting strategy. Selective web archiving was not pursued as a rejection of the domain harvesting approach but, rather, as a practical step towards collecting web content as soon as possible with available resources and low-cost infrastructure development. The NLA in

---

[3]For detail concerning the establishment and early activities of the NLA's web archiving programme, PANDORA, see: Cathro et al. (2001); Phillips (2002); and Webb (2001).

fact began exploring options for domain harvesting soon after establishing an operational selective web archiving programme. Later the Library adopted the approach of contracting the Internet Archive to undertake custom scoped .au level domain harvests to supply to the Library for preservation, indexing and access. The practicality of this latter arrangement became cogent in 2005 when the Internet Archive released its purpose-built archival web harvester, Heritrix, and funding arrangements within the NLA made capital funding available to purchase domain harvest collections. This offered a way forward for the Library to increase the scale of collecting by outsourcing the harvesting of the Australian web domain, which could then be purchased as a collection item. Large-scale domain harvesting was not established in-house since operational budgets remained un-supplemented and unavailable for the required infrastructure and expertise.

Like all national collecting institutions, the NLA's functions are writ in legislation, specifically the *National Library Act* (1960), which includes the mandate to maintain and develop a comprehensive collection of library materials relating to Australia and Australians and to make the collection available "to the most advantageous use of the collection in the national interest". Unlike many other jurisdictions, enabling legislation requiring publishers to deliver material to the library, generally known as "legal deposit" provisions, are not contained in the *National Library Act* but rather in the Australian Commonwealth *Copyright Act* (1968), legislation over which the Library had little influence for change. The original act only clearly applied the legal deposit requirements to print format library materials and the difficulty in influencing change meant that legal deposit in Australia was not extended to digital materials (including, specifically, online materials) until March 2016.[4] Thus, while the Library's establishing legislation framed its comprehensive collecting function, legal deposit legislation constrained comprehensive collecting for the first 20 years of the web archiving programme's operation because it did not extend to online content.[5]

Since legislation not only enables but may also constrain collecting, an institution's approach to risk in managing and extending its collecting within the legislative framework becomes important. Prior to the extension of legal deposit to online materials, the NLA's primary web archiving activity involved curated selection which was only pursued to a collecting and archiving stage when explicit permissions—copyright licences—were received from publishers. Permission negotiations were conducted by email, so they were usually quick and mostly resulted in agreement, at least where responses could be obtained. In the context of a publications-focused approach to collecting online materials, the permissions based, selective regime was largely successful. However, under this regime, significant

---

[4]Fortuitously, though untypically, this was a time when the Attorney-General responsible for the *Copyright Act* also had portfolio responsibility for the National Library—a situation that facilitated the progress of legislative changes.

[5]Copyright and legal deposit issues in the early years of the PANDORA web archiving programme are briefly outlined in Phillips and Koerbin (2004) and in more detail by Gatenby (2002).

material that was identified and selected for collection would not be pursued if permission was not forthcoming, as was the case with a seminal election campaign website called jeff.com.au in 1999.[6] As Winters (2019, p. 76) rightly states, "inconsistency of selection and capture is thus not accidental but central to the nature" of essentially patchwork collections. While Winters was referring specifically to a patchwork of various collections (in the UK), this temporal and artefactual patchwork exists within the very collections themselves.

It was common to hear speakers at conferences and forums in the early years of web archiving talk about "time travel" in terms holding out the prospect of a future when we could choose to surf the Web as it was at any point in time— as if all archived content would continue to exist in its original form, context, completeness and functionality. This idea persists to some degree as the ultimate objective. However, such virtual time travel is dependent upon the time coordinates of the artefacts that are collected from the Web—and like oral culture, websites do not exist as artefacts until and unless collected[7]—and thus upon the date-stamp that becomes a defining dimension of the artefact. The technical processes of collecting online content necessarily limit what is represented in the archival collection, so that even the largest scale collecting remains selective, especially when considering the timing and frequency of collecting and the period of time over which the "snapshot" is harvested. There is a curatorial effect (or bias) on collecting no matter what scale of effort is achieved.

When the NLA extended its web archiving programme to domain-level collecting in 2005 (and in-house bulk collecting of government websites from 2011), it was to build scale within the collection and to address curatorial biases and blind spots. It also represented a willingness to manage risk since the legislation at the time was ambiguous in its warrant for such an expansion of web collecting and preservation. While exemption under the *Copyright Act* (s. 200AB)[8] exists to allow libraries to conduct their business and function as a library, in accordance with Article 13 of the TRIPS Agreement,[9] it does not have the same clarity as legal deposit. As well as the objective to increase the scale of collecting, the move to domain harvesting addressed the Library's need to understand the scale and nature of the content published on the .au domain using the empirical evidence of the harvested content. Domain harvesting was also pursued as soon as feasible as a necessary step in developing in-house experience in managing large-scale web archive content.

Collecting the websites published on the country code top-level domain (ccTLD) is an obvious and relatively straightforward objective for national collecting. The

---

[6]For a detailed discussion of this particular case and other constraints in relation to collecting content for the PANDORA web archive, see Koerbin (2017).

[7]See Koerbin (2017).

[8]For a useful overview of these provisions, see the Australian Libraries Copyright Committee (2008).

[9]See the World Trade Organization's Agreement on Trade-Related Aspects of Intellectual Property Rights (1995).

ccTLD represents published material clearly identified with a country, at least for larger nations, since some smaller nations offer their ccTLD as one of the few international commercial assets they have. For nations like Australia undertaking national web archiving, collecting the ccTLD is central to any approach to comprehensive collecting. It is relatively easy, since scoping covers all content appearing on the .au domain and can readily include embedded content, that is, the links on pages that bring in content, whether on the .au domain or not, that are essential for an accurate rendering of the webpage. Nor is it required to compile a complete seed list of published websites, for example from domain registrations that do not necessarily accurately reflect what is published, since many domains may be registered but never used. In collecting the published record it is what actually exists on the .au domain that is of primary interest since that is what forms (or formed) part of the social and cultural discourse. Consequently, a substantial representative URL list will serve to seed the harvest that is then scoped to follow and include any content found on the .au domain through the harvest crawl process. This process, if run for sufficient time, is the best evidence of the ccTLD, though never a complete record since the harvest must be terminated at some point and is never really completed. Typically, the annual harvests of the .au domain contracted by the NLA, and run by the Internet Archive, run for around 2 months, collecting a representative 800 million to 1 billion documents and data in the order of 60–70 terabytes.

Domain harvesting, as suggested above, supplements and to some degree balances out the curatorial biases of selective archiving, since, within the scope of the harvest, the robots collect without discrimination. Nevertheless, this process, while a critical element of a comprehensive approach to collecting national web content, has some significant limitations. What is collected is dependent upon what the robot identifies and is actually able to successfully harvest. To mitigate risk, large harvests generally follow robots.txt disallow rules and, consequently, much content may not be collected. Other content resists harvesting because of technical complexity or server configurations. Moreover, the scale of domain harvesting means it is very difficult—for both resource and technical reasons—to collect content frequently and in a timely (or time-specific) manner. Domain harvesting is efficient but not entirely effective per se.

Perhaps the principal limitation of ccTLD harvesting is that there is a large amount of content that is intellectually within scope for the national collection that is not published on the .au domain. Not only a large number of personal websites such as blogs that are published on services on international domains, but many Australian-based or Australian-focused organisations, businesses, online news sites, even academic institutions and government bodies have websites on non .au domains.[10] In addition, the modern Australian citizen's online world does not stop at the jurisdictional borders but ranges wherever it may through the borderless Web and of course into social media, where the concepts and boundaries of publication

---

[10]Webster (2019) suggests that as much as a third of the UK Web exists outside the ccTLD, that is, those hosts located in the UK but not on the .uk domain.

and communication are blurred or non-existent. International publishing platforms and social media services often offer the simplest access to online expression but can be the most challenging formats for web archivists both technically and in jurisdictional terms.

The warrant of legal deposit has jurisdictional boundaries and a collection representing a nation and its people is fundamentally constrained by the reach of this remit. While the nature of the Web itself does not sit entirely comfortably with archiving along national jurisdictions—and the mission of the Internet Archive indeed does try to overleap that constraint—national institutions by the fiat of this same remit remain the driving, sustaining and responsible organisations for the task. When the practical outcomes of the comprehensive collecting objective are considered, we must recognise that it is not about collecting all and every resource, in every form at every point in time, but rather using available methodologies, technologies and warrant to collect in sufficient scale and time to provide an intelligible representation of the whole.

3 Comprehensive Access

In March 2019, the NLA released its entire web archive holdings to open public access under the banner of the Australian Web Archive (AWA) through its Trove discovery service. The AWA includes content from the selective curated PANDORA Archive and the bulk harvested Australian Government Web Archive (AGWA).[11] Both these collections were already searchable and publicly available, PANDORA since 1998 and AGWA since 2014. Most significantly, the AWA also made accessible the entire content of the Australian domain harvests collected since 2005 as well as older .au content from 1996 to 2004 obtained from the Internet Archive. The Australian domain harvests comprise around 85% of the entire corpus; thus, the release of AWA through Trove was a significant step towards providing comprehensive access to the web archive.[12]

As stated above, the NLA's statutory function is not only to collect and preserve Australia's documentary heritage but also to make it available for use in the public interest. The purpose of collecting and preservation is only truly realised through access, and access is the real test of the national institution's commitment to the task since it exposes the organisation to a greater amount of legal and reputational risk. The extent to which the institution is able or willing to expose its web archive content is not only determined (and constrained) by legislation, but also by the degree of organisational aversion to risk.

---

[11] The Australian Government Web Archive was a prototype web archiving programme established by the NLA in 2011 with the objective to introduce in-house some infrastructure capacity for larger scale bulk harvesting and in doing so also to comprehensively collect Australian Government websites.

[12] At the time of its public release in March 2019, the Australian Web Archive consisted of around 8 billion documents amounting to a little over 600 terabytes of data.

Building on a two-decade history of providing access to its selective web archive, the NLA's approach to the expanded AWA was to provide open search access to content through both full text and URL indexing. This gives primacy to the content as documents as encountered by individual users and does not treat the corpus as essentially a dataset. Moreover, facilitating the personal encounter between user and intellectual content for which the Library was neither the creator nor first publisher may yet be considered an act of publication. In that context, actions to ameliorate risk associated with privacy, copyright and potentially illegal, defamatory or offensive material—including takedown processes—were implemented.

In exposing the complete web archive collection, the NLA took a number of actions to reduce reputational and legal risks including significant work on search results ranking, including Bayesian analysis of content, to push possible offensive content down the results rankings. This is preferable to a censorship approach but it should also be understood as bringing further curatorial bias to the collection as presented to the user. Another important action to mitigate risk is to limit unintentional exposure to the archive. While the entire web archive is openly accessible through the Trove Australian Web Archive portal, content is exposed neither to search engines nor to the Trove single discovery function that interrogates multiple collections in a single search. Thus, accessing the archive has to be a conscious and intentional act by the user.

In providing open access to the web archive content, the NLA does not identify or privilege any particular target user group. In the spirit of its legislated function, access is provided for the use of all Australians generally. This, certainly, means that the specific needs of potentially high-value research users are not necessarily met. For example, at the time of writing, there is no API available to researchers to interrogate the web archive metadata or content.

Like the Library's other collections of printed and digital materials relating to Australia and Australians, the national web archive serves to represent Australian culture to the world. As an online collection accessible over the Web, the AWA— like the Library's digitised collections—is at the forefront of how the Library presents Australian culture. The opportunity for such a collection to be curated with value-adding pathways, collections and analytics is considerable since metadata is collected or created at various stages of the curation process. The NLA has done little to exploit this opportunity while focusing on establishing the basic search facility. While the opportunity to build additional research access tools, curated pathways and analysis exists, the significant human and technical resources required to provide these value-added services continue to be a constraint for an organisation with its business committed to many services. This is not simply a technical matter but goes to the core of corporate planning and priorities.

The NLA's approach to developing its web archiving, from collecting to maintaining to providing fully open access, has been described by the Library's Director-General Marie-Louise Ayres as "radical incrementalism"—that is, taking the small and achievable steps, learning and evaluating along the way, and working within inevitable constraints that nevertheless lead, over time, to profound change. This allows the organisation "to achieve goals that would have previously sounded too big, ambitious or risky ... setting a course and then sticking to it for the long term" (Easton 2019).

4 Conclusions

National web archiving programmes are long-standing, prominent and critical components in the international efforts to preserve the Web because the national libraries (and archives) that establish and maintain them are statutory institutions with the functional mandate to collect national documentary heritage. Moreover, they bring long experience and established expertise in collecting materials in a variety of formats, often supported by legal deposit legislation (or, if not, an approach resembling the purpose of legal deposit), and a sustainable vision supported by institutional robustness. Certainly, the National Library of Australia's web archiving programme could be characterised in these terms. Each national institution will, of course, have its own history, culture, resource priorities and structures that shape the nature of their individual web archiving programmes. For the NLA, whose web archiving programme spans the entire historical period of web archiving activity commencing in the mid-1990s, comprehensive collecting and comprehensive access have continued to be the objective, though how comprehensiveness has been conceptualised has necessarily changed over time. It may have been to see collecting web resources as completing gaps in the broader national collection; or achieving national scale by collecting the entire .au web domain; or understanding that the remit to collect published material should also include social media. Comprehensive national collecting is really a process of turning a statutory function into strategic objectives to collect from the elusive and protean Web the artefacts created and shaped by the technical, resource and legal constraints. In other words, national web archiving is fundamentally a strategic attempt to collect a functional representation of a comprehensive national collection of online publication. The success or otherwise of such attempts will ultimately depend on the engagement of the user with the collection. For the user seeking a specific document, this perspective may be different from a researcher looking to interrogate the archive as a coherent and complete dataset.

References

Agreement on Trade-Related Aspects of Intellectual Property Rights (1995) https://www.wto.org/english/docs_e/legal_e/27-trips.pdf. Accessed 14 November 2019
Australian Libraries Copyright Committee (2008) A user's guide to flexible dealing provisions for libraries, educational institutions and cultural institutions. Section 200AB of the Copyright Act 1968 (Cth). Australian Libraries Copyright Committee and the Australian Digital Alliance, Kingston, ACT

Brügger N, Laursen D (2019) The historical web and digital humanities: the case of national web domains. Routledge, London

Cathro W, Webb C, Whiting J (2001) Archiving the web: the PANDORA Archive at the National Library of Australia. Paper presented at the Preserving the Present for the Future, Web Archiving Conference, Copenhagen, 18–19 June 2001

Easton S (2019) Australia's top librarian tells how the National Library fosters a culture of in-house innovation. In two words: 'radical incrementalism'. The Mandarin. https://www.themandarin.com.au/110303-australias-top-librarian-tells-how-the-national-library-fosters-a-culture-of-in-house-innovation-in-two-words-radical-incrementalism/

Gatenby P (2002) Legal deposit, electronic publications and digital archiving: the National Library of Australia's experience. A paper presented at the 68th IFLA General Conference and Council, Glasgow, 2002. http://pandora.nla.gov.au/pan/21336/20080620-0137/www.nla.gov.au/nla/staffpaper/2002/gatenby1.html. Accessed 14 November 2019

Koerbin P (2010) Issues in business planning for archival collections of web materials. In: Collier M (ed) Business planning for digital libraries: international approaches. Leuven University Press, Leuven, pp 101–111

Koerbin P (2017) Revisiting the world wide web as artefact: case studies in archiving small data for the National Library of Australia's PANDORA archive. In: Brügger N (ed) Web 25: histories from the first 25 years of the world wide web. Peter Lang, New York, pp 191–206

Lyman P, Kahle B (1998) Archiving digital cultural artifacts: organizing and agenda for action. D-Lib Magazine, 4(7/8). http://www.dlib.org/dlib/july98/07lyman.html. Accessed 14 November 2019

Phillips M (2002) Archiving the web: the national collection of Australian online publications. Paper presented at the International Symposium on Web Archiving, National Diet Library, Tokyo, 30 January 2002

Phillips M, Koerbin P (2004) PANDORA, Australia's web archive: how much metadata is enough? J Internet Catalog 7(2):19–33

Webb C (2001) The National Library of Australia's digital preservation agenda. RLG DigiNews: 5(1). http://worldcat.org/arcviewer/1/OCC/2007/08/08/0000070511/viewer/file1108.html#feature1. Accessed 14 November 2019

Webster P (2019) Understanding the limitations of the ccTLD as a proxy for the national web: lessons from cross-border religion in the northern Irish web sphere. In: Brügger N, Laursen D (eds) The historical web and digital humanities: the case of national web domains. Routledge, London, pp 110–123

Winters J (2019) Negotiating the archives of the UK web space. In: Brügger N, Laursen D (eds) The historical web and digital humanities: the case of national web domains. Routledge, London, pp 75–88

Web Archiving in Singapore: The Realities of National Web Archiving

Ivy Huey Shin Lee and Shereen Tay

Abstract This chapter describes the challenges of web archiving in Singapore, where awareness about web archiving is low. It focuses on the legislation amendments, infrastructure enhancements and public engagement activities required to facilitate web archiving work at a national scale.

1 Background

The National Library, Singapore (NLS) is a knowledge institution under the National Library Board (NLB). The NLB manages 26 public libraries, the National Library, the National Archives and the Asian Film Archives. NLS is the custodian of Singapore's documentary heritage and has a mandate to preserve the published heritage of the nation through the legal deposit of works published in Singapore. This mandate came into force in 1958 through the enactment of the Raffles National Library Ordinance, which eventually came under the NLB Act in 1995. The legal deposit scheme has served NLS well in the last 60 years, enabling the library to systematically collect and preserve more than 1.3 million items over time. However, this mandate is limited to physical items and does not extend to electronic formats such as e-books and online materials. NLS can thus only encourage publishers of such electronic publications to deposit these materials voluntarily as it cannot legally enforce this under the legal deposit scheme that covers only physical materials. While NLS can use web archiving tools to capture online content, it has to seek the written consent of website owners before doing so, which is administratively cumbersome and yields a low response rate. As the volume of digital content explodes, it has become a priority for NLS to update its legislation to save materials from disappearing into the digital black hole.

I. H. S. Lee (✉) · S. Tay
Statutory Functions and Research, National Library, Singapore, Singapore
e-mail: Ivy_LEE@nlb.gov.sg

Electronic and Internet materials are increasingly important resources that capture national identity and culture; hence, it is essential for NLS to have a legal mandate to collect digital content. This is especially true for materials published on the Web. As of December 2019, there are more than 181,000 websites in Singapore (.sg domain),[1] and this number is growing rapidly. If published materials on the Web are not systematically collected in a timely manner, there will be a permanent loss of Singapore's published cultural heritage.

2   Amendments to the Legislation

NLS takes its cue from forerunners at other national libraries who have in place legislation and processes that facilitate the collection of digital legal deposit materials and web archiving. In the drafting of legislative provisions, NLS became aware of the common issues that other national libraries encountered, especially those based in developed economies. Privacy concerns and copyright matters consistently turn up at the top of the list and need to be addressed. Bearing in mind these two key areas of concern, NLS drafted proposed amendments to balance the rights of content creators and publishers while also meeting the library's mandate to preserve digital cultural heritage and provide access to the public.

Guidelines were also prepared for handling operational matters which the law may not cover in detail, such as the number of access points and takedown requests for the materials. According to these guidelines, NLS will provide two terminals (or two concurrent accesses) on the library's premises for viewing digital legal deposit materials and archived websites. Two access points were chosen as this mirrors the way in which the physical legal deposit collection is available to the public in Singapore, that is, two copies. This restricted access will help to protect the content owners' commercial interests while also ensuring that members of the public have access to these materials.

Based on NLS's research and findings, it proposed four main areas for update to the legislation:

(a) To extend the scope of NLS's legal deposit scheme to incorporate digital materials, including electronic counterparts of print publications as well as online content.
(b) To empower NLS to collect online materials through web harvesting without requiring it to seek written consent from the owners/producers. Without amending the NLB Act to authorise NLS to collect online content, the library would have no protection against potential legal liabilities such as copyright infringement. NLS will only collect online content within the .sg domain, as its focus is on Singapore. In addition, the library will not harvest protected online

---

[1] See Singapore Network Information Centre (SGNIC) at www.sgnic.sg

publications and materials (e.g. sites protected by password), unless they are voluntarily deposited by the website publisher or owner.

(c) To give NLS the right to digitise, copy, preserve and use the deposited materials for non-commercial purposes. This is important for NLS to carry out tasks like digital preservation, where content will need to be preserved digitally (including migration to new formats, as old formats become obsolete due to technological advancements) to enable perpetual access.

(d) To enable digital materials collected/archived by NLS to be accessible to researchers.

NLS also consulted legal agencies in Singapore and was advised that a complementary amendment to Singapore's Copyright Act would be necessary. A decision was made to include updates to the Copyright Act simultaneously.

In July 2018, the Bill to amend the NLB Act was passed by the Singapore Parliament and the changes came into effect on 31 January 2019. The updated NLB Act now empowers NLS to collect, preserve and provide access to digital legal deposit publications, as well as to Singapore websites.

3 Engagement with Stakeholders

During the drafting of the legislation, NLS engaged with stakeholders and the general public to get feedback and support for the proposed amendments. In Singapore, it is common practice to seek inputs from stakeholders and the general public via a public consultation exercise whenever government bodies implement or amend legislation.

Due to the complexity of the legislative amendments, NLS designed a series of infographics to explain the benefits of the legislative changes to stakeholders in easily understood pictorial forms (see an example on Fig. 1).

NLS began with a shortlist of key stakeholders who would be most affected by the proposed legislative amendments, to invite them for focus group discussions. The objective was to judge sentiment on the ground, to gain feedback on the legislative changes and to obtain buy-in, as well as to identify advocates for future media interviews when the legislation change was made public. Several sessions were conducted from November 2017 to February 2018 with publishers, writers, academics, heritage researchers and website owners. A dialogue session was subsequently extended to other members of the same group of stakeholders so as to widen NLS's reach and ensure that as many voices as possible could be heard and addressed. Both content providers (publishers, writers and website owners) and users (researchers and academics) were generally supportive of the proposed amendments and appreciated the custodian role that NLS plays in preserving documentary heritage. They were in favour of the web archiving initiative and suggested that NLS should archive websites more frequently and provide greater access to these materials. Stakeholders also encouraged NLS to consider archiving

WEB ARCHIVING

Web archiving is the process of taking a snapshot of a website at a specific point in time and preserving it for research. Online publications constitute an important part of Singapore's heritage and memories, and we need to preserve them before they are lost.

WHY IS WEB ARCHIVING IMPORTANT?

Works published on websites will be lost if not collected and preserved.

Current and future generations should have access to these archived websites to understand the life and times of our nation.

WHAT WILL BE ARCHIVED?

Singapore websites (.sg) that are freely open for public access

Content hosted within the website

WHAT WILL NOT BE ARCHIVED?

Password protected websites

Intranet sites

Content hosted outside the website

WHAT ABOUT NON-SINGAPORE DOMAIN (.SG) WEBSITES?

Permission will be sought to archive non .sg websites with Singapore content of heritage value and which are important to preserve for future generations.

HOW OFTEN WILL ARCHIVING BE DONE?

At least once a year.

More frequently during key events in Singapore, such as National Day.

WHAT WILL WEBSITE OWNERS BE REQUIRED TO DO?

No action is required from the website owners. Auto-archiving will be done by the National Library Board.

HOW WILL ARCHIVED WEBSITES BE ACCESSED?

Archived websites can be viewed for research and reference at the National Library. With permission from website owners, some will be made available online.

Fig. 1 Infographics explaining the legislative changes to stakeholders and members of the public

non .sg websites that contain Singapore content. A public consultation exercise was conducted simultaneously to seek feedback from members of the public. The consultation paper detailing the proposed amendments was published through the Singapore government's feedback unit, REACH (www.reach.gov.sg), for a month at the end of 2017. At the end of the consultation period, feedback received included general support for the amendments and some technical queries pertaining to web archiving because the general public is not familiar with the web archiving process.

The key takeaway from the engagement with stakeholders and the public consultation exercise was that established good working relationships with publishers and researchers were advantageous, as both parties were willing to have open discussions and share their concerns. The challenge, however, was engaging stakeholders with whom NLS had less association, that is, website owners. It took multiple attempts to reach out to them before feedback was received, but after a connection was made, website owners lent their support and gave NLS the necessary encouragement to push forward with the update to the legislation.

4 System Enhancements to Support the Legislative Changes

Apart from legislative changes and engagement with stakeholders, NLS also looked at improving its systems and infrastructure so that it would be better able to process and support the web archive collection. Web Archive Singapore (WAS) (eresources.nlb.gov.sg/webarchives) hosts NLS's collection of archived Singapore websites.

As the number of archived websites increased exponentially, from a handful to about 180,000 registered .sg websites a year, effort was focused on rebuilding WAS. The increase in volume of data called for a review of the existing workflow, policies, budgetary requirements and manpower needs. WAS was launched in 2006 when NLS first embarked on collecting Singapore websites. The portal had two functions—keyword search and subject browsing. Websites are harvested with Heritrix and displayed via the OpenWayback.[2]

A project to revamp the WAS portal started in late 2017. Figure 2 presents a screenshot of the WAS portal. An environmental scan was done of other established web archiving portals, such as the British Library, the National Library of Australia and the Library of Congress, to baseline what functionality the redesigned WAS website could adopt and improve upon.

Five new functions were added to the new website—curation, full-text search, the public nomination of websites, a data visualiser and rights management. Curation takes centre stage on the homepage of the new website, with the showcasing of highlights from the collection. This helps to generate interest and encourage further exploration of the website. Figure 3 illustrates that there are two types of curation activities: Special Collections, which cover a significant event or topic relating to

---

[2]https://github.com/iipc/openwayback

Fig. 2 The revamped Web Archive Singapore portal, https://eresources.nlb.gov.sg/webarchives/, 2018

Fig. 3 Two types of curations are available—Special collections and Librarian's Pick, 2018

Singapore (e.g. National Day Parade General Elections) and Librarian's Pick, a monthly highlight of an archived website related to a topic or event of interest for that month (e.g. Singapore Arts Festival). The selection of the topics and curation of archived websites are done by librarians.

The search function, based on Solr,[3] has been enhanced and facilitates full-text search right down to the individual webpages and files within an archived website. Facets are also included to enable users to refine their search results by format (e.g. websites, documents or images), year, subject category and URL.

To encourage public participation, an online nomination form was included so that the public could recommend Singapore websites from non .sg domains for NLS's consideration. This will help librarians to build the web archives collection and also allow members of the public to contribute to NLS's published heritage through their nominations.

Figure 4 presents another new feature of the portal is a data visualiser, which charts the frequency of a keyword or phrase written in archived documents over a period of time. This visual representation may be a useful resource for researchers who are interested in studying trends in the use and frequency of certain words. NLS is exploring other features that will be of use to researchers, in particular the provision of derivative data that highlights the unique voices of Singaporeans through the country's websites.

Finally, the new WAS has also built in rights management to control access to the collection. Although NLS now has the mandate to collect .sg websites, these by default are only viewable within the library's premises due to prevailing copyright

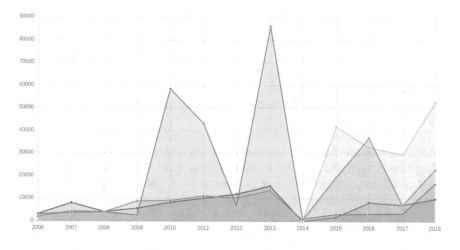

Keyword Search

Enter your keyword(s) below, maximum of 5 tags at a time. Use a comma(',') to separate keyword(s). Click Generate to view the chart.

NDP ✕   Haze ✕   SG50 ✕   Elections   Add a keyword

Fig. 4 Users can trace the frequency of use of a keyword or phrase over a period of time

---

[3]https://lucene.apache.org/solr/

laws. A simple lock icon will be displayed for archived websites that can only be viewed onsite.

5 Building a Comprehensive Collection of Singapore Websites

With the implementation of the new law, NLS has adopted a multi-prong approach to archiving the nation's online published works. NLS conducts both domain and selective archiving to ensure that the breadth and depth of online information is captured. This includes annual domain archiving, quarterly archiving of pre-identified subjects and monthly thematic archiving.

A domain crawl of .sg websites will be conducted at least once a year. This is done via a Memorandum of Understanding with the Singapore Network Information Centre, the national registry of .sg websites in Singapore, which allows NLS to obtain a yearly list of registered .sg websites. For selective archiving, NLS conducts quarterly archiving of websites from pre-identified subjects that contain substantial heritage value for Singapore, such as government websites, the arts, heritage, culture and politics. A quarterly frequency has been chosen as it strikes a good balance between capturing new content as well as ensuring that the web crawler does not affect the websites' performance.

NLS also conducts thematic archiving of websites that are event-driven. Event-based websites with a short lifespan will be archived more often to allow timely capture and minimise loss in case they are taken down or updated frequently. Examples of such topics are annual National Day celebrations, the Southeast Asian Games, new government policies and trending events that have substantial news and social media coverage.

While these three approaches help to build a good collection of .sg websites, NLS is also aware that there are many non .sg websites that contain significant Singapore content. As non .sg websites are excluded under the new legislation, NLS is still required to seek written consent from website owners before these can be archived. NLS will continually identify Singapore websites from the non .sg domain strategically. It has written to thousands of Singapore businesses and registered societies from non .sg domains for permission to archive their websites. This may be a tedious process and one which might not yield a high success rate, as NLS had experienced before the legislation was amended, but it will help the library to build a more comprehensive collection of Singapore websites. To help ease the permission-seeking process, NLS has also enhanced its public nomination form to allow website owners to grant permission directly to archive their websites. With enhanced marketing and promotion efforts, NLS hopes that this channel will encourage more Singaporeans and local companies to join it in preserving their institutional memories.

6 Public Education on Web Archiving and Legal Deposit

The passing of the NLB Act amendment Bill in July 2018 was a milestone event for NLS. Momentum arising from coverage in the media and public attention was harnessed for the purposes of public education and to strengthen the National Library's position as the custodian for Singapore documentary heritage. This was a "once-in-a-lifetime" opportunity afforded only by the timing of the legislative amendments. NLS seized the opportunity and organised an outdoor event at the National Library Building, as well as roving exhibitions with supporting programmes at NLB's three regional public libraries, to launch the implementation of digital legal deposit and domain web archiving, which are the primary components of the amendments to the legislation. The event was positioned to achieve the objective of creating greater public awareness of and appreciation for Singapore's published heritage and web archiving, as well as to encourage the public to contribute towards this collection.

A 2-day event in November 2018 was held at the National Library Building that included a showcase of legal deposit and web archive content, public talks and performances, Instagram-worthy backdrops and photo booths to attract young people and families (see Fig. 5). The event was attended by about 1800 people, who came to enjoy the activities and soak in the carnival-like atmosphere. A public talk by Mr. Brown, Singapore's most famous blogger, that highlighted the role of web archiving to preserve online materials was standing-room only in a venue that can hold 300 people.

Fig. 5 Elderly guests from nearby communities having fun at the "Instagram-worthy" photo booth

7 Conclusions

NLS's journey to extend the remit of the legal deposit scheme to the digital realm required perseverance to push through the proposed legislation. Through this process of amending the legislation, NLS learnt many valuable lessons, such as the importance of investing time and effort to cultivate relationships and goodwill with content creators, publishers and website owners so that they can be persuaded to support web archiving initiatives. It was also essential to keep up with the developments of the various laws governing copyright and privacy worldwide as these could potentially impact how the legislation was drafted. Internally, NLS had to make a convincing case to persuade the relevant ministries to support the long-term activities of archiving and preserving digital works in annual budgets.

The journey does not end now that the legislation has been passed. NLS will need to continually fine-tune its work process and systems, train its personnel and develop their skillset. Externally, it will be an ongoing uphill task for NLS to create awareness of web archiving, in order to maintain its relationship with content creators and publishers. It will be a long road ahead, but NLS takes heart that at least it has started on the right track and is positive that its work will create a lasting legacy for future generations of Singaporeans and researchers.

Archiving Social Media: The Case of Twitter

Zeynep Pehlivan, Jérôme Thièvre, and Thomas Drugeon

Abstract Around the world, billions of people use social media like Twitter and Facebook every day, to find, discuss and share information. Social media, which has transformed people from content readers to publishers, is not only an important data source for researchers in social science but also a "must archive" object for web archivists for future generations. In recent years, various communities have discussed the need to archive social media and have debated the issues related to its archiving. There are different ways of archiving social media data, including using traditional web crawlers and application programming interfaces (APIs) or purchasing from official company firehoses. It is important to note that the first two methods bring some issues related to capturing the dynamic and volatile nature of social media, in addition to the severe restrictions of APIs. These issues have an impact on the completeness of collections and in some cases return only a sample of the whole. In this chapter, we present these different methods and discuss the challenges in detail, using Twitter as a case study to better understand social media archiving and its challenges, from gathering data to long-term preservation.

1 Introduction

Social media, such as Twitter and Facebook, provides an important data source for social science and other research (Mejova et al. 2015; McCormick et al. 2017; Sloan and Quan-Haase 2017). Its popularity and great potential as a historical data source for further research has also made it an important source for web archiving initiatives (Marshall and Shipman 2012; Hockx-Yu 2014). However, there is no existing standard for collecting and preserving social media data. Different methods are used by web archiving initiatives, including deploying traditional web crawlers,

Z. Pehlivan (✉) · J. Thièvre · T. Drugeon
Institut National de l'Audiovisuel, Bry-sur-Marne, France
e-mail: zpehlivan@ina.fr; jthievre@ina.fr; tdrugeon@ina.fr

© Springer Nature Switzerland AG 2021
D. Gomes et al. (eds.), *The Past Web*,
https://doi.org/10.1007/978-3-030-63291-5_5

43

using application programming interfaces (APIs) or purchasing from official data sellers.

None of these existing methods will result in a complete historical dataset, without any filters applied, because of technical or budgetary restrictions. The United States Library of Congress is the only institution to have made an agreement with Twitter that allowed it to retrieve "everything that has been sent and declared public" directly from the source servers (Zimmer 2015). This aside, whatever method is used to archive Twitter, there is an initial and crucial step: selection. As in web archiving (Milligan et al. 2016), this requires meticulous and reactive work from curators to choose the initial user accounts, hashtags, keywords, etc. Lots of web archiving institutions have developed topic-centric collections, so that they can be more comprehensive, like the Brexit archive of the British Library.[1]

We would like to make a distinction between archiving social media data for a specific research purpose (scholar uses) and institutional archiving. The first consists of collecting social media data for research depending on researchers and is usually carried out as a one-off collecting process for a given period. By contrast, we use the term "institutional archiving" to describe social media/web archiving independent of any specific research needs, but rather to ensure the preservation of cultural heritage, for example as part of legal deposit collecting. Both of these approaches have questions in common, for example how precisely to collect, but institutional archiving has to deal with additional questions around continuity of the archiving process, authenticity, methods of access, preservation and obsolescence (Bruns and Weller 2016).

In this chapter, we will give a brief introduction to social media archiving, using Twitter as a case study, but the questions and the issues can be applied to other social media platforms. In the next section, we will explain different ways of archiving social media data. In Sect. 3, the related work and issues concerned with accessing and analysing archived Twitter data are discussed. Next, the preservation step is presented. Before concluding, we present our procedure for archiving Twitter at the Institut national de l'audiovisuel (INA) in France.

2   How to Archive Social Media?

The initial step of archiving is to decide what to archive, before choosing between different archiving methods. Almost all archiving methods require an initial query, for example a list of hashtags to archive. The interactive nature of social media (likes, replies, retweets, etc.) makes it difficult to identify selection criteria. In both research and institutional archiving, defining a collection around a topic (e.g. Brexit, the Olympics) is used as a way of managing this selection step better. A

---

[1]https://www.webarchive.org.uk/en/ukwa/collection/911.

list of hashtags, keywords, user accounts, etc., related to a topic can be used as an initial query, but one should be aware that there is no guarantee that the data matching the selection criteria represents all the data on this topic. For example, related hashtags can be easily missed or relevant information can be posted without using a hashtag. Another problem is that when a topic becomes a trend, related selection criteria can also bring lots of noise to the collection, which requires data cleaning. At most of the archiving institutions, this task is undertaken by curators.

We will now explain different ways of archiving social media data, taking Twitter as an example. Twitter, founded in 2007, is a microblogging service that allows users to send and read messages of up to limited number of characters. These messages are called "tweets". It has established itself as an important social media platform and plays a particularly significant role not only in broadcasting information but also in reacting live to current events.

2.1   Web Crawling

A web crawler is typically defined as "a system for the bulk downloading of web pages" (Olston and Najork 2010). The basic web crawling algorithm, the crawler, downloads all of the webpages addressed by a given a set of seed Uniform Resource Locators (URLs), extracts the hyperlinks contained in the pages and iteratively downloads the webpages addressed by these hyperlinks. Twitter webpages for user timelines or search results can be archived using traditional web archiving approaches. Several institutions such as the Bibliothèque nationale de France or the State Library of North Carolina use the Internet Archive's Heritrix crawler (Liu and Fan 2011) to archive Twitter pages. If the Twitter webpage is considered as a canonical representation of tweets, this method helps to keep the presentation of archived tweets, which can be the core of some research projects.

However, this approach also has disadvantages for archiving Twitter and social media platforms in general. The data, like text, screen name, date or number of likes, displayed on the page for each tweet must be extracted in order to perform analyses or aggregation. On the other hand, the metadata of a tweet is richer than the displayed data; it contains more than 30 different types of metadata per tweet, like geo-location, time zone, language, and device as seen in Fig. 1. In addition, archiving by robots causes certain problems, such as the inability to browse all the tweets displayed dynamically on a page, and crawlers should respect certain rules imposed by the service providers. In fact, without the right safety mechanisms, a high-throughput crawler can inadvertently carry out a denial-of-service attack (Olston and Najork 2010).

```
▼ object {1}
    ▼ array {30}
        created_at : Fri Sep 01 13:19:27 +0000 2017
        id       : 903608241283891200
        id_str : 903608241283891200
        text : #Hommage à #SimoneVeil - une Niçoise unique. \n5 Septembre 2017, 19h30 av
               @YvanGastaut @Univ_Nice… https://t.co/VewReLA4mK
        ▶ display_text_range [2]
        source : <a href=\"http://twitter.com\" rel=\"nofollow\">Twitter Web Client</a>
        truncated : true
        in_reply_to_status_id : null
        in_reply_to_status_id_str : null
        in_reply_to_user_id : null
        in_reply_to_user_id_str : null
        in_reply_to_screen_name : null
        ▶ user  {39}
        geo   : null
        coordinates : null
        place : null
        contributors : null
        is_quote_status : false
        ▶ extended_tweet {4}
        quote_count : 0
        reply_count : 0
        retweet_count : 0
        favorite_count : 0
        ▶ entities {4}
        favorited : false
        retweeted : false
        possibly_sensitive : false
        filter_level : low
        lang : fr
```

Fig. 1 Example of Twitter metadata obtained via API

2.2 Web Scraping

Web scraping consists of using automated programs to process webpages and extract specific pieces of information, for example the content of a tweet. Web-scraped data will only include whatever information is available to the browser, which may be different from data obtained directly from official APIs. There are several applications offering web scraping, like Octoparse[2] and ParseHub.[3] A recent study (Sobrinho et al. 2019) shows how elementary data from a public user profile in Instagram can be scraped and loaded into a database without any consent. Twitter and most other social media platforms do not like getting scraped, but they tolerate "polite" crawlers.

2.3   Accessing Application Programming Interfaces

Twitter, like other social media platforms, is different from traditional websites because it also provides "Application Programming Interfaces" (APIs), which offer a series of options to third-party developers, allowing them to use certain features or access data on the site. Using these APIs to archive social media data is a common practice, which brings with it both advantages and disadvantages.

There is not a strictly canonical form to access Twitter data. A tweet can be read from the Twitter website, through a mobile application, or on a third-party webpage containing an embedded social-media ticker that displays tweets. Plus, the Twitter APIs provide access to rich additional metadata which is not visible on the Twitter website. Thus, several institutions opt to archive Twitter data through its APIs. Twitter offers different APIs: the standard (free) Twitter APIs consist of a Sample API, a REST API and a Streaming API; in addition, the enterprise (paid subscription) APIs include advanced filters, historical search and engagement APIs, via Gnip, which give full access to historical data.[4]

Twitter also provides several public free APIs to query its database and to allow the building of services on top of its platform. However, Twitter has been imposing more restrictive rules on its API users. API end-points and limitations changed frequently, so users should check Twitter's official developer website before starting to archive data.[5] The APIs have to be regarded as a "black box" (Driscoll and Walker 2014) as Twitter does not reveal in detail how data sampling is handled.

The Sample API offers 1% of all public tweets randomly in real time, but it does not allow the filtering of this data through a query. The Streaming API does not include historical tweets, but once set up it allows the retrieval of all tweets responding to a request. The value of this advanced API is that it allows access to large volumes of data and is less constrained by Twitter's access and query limits. The Streaming API is actually a constant stream of tweets representing

---

[2]https://www.octoparse.com/tutorial-7/scrape-tweets-from-twitter. Accessed 30 July 2019.

[3]https://www.parsehub.com/. Accessed 30 July 2019.

[4]Gnip, Inc. is a social media API aggregation company, acquired by Twitter in 2014 to offer more sophisticated datasets and better data enrichment. Gnip APIs https://support.gnip.com/apis/ (accessed 30 July) offer different access methods for gathering data, including real-time, historical and reliability features, etc.

[5]https://developer.twitter.com/. Accessed 30 June 2019.

approximately 1% of the global stream (all published tweets) circulating on the platform. Regular hashtags and keywords never exceed 1% of the global flow, that is, all tweets can be archived (Tromble et al. 2017). However, keywords related to events (e.g. terrorist attacks, the Olympic games) are affected by this restriction. The REST API provides access to different endpoints. The Search API, as part of the REST API, returns tweets from the past week, a notably smaller sample of tweets than the Streaming API because, as explained by Twitter, "the standard Search API is focused on relevance and not completeness". It is not meant to be an exhaustive source of tweets. There has been a lot of scientific research to understand the sampling of Twitter APIs (Joseph et al. 2014; Gerlitz and Rieder 2013; Morstatter et al. 2014; Campan et al. 2018; Lamba et al. 2015; Hino and Fahey 2019). A recent study (Pfeffer et al. 2018) demonstrates that, due to the nature of Twitter's sampling mechanism, it is possible to deliberately influence these samples, the extent and content of any topic, and consequently to manipulate the analyses of researchers and journalists, as well as market and political analysts who analyse these data sources.

Different "open-source" applications and libraries are developed to archive tweets by APIs, like Twarc,[6] Social Feed Manager (Littman et al. 2018),[7] TAGS,[8] Digital Methods Initiatives[9] and TSViz (Rios et al. 2017). These approaches mostly respond to one-off requests and require researchers or web archivists to be able to code. On the other hand, only one of them (Littman et al. 2018) takes archiving issues into account. From an institutional archiving point of view, just getting raw data from an API is not enough, because a tweet may contain other objects, like images, videos or URLs. To guarantee the authenticity of a tweet, each of these objects should be archived and made accessible.

3   How to Access Social Media Archives?

Social media archiving, like web archiving, consists not only of archiving data but also of giving efficient access to these collections. Access to these archives is also closely tied to social media platforms. Thus, the platforms' agreements and policies on how data may be accessed, collected and used play a major role in all phases of social media archiving. Twitter data may not be shared in the form of full-text tweets with their metadata, but only in the form of lists of tweet IDs.

If the data is archived via web crawlers, full-text search and "Wayback machine-like" access can be provided easily (Tofel 2007). This will let users search and read archived tweets like webpages. However, getting statistics like top hashtags for a corpus will require additional information extraction steps. When we study the

---

[6]https://github.com/DocNow/twarc. Accessed 30 July 2019.

[7]https://gwu-libraries.github.io/sfm-ui/. Accessed 30 July 2019.

[8]https://tags.hawksey.info/. Accessed 30 July 2019.

[9]https://digitalmethodsinitiative/dmi-tcat. Accessed 30 July 2019.

research done using Twitter data in the social sciences, we see that there is a need for data mining tools. The most common ways of studying Twitter data in the social sciences are:

- Timelines that show the distribution of the number of tweets over time
- Top entities to get the most popular entities, e.g. top hashtags, top mentions, top users, top URLs, top emojis, top images, etc.
- General statistics like the distribution of retweets, language, geo-location
- Word clouds to analyse the discourse around a subject
- Network graphs to visualise the relations between users, hashtags, etc.

These five methods are essential for providing efficient access to social media archives, in addition to other advanced studies like topic detection or sentiment analysis. The limits of APIs have an impact on the completeness of collections. Thus, it is important to be able to visualise this gap during access, but this issue has not been studied so far. Providing an efficient search interface combined with filters based on metadata (e.g. dates, hashtags, mentions, etc.), together with full-text search, to create subcollections is very important for analysing archived social media. In Littman et al. (2018), Kibana[10] is proposed as a possible access interface.

Access tools should also let users see information related to the archiving procedure for each tweet, like the date at which it was archived and which API was used. It is important to know, for example, that tweets archived using the Streaming API have no retweet, like or favourite counts because the system archives the data as soon as it is published. On the other hand, the same tweet archived using the REST API can contain this information, which reflects the state of the tweet at the archived time.

4   How to Preserve Social Media?

Social media archives must be protected through a long-term preservation strategy, as for web archives, but it is more complicated than preserving common webpages.

The WARC (Web ARChive), a file format for the long-term preservation of digital data, is the predominant format in web archiving and is an International Organization for Standardization or ISO (ISO 2017). The principle is that all interactions between a browser (web client) and a website (a web server) are recorded in a WARC file. It also preserves data gathered from social media APIs based on HTTP transactions.

It is important to note that the WARC is a protocol-oriented archiving format, with each HTTP interaction being archived as request and response records embodying the entirety of the transaction, including transfer-specific headers. Understanding and accessing these records requires, on top of the WARC format

---

[10]https://www.elastic.co/products/kibana. Accessed 30 July 2019.

and content themselves, an understanding of the protocol specifics. That situation is pretty well controlled when it comes to typical webpage archiving, as the vast majority of resources are accessed by URL through an HTTP request. Typical shortcomings such as chunk-encoding[11] removal are well known and accounted for in access tools.

The situation gets more complicated when tweets are acquired via web scraping or APIs. The latter can be addressed by simply archiving API access as HTTP transactions, adding an understanding of the API to the list of requirements when accessing the archive, on top of the WARC format, HTTP protocol and the content itself. However, the WARC format was designed considering the specifications of the first versions of HTTP (HTTP 1.0 and 1.1). HTTP/2 is already being used by many websites like Google and HTTP/3 is being developed. These are multiplexed and binary protocols that would require a specific approach. For example, when we observe the network activity of requests from Google Chrome to Google.com, they use faked HTTP/1-like headers that are recreated based on HTTP/2 metadata. Another example is related to the Twitter HTTP streaming API where the request is potentially infinite, which would make little sense to be archived as-is in WARC records. Twitter APIs are using HTTP as a commodity. The "real" protocol are the APIs where the complexity and information are. Twitter APIs could as well be implemented through raw TCP sockets or another compression or serialisation format. As Twitter APIs are multiple and evolving, this is an undoubted challenge when considering long-term preservation. There is also the possibility that Twitter might in the future drop HTTP altogether and consider (or create) another protocol to serve its APIs, making WARC storage impossible without a change in specifications or without mimicking HTTP transactions. This situation already exists for tweets acquired via web scraping, when the extracted data for each tweet has to be stored without being served by any protocol. By scraping in this context, we mean extracting multiple independent objects (tweets) from an HTML page. Thus, there cannot be a validated HTTP header for this transaction describing for example values for the HTTP fields Content-Length or Content-Type of each extracted tweet.

There is another level to consider when preserving Twitter data: the tweet data itself is evolving in its structure, with the appearance of new properties and changes in meaning of others, and this also has to be considered when accessing archived tweets for a given period of time (Bruns and Weller 2016).

It is also important to consider that access to Twitter data is typically restricted and limited. These limitations are not easily apprehended when crawling and scraping pages but are explicitly stated in the different API access documentation, and materialised as specific information within the transaction. This information, albeit not as important as the data itself, is of interest for the correct interpretation of the archived data. Information about the data being requested (e.g. the tracking of a given keyword using the streaming API) is an important element to preserve.

---

[11] https://en.wikipedia.org/wiki/Chunked_transfer_encoding

These metadata should be extracted separately and considered at the same level as other crawling metadata, for example crawler logs and crawl commands.

At INA, the DAFF (digital archiving file format) has been developed and used (Drugeon 2005). The description of the format is outside the scope of this chapter, but suffice to say that it is not a transaction-oriented archiving format. In the DAFF, each piece of content is archived in a record, independently of the protocol serving it, and identified by its statistically unique SHA-256 digest. Metadata is normalised in a different record in a way that any protocol can lend itself to, including ex nihilo content from extractions or conversion. Metadata about a content preserved in DAFF format are not the responses received through HTTP headers during the HTTP transaction (e.g. transfer encoding, content encoding, range, etc.) but the metadata about the content itself (e.g. URI, date, length, type, status). It is a simplified model when compared to storing all HTTP headers but enough to create HTTP headers to store any type of object independently of transaction type (HTTP, FTP, APIs, scraping, etc.) and to enable later access to the preserved content. Instead of faking (or modifying) headers from a given protocol, we simply keep and normalise a relevant set metadata about the preserved content. In a way, we could consider that WARC archives HTTP transactions, whereas DAFF archives objects identified by URIs, regardless of the protocol used to obtain them. Consequently, INA has chosen to archive each tweet as JSON data. Tweets are typically acquired through the different APIs, and each tweet object is separated in its own record. Tweets acquired through other means (web scraping, data import from other sources, etc.) can also be addressed in the same manner, while acknowledging that some properties of the tweet object might be missing or altered.

It is also important to choose the most adequate digital preservation and metadata standard to describe the archived data such as OAIS (ISO 2012) or Dublin Core (DCMI Usage Board 2006). OAIS is the first and widely used reference model for digital data preservation, which became a standard in 2002. One of the key elements of this model is its fixity, which guarantees that the digital object in the archive has not been modified since its deposit, something which can be computationally verified. As discussed in Acker and Kreisberg (2019), social media that provides activity streams and allows user engagement with multimedia and multi-temporal content is a challenge for the OAIS-based understanding of digital preservation.

5 Archiving Twitter at INA

This section explains the architecture of Twitter archiving at the Institut national de l'audiovisuel (INA) in France. French legal deposit legislation was extended in scope to cover online public web contents in 2006, and the DLWeb (legal deposit web) team at INA is responsible for the collection and preservation of French websites concerned with media and audiovisual content. Tweets have also been

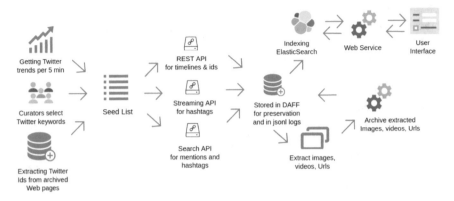

Fig. 2 Overall architecture of the Twitter archiving process at INA

archived as part of legal deposit since 2014. Using Twitter APIs, more than 13,000 user timelines and 600 hashtags are archived 24 h a day. This collection exceeded one million tweets in June 2019, and an average of 300,000 new tweets are added every day.

Figure 2 shows the architecture of the Twitter archiving process at INA. The seed list that contains hashtags, user accounts and keywords is created based on three sources: (1) Curators select the content to archive, (2) Tweet IDs are extracted from archived webpages and (3) Twitter trends in France are tracked every 5 min and all the hashtags and keywords in trends are archived. This selection is used in order not to miss the hashtags or keywords that emerge during special events or outside working hours. The tweets archived as part of trends are not fully indexed but are used to complete the official archive. Different APIs are used based on the nature of the entity in the seed list: the REST API for timelines, the Streaming API for hashtags and the Search API for mentions and hashtags if necessary. All of this data gathered in JSON format is stored in DAFF files for preservation. In addition, logs related to collection, like API warnings, rate limit errors, etc., are kept in JSONL files.

As a next step, the images, videos and URLs are extracted from tweet metadata, archived and stored in DAFF files. In parallel, the tweets are indexed using Elasticsearch,[12] and communication between the resulting index and the user interface is implemented via a web service.

Access to Twitter archives is provided in two ways. The first one is the Social TV approach allows for the visualisation of Twitter and television archives in a synchronous way that will be detailed in Chapter "Linking Twitter Archives with Television Archives". Another approach is an interface to display archived tweets and to enable the aggregation of metadata. Providing an efficient search interface, combined with multiple filters (e.g. dates, hashtags, mentions), is very important

---

[12]https://www.elastic.co/

while working with archived data. This search interface combines search queries and filters, as shown in Fig. 3. Mining Twitter data requires not only full-text search but also data aggregation at different levels. We need to offer generic solutions to satisfy diverse research needs. Figure 4 illustrates our third approach to enable access to Twitter archives at INA. By using aggregations, we are able to provide diverse analytics (e.g. timelines, top hashtags, top distributions) for a given query with a high performance. In addition, users can do complex queries by using search area in Kibana, for example media.type:"video" will get all tweets containing an embedded video.

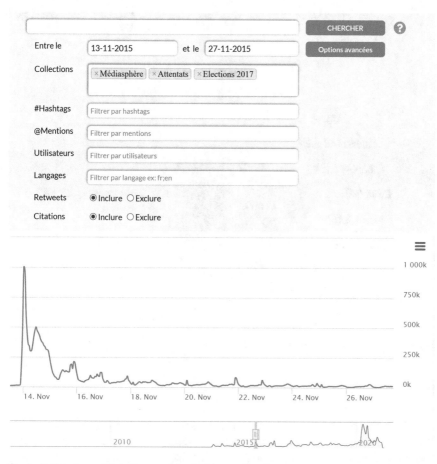

Fig. 3 Full-text search interface combined with metadata filters

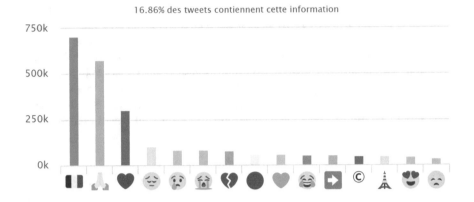

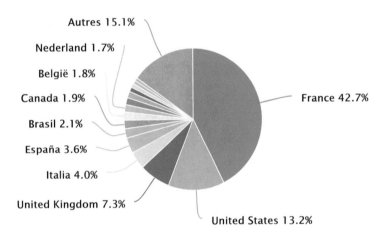

Fig. 4 Data mining user interface to aggregate tweets

6 Conclusions

Social media has become an important source for researchers and web archivists. While there is great enthusiasm for this new source of social data, and Twitter in particular, concerns are also expressed about appropriate archiving and preservation methods. In this chapter, we provided an overview of social media archiving processes based on web crawling, scraping and APIs using Twitter and the archiving system at INA as case studies.

As discussed, each type of approach for archiving social media has different limitations. The needs should be specified clearly before starting to archive social media and the appropriate approach should be identified. For web archiving institutions, different access methods and long-term preservation plans should be discussed in detail. Whatever method is chosen, it is very important to understand its technical advantages and disadvantages, and to be able to clearly communicate them to users. Increasing attention has been given to developing better understanding of the construction and circulation of social media data, in order to evaluate its potential uses (Bruns and Weller 2016; Halford et al. 2018). The challenging part now is to preserve information about the construction of social media archives for future generations, and to find new access methods.

References

Acker A, Kreisberg A (2019) Social media data archives in an API-driven world. Arch Sci:1–19

Bruns A, Weller K (2016) Twitter as a first draft of the present: and the challenges of preserving it for the future. In: Proceedings of the 8th ACM conference on web science, WebSci '16. ACM, New York, pp 183–189

Campan A, Atnafu T, Truta TM, Nolan JM (2018) Is data collection through Twitter streaming API useful for academic research? In: 2018 IEEE international conference on big data (Big Data), pp 3638–3643

DCMI Usage Board (2006) DCMI metadata terms. DCMI recommendation, Dublin Core Metadata Initiative. http://dublincore.org/documents/2006/12/18/dcmi-terms/

Driscoll K, Walker S (2014) Big data, big questions| working within a black box: Transparency in the collection and production of big Twitter data. Int J Commun 8(2014):1745–1764

Drugeon T (2005) A technical approach for the French web legal deposit. In: International workshop on web archiving IWAW'05

Gerlitz C, Rieder B (2013) Mining one percent of Twitter: collections, baselines, sampling. M/C J 16(2):1–18. https://doi.org/10.5204/mcj.620

Halford S, Weal M, Tinati R, Carr L, Pope C (2018) Understanding the production and circulation of social media data: Towards methodological principles and praxis. New Media Soc 20(9):3341–3358

Hino A, Fahey RA (2019) Representing the Twittersphere: archiving a representative sample of Twitter data under resource constraints. Int J Inf Manag 48:175–184

Hockx-Yu H (2014) Archiving social media in the context of non-print legal deposit. In: IFLA WLIC 2014 - Lyon - libraries, citizens, societies: confluence for knowledge in session 107 - national libraries.IFLA WLIC 2014

ISO 14721:2012 (2012) Space data and information transfer systems - Open archival information system (OAIS) – Reference model. Standard, International Organization for Standardization, Geneva, CH

ISO 28500:2017 (2017) Information and documentation – WARC file format. Standard, International Organization for Standardization, Geneva, CH

Joseph K, Landwehr PM, Carley KM (2014) Two 1%s don't make a whole: comparing simultaneous samples from Twitter's streaming API. In: Social computing, behavioral-cultural modeling and prediction, Lecture Notes in Computer Science. Springer International Publishing, Cham, pp 75–83

Lamba H, Malik MM, Pfeffer J (2015) A tempest in a teacup? Analyzing Firestorms on Twitter. In: Proceedings of the 2015 IEEE/ACM International conference on advances in social networks analysis and mining 2015, ASONAM '15. ACM, pp 17–24

Littman J, Chudnov D, Kerchner D, Peterson C, Tan Y, Trent R, Vij R, Wrubel L (2018) API-based social media collecting as a form of web archiving. Int J Digit Libr 19(1):21–38

Liu DF, Fan XS (2011) Study and application of web crawler algorithm based on Heritrix. In: Advanced research on information science, automation and material system. Advanced materials research, vol 219. Trans Tech Publications Ltd, pp 1069–1072

Marshall CC, Shipman FM (2012) On the institutional archiving of social media. In: Proceedings of the 12th ACM/IEEE-CS joint conference on digital libraries, JCDL '12. ACM, New York, pp 1–10

McCormick TH, Lee H, Cesare N, Shojaie A, Spiro ES (2017) Using Twitter for demographic and social science research: tools for data collection and processing. Sociol Methods Res 46(3):390–421

Mejova Y, Macy MW, Weber I (2015) Twitter: a digital socioscope. Cambridge University Press, Cambridge

Milligan I, Ruest N, Lin J (2016) Content selection and curation for web archiving: The gatekeepers vs. the masses. In: 2016 IEEE/ACM joint conference on digital libraries (JCDL), pp 107–110

Morstatter F, Pfeffer J, Liu H (2014) When is It Biased?: Assessing the representativeness of Twitter's streaming API. In: Proceedings of the 23rd international conference on world wide web, WWW '14 companion. ACM, New York, pp 555–556

Olston C, Najork M (2010) Web crawling. Found Trends Inf Retr 4:175–246

Pfeffer J, Mayer K, Morstatter F (2018) Tampering with Twitter's sample API. EPJ Data Science 7(1):50

Rios RA, Pagliosa PA, Ishii RP, de Mello RF (2017) TSViz: a data stream architecture to online collect, analyze, and visualize tweets. In: Proceedings of the symposium on applied computing, SAC '17. ACM, pp 1031–1036

Sloan L, Quan-Haase A (2017) The SAGE handbook of social media research methods. SAGE, Philadelphia

Sobrinho JLV, Júnior GdC, Vinhal CDN (2019) Web crawler for social network user data prediction using soft computing methods. SSRN Scholarly Paper, Social Science Research Network

Tofel B (2007) Wayback for accessing web archives. In: International workshop on web archiving IWAW'07

Tromble R, Storz A, Stockmann D (2017) We don't know what we don't know: when and how the use of Twitter's public APIs biases scientific inference. SSRN Scholarly Paper, Social Science Research Network, Rochester, NY

Zimmer M (2015) The Twitter archive at the library of congress: challenges for information practice and information policy. First Monday 20(7). http://dx.doi.org/10.5210/fm.v20i7.5619

Creating Event-Centric Collections from Web Archives

Elena Demidova ⓘ **and Thomas Risse** ⓘ

Abstract Web archives are an essential information source for research on histo-rical events. However, the large scale and heterogeneity of web archives make it difficult for researchers to access relevant event-specific materials. In this chapter, we discuss methods for creating event-centric collections from large-scale web archives. These methods are manifold and may require manual curation, adopt search or deploy focused crawling. In this chapter, we focus on the crawl-based methods that identify relevant documents in and across web archives and include link networks as context in the resulting collections.

1 Introduction

Web archive materials are of high relevance for research on historical events, such as the Olympic Games, political elections and traumatic incidents with high societal impact. Research on the past events is of interest for many disciplines, including digital humanities, history, law and journalism (Risse et al. 2014b). Given an event of interest and a large-scale web archive, researchers have difficulty in identifying relevant archived content accurately and efficiently. In this chapter, we discuss methods that automatically create focused, event-centric collections for studies on historical events from large-scale web archives.

E. Demidova (✉)
Data Science & Intelligent Systems, Computer Science Institute, University of Bonn, Bonn, Germany

L3S Research Center, Leibniz University of Hannover, Hannover, Germany
e-mail: demidova@L3S.de

T. Risse
University Library J. C. Senckenberg, Goethe University Frankfurt, Frankfurt am Main, Germany
e-mail: t.risse@ub.uni-frankfurt.de

© Springer Nature Switzerland AG 2021
D. Gomes et al. (eds.), *The Past Web*,
https://doi.org/10.1007/978-3-030-63291-5_6

Services for the creation of event-centric or topical collections may require manual curation (e.g. the Archive-It service[1]), as well as adopt search and focused crawling (e.g. Farag et al. 2018; Gossen et al. 2015a). These methods, initially developed for the live Web, are increasingly adopted to the creation of event-centric collections derived from web archives.

Manual curation typically means that the user specifies the web addresses (Uniform Resource Identifiers [URIs]) of interest to be included in the collection. A variation of this method can include search, where the URIs retrieved by a search engine are verified by the user and included in the collection. Manual curation can be very precise, in particular in cases where the intended collection covers only a few relevant URIs known in advance. It also allows for the preservation of the link context of a document. However, manual curation becomes unfeasible as the number of relevant URIs increases and as the temporal gap grows between the event and the time of collection creation. Nevertheless, manual curation can provide valuable input for automatic collection-creation methods. This includes, for example, the seed URIs for crawl-based approaches, which are discussed later in this chapter.

Search-based collection-creation methods can make use of full-text search over the archived documents (see chapter "Full-Text and URL Search" for more details), or of keyword search in the lightweight indexes constructed over the URIs that have been proposed in Souza et al. (2015). In these cases, a collection corresponds to a set of search results retrieved from a web archive and consists of snapshots of web resources. While search-based approaches can appear intuitive, as they correspond to the way users look for information on the live Web, they have several shortcomings. First, in the search-based methods, users' intent is typically expressed as a keyword query. However, keyword queries possess low expressivity and do not adequately capture the complex semantics of event-centric collections. Second, search retrieves document snapshots in isolation and does not provide contextual information for the linked documents. Finally, search-based methods require a priori full-text indexing of the archived resources, which is still not supported by many web archives.

In contrast, the crawl-based methods recently proposed by Gossen et al. (2017, 2020) and extended by Klein et al. (2018) adapt focused crawling, initially designed for the live Web, to web archives. These methods address the shortcomings discussed earlier and provide the following advantages: first, crawl-based techniques allow for more expressive collection specification, which reflects the topical and temporal properties of the events; second, event-centric collections created through crawl-based methods preserve the document linking structure within the archived web graph, thus providing context; and third, crawl-based methods do not require any full-text indexes. Recently, crawl-based methods have been applied to create event-centric collections from a single web archive (Gossen et al. 2017, 2020) as well as to create collections combining relevant documents from several web archives (Klein et al. 2018).

---

[1] http://archive-it.org.

This chapter summarises recent works on the creation of event-centric collections from large-scale web archives, with a focus on crawl-based methods. In the following sections, we discuss the definition and specification of event-centric collections, present collection-creation methods in more detail and discuss open challenges.

2 Definitions of Event-Centric Collections

The aim of creating event-centric collections from web archives is to gather documents relevant to a given historical event. Such collections can contain—as a result—a set of identifiers of the archived documents (URIs) or a set of snapshots of the archived webpages.

When defining event-centric collections, we distinguish between the event and its representation on the Web. The philosopher Kim defined an event as a happening that has a finite duration and changes object's properties or relations (Kim 1976). Westermann and Jain proposed a more formal model that defined an event as a tuple of aspects (Westermann and Jain 2007). These aspects are informational (e.g. entities), structural (e.g. sub-events), spatial (e.g. places, regions, coordinates), temporal (e.g. physical time), causal (chain of causing events) and experiential (e.g. documenting media, sensor data). Farag et al. adopted this model for event-centric collection creation by crawling webpages on the live Web (Farag et al. 2018). There are many other variations of event definition in the literature. In this chapter, we adopt Kim's view.

Events can exhibit different granularity and significance. The target user group for the creation of event-centric collections from web archives are researchers in digital humanities, history, law, journalism and other disciplines. These researchers are typically concerned with more significant events that are reflected on the Web and are of some interest for society. Therefore, events considered in this chapter are happenings of historical relevance, such as the Olympic Games, political elections and traumatic incidents with high societal impact. In contrast, fine-grained events like Mrs Smith moved to Berlin will rarely be reflected on the Web, unless Mrs Smith was a prominent person. A focus on events of societal significance raises the chance that at a later point in time an overview, a summary page or an article will appear, e.g. on Wikipedia, that summarises the event and provides pointers to other relevant materials. These pointers can be used in the crawl specification as a starting point to collect related documents (i.e. as an initial seed list, as discussed later in Sect. 4).

According to Kim's event definition, time and objects changing their properties are essential event characteristics. In the case of significant events, the Web typically adequately reflects such crucial event properties. Shortly after the beginning of an event, the number of mentions of related objects rapidly increases on the Web and decreases subsequently, depending on the level of public interest. Primarily, this is the case for unexpected events such as natural disasters and terrorist attacks.

Gossen et al. observed that for planned, and in particular for recurring events (sport competitions, political elections), relevant documents often appear ahead of the actual start of an event, during the event lead time, and are still published after the completion of the event, during the cool-down time (Gossen et al. 2017, 2020).

Another aspect of collection creation is the user perspective on collection usage. Holzmann and Risse identified three views: user-, data- and graph-centric (Holzmann and Risse 2017). In the user-centric view, users access the archived pages by specifying a URI and time, or by using full-text search. The focus is on the full presentation of a single page for close reading. In the data-centric view, webpages are considered as single resources and treated as raw data, such as text or images. Collections following the data-centric view consist of mostly isolated pages that are not necessarily connected. Finally, in the graph-centric view, single pages or websites, consisting of multiple resources, are considered as nodes in a graph, without taking their contents into account. In such a graph, edges between the nodes represent the links among the pages. Chapter "A Holistic View on Web Archives" discusses these views in more detail.

The user perspective identified by Holzmann and Risse (2017) can provide an essential basis for the collection-creation strategy. For example, a special kind of collection that follows the user-centric view is the storytelling proposed by AlNoamany et al. (2017). This method summarises smaller events and turns them into a story. The stories are built by sampling the most relevant pages from the collection and ordering them by time. The users can access the results via a storytelling social media interface like Adobe Livefyre (previously Storify). Search-based methods can appropriately support the data-centric view. For example, Nanni et al. (2017) followed the data-centric view and selected specific isolated documents. In contrast, the graph-centric view requires a crawl-based method, which preserves the links in the archived web graph. Gossen et al. (2017, 2020) proposed a crawl-based approach that facilitates the graph-centric view. Klein et al. extended this work to accumulate data from several distributed web archives in the resulting collection (Klein et al. 2018).

3 Event-Centric Collection Specification

To create an event-centric collection from a web archive, the user needs to define the desired collection characteristics and the parameters required to configure the specific collection-creation method.

Relevant characteristics of the target collection can include the topical relevance and the temporal scope of the documents as well as the domains of interest. Methods for collection creation can be search or crawl based or involve manual curation. Parameters that delimit a crawl-based collection can include seed URIs of relevant pages to start the crawling process, as well as further restrictions like the number of links followed from the seed URIs.

To facilitate a canonical specification of these characteristics and parameters, Gossen et al. introduced a Collection Specification (Gossen et al. 2017, 2020). This specification, initially developed for crawl-based collection creation, provides a rather generic view, whereas other collection-creation methods typically adopt a subset of the characteristics and parameters specified in the Collection Specification. An exemplary Collection Specification for the event *Snowden leaks* from Gossen et al. (2020) is presented in Example 1.

Example: Collection Specification 1 (Snowden Leaks) *This collection can be described as:*

- *Topical Scope:*

  - *reference documents: wikipedia:Edward_Snowden*
  - *keywords: nsa, edward snowden, ...*

- *Temporal Scope:*

  - *time span of the event: [2013-06-01, 2013-06-30];*
  - *duration of the lead time $T_l = 0$;*
  - *duration of the cool-down time $T_r = 1$ year.*

The Collection Specification describes the topical and temporal scope of relevant documents to be included in the event-centric collection. Like the approaches for search and focused crawling on the live Web proposed in Gossen et al. (2015b), a Collection Specification can indicate the intended topical scope through keywords and named entities. Furthermore, examples of relevant documents can narrow down the collection scope. Recent approaches to event-centric collection creation typically adopt Wikipedia articles on the event of interest as examples (Gossen et al. 2017, 2020; Klein et al. 2018), whereas in general any relevant documents can be named.

The temporal scope is the time interval during which relevant documents appear on the live Web or are stored in a web archive. In the case of events, the relevant time frame depends on the time at which the event took place as well as on the nature of the event (see Table 1). For example, regularly recurring events (e.g. sport competitions), planned special events (e.g. concerts) or unexpected events (e.g. natural disasters) indicate specific temporal reporting patterns (Gossen et al. 2020). Therefore, existing approaches include in the Collection Specification the lead time,

Table 1 Examples of temporal event characteristics

Event	Type	Duration	Lead time	Cool-down time
Olympic Games	Recurring	2 weeks	Weeks	Days
Federal election	Recurring	1 day	Months	Weeks
Fukushima accident	Non-recurring	1 week	–	Months
Snowden leaks	Non-recurring	1 day	–	Years

i.e. the time ahead of the event, and the cool-down time after the completion of the event during which relevant documents appear on the Web.

Furthermore, a Collection Specification for crawl-based collection creation can include specific instructions and parameters for the crawling procedure. For example, the Collection Specification may include seed pages for the crawler and crawl depth (Gossen et al. 2017, 2020; Klein et al. 2018). The seed URIs may constitute the entire collection, like the manually curated services of Archive-It, or serve as starting points for web archive crawling. Web archive crawling may adopt existing link collections as seed URIs. For example, recent approaches utilise links extracted from Wikipedia event articles as seeds for the focused archive crawler (Gossen et al. 2017, 2020; Klein et al. 2018). In future work, possible extensions might include the use of search results as seed URIs, like (Bicho and Gomes 2016), thus combining search-based and crawl-based collection-creation methods.

The choice of the relevant version of the Wikipedia article from which to obtain an appropriate event representation varies across the approaches. For example, Gossen et al. selected the most recent version of the Wikipedia article, assuming it to be more complete (Gossen et al. 2017, 2020). In contrast, Klein et al. adopted temporal heuristics based on the article's editing behaviour to pick the version reflecting the original event representation (Klein et al. 2018).

Further relevant parameters are the intended collection size and the relevance threshold for the included documents. Termination conditions may include a time limit for the collection creation. Gossen et al. developed a user interface to support the specification of crawl-based event-centric collections for the live Web (Gossen et al. 2015b). Such interfaces may be adapted to define the Collection Specification for web archives in the future.

4 Methods to Create Event-Centric Collections

In this section, we briefly discuss methods to create event-centric collections from web archives, including manual curation, search and crawling.

One rather straightforward method to create collections is to search the content of the web archive or its metadata. Existing web archives, such as the UK Web Archive,[2] the Arquivo.pt[3] archive or the Internet Archive,[4] increasingly support full-text search, or metadata search as described in chapter "Full-Text and URL Search". Search results can directly provide a data-centric view of the archived data (see Sect. 2), but the surrounding context of a page might be missing. Nanni et al. (2017) expanded the collections to include related aspects found in knowledge bases like DBpedia (Lehmann et al. 2015). Here, specialised event-centric knowledge

---

[2]https://www.webarchive.org.uk/ukwa/.

[3]https://arquivo.pt/?l=en.

[4]https://archive.org/.

graphs, such as EventKG (Gottschalk and Demidova 2018, 2019), can potentially provide an important source of information regarding events and their temporal relations. One particular case of metadata search is semantic URI search, which adopts named entities mentioned in the URIs of the archived documents to identify relevant documents efficiently while relying on a lightweight index structure, as opposed to full-text indexing (Souza et al. 2015).

Strategies that aim at a graph-centric or user-centric view need to follow the link structure in the web archive, like regular web crawlers. Whereas Gossen et al. created crawl-based collections from a single web archive (Gossen et al. 2020, 2017), Klein et al. (2018) used the Memento protocol (Bornand et al. 2016) to facilitate collection creation from 22 web archives. Web archive crawlers have five main phases: seed selection, content fetching, content assessment, link extraction and prioritisation. The crawlers typically fetch and analyse the pages one by one. Alternatively, a crawler may fetch all pages of the seed list at once and apply all the subsequent steps in the same way (e.g. Nanni et al. (2017)).

Seed selection may be performed manually, by utilising a reference source like a Wikipedia article with manually curated links to relevant documents, or by using a search engine. All methods have their pros and cons. Fully manual curation of the seed list provides collection curators with the highest level of control. However, this strategy will fail to include relevant seeds not known to the curators. A prominent example of manually curated web archive collections is Archive-It,[5] even though the seed list of this service is used for live web crawling. Manual curation approaches are in principle feasible for web archive collections, although not widely adopted. A semi-automatic approach is to draw on a Wikipedia article of the event of interest and utilise the links that it contains as seeds (Gossen et al. 2017; Klein et al. 2018). However, Wikipedia-based seed selection is only possible for significant events regularly curated in Wikipedia. Web search engines typically index major parts of the Web, such that their search results probably include the relevant seeds for essential events. However, the factors influencing their result ranking are not transparent. Nonetheless, web search engines can provide useful hints for a seed list. As web search engines operate on today's Web, past content is often not visible to them. Search engines operating directly on web archive content can circumvent this problem.

The content-fetching phase in web archives is similar to content fetching on the Web. Given a URI, the crawler selects the corresponding archived page. Nevertheless, the ephemeral nature of webpages leads to substantial differences while crawling these media. The live Web contains only one, the most recent version of a page. In contrast, web archives contain different versions of the same page, as a crawler might visit a page at multiple points in time. Therefore, the evolution of a page, e.g. a live blog about an event, is documented at different times. The question that arises is which version should be selected. However, this cannot be answered in general, as it depends on the anticipated usage of the collection. For

---

[5]https://archive-it.org/.

example, to analyse the evolution of perception of an event, it might be interesting to observe the evolution of individual page content over time. In contrast, to obtain a comprehensive event overview, the newest version of a page might be a better choice as it typically contains the most recent updates.

Content assessment is a crucial phase in the collection-creation process. In this phase, given the Collection Specification, the crawler will assess the relevance of a page. The result of the assessment is a relevance score, used to decide if a page will become part of the collection. The threshold for this decision depends on collection intent. A high threshold leads to a precise page selection, with the risk of leaving out relevant pages. With a lower threshold, the number of relevant pages increases. However, a lower threshold will also lead to the inclusion of further non-relevant pages. Identification of a suitable threshold value typically requires some experimentation to tune the selection and crawl parameters.

There are different approaches to content assessment. Gossen et al. and Klein et al. used a vector representation of an event (Gossen et al. 2017; Klein et al. 2018). Gossen et al. created an event vector from the Wikipedia event article and used this vector as a reference to judge the relevance of the crawled pages (Gossen et al. 2017). They created a candidate vector for each crawled page, similar to the creation of the event vector. The crawler then calculated the relevance score as the cosine similarity between the event vector and the candidate vector. The impact of specific terms mentioned in the Collection Specification on relevance estimation can be increased by additional factors such as the inverse document frequency (IDF). IDF values can be obtained, for example, from the Google NGram datasets.[6]

To our knowledge, machine learning has not yet been applied in the context of crawl-based collection creation from web archives. In contrast, on the live Web, several approaches have been developed for topic-centric crawling of webpages. Such focused crawlers use text classification to learn a model to estimate the relevance of an unseen page (Chakrabarti et al. 1999; Pant and Srinivasan 2005). Reinforcement learning is used in Rennie and McCallum (1999) and Singh et al. (2012) by modelling the crawling process as a Markov decision process. Menczer and Monge combined genetic programming and reinforcement learning to estimate page relevance (Menczer and Monge 1999). Adoption of machine learning to crawl-based collection creation in web archives is a promising direction for future research.

Besides content relevance, temporal relevance also plays an important role. Event-related documents are published not only during the event time interval but also before and after. Consequently, we need to estimate the relevance of a document based on the Collection Specification and a time point associated with the web document (e.g. the creation, last modification or capture date). Like Kanhabua and Nørvåg (2011), Gossen et al. assumed that the relevance of documents decreases rapidly as the distance from the event increases and therefore defined a temporal relevance function based on the exponential decay function (Gossen et al. 2020).

---

[6]https://books.google.com/ngrams.

The document time point can be estimated using the *document focus time* discussed in Jatowt et al. (2013).

The link extraction phase extracts all links included in the page. These are the links to related pages, pictures, layout information and scripts. If the collection adopts a user-centric or a graph-centric view, this collection should include layout information of the pages. The crawler adds the extracted links to the crawl queue and can also apply prioritisation, e.g. based on the page score or through further content analysis.

Demidova et al. proposed methods for semantic enrichment of event-centric collections using knowledge bases (Demidova et al. 2014). They applied these methods to event-centric collections created from the live Web in the ARCOMEM project (Risse et al. 2014a). Further development of these methods to enrich event-centric collections created from web archives, in particular through the adoption of event-centric knowledge graphs such as EventKG (Gottschalk and Demidova 2018, 2019), is a promising direction for future research.

5   Discussion and Open Research Directions

In this chapter, we discussed methods aimed at the creation of event-centric collections from web archives. One important consideration when selecting a specific approach for collection creation is the purpose of the collection from the user's perspective, where we differentiate among the user-, data- and graph-centric views proposed by Holzmann and Risse (2017). This view determines the parameters of the creation method and the characteristics of the selected pages, in particular concerning their interlinking and relevant context in the archived web graph.

Furthermore, the collection-creation methods may be classified as manual curation, search-based or crawl-based. In this chapter, we paid particular attention to crawl-based techniques. We observe that existing processes for the creation of collections from the live Web can successfully be adapted to web archives. In addition, aspects such as temporal relevance, to select the suitable version of a document, and seed selection, to reach documents that may not exist on the live Web, should be addressed.

Finally, we observed that state-of-the-art methods in the area of machine learning have not yet been widely adopted in the context of collection creation from web archives. Here, we see significant potential for future research. Furthermore, recently proposed event-centric knowledge bases, like EventKG (Gottschalk and Demidova 2018, 2019), or entity-centric knowledge bases, like DBpedia (Lehmann et al. 2015) and Wikidata (Vrandecic and Krötzsch 2014), provide a rich source of event- and entity-centric semantic information to complement archived materials and to facilitate further advances in event-centric collection creation.

References

AlNoamany Y, Weigle MC, Nelson ML (2017) Generating stories from archived collections. In: Proceedings of the 2017 ACM conference on web science, ACM, WebSci '17, pp 309–318

Bicho D, Gomes D (2016) Preserving websites of research & development projects. In: Proceedings of the 13th international conference on digital preservation, iPRES 2016

Bornand NJ, Balakireva L, de Sompel HV (2016) Routing memento requests using binary classifiers. CoRR abs/1606.09136

Chakrabarti S, van den Berg M, Dom B (1999) Focused crawling: a new approach to topic-specific Web resource discovery. Comput Netw 31(11–16):1623–1640

Demidova E, Barbieri N, Dietze S, Funk A, Holzmann H, Maynard D, Papailiou N, Peters W, Risse T, Spiliotopoulos D (2014) Analysing and enriching focused semantic web archives for parliament applications. Fut Intern 6(3):433–456

Farag MMG, Lee S, Fox EA (2018) Focused crawler for events. Int J Digit Lib 19(1):3–19

Gossen G, Demidova E, Risse T (2015a) iCrawl: improving the freshness of web collections by integrating social web and focused web crawling. In: Proceedings of the 15th ACM/IEEE-CE joint conference on digital libraries. ACM, New York, pp 75–84

Gossen G, Demidova E, Risse T (2015b) The iCrawl wizard - supporting interactive focused crawl specification. In: Proceedings of the 37th European conference on IR research, ECIR 2015. Lecture Notes in Computer Science, vol 9022, pp 797–800

Gossen G, Demidova E, Risse T (2017) Extracting event-centric document collections from large-scale web archives. In: Proceedings of the 21st international conference on Theory and Practice of Digital Libraries, TPDL 2017, pp 116–127

Gossen G, Demidova E, Risse T (2020) Towards extracting event-centric collections from Web archives. Int J Digit Lib 21(1):31–45

Gottschalk S, Demidova E (2018) EventKG: a multilingual event-centric temporal knowledge graph. In: Proceedings of the ESWC 2018, pp 272–287

Gottschalk S, Demidova E (2019) EventKG - the hub of event knowledge on the web - and biographical timeline generation. Seman Web 10(6):1039–1070

Holzmann H, Risse T (2017) Accessing web archives from different perspectives with potential synergies. In: Researchers, practitioners and their use of the archived web (London, 2017)

Jatowt A, Yeung CA, Tanaka K (2013) Estimating document focus time. In: Proceedings of the 22nd ACM international conference on information and knowledge management, CIKM'13. ACM, New York, pp 2273–2278

Kanhabua N, Nørvåg K (2011) A comparison of time-aware ranking methods. In: Proceeding of the 34th international ACM SIGIR conference on research and development in information retrieval, SIGIR 2011. ACM, New York, pp 1257–1258

Kim J (1976) Events as property exemplifications. Springer Netherlands, Dordrecht, pp 159–177

Klein M, Balakireva L, de Sompel HV (2018) Focused crawl of web archives to build event collections. In: Proceedings of the 10th ACM conference on web science, WebSci 2018. ACM, New York, pp 333–342

Lehmann J, Isele R, Jakob M, Jentzsch A, Kontokostas D, Mendes PN, Hellmann S, Morsey M, van Kleef P, Auer S, Bizer C (2015) DBpedia - a large-scale, multilingual knowledge base extracted from Wikipedia. Seman. Web 6(2):167–195

Menczer F, Monge AE (1999) Scalable web search by adaptive online agents: an InfoSpiders case study. In: Klusch M (ed) Intelligent information agents. Springer, Berlin, Heidelberg, pp 323–347. https://doi.org/10.1007/978-3-642-60018-0_17

Nanni F, Ponzetto SP, Dietz L (2017) Building entity-centric event collections. In: Proceedings of the 2017 ACM/IEEE joint conference on digital libraries, JCDL 2017. IEEE Computer Society, Washington, pp 199–208

Pant G, Srinivasan P (2005) Learning to crawl: comparing classification schemes. ACM Trans Inf Syst 23(4):430–462

Rennie J, McCallum A (1999) Using reinforcement learning to spider the web efficiently. In: Proceedings of the sixteenth international conference on machine learning (ICML 1999). Morgan Kaufmann, Burlington, pp 335–343

Risse T, Demidova E, Dietze S, Peters W, Papailiou N, Doka K, Stavrakas Y, Plachouras V, Senellart P, Carpentier F, Mantrach A, Cautis B, Siehndel P, Spiliotopoulos D (2014a) The ARCOMEM architecture for social- and semantic-driven web archiving. Fut Intern 6(4):688–716

Risse T, Demidova E, Gossen G (2014b) What do you want to collect from the web? In: Proceedings of the building web observatories workshop (BWOW) 2014

Singh N, Sandhawalia H, Monet N, Poirier H, Coursimault JM (2012) Large scale URL-based classification using online incremental learning. In: Proceedings of the 2012 11th international conference on machine learning and applications, ICMLA '12, vol 02. IEEE Computer Society, Washington, pp 402–409

Souza T, Demidova E, Risse T, Holzmann H, Gossen G, Szymanski J (2015) Semantic URL analytics to support efficient annotation of large scale web archives. In: First COST Action IC1302 International KEYSTONE conference IKC, 2015. Lecture notes in computer science, vol 9398. Springer, New York, pp 153–166

Vrandecic D, Krötzsch M (2014) Wikidata: a free collaborative knowledgebase. Commun ACM 57(10):78–85

Westermann U, Jain R (2007) Toward a common event model for multimedia applications. IEEE MultiMedia 14(1):19–29

Part III
Access Methods to Analyse the Past Web

Elena Demidova

Numerous organisations around the globe, including national libraries and academic institutions, as well as individuals, operate web archives. The oldest and the most prominent example is the Internet Archive, with a collection including over 20 years of web history and more than 475 billion webpages as of February 2021.[1] Other prominent web archives include Arquivo.pt,[2] with more than 10 billion documents, and the UK Web Archive.[3] Web archives contain information that is extremely valuable for researchers and information professionals in various disciplines, including digital humanities, social sciences, web science, history, law and journalism. However, this information is exceedingly hard to access.

The development of effective and efficient methods to access the past Web poses significant challenges. These challenges result from the large scale, heterogeneity and temporal properties of the archived materials. Furthermore, the large variety in users' disciplinary backgrounds requires a range of different access methods. Finally, a critical part of the problem is technological barriers. The investment and expertise needed to maintain efficient access to the archived materials at scale significantly restrict access to web archives. Overall, this results in substantial differences in the access methods provided by existing web archives. In this part of the book, we present a selection of recently developed access methods aiming to address these challenges.

---

[1] http://archive.org/about
[2] https://arquivo.pt/?l=en
[3] https://www.webarchive.org.uk/ukwa/

E. Demidova (✉)
Data Science & Intelligent Systems, Computer Science Institute, University of Bonn, Bonn, Germany

L3S Research Center, Leibniz University of Hannover, Hannover, Germany
e-mail: elena.demidova@cs.uni-bonn.de

Full-text search and search based on Uniform Resource Identifiers (URIs) are methods directly adapted to web archives from the live Web, while addressing the additional challenges of handling the temporal dimension of web archives. We present these methods in the chapter "Full-Text and URL Search". The content of a web archive may be viewed as snapshots of the archived webpages, as data or metadata extracted from a collection of archived webpages and as a graph connecting archived web resources. In the chapter "A Holistic View on Web Archives", we discuss such different perspectives on web archives, namely, a user-centric view, a data-centric view and a graph-centric view. Archived materials relevant to particular studies are often fragmented and spread across several archives. The chapter "Interoperability for Accessing Versions of Web Resources with the Memento Protocol" presents the Memento protocol, which facilitates unified and standardised access to data spread across several archives. This protocol, developed by the Internet Archive, is currently supported by more than 20 memory organisations. The chapter "Linking Twitter Archives with Television Archives" presents a novel application, developed at the Institut national de l'audiovisuel, which links Twitter and television archives to facilitate a social television experience. Finally, in the chapter "Image Analytics in Web Archives", we present an approach that leverages deep learning techniques for the identification of public personalities in the images stored in the Internet Archive.

Full-Text and URL Search Over Web Archives

Miguel Costa

Abstract Web archives are a historically valuable source of information. In some respects, web archives are the only record of the evolution of human society in the last two decades. They preserve a mix of personal and collective memories, the importance of which tends to grow as they age. However, the value of web archives depends on their users being able to search and access the information they require in efficient and effective ways. Without the possibility of exploring and exploiting the archived contents, web archives are useless. Web archive access functionalities range from basic browsing to advanced search and analytical services, accessed through user-friendly interfaces. Full-text and URL search have become the predominant and preferred forms of information discovery in web archives, fulfilling user needs and supporting search APIs that feed third-party applications. Both full-text and URL search are based on the technology developed for modern web search engines. However, while web search engines enable searching over the most recent web snapshot, web archives enable searching over multiple snapshots from the past. This means that web archives have to deal with a temporal dimension that is the cause of new challenges and opportunities, discussed throughout this chapter.

1 Introduction

The World Wide Web has a democratic character, and everyone can publish all kinds of information using different types of media. News, blogs, wikis, encyclopaedias, photos, interviews and public opinion pieces are just a few examples. Some of this information is unique and historically valuable. For instance, online newspapers reporting the speech of a president after winning an election or announcing an imminent invasion of a foreign country might become as valuable in the future as

M. Costa (✉)
Vodafone, Lisbon, Portugal
e-mail: miguel.costa2@vodafone.com

© Springer Nature Switzerland AG 2021   71
D. Gomes et al. (eds.), *The Past Web*,
https://doi.org/10.1007/978-3-030-63291-5_7

ancient manuscripts are today. Historical interest in these documents is also growing as they age, becoming a unique source of past information for many areas, such as sociology, history, anthropology, politics, journalism, linguistics or marketing.

Much of the effort invested in web archive research and development focused on acquiring, storing, managing and preserving data (Masanès 2006). However, to make historical analysis possible, web archives must turn from mere document repositories into accessible archives. Full-text search, i.e. finding documents with text that match the given keywords or sentences, has become the dominant form of information access, especially thanks to web search engines such as Google, which have a strong influence on how users search in other systems. In web archives, full-text queries (e.g. Iraq war) can be narrowed to a user-specified time interval (e.g. year 2003). The matching document versions, sometimes in the order of millions, are then ranked according to their relevance to the query and time interval. Surveys indicate that full-text search is the preferred method for accessing web archive data, and the most used when supported (Costa and Silva 2011; Ras and van Bussel 2007). As a result, despite the considerably high computational resources required to provide full-text search over large-scale web collections, 63% of worldwide web archives provide it for at least a part of their collections (Costa et al. 2016).

As a result of the challenges of creating effective and efficient mechanisms to match and rank all document versions, the prevalent discovery method in web archives is based on URL (Uniform Resource Locator) search. Users can search for a web document of interest by submitting its URL and narrow the obtained document versions by date range. A list of chronologically ordered versions is then returned for that URL, such as in the Internet Archive's Wayback Machine.[1] This allows, for instance, a search for stored versions of a webpage by using its original web address. Around 80% of worldwide web archives support URL of search, which requires much less computational resource than full-text search. On the other hand, URL search is limited, as it forces users to remember URLs that may have ceased to exist a long time ago.

Metadata search, i.e. a search by metadata attributes, such as category, language and file format, is another type of search that complements the previous two examples. For instance, the Library of Congress Web Archive[2] supports search on the bibliographic records of its collections. Other web archives include metadata filters in their advanced search user interfaces along with full-text or URL search. The manual creation of metadata describing the curated collections and their artefacts is a time-consuming and expensive process, which makes it a non-viable option for large-scale web archives. In this case, most of the metadata must be created automatically. Metadata search is provided by 72% of worldwide web archives.

These three types of search are available in most web archives, complementing each other. Full-text, URL and metadata search are the most common forms of

---

[1] https://web.archive.org.

[2] https://www.loc.gov/webarchiving.

information discovery in web archives. Technology is adapted from the typical search functionalities provided by modern web search engines and developed to enable search over multiple snapshots from the past Web. The main advantage of this approach is that the users of search engines can easily replicate their search behaviour to find information in web archives. The main disadvantage is that this technology tends to provide unsatisfactory results, because the data characteristics of web archives and the information needs of their users are different from web search engines (Costa and Silva 2010). Hence, the web archiving community has been working on search tools and user interfaces that better satisfy web archive users.

The remainder of this chapter is organised as follows. Section 2 presents the typical search user interfaces offered by web archives, giving an overview of web archive access functionalities. Section 3 characterises users' search behaviours that determine development decisions and suggests new research directions. Section 4 explains how current search technology locates the desired information and fulfils users' information needs, and Sect. 5 draws the conclusions of this research.

2 Search User Interfaces Over Web Archives

Most web archives are accessible from the live Web through a web browser. Their digital collections, to which access may be restricted, are searchable via a graphical user interface (GUI). Despite the particularities and different layouts, these GUIs generally provide similar functionalities. The GUIs mostly comprise a search box complemented with a date range filter to narrow the search results to a specific time interval. The GUIs of the three web archives depicted in this section are illustrative of this arrangement, namely, the Internet Archive,[3] Arquivo.pt (a.k.a. the Portuguese web-archive)[4] and the Library of Congress Web Archive.[5] The Internet Archive, created in 1996, was one of the first web archives and leads the most ambitious initiative, with more than 400 billion webpages saved worldwide over time. Its Wayback Machine is probably the most used system for searching and accessing archived content, along with its open-source counterpart OpenWayback,[6] used by most web archives. Because of the huge amount of data, full-text search is only available in beta mode for a few million documents.[7] Currently, URL search is the main method to find information in the Internet Archive.

---

[3]https://archive.org.

[4]https://arquivo.pt/?l=en.

[5]https://loc.gov/websites.

[6]https://github.com/iipc/openwayback.

[7]https://blog.archive.org/2016/10/26/searching-through-everything/.

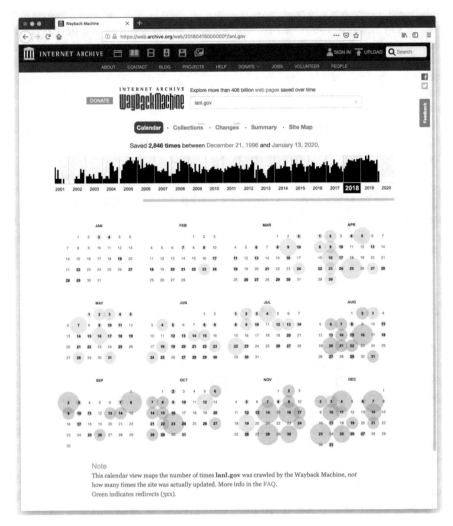

Fig. 1 User interface of the Internet Archive's Wayback Machine after a URL search (netpreserve.org was submitted and 2018 selected to narrow the archived versions to this year)

Figure 1 depicts the GUI of the Wayback Machine after searching a URL, without protocol (e.g. http), which in this example is netpreserve.org. A calendar view is presented with circles around the days when the corresponding webpage was archived. The size of the circle is proportional to the number of versions archived on a given day. A total of 567 versions were archived between 2004 and 2019. A time slider at the top of the GUI shows the distribution of the number of archived versions throughout the years and enables the user to select a year and narrows the calendar view to that period. In this example, the selected year is 2018. Users can then click on the versions to view and navigate them as if they were in the past.

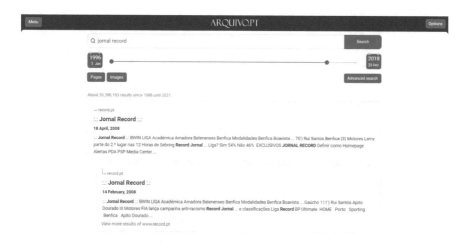

Fig. 2 User interface of Arquivo.pt presenting the first two full-text search results for the query "jornal record" (record newspaper). The search results were restricted to the time interval between 1996 and 2018

The Memento project adds a temporal dimension to the HTTP protocol so that archived versions of a document can be served by the web server holding that document or by existing web archives that support the Memento API (application programming interface), such as the Internet Archive (Van de Sompel et al. 2009). The Time Travel portal[8] uses this protocol to propagate URL queries to the aforementioned systems and redirects users to the archives that host the versions of a given URL. For each archive, the version closest to the requested date is shown, along with the first, last, previous and next versions. The portal works as a metasearch engine for web archives.

Arquivo.pt, also informally known as the Portuguese web-archive, was created in 2007 and focuses its activities on the preservation of the Portuguese Web, which is broadly defined as the web content of most interest for the Portuguese community. It provides access to more than 10 billion documents written in several languages, searchable by full-text and URL via a unique web form. The GUI of the Arquivo.pt automatically interprets the type of query and presents the results accordingly. When the Arquivo.pt receives a full-text query, which can be restricted by a date range, it returns a results page containing a list of 10 webpages matching the query and the time interval, as illustrated in the example of Fig. 2. User interaction with the system and the results layout are similar to commercial web search engines. The results are ranked by relevance to the query, determined by a customised ranking model. Each result includes the title, URL and crawled date of the webpage, along with a snippet of text containing the query terms. The user can then click on the links of

---

[8]https://timetravel.mementoweb.org.

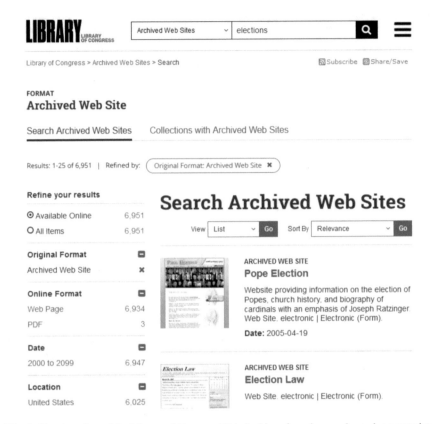

Fig. 3 User interface of the Library of Congress Web Archive after a keyword search on metadata (*elections* was submitted to search on the indexed *Archived Web Sites*)

the archived webpages to browse them. In addition, the user can click to see a list of all archived versions chronologically ordered for each webpage.

Both the Wayback Machine and Arquivo.pt offer an advanced interface for their users to conduct metadata search by applying multiple filters (e.g. file format, domain name) or by restricting the search to special operators (e.g. exact phrases, word exclusion). Another example of metadata search is the Library of Congress Web Archive, which was set up in 2000 and since then has been creating collections of archived websites on selected topics, such as the US elections or the Iraq War. It enables users to search for keywords in the bibliographic records of their collections and then to refine results by multiple filters, such as format type, location, subject, language and access conditions. Figure 3 shows the GUI of the Library of Congress Web Archive with some of these filters available on the left menu.

In addition to GUIs, several APIs implemented as web services have been provided to facilitate interoperability between web archives and external applications. These APIs specify how to search and access web archive collections automatically.

Examples include the Internet Archive API,[9] the Arquivo.pt API[10] and the Memento Time Travel API.[11] They are essential services to feed innovative applications developed by third-parties that need to search historical web data.

3 Why, What and How Do Users Search?

Search is a way to achieve users' goals and not an end in itself. Understanding these goals along with all other aspects of user behaviour is key to the success of web archives. This knowledge enables the development of technology, the design of GUIs and the tailoring of search results that better satisfy users. To this end, a few studies have been conducted to understand why, what and how users search in web archives.

Let me first introduce the taxonomy proposed by Broder, which is common to information retrieval researchers and used to investigate different search systems, of which web search engines are the most studied (Broder 2002). Broder classified web search engine queries into three broad categories according to user goal: (1) *navigational* to reach a particular webpage or site (e.g. www.europa.eu), (2) *informational* to collect information about a topic, usually from multiple pages, without having a specific one in mind (e.g. Brexit) and (3) *transactional* to perform a web-mediated activity (e.g. shopping, downloading a file, finding a map).

Quantitative and qualitative studies investigated the information needs of general web archive users (i.e. why they are searching). Three studies presented in the same research article, namely, a search log analysis, an online questionnaire and a laboratory study, found similar results (Costa and Silva 2010). The information needs of web archive users are mainly navigational, then informational and lastly, transactional. Overall, these needs are aligned with the available functionalities. URL search is a perfect match to fulfil navigational needs when URLs are submitted, which occurs on a significant percentage of occasions (26% reported in Costa and Silva 2011). In addition, full-text search can be used as a generic tool to fulfil all three needs. In sum, the search technology provided by web archives can support the main informational needs of their users. On the other hand, web archives fail in efficiently supporting some specific needs, such as exploring the evolution of the content of a website that may present thousands of different versions archived along time.

Full-text and URL search are also limited when analysing complex information needs, such as those of historians or journalists. For instance, they fail to provide answers to questions such as "Who were the most discussed politicians during 2005?", "What were the top sporting events in the last decade?" or "What were

---

[9]https://archive.org/services/docs/api.

[10]https://github.com/arquivo/pwa-technologies/wiki/APIs.

[11]https://timetravel.mementoweb.org/guide/api.

the most popular time periods related to Barack Obama?" Users would have to submit many queries without guarantees of full coverage of all relevant content. The search functionalities of web archives lack expressive power to query an entity (e.g. a person) or an event (e.g. September 11) by its properties or relations with other entities and events (Fafalios et al. 2018). Researchers find it difficult to meet these complex information needs when they use web archives as a source of research data (Brügger and Milligan 2018; Dougherty et al. 2010; Singh et al. 2016b).

When we look at what users search to understand what is relevant for them, results show that nearly half of their informational needs are focused on names of people, places or things. Many navigational queries only contain the names of companies or institutions. People tend to remember short names that they use as keywords for searching. When analysing by topic, navigational queries refer mostly to websites about commerce, computers or the Internet, such as blogs, and about education, such as universities. Informational queries refer mostly to people, health and entertainment. This search analysis was conducted on the general use of the Arquivo.pt (Costa and Silva 2011). Another study on the Wayback Machine indicates that its users mostly request English pages, followed by pages written in European languages (AlNoamany et al. 2014). Most of these users probably search for pages archived in the Wayback Machine because the requested pages no longer exist on the live Web.

Studies about the ways in which users search indicate that they do not spend much time and effort searching the past Web (AlNoamany et al. 2013; Costa and Silva 2011). Users prefer short sessions, which comprise short queries and few clicks. Full-text search is preferred to URL search, but both are frequently used. This preference is understandable because URL search requires users to remember the exact URL, which in some cases became unavailable a long time ago. User interactions in the form of queries, query terms, clicked rankings and viewed archived pages follow a power law distribution. This means that all these interactions have a small percentage that is repeated many times and can be exploited to increase the performance of web archives (e.g. using cache mechanisms) and the quality of their results (e.g. learning a higher ranking for the most viewed pages). There is a strong evidence that users prefer the oldest documents over the newest. However, they do not search applying any temporal restriction or use temporal expressions (Costa and Silva 2014). This is an intriguing result, since all information needs are focused on the past but not even large time intervals were used to narrow queries. Also surprising is the fact that web archive users said they wanted to see the evolution of a page over time, but they tended to click on just one or two versions of each URL. The main conclusion is that web archive users search as they would in web search engines. These behaviours may be the result of offering similar GUIs, leading users to search in a similar way. Another example of this behaviour is that almost all users of both web archives and web search engines do not use metadata filters available as advanced search functions.

Lastly, specific types of researchers, such as historians, present different search behaviours (Singh et al. 2016b). They require a comprehensive understanding of a subject, so they usually start with broader queries about that subject, which are reformulated several times to get an overview of the areas of interest. More specific queries are then submitted on each research aspect in order to gain deeper knowledge.

4 Finding Relevant Results

Finding the desired information to fulfil the information need of web archive users is a complex process that passes through several stages. This section explains them very succinctly and gives a glimpse of the associated challenges.

4.1 From Archived Data to Search Results

URL search matches all archived versions of the content obtained along time from a given URL and its possible aliases (i.e. different URLs referring to the same resource). URLs are first normalised to a canonical form and then indexed to speed up the matching phase. For instance, https://www.example.com, https://example.com:80 and https://example.com/index.html tend to refer to the same webpage and can be normalised to https://example.com. The matching versions are traditionally presented in a chronological view, such as shown in Fig. 1. The versions are ranked by their timestamp, which usually refers to the content acquisition date but may also refer to the creation or publication date. This ranking enables users easily to jump between the oldest and most recent versions.

URL search can be implemented without processing the full content of archived documents, using for instance just the crawl logs. Creating a full-text search service is much more complex. All data must be processed beforehand, for example broken up into words (tokenised) and syntactically analysed (parsed) to separate text from metadata and identify the structural elements to which each segment of text belongs (e.g. title, headings, image). This processing is performed over content coded using many different file formats that continue to evolve, such as HTML, PDF and Microsoft Office formats. Further processing is usually carried out, such as link extraction for graph analysis algorithms (e.g. PageRank by Page et al. 1998) and the enhancement, with anchor text, of the content of web documents to which the links point. Then, index structures are created over the words and metadata to speed up the matching process between documents and queries. This matching depends on the implemented retrieval model. Usually, for very large-scale collections such as those preserved in web archives, a retrieval model is chosen, where all query terms or semantically related terms must occur in the documents. This works as a selection stage for candidate documents relevant to the query. Still, millions of documents may be retrieved, which makes it extremely hard for a user to explore and find relevant information. To overcome this problem, ranking models estimate document relevance based on how well documents match user queries. Documents are then sorted in descending order by their relevance score as a means for users to find information effectively and efficiently.

4.2 Ranking Search Results

A ranking model combines a set of ranking features (a.k.a., factors or signals). Some of these features estimate the documents' relevance according to a given query. Examples include query term proximity in documents, where closer terms tend to be more related than terms that are further apart, or the TF-IDF and BM25 functions (Robertson et al. 2009), which measure the relevance of query terms to a document based on the number of times the terms occur in the document and collection. Other features are independent from the query and estimate a static measure of importance, quality or popularity for a document. Examples include the number of links a document receives or the number of times a document was visited by users. There are many other proven ranking features that can be used alone or combined (Baeza-Yates and Ribeiro-Neto 2011).

Creating precise ranking models for a new type of search, such as for web archives, brings many challenges. First, it requires a comprehensive knowledge of users' needs and behaviours. Second, it is necessary to quantify the perception of relevance to the users by applying the proper ranking features, some of which need to be created or redesigned for the new context. Third, all features need to be combined into one ranking model optimised towards a goal (e.g. an evaluation metric aligned with users' perceived relevance of the obtained search results). Combining them manually is not trivial, especially when there are hundreds of potential features. In addition, manual tuning can lead to overfitting, i.e. the model fits training data closely, but fails to generalise to unseen test data. Hence, supervised learning-to-rank (L2R) algorithms have been employed to automatically find the best way to combine ranking features, resulting in significant improvements (Liu 2009). Deep learning extends L2R algorithms with novel techniques with novel capabilities that can automatically learn representations of queries and documents for matching in a latent semantic space (Mitra and Craswell 2018). In addition, end-to-end ranking models can be learned directly from data without the need to build hand crafted features or even manually labelling datasets.

4.3 Web Archive Information Retrieval

All steps necessary to provide ranked search results require significant time and effort. This is the reason why most web archives use web search engine technology to support full-text search on their collections. Most of this technology uses

Lucene[12] or its extensions for distributed processing, such as Solr,[13] ElasticSearch[14] and NutchWAX.[15] However, by default all these technologies ignore the specificities of web archives, and the consequence is that the search results generated are poorly ranked and fail to satisfy users (Costa et al. 2014).

Web archive information retrieval is a recent field which is still developing solutions for web archive users. As a result, some of the approaches have come from the field of temporal information retrieval, which also considers both topical and temporal criteria of relevance (Campos et al. 2015; Kanhabua et al. 2015). An idea shared between both fields is that the distribution of document dates can be exploited, since it reveals time intervals that are likely to be of interest to the query (Jones and Diaz 2007; Singh et al. 2016b). For instance, when searching for *tsunami*, the peaks in the distribution may indicate when tsunamis occurred. Another idea is to attribute additional relevance to the documents that changed their content more often or to a greater degree (Elsas and Dumais 2010). More popular and revisited documents are also more likely to change (Adar et al. 2009). On the other hand, the most persistent terms along several versions of a document are potentially descriptive of the main topic addressed in the document text and are probably used early in the life of a document. These persistent terms are especially useful for matching navigational queries, because the relevance of documents for these queries is not expected to change over time.

This type of knowledge about what is relevant for users is core for the engineering of better ranking features for web archives. A different type of improvement can be achieved by training temporal ranking models. For instance, multiple models trained and optimised for specific time periods showed better performance than using just one single model to fit all data (Costa et al. 2014). A simpler way to take advantage of multiple models is to allow users to select the one that is better suited for their particular information need (Singh et al. 2016a). Scholars, for instance, initially want an overview of the research topic, preferring more diversified results, and later on in the process they need more focused results. Different models can support these different needs.

4.4 Scalability Challenges

Creating a full-text search service on the huge and rapidly growing amount of archived web data presents many scalability challenges. Users expect immediate responses and optimal search results (like Google provides), but the budgets assigned to the web archiving institutions is insignificant in comparison to the

---

[12]https://lucene.apache.org.

[13]https://lucene.apache.org/solr.

[14]https://www.elastic.co.

[15]https://archive-access.sourceforge.net.

Internet giants that manage commercial search engines. Thus, some creative alternatives have been proposed, such as simply indexing the anchor texts, which are many orders of magnitude smaller (Holzmann et al. 2017). Anchor text is the set of words contained in a hyperlink, typically the blue underlined words in a page. Anchor texts to a web document are short and concise descriptions that together represent the collective perception of other content authors.

Besides anchor texts, URLs may contain hints about the content of documents, such as their language (Baykan et al. 2008), topic (e.g. sport) (Baykan et al. 2009) and genre (e.g. blog) (Abramson and Aha 2012). Named entities can be extracted from URLs to annotate documents accurately (Souza et al. 2015). Features additional to the webpage content when combined provide better search results than when used individually. They may include metadata extracted from crawl logs (e.g. number of archived versions), hyperlinks (e.g. number of inlinks), URL strings (e.g. URL depth measured by counting the number of embedded slashes) and anchors (e.g. frequency of the query terms in the anchor text) (Vo et al. 2016).

A completely different approach to address scalability challenges is to use commercial web search engines (e.g. Bing) to retrieve lists of ranked results from the live Web (Kanhabua et al. 2016). Results are then linked to the Wayback Machine to support browsing in the archived versions. This solution supports full-text search almost without developing any technology. The downside is that only a small part of the archived Web is covered by commercial web search engines, and this tends to worsen over time as more pages become permanently unavailable. Moreover, this technology is not tailored for web archive users. For instance, it is known that web search engines favour fresh content, while web archives focus on content from the past Web.

5 Conclusions

Full-text and URL search turned web archives into useful data sources for a wide range of users and applications. Currently, these forms of search are the best and most available forms of information discovery in web archives. They are an amazing feat of engineering, able to process billions of archived versions of documents to enable discovery of the desired information almost immediately. Nevertheless, web archives continue to adopt web search engine technology that ignores the particularities of their users and preserved collections. As a result, the quality of search results, and thus user satisfaction, is far from ideal.

The web archiving community has offered some improvements, such as better GUIs, search tools and ranking algorithms. One of the reasons for these improvements is a better understanding of the web archive users, such as knowing why are they searching, what is relevant for them and how they search to fulfil their information needs. Another reason is the joint efforts of the community to develop common tools and data formats for web archives. These are promising advances to make digital memories easier to find and exploit.

References

Abramson M, Aha DW (2012) What's in a URL? Genre classification from URLs. In: Proceedings of the workshops at the twenty-sixth AAAI conference on artificial intelligence

Adar E, Teevan J, Dumais S, Elsas J (2009) The web changes everything: understanding the dynamics of web content. In: Proceedings of the 2nd ACM international conference on web search and data mining, pp 282–291

AlNoamany YA, Weigle MC, Nelson ML (2013) Access patterns for robots and humans in web archives. In: Proceedings of the 13th ACM/IEEE-CS joint conference on digital libraries, pp 339–348

AlNoamany Y, AlSum A, Weigle MC, Nelson ML (2014) Who and what links to the internet archive. Int J Digit Libr 14(3–4):101–115

Baeza-Yates R, Ribeiro-Neto B (2011) Modern information retrieval: the concepts and technology behind search. Addison-Wesley Professional, Boston

Baykan E, Henzinger M, Weber I (2008) Web page language identification based on URLs. Proc VLDB Endowm 1(1):176–187

Baykan E, Henzinger M, Marian L, Weber I (2009) Purely URL-based topic classification. In: Proceedings of the 18th international conference on world wide web, pp 1109–1110

Broder A (2002) A taxonomy of web search. SIGIR Forum 36(2):3–10

Brügger N, Milligan I (2018) The SAGE handbook of web history. SAGE Publications Limited, Thousand Oaks

Campos R, Dias G, Jorge AM, Jatowt A (2015) Survey of temporal information retrieval and related applications. ACM Comput Surv 47(2):15

Costa M, Silva MJ (2010) Understanding the information needs of web archive users. In: Proceedings of the 10th international web archiving workshop, pp 9–16

Costa M, Silva MJ (2011) Characterizing search behavior in web archives. In: Proceedings of the 1st international temporal web analytics workshop, pp 33–40

Costa M, Couto F, Silva M (2014) Learning temporal-dependent ranking models. In: Proceedings of the 37th international ACM SIGIR conference on research & development in information retrieval. ACM, New York, pp 757–766

Costa M, Gomes D, Silva MJ (2016) The evolution of web archiving. Int J Digit Libr 18(3):1–15

Dougherty M, Meyer E, Madsen C, Van den Heuvel C, Thomas A, Wyatt S (2010) Researcher engagement with web archives: state of the art. Tech. rep., Joint Information Systems Committee (JISC)

Elsas J, Dumais S (2010) Leveraging temporal dynamics of document content in relevance ranking. In: Proceedings of the 3rd ACM international conference on web search and data mining, pp 1–10

Fafalios P, Holzmann H, Kasturia V, Nejdl W (2018) Building and querying semantic layers for web archives (extended version). Int J Digit Libr 19:1–19

Holzmann H, Nejdl W, Anand A (2017) Exploring web archives through temporal anchor texts. In: Proceedings of the 2017 ACM on web science conference. ACM, New York, pp 289–298

Jones R, Diaz F (2007) Temporal profiles of queries. ACM Trans Inf Syst 25(3):14

Kanhabua N, Blanco R, Nørvåg K, et al. (2015) Temporal information retrieval. Found Trends Inf Retr 9(2):91–208

Kanhabua N, Kemkes P, Nejdl W, Nguyen TN, Reis F, Tran NK (2016) How to search the internet archive without indexing it. In: International conference on theory and practice of digital libraries. Springer, New York, pp 147–160

Liu T (2009) Learning to rank for information retrieval. In: Foundations and trends in information retrieval, vol 3. Now Publishers Inc., Boston

Masanès J (2006) Web archiving. Springer, New York

Mitra B, Craswell N (2018) An introduction to neural information retrieval. Found Trends Inf Retr 13(1):1–126

Page L, Brin S, Motwani R, Winograd T (1998) The PageRank citation ranking: bringing order to the web. Tech. rep., Stanford Digital Library Technologies Project

Ras M, van Bussel S (2007) Web archiving user survey. Tech. rep., National Library of the Netherlands (Koninklijke Bibliotheek)

Robertson S, Zaragoza H, et al. (2009) The probabilistic relevance framework: BM25 and beyond, vol 3. Now Publishers Inc., Boston

Singh J, Nejdl W, Anand A (2016a) Expedition: a time-aware exploratory search system designed for scholars. In: Proceedings of the 39th International ACM SIGIR conference on Research and Development in Information Retrieval, pp 1105–1108

Singh J, Nejdl W, Anand A (2016b) History by diversity: helping historians search news archives. In: Proceedings of the 2016 ACM on conference on human information interaction and retrieval, pp 183–192

Souza T, Demidova E, Risse T, Holzmann H, Gossen G, Szymanski J (2015) Semantic URL analytics to support efficient annotation of large scale web archives. In: Proceedings of the international KEYSTONE conference on semantic keyword-based search on structured data sources, pp 153–166

Van de Sompel H, Nelson ML, Sanderson R, Balakireva LL, Ainsworth S, Shankar H (2009) Memento: time travel for the web. CoRR abs/0911.1112

Vo KD, Tran T, Nguyen TN, Zhu X, Nejdl W (2016) Can we find documents in web archives without knowing their contents? In: Proceedings of the 8th ACM conference on web science, pp 173–182

A Holistic View on Web Archives

Helge Holzmann and Wolfgang Nejdl

Abstract In order to address the requirements of different user groups and use cases of web archives, we have identified three views to access and explore web archives: user-, data- and graph-centric. The user-centric view is the natural way to look at the archived pages in a browser, just like the live Web is consumed. By zooming out from there and looking at whole collections in a web archive, data processing methods can enable analysis at scale. In this data-centric view, the Web and its dynamics as well as the contents of archived pages can be looked at from two angles: (1) by retrospectively analysing crawl metadata with respect to the size, age and growth of the Web and (2) by processing archival collections to build research corpora from web archives. Finally, the third perspective is what we call the graph-centric view, which considers websites, pages or extracted facts as nodes in a graph. Links among pages or the extracted information are represented by edges in the graph. This structural perspective conveys an overview of the holdings and connections among contained resources and information. Only all three views together provide the holistic view that is required to effectively work with web archives.

1 Introduction

By offering unique potential for studying past events and temporal evolution, web archives provide new opportunities for various kinds of historical analysis (Schreibman et al. 2008), cultural analysis and Culturomics (Michel et al. 2010), as well as analytics for computational journalism (Cohen et al. 2011). Consequently, with

H. Holzmann (✉)
Consultant, Hannover, Germany
e-mail: consulting@helgeholzmann.de

W. Nejdl
L3S Research Center, Leibniz Universität Hannover, Hannover, Germany
e-mail: nejdl@L3S.de

© Springer Nature Switzerland AG 2021
D. Gomes et al. (eds.), *The Past Web*,
https://doi.org/10.1007/978-3-030-63291-5_8

the growing availability of these collections and the increasing recognition of their importance, an increasing number of historians, social and political scientists, and researchers from other disciplines see them as rich resources for their work (Hockx-Yu 2014).

However, as web archives grow in scope and size, they also present unique challenges in terms of usage, access and analysis that require novel, effective and efficient methods and tools for researchers as well as for the average user (Holzmann 2019). In this chapter, we tackle these challenges from three different perspectives: the *user-centric view*, the *data-centric view* and the *graph-centric view*. One natural way of conceiving these views is as different levels of magnification for looking at the same archival collection, as illustrated in Fig. 1, starting with the user-centric view that targets single documents to be examined by regular users. By zooming out to the data-centric view, one can scale the examination up to the whole archival collection or subsets of it. In contrast, the broadest zoom level, the graph-centric view, does not focus on the individual documents but deals with the underlying structures that span an archive as graphs. These are the foundational models for most downstream applications, such as search and data analysis, as well as models to guide users in user-centric views.

Another way of conceiving the relationships among the views is by considering their levels of abstraction. While the data-centric view is rather low level, closest to the data as well as to computational resources, both the graph- and user-centric views may be considered as more abstract. The graph-centric view is a conceptual layer, dealing with underlying conceptual models, facts and information contained in the archive and the relationships among them. The user-centric view, on the other hand, focuses on the users who interact with the archive without any particular technical or data science skills required. Both views attempt to hide the underlying data access and processing complexities from the targeted user group. This understanding leads to another distinguishing factor of the three views, namely, the types of challenges they cause. While we care about usability as well as

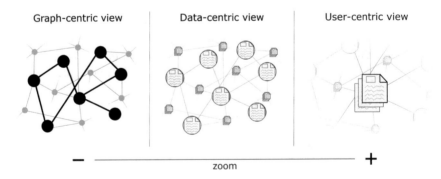

Fig. 1 Three views on web archives, representing different levels of magnification for looking at the archived data by "zooming out" (−) and "zooming in" (+)

exploration in the user-centric view, technical and fundamental questions are raised to a much larger extent by both other views. However, all three views are connected and synergies exist. According to the previous discussion, the following user roles may be assigned to the different views:

- User-centric view: web users, close-reading researchers, managers, etc.
- Data-centric view: data engineers, computer scientists, web archive experts, etc.
- Graph-centric view: data scientists, distant-reading/digital researchers, analysts, software (clients, agents, APIs, downstream applications), etc.

2   User-Centric View: Browsing the Past Web

The most common way to explore a web archive is through a web browser, just as regular users explore the live Web. This is what we consider the *user-centric view*: access with a focus on users and their needs, without requiring additional infrastructure or knowledge about the underlying data structures.

The most common way to access a web archive from a user's perspective is the Wayback Machine,[1] the Internet Archive's replay tool to render archived webpages, as well as its open-source counterpart OpenWayback,[2] which is available for many web archives.

These tools are made for common web users who just want to browse a webpage from the past as if it would be still online but also for scholarly users who closely read individual webpages to understand their content and the context, rather than or before, zooming out and analysing collections in a data analysis or distant reading fashion (Moretti 2005). Similar to the live Web, where users either directly enter the URL of a webpage in a browser, click a link or utilise search engines to find the desired page, the use of web archives from a user's perspective can be distinguished as *direct access* and *search*.

2.1   *Direct Access*

Direct access to an archived webpage through the Wayback Machine requires the user to enter a target URL first, before selecting the desired version of the corre-

---

[1] https://web.archive.org.

[2] https://github.com/iipc/openwayback.

sponding webpage from a calendar view, which gives an overview of all available snapshots of a URL per day, month and year. As URLs can be cumbersome, users on the live Web often prefer to use search engines rather than remember and type URLs manually. The Internet Archive's Wayback Machine provides search only in a very rudimentary way (Goel 2016). While the *site search* feature is a great improvement over plain URL lookups, this approach is pretty limited as it neither surfaces deep URLs to a specific page under a site nor supports temporal search, i.e. users cannot specify a time interval with their queries.

An alternative to search, if a URL is not known, is to follow hyperlinks from other pages. As web archives are temporal collections, such links need to carry a timestamp in addition to the URL. Within the Wayback Machine, links automatically point to the closest page or capture of the one that is currently viewed. However, it is also possible to link an archived page from the live Web. In this case, the timestamp needs to be set explicitly. One way to do this is by manually pointing to a particular capture in a web archive, as is done in Wikipedia in order to keep references working.[3] Another approach to form such temporal hyperlinks is by incorporating time information that can be associated with the link, e.g. when software is referenced by its website in a research paper, the publication time of the paper can be used as a close estimator or upper bound to look up the software's website at the time that best represents the version used in the research (Holzmann et al. 2016d,e). While this example is very domain-specific to software, the same idea can be applied to other scenarios, such as preserving and referencing the evolution of people by archiving their blogs and social network profiles (Kasioumis et al. 2014; Marshall and Shipman 2014; SalahEldeen and Nelson 2012).

2.2 Search

Web archives can provide access to historical information that is absent on the current Web, for companies, products, events, entities, etc. However, even though they have been in existence for a long time, web archives are still lacking the search capabilities that would make them truly accessible and usable as temporal resources. *Web archive search* may be considered a special case of temporal information retrieval (temporal IR) (Kanhabua et al. 2015). This important subfield of IR has the goal of improving search effectiveness by exploiting temporal information in documents and queries (Alonso et al. 2007; Campos et al. 2015). The temporal dimension leads to new challenges in query understanding (Jones and Diaz 2007)

---

[3]https://blog.archive.org/2018/10/01/more-than-9-million-broken-links-on-wikipedia-are-now-rescued.

and retrieval models (Berberich et al. 2010; Singh et al. 2016), as well as temporal indexing (Anand et al. 2011, 2012). However, most temporal indexing approaches treat documents as static texts with a certain validity, which does not account for the dynamics in web archives where webpages change over time, and hence their relevance to a query may also change over time. Furthermore, while information needs in IR are traditionally classified according to the taxonomy introduced by Broder (2002), users' intentions are different for web archives, as studied by Costa and Silva (2010). In contrast to the majority of queries on the live Web, which are informational, queries in web archives are predominantly navigational, because users often look for specific resources in a web archive by a temporal aspect rather than searching for general information that is commonly still available on the current Web. Costa et al. (2013) presented a survey of existing web archive search architectures, and Hockx-Yu (2014) identified 15 web archives that already featured full-text search capabilities in 2014. With the incorporation of live web search engines, ArchiveSearch demonstrates how to search a web archive without the expensive indexing phase (Kanhabua et al. 2016).

One specific goal that is often sought by web archive search systems is to provide true *temporal archive search*: given a keyword query together with a time interval we want to find the most authoritative pages, e.g. "what were the most representative webpages for Barack Obama before he became president in 2005?". This would bring up Obama's senatorial website rather than his current website and social media accounts. Such temporal semantics can often not be derived from the webpages under consideration and require external indicators. A proof of concept of this approach was implemented by Tempas, which in its first version incorporated tags attached to URLs on the social bookmarking platform Delicious as temporal cues (Holzmann and Anand 2016). Its ranking was based on the frequency of a tag used with a URL, an approach that we could show results in a good temporal recall with respect to query logs from AOL and MSN (Holzmann et al. 2016b). Unfortunately, since Delicious has now closed, the available data was limited and our dataset only covers the period from 2003 to 2011. We also found that it shows a strong bias towards certain topics, like technology. For these reasons, a second version of Tempas was developed, based on hyperlinks and anchor texts. Using a graph-based query model, Tempas v2 exploits the number of websites and corresponding anchor texts linking to a URL in a given time interval, as shown in Fig. 2. Its temporally sensitive search for authority pages for entities in web archives has been shown to be very effective in multiple scenarios (Holzmann et al. 2017b), like tracing the evolution of people on the Web or finding former domains of websites.

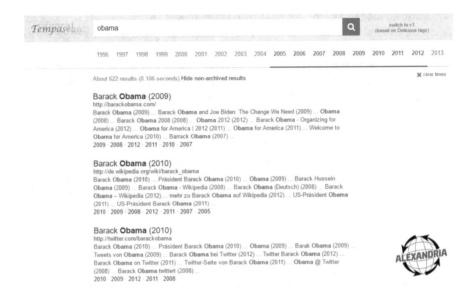

Fig. 2 Tempas v2 screenshot for query "*obama*" in period 2005–2012

3 Data-Centric View: Processing Archival Collections

In contrast to accessing web archives by close reading pages as human users do, archived contents may also be processed at scale enabling evolution studies and big data analysis as it will be shown in Parts 4 and 5 of this book. In the *data-centric view*, webpages are not considered as self-contained units with a layout and embeddings. The independent resources that compose a webpage (e.g. embedded images) are treated as raw data. Web archives are commonly organised in two data formats: WARC *files* (Web ARChive files) store the actual archived contents, while CDX *files* (Capture Index) comprise lightweight metadata records. The data-centric view approaches web archives from the low-level perspective of these files, which is how data engineers would typically look at it. This perspective provides a more global point of view, looking at whole collections rather than individual records. On the downside, we have to deal with higher complexity at this level, instead of pages being nicely rendered in a web browser.

When analysing archived collections, "What persons co-occur on the archived pages most frequently in a specific period of time?" is only one example of the kinds of questions that can be asked (Shaltev et al. 2016). Studies like this are typical cases for the graph-centric view. However, answering such questions does not usually require a whole web archive, but only pages from a specific time period, certain data types or other criteria to pre-filter a dataset in this data-centric perspective before the graph extraction. One way to accomplish this is ArchiveSpark, a tool for building research corpora from web archives that operates using standard formats and facilitates the process of filtering as well as data extraction and derivation at scale in a very efficient manner (Holzmann et al. 2016a). While ArchiveSpark should be considered a tool that operates on the data-centric view, the resulting datasets consist of structured information in the form of graphs that can be used by data scientists and researchers in the graph-centric view.

We distinguish between two sorts of data that can be studied: (1) derived, extracted or descriptive metadata, representing the Web and archived records, which reflects the evolution of the Web and its dynamics; and (2) contents of archived webpages, from which can be derived insights into the real world, which is commonly referred to as *Web Science* (Hall et al. 2017). The latter should be considered a graph-centric task, focusing on the required facts, after these have been prepared by data engineers from a data-centric perspective.

3.1 Metadata Analysis

Web archives that span multiple years constitute a valuable resource for studying the evolution of the Web as well as its dynamics. In previous works on web dynamics, suitable datasets had to be crawled first, which is tedious and can only be done for shorter periods (Cho and Garcia-Molina 2000; Fetterly et al. 2003; Koehler 2002; Ntoulas et al. 2004; Adar et al. 2009). With access to existing archives, more recent studies of the Web were conducted retrospectively on available data (Hale et al. 2014; Agata et al. 2014; Alkwai et al. 2015), commonly with a focus on a particular subset, such as national domains or topical subsets. These kinds of works are typical data-centric tasks as they require access to archived raw data or metadata records.

An example of such a study is an analysis we conducted in 2016 of the dawn of today's most popular German domains over 18 years, i.e. the top-level domain .de from 1996 to 2013, with the required data provided by the Internet Archive (Holzmann et al. 2016c). This investigation was carried out purely by studying metadata describing the archived records, without analysing actual contents of archived webpages. Based on that, we introduced properties to explore the evolution of the Web in terms of age, volume and size, which can be used to replicate similar studies using other web archive collection. These properties deliver insights into the development and current state of the Web. One of our findings was that the majority of the most popular educational domains, like universities, have already existed for more than a decade, while domains relating to shopping and games have emerged steadily. Furthermore, it could be observed that the Web is getting older, not in its entirety, but with many domains having a constant fraction of webpages that are more than 5 years old and ageing further. Finally, we could see that popular websites have been growing exponentially since their inception, doubling in volume every 2 years, and that newborn pages have become bigger over time.

3.2   Web Archive Data Processing

In order to study structures of link graphs or characteristics of Web contents, the actual archived payloads have to be processed. Because of the sheer size of web archives, in the order of multiple terabytes or even petabytes, this requires distributed computing facilities to process archived web data efficiently. Common operations, like selection, filtering, transformation and aggregation, may be performed using the generic MapReduce programming model (Dean and Ghemawat 2010), as supported by Apache Hadoop[4] or Apache Spark[5] (Zaharia et al. 2010). AlSum (2014) presents ArcContent, a tool developed specifically for web archives using the distributed database Cassandra (Lakshman and Malik 2010). In this approach, the records of interest are selected by means of the CDX metadata records and inserted into the database to be queried through a web service. The Archives Unleashed Toolkit (AUT), formerly known as Warcbase, by Lin et al. (2014), used to follow a similar approach based on HBase, a Hadoop-based distributed database system, which is an open-source implementation of Google's Bigtable (Chang et al. 2008). While being very efficient for lookups, major drawbacks of these database solutions are their limited flexibility as well as the additional effort to insert the records, which is expensive both in terms of time and resources. In its more recent version, AUT loads and processes (WARC) files directly using Apache Spark in order to avoid the HBase overhead, for which it provides convenient functions to work with web archives. With the Archives Unleashed Cloud (AUK), there even exists a hosted service for a limited number of analyses based on WARC files.

ArchiveSpark introduces a novel data processing approach for web archives and other archival collections that exploits metadata records for gains in efficiency while not having to rely on an external index (Holzmann et al. 2016a). ArchiveSpark is a tool for general web archive access based on Spark. It supports arbitrary filtering and data derivation operations on archived data in an easy and efficient way. Starting from the small and lightweight CDX metadata records, it can run basic operations, such as filtering, grouping and sorting very efficiently, without touching the actual data contents of archived webpages. In a step-wise approach, the records are enriched with additional information by applying external modules that can be customised and shared among researchers and tasks, even beyond web archives (Holzmann et al. 2017a). In order to extract or derive information from archived resources, third-party tools can be integrated. It is only at this point that ArchiveSpark seamlessly integrates the actual data for the records of interest stored in WARC files. Internally, ArchiveSpark documents the lineage of all derived and extracted information, which can serve as a source for additional filtering and processing steps or be stored in a convenient output format to be used as a

---

[4]https://hadoop.apache.org.

[5]https://spark.apache.org.

research corpus in further studies. Benchmarks show that ArchiveSpark is faster than competitors, like AUT/Warcbase and pure Spark, in typical use case scenarios when working with web archive data (Holzmann et al. 2016a).

4 Graph-Centric View: Exploring Web Archive Content

The last perspective, besides the *user-centric* and *data-centric views*, is referred to as the *graph-centric view*. This view enables the exploration of web archives from a more structural perspective, which constitutes the foundational model for most downstream applications and studies run by researchers, data scientists and others who are not as close to the data as engineers. In contrast to the views discussed above, the focus here is not on content or individual archived records but on the facts and information contained within them and the relationships among them. In the context of the Web, the most obvious relationships are the hyperlinks that connect webpages by pointing from one to another. However, there is a lot more valuable data on the Web that is less obvious. Looking at hyperlinks from a more coarse-grained perspective, multiple links can be combined to connections among hosts, domains or even top-level domains, revealing connections among services, organisations or the different national regions of the Web. Furthermore, by zooming out to the graph perspective after processing the archived data from a data-centric view, even relationships among persons or objects mentioned on the analysed pages can be derived (Shaltev et al. 2016; Fafalios et al. 2017, 2018).

The holistic view of archival collections provided by graphs is very helpful in many tasks and generates synergies with the other views. The broad zoom level is crucial to get an overview of available records in an archive and to find the right resources to run analyses and power applications. Hyperlinks among the archived pages can point users or algorithms in search or data analysis tasks to the desired entry points within the big and often chaotic web archive collections. As shown before, we make use of this with our web archive search engine Tempas (see Sect. 2). The effectiveness of hyperlinks and attached anchor texts for this task has already been shown by previous works (Craswell et al. 2001; Kraaij et al. 2002; Ogilvie and Callan 2003; Koolen and Kamps 2010).

4.1 Data Analysis

The approaches for exploring web archives through graphs that are described here allow for queries on a structural level (cf. Fig. 1). Once a set of documents that match a query has been identified, a data engineer might be involved to zoom in to the contents in order to extract new structured knowledge graphs from a data-centric perspective, to be processed further by data scientists or the like. Quite commonly, such workflows also involve manual inspection of the records under consideration

Graph-centric   **Data-centric**   **User-centric**

graph analysis / search   data access   processing / presentation

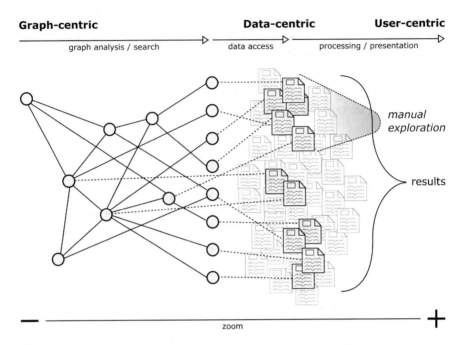

Fig. 3 Combining different views on web archives for systematic data analysis by "zooming out"
(−) and "zooming in" (+)

from a user-centric view. This is helpful to get an understanding of the data that is
being studied. Ultimately, derived results need to be aggregated and presented to the
user in an appropriate form.

Figure 3 shows this generic analysis schema that outlines a systematic way to
study web archives. This schema can be adopted and implemented for a range of
different scenarios. In such a setting, the graph-centric view is utilised to get an
overview and find suitable entry points into the archive. This may initially be done
manually by the user, to get a feeling for the available data using a graph-based
search engine like Tempas, but can also be integrated as the first step in a data-
processing pipeline to (semi-)automatically select the corpus for further steps. Next,
the selected records can be accessed from a data-centric view at scale, using a tool
like ArchiveSpark (see Sect. 3), to extract the desired information, compute metrics
or aggregate statistics. Finally, the results are presented to the user. A concrete
implementation of this pipeline is outlined in Holzmann et al. (2017b), where we
describe the example of analysing restaurant menus and compare prices before and
after the introduction of the Euro as Europe's new currency in Germany in 2001–
2002.

4.2 Open Challenges

The reason for addressing the graph-centric view at the end of this chapter is because it requires a certain understanding of the eventual task or study in order to evaluate its utility. Graphs enable completely different kinds of analysis, such as centrality computations with algorithms like PageRank (Page et al. 1999). However, scientific contributions in this area specific to web archives are very limited and results are less mature. Although scientists have looked into graph properties of the Web in general, both in static (Albert et al. 1999; Broder et al. 2000; Adamic et al. 2000; Suel and Yuan 2001; Boldi and Vigna 2004) and evolving graphs (Huberman and Adamic 1999; Leskovec et al. 2005, 2007), we found that certain traits of web archives lead to new kinds of questions. For instance, as we show in Holzmann et al. (2018, 2019), the inherent incompleteness of archives can affect rankings produced by graph algorithms on web archive graphs.

5 Summary

Web archives have been instrumental in the digital preservation of the Web and provide great opportunities for the study of the societal past and its evolution. These archival collections are massive datasets, typically in the order of terabytes or petabytes, spanning time periods of up to more than two decades and growing. As a result of this, their use has been difficult, as effective and efficient exploration and methods of access are limited. We have identified three views on web archives, for which we have proposed novel concepts and tools to tackle existing challenges: user-, data- and graph-centric. Depending on who you are, these provide you with the right perspective from which to approach archived web data for your needs, with suitable abstractions and simplifications. Switching between roles and combining different views provides a holistic view on web archives.

Acknowledgments This work was partially funded by the EU Horizon 2020 under ERC grant "ALEXANDRIA" (339233).

References

Adamic LA, Huberman BA, Barabási AL, Albert R, Jeong H, Bianconi G (2000) Power-law distribution of the world wide web. Science 287(5461):2115. https://doi.org/10.1126/science. 287.5461.2115a

Adar E, Teevan J, Dumais ST, Elsas JL (2009) The web changes everything: understanding the dynamics of web content. In: Proceedings of the 2nd ACM international conference on web search and data mining - WSDM '09. ACM Press, New York, pp 282–291. https://doi.org/10. 1145/1498759.1498837

Agata T, Miyata Y, Ishita E, Ikeuchi A, Ueda S (2014) Life span of web pages: a survey of 10 million pages collected in 2001. Digit Libr pp 463–464. https://doi.org/10.1109/JCDL.2014. 6970226

Albert R, Jeong H, Barabási AL (1999) Internet: diameter of the world-wide web. Nature 401(6749):130–131. https://doi.org/10.1038/43601

Alkwai LM, Nelson ML, Weigle MC (2015) How well are Arabic websites archived? In: Proceedings of the 15th ACM/IEEE-CS joint conference on digital libraries - JCDL '15. ACM, pp 223–232. https://doi.org/10.1145/2756406.2756912

Alonso O, Gertz M, Baeza-Yates R (2007) On the value of temporal information in information retrieval. ACM SIGIR Forum 41(2):35–41. https://doi.org/10.1145/1328964.1328968

AlSum A (2014) Web archive services framework for tighter integration between the past and present web. PhD thesis, Old Dominion University

Anand A, Bedathur S, Berberich K, Schenkel R (2011) Temporal index sharding for space-time efficiency in archive search. In: Proceedings of the 34th international ACM SIGIR conference on research and development in information retrieval - SIGIR '11. ACM, New York, NY, pp 545–554. https://doi.org/10.1145/2009916.2009991

Anand A, Bedathur S, Berberich K, Schenkel R (2012) Index maintenance for time-travel text search. In: Proceedings of the 35th international ACM SIGIR conference on research and development in information retrieval - SIGIR '12, Portland, Oregon, pp 235–244. https://doi.org/10.1145/2348283.2348318

Berberich K, Bedathur S, Alonso O, Weikum G (2010) A language modeling approach for temporal information needs. In: Proceedings of the 32nd European conference on advances in information retrieval (ECIR), Springer-Verlag, Berlin, Heidelberg, ECIR'2010, pp 13–25. https://doi.org/10.1007/978-3-642-12275-0_5

Boldi P, Vigna S (2004) The WebGraph framework I: compression techniques. In: Proceedings of the 13th conference on world wide web - WWW '04, ACM. ACM Press, Manhattan, pp 595–602. https://doi.org/10.1145/988672.988752. http://law.di.unimi.it/datasets.php

Broder A (2002) A taxonomy of web search. In: ACM Sigir forum, ACM. Association for Computing Machinery (ACM), New York, vol 36, pp 3–10. https://doi.org/10.1145/792550.792552

Broder A, Kumar R, Maghoul F, Raghavan P, Rajagopalan S, Stata R, Tomkins A, Wiener J (2000) Graph structure in the web. Comput Netw 33(1):309–320. https://doi.org/10.1016/s1389-1286(00)00083-9

Campos R, Dias G, Jorge AM, Jatowt A (2015) Survey of temporal information retrieval and related applications. ACM Comput Surv (CSUR) 47(2):15

Chang F, Dean J, Ghemawat S, Hsieh WC, Wallach DA, Burrows M, Chandra T, Fikes A, Gruber RE (2008) Bigtable: a distributed storage system for structured data. ACM Trans Comput Syst (TOCS) 26(2):4. https://doi.org/10.1145/1365815.1365816

Cho J, Garcia-Molina H (2000) The evolution of the web and implications for an incremental crawler. In: Proceedings of the 26th international conference on very large data bases, VLDB '00

Cohen S, Li C, Yang J, Yu C (2011) Computational journalism: a call to arms to database researchers. In: Proceedings of the 5th Biennial conference on innovative data systems research, pp 148–151

Costa M, Silva MJ (2010) Understanding the information needs of web archive users. In: Proceedings of the 10th international web archiving workshop

Costa M, Gomes D, Couto F, Silva M (2013) A survey of web archive search architectures. In: Proceedings of the 22nd international conference on world wide web - WWW '13 companion. ACM Press, New York, NY, pp 1045–1050. https://doi.org/10.1145/2487788.2488116

Craswell N, Hawking D, Robertson S (2001) Effective site finding using link anchor information. In: Proceedings of the 24th international ACM SIGIR conference on research and development in information retrieval - SIGIR '01, ACM. ACM Press, New York. https://doi.org/10.1145/383952.383999

Dean J, Ghemawat S (2010) MapReduce: a flexible data processing tool. Commun ACM 53(1):72–77. https://doi.org/10.1145/1629175.1629198

Fafalios P, Holzmann H, Kasturia V, Nejdl W (2017) Building and querying semantic layers for web archives. In: Proceedings of the 17th ACM/IEEE-CS joint conference on digital libraries - JCDL '17. IEEE, Piscataway. https://doi.org/10.1109/jcdl.2017.7991555

Fafalios P, Holzmann H, Kasturia V, Nejdl W (2018) Building and querying semantic layers for web archives (extended version). Int J Digit Libr. https://doi.org/10.1007/s00799-018-0251-0

Fetterly D, Manasse M, Najork M, Wiener J (2003) A large-scale study of the evolution of web pages. In: Proceedings of the 12th international conference on world wide web - WWW '03, pp 669–678. https://doi.org/10.1002/spe.577

Goel V (2016) Beta Wayback machine - now with site search!. https://blog.archive.org/2016/10/24/beta-wayback-machine-now-with-site-search. Accessed 16 Mar 2017

Hale SA, Yasseri T, Cowls J, Meyer ET, Schroeder R, Margetts H (2014) Mapping the UK webspace: fifteen years of British universities on the web. In: Proceedings of the 2014 ACM conference on web science - WebSci '14, WebSci '14. ACM Press, New York. https://doi.org/10.1145/2615569.2615691

Hall W, Hendler J, Staab S (2017) A manifesto for web science @10. arXiv:170208291

Hockx-Yu H (2014) Access and scholarly use of web archives. Alexandria J Natl Int Library Inf Issues 25(1–2):113–127. https://doi.org/10.7227/alx.0023

Holzmann H (2019) Concepts and tools for the effective and efficient use of web archives. PhD thesis, Leibniz Universität Hannover. https://doi.org/10.15488/4436

Holzmann H, Anand A (2016) Tempas: temporal archive search based on tags. In: Proceedings of the 25th international conference companion on world wide web - WWW '16 companion. ACM Press, New York. https://doi.org/10.1145/2872518.2890555

Holzmann H, Goel V, Anand A (2016a) Archivespark: efficient web archive access, extraction and derivation. In: Proceedings of the 16th ACM/IEEE-CS joint conference on digital libraries - JCDL '16,. ACM, New York, pp 83–92. https://doi.org/10.1145/2910896.2910902

Holzmann H, Nejdl W, Anand A (2016b) On the applicability of delicious for temporal search on web archives. In: Proceedings of the 39th international ACM SIGIR conference on research and development in information retrieval - SIGIR '16. ACM Press, Pisa. https://doi.org/10.1145/2911451.2914724

Holzmann H, Nejdl W, Anand A (2016c) The dawn of today's popular domains - a study of the archived German web over 18 years. In: Proceedings of the 16th ACM/IEEE-CS joint conference on digital libraries - JCDL '16. IEEE/ACM Press, Newark/New Jersey, pp 73–82. https://doi.org/10.1145/2910896.2910901

Holzmann H, Runnwerth M, Sperber W (2016d) Linking mathematical software in web archives. In: Mathematical software – ICMS 2016. Springer International Publishing, Cham, pp 419–422. https://doi.org/10.1007/978-3-319-42432-3_52

Holzmann H, Sperber W, Runnwerth M (2016e) Archiving software surrogates on the web for future reference. In: Research and advanced technology for digital libraries, 20th international conference on theory and practice of digital libraries, TPDL 2016, Hannover. https://doi.org/10.1007/978-3-319-43997-6_17

Holzmann H, Goel V, Gustainis EN (2017a) Universal distant reading through metadata proxies with archivespark. In: 2017 IEEE international conference on big data (Big Data). IEEE, Boston, MA. https://doi.org/10.1109/bigdata.2017.8257958

Holzmann H, Nejdl W, Anand A (2017b) Exploring web archives through temporal anchor texts. In: Proceedings of the 2017 ACM on web science conference - WebSci '17. ACM Press, Troy, New York. https://doi.org/10.1145/3091478.3091500

Holzmann H, Anand A, Khosla M (2018) What the HAK? Estimating ranking deviations in incomplete graphs. In: 14th International workshop on mining and learning with graphs (MLG) - co-located with 24th ACM SIGKDD international conference on knowledge discovery and data mining (KDD), London

Holzmann H, Anand A, Khosla M (2019) Delusive pagerank in incomplete graphs. In: Complex networks and their applications, vol VII. Springer International Publishing, Cham

Huberman BA, Adamic LA (1999) Internet: growth dynamics of the world-wide web. Nature 401(6749):131

Jones R, Diaz F (2007) Temporal profiles of queries. ACM Trans Inf Syst 25(3):14–es. https://doi.org/10.1145/1247715.1247720

Kanhabua N, Blanco R, Nørvåg K, et al (2015) Temporal information retrieval. Found Trends Inf Retrieval 9(2):91–208. https://doi.org/10.1145/2911451.2914805

Kanhabua N, Kemkes P, Nejdl W, Nguyen TN, Reis F, Tran NK (2016) How to search the internet archive without indexing it. In: Research and advanced technology for digital libraries. Springer International Publishing, Hannover, pp 147–160. https://doi.org/10.1007/978-3-319-43997-6_12

Kasioumis N, Banos V, Kalb H (2014) Towards building a blog preservation platform. World Wide Web J 17(4):799–825. https://doi.org/10.1007/s11280-013-0234-4

Koehler W (2002) Web Page change and persistence-a four-year longitudinal study. J Am Soc Inf Sci Technol 53(2):162–171. https://doi.org/10.1002/asi.10018

Koolen M, Kamps J (2010) The importance of anchor text for ad hoc search revisited. In: Proceeding of the 33rd international ACM SIGIR conference on research and development in information retrieval - SIGIR '10, ACM. ACM Press, pp 122–129. https://doi.org/10.1145/1835449.1835472

Kraaij W, Westerveld T, Hiemstra D (2002) The importance of prior probabilities for entry page search. In: Proceedings of the 25th annual international ACM SIGIR conference on research and development in information retrieval - SIGIR '02. ACM, New York. https://doi.org/10.1145/564376.564383

Lakshman A, Malik P (2010) Cassandra: a decentralized structured storage system. ACM SIGOPS Oper Syst Rev 44(2):35–40. https://doi.org/10.1145/1773912.1773922

Leskovec J, Kleinberg J, Faloutsos C (2005) Graphs over time: densification laws, shrinking diameters and possible explanations. In: Proceeding of the 1th ACM SIGKDD international conference on knowledge discovery in data mining - KDD '05, ACM. ACM Press, pp 177–187. https://doi.org/10.1145/1081870.1081893

Leskovec J, Kleinberg J, Faloutsos C (2007) Graph evolution: densification and shrinking diameters. ACM Trans Knowl Discov Data (TKDD) 1(1):2. https://doi.org/10.1145/1217299.1217301

Lin J, Gholami M, Rao J (2014) Infrastructure for supporting exploration and discovery in web archives. In: Proceedings of the 23rd international conference on world wide web - WWW '14 companion. ACM Press, New York. https://doi.org/10.1145/2567948.2579045

Marshall CC, Shipman FM (2014) An argument for archiving Facebook as a heterogeneous personal store. In: Proceedings of the 14th ACM/IEEE-CS joint conference on digital libraries - JCDL '14. IEEE Press, Piscataway, pp 11–20. https://doi.org/10.1109/jcdl.2014.6970144

Michel JB, Shen YK, Aiden AP, Veres A, Gray MK, Pickett JP, Hoiberg D, Clancy D, Norvig P, Orwant J, Pinker S, Nowak MA, and ELA (2010) Quantitative analysis of culture using millions of digitized books. Science 331(6014):176–182. https://doi.org/10.1126/science.1199644

Moretti F (2005) Graphs, maps, trees: abstract models for a literary history. Verso

Ntoulas A, Cho J, Olston C (2004) What's new on the web?: The evolution of the web from a search engine perspective. In: Proceedings of the 13th conference on world wide web - WWW '04. ACM Press, New York, pp 1–12. https://doi.org/10.1145/988672.988674

Ogilvie P, Callan J (2003) Combining document representations for known-item search. In: Proceedings of the 26th annual international ACM SIGIR conference on research and development in information retrieval - SIGIR '03, ACM. ACM Press, New York. https://doi.org/10.1145/860435.860463

Page L, Brin S, Motwani R, Winograd T (1999) The PageRank citation ranking: bringing order to the web. InfoLab

SalahEldeen HM, Nelson ML (2012) Losing my revolution: how many resources shared on social media have been lost? In: Theory and practice of digital libraries, TPDL'12. Springer, Paphos, Cyprus, pp 125–137. https://doi.org/10.1007/978-3-642-33290-6_14

Schreibman S, Siemens R, Unsworth J (2008) A companion to digital humanities. Blackwell Publishing, Malden

Shaltev M, Zab JH, Kemkes P, Siersdorfer S, Zerr S (2016) Cobwebs from the past and present: extracting large social networks using internet archive data. In: Proceedings of the 39th international ACM SIGIR conference on research and development in information retrieval - SIGIR '16, Pisa. https://doi.org/10.1145/2911451.2911467

Singh J, Nejdl W, Anand A (2016) History by diversity: helping historians search news archives. In: Proceedings of the 2016 ACM on conference on human information interaction and retrieval - CHIIR '16. ACM Press, New York, pp 183–192. https://doi.org/10.1145/2854946.2854959

Suel T, Yuan J (2001) Compressing the graph structure of the web. In: Data compression conference

Zaharia M, Chowdhury M, Franklin MJ, Shenker S, Stoica I (2010) Spark: cluster computing with working sets. In: Proceedings of the 2nd USENIX conference on Hot topics in cloud computing, vol 10, p 10

Interoperability for Accessing Versions of Web Resources with the Memento Protocol

Shawn M. Jones (ID), **Martin Klein** (ID), **Herbert Van de Sompel** (ID),
Michael L. Nelson (ID), and **Michele C. Weigle** (ID)

Abstract The Internet Archive pioneered web archiving and remains the largest publicly accessible web archive hosting archived copies of webpages (Mementos) going back as far as early 1996. Its holdings have grown steadily since, and it hosts more than 475 billion URIs as of September 2019. However, the landscape of web archiving has changed significantly over the last two decades. There are more than 20 web archives around the world. This diversity contributes to the preservation of archived content that documents the past Web but requires standards to enable interoperability among them. The Memento Protocol is one of the main enablers of interoperability among web archives. We describe this protocol and present a variety of tools and services that leverage the broad adoption of the Memento Protocol and discuss a selection of research efforts made possible by these interoperability standards. In addition, we outline examples of technical specifications that enhance machines to access resource versions on the Web in an automatic, standardised and interoperable manner.

1 Introduction

The Internet Archive pioneered web archiving and remains the largest publicly accessible web archive preserving copies of pages from the past Web (Mementos) going back as far as early 1996. Its holdings have grown steadily since, and it hosts more than 475 billion URIs as of September 2019. However, the landscape of web

S. M. Jones (✉) · M. Klein
Los Alamos National Laboratory, Los Alamos, NM, USA
e-mail: smjones@lanl.gov; mklein@lanl.gov

H. Van de Sompel
Data Archiving and Networked Services (DANS), Den Haag, The Netherlands
e-mail: herbert.van.de.sompel@dans.knaw.nl

M. L. Nelson · M. C. Weigle
Old Dominion University, Norfolk, VA, USA
e-mail: mln@cs.odu.edu; mweigle@cs.odu.edu

© Springer Nature Switzerland AG 2021
D. Gomes et al. (eds.), *The Past Web*,
https://doi.org/10.1007/978-3-030-63291-5_9

archiving has changed significantly over the last two decades. Today we can freely access Mementos from more than 20 web archives around the world, operated by for-profit and nonprofit organisations, national libraries and academic institutions, as well as individuals. The resulting diversity improves the odds of the survival of archived records but also requires technical standards to ensure interoperability between archival systems. To date, the Memento Protocol and the WARC file format are the main enablers of interoperability between web archives. Before the Memento Protocol (Van de Sompel et al. 2013; Nelson and Van de Sompel 2019), there was no standard way to answer some basic questions about archived web resources, such as:

- Is this web resource, identified by a specific Uniform Resource Identifier (URI), an archived web resource (Memento)?
- From what URI was this Memento created?
- When was this Memento captured?
- Given the URI for a web resource and a datetime, how do we find a Memento from that datetime?
- Given the URI for a web resource, how do we locate all of the Mementos for that URI at an archive?
- What about across all archives?

1.1 Answering Questions Without the Memento Protocol

This section outlines several scenarios that illustrate the difficulties in answering the above questions without the Memento Protocol. Consider the process that a human user would follow to acquire a Memento from a web archive running OpenWayback (Ko 2019), the most common web archival replay software. The web archive presents the user with a search page. The users enter their desired URI, and the system delivers them a page consisting of a series of calendars containing highlighted dates, as seen in Fig. 1. These dates represent the capture datetimes for that URI (Gomes and Costa 2014). To view the Memento, the user clicks on one of these capture datetimes. This tedious process requires that the user manually click through calendars of dates to find the datetime of interest before finding their Memento.

Behind the scenes, the Memento is stored as a record in a Web ARChive (WARC) file (ISO 2009), the standard web archive file format. Web archives routinely generate one or more Crawl Index (CDX) (International Internet Preservation Coalition 2006) files to help the playback system locate Mementos. When the user clicks on a date, the archive's playback system searches CDX files for the corresponding WARC file and the position of the Memento record in that file. Based on this information, the system then locates the WARC record and presents the Memento to the user, that is, the content of a page from the past as it was in the datetime when it was captured. This process provides data for the user interface, but how would a machine client acquire a Memento?

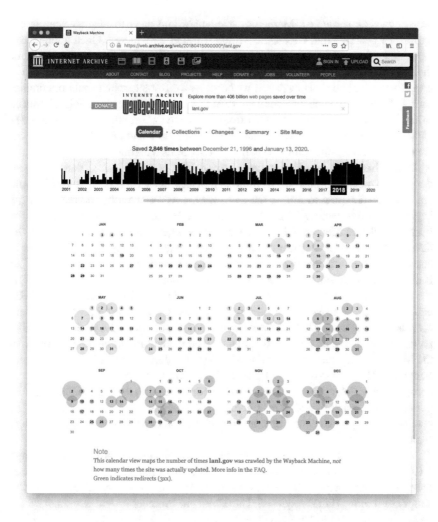

Fig. 1 Links to Mementos of http://www.lanl.gov for 2018 exist in the calendar interface employed by the Internet Archive

Given a URI, how does a software executed by a client machine know that the resource is a Memento? How does it determine the capture datetime of this resource given that the capture datetime is not necessarily the same as the last modification date (Nelson 2010), which datetime is available in the resource's archived HTTP header? How does the client machine determine the URI that the web archive captured? The home page of the Internet Archive's Wayback Machine, https://web.archive.org, is not a Memento, nor are the various images, scripts and stylesheets used to build the web archive's page banners (e.g. https://web.archive.org/_static/js/toolbar.js). However, the page at https://web.archive.org/web/20191210234446/

https://www.lanl.gov/ is a Memento. A client would need to identify the pattern applied to generate this URI to know that it found a Memento. Once a client can parse this pattern, it can screen for Memento URIs, identify the capture datetime of the Memento (i.e. 20191210234446) and the URI that the archive had captured (i.e. https://www.lanl.gov/). However, if we consider a different archive that does not use such URI patterns, such as Perma.cc, then this approach is not feasible. Perma.cc stores a Memento for that same URI from that same date at https://perma.cc/Q938-LPMG. How does a client know that this is a Memento and https://perma.cc/about is not? How does a client find the captured URI or its datetime?

If the client software knows the captured URI and the desired datetime, how does it find the temporally closest Memento in an archive for that datetime? It could employ web scraping to mimic the tedious process executed by the human at the beginning of this section. Then it could create a list of all captures and search the list for the closest Memento. Because web archives have different user interfaces, the developer of the client software would need to update this scraper for all changes to any archive. Web archives may not share CDX files for technical or legal reasons, but if the archive does share its CDX files, then a machine client could parse each CDX file to find the location of the Memento at the archive. CDX files list captured URIs and not the URIs of Mementos. So even with the CDX record, how does a client software discover the URI of the Memento? If a web archive uses a known URI pattern to reference its preserved contents, then a client might be able to construct the Memento URI, but how does it work when an archive, such as Perma.cc, did not base the URI structure on the CDX data? What if the client software wants to search across archives? A client would need to be able to perform the aforementioned URI parsing, CDX parsing and screen scraping for several archives and combine the results. This approach would be time consuming and expensive to maintain at large scale.

What if web archives could keep their own customised user interfaces and URI structures, control access to their CDX files, but still be able to answer these questions? What if the machine client could obtain responses effectively by simply executing HTTP requests? The Memento Protocol provides a standard for answering questions about individual Mementos and the means for interoperability across archives.

1.2   Answering These Questions with the Memento Protocol

In order to understand how Memento answers these questions, we first describe how the Memento Protocol works. To provide a standard and consistent method of access across web archives, the Memento Protocol introduces the following components:

- **Original Resource**: A web resource as it exists or used to exist on the Web. A **URI-R** (e.g., http://lanl.gov) denotes the URI of an Original Resource.

- **Memento**: A capture of an Original Resource from a specific point in time. A **URI-M** (e.g., https://webarchive.loc.gov/all/19990125090547/http://lanl.gov/) denotes the URI of a Memento.
- **Memento-Datetime**: The capture datetime (e.g., Mon, 25 Jan 1999 09:05:47 GMT) of the Original Resource for the given Memento.
- **TimeGate**: A web resource that helps clients find the temporally closest Memento for an Original Resource given a specific datetime using datetime negotiation, a process described below. A **URI-G** (e.g., https://webarchive.loc. gov/all/http://lanl.gov/) denotes the URI of a TimeGate.
- **TimeMap**: A resource that contains a list of the URI-Ms for an Original Resource. A **URI-T** (e.g., https://webarchive.loc.gov/all/http://lanl.gov/) denotes the URI of a TimeMap.

The remainder of this section details how these components answer the questions posed in the introduction. Table 1 summarises these questions and the components that support answering them.

The Memento Protocol conforms to REST (Fielding 2000) and thus uses HTTP (Fielding et al. 2014a,b; Fielding and Reschke 2014a,b,c,d) to help clients answer questions about Mementos. Figure 2 displays the HTTP response headers for a single Memento from the United States Library of Congress web archive. The presence of the `Memento-Datetime` header indicates that this resource is a

Table 1 The questions addressed by the Memento Protocol

Question	Memento feature addressing question
Is this resource a Memento?	`Memento-Datetime` header in the Memento's HTTP response header
From what URI was this Memento created?	`original` relation in the Memento's HTTP `Link` response header
When was this Memento captured?	`Memento-Datetime` in the Memento's HTTP response header
How do we locate all of the Mementos for a URI at an archive?	TimeMap
How do we locate all of the Mementos for a URI across all archives?	TimeMap aggregator (see Sect. 2.2)
How do we find an Original Resource's TimeGate?	`timegate` relation in the Original Resource's HTTP `Link` response header (if available)
How do we find the temporally closest Memento for a given datetime and URI?	TimeGate
How do we find the temporally closest Memento across all web archives for a given datetime and URI?	TimeGate aggregator (see Sect. 2.2)
How do we find a Memento's TimeGate?	`timegate` relation in the Memento's HTTP `Link` response header
How do we find a Memento's TimeMap?	`timemap` relation in the Memento's HTTP `Link` response header

```
HTTP/1.1 200 OK
Date: Thu, 19 Dec 2019 20:38:53 GMT
Server: Apache-Coyote/1.1
Memento-Datetime: Mon, 25 Jan 1999 09:05:47 GMT
Link: <http://lanl.gov/>
    ; rel="original",
  <https://webarchive.loc.gov/all/timemap/link/http://lanl.gov/>
    ; rel="timemap"; type="application/link-format",
  <https://webarchive.loc.gov/all/http://lanl.gov/>
    ; rel="timegate",
  <https://webarchive.loc.gov/all/19961221031231/http://lanl.gov/>
    ; rel="first memento"; datetime="Sat, 21 Dec 1996 03:12:31 GMT",
  <https://webarchive.loc.gov/all/19990117083819/http://lanl.gov/>
    ; rel="prev memento"; datetime="Sun, 17 Jan 1999 08:38:19 GMT",
  <https://webarchive.loc.gov/all/19990125090547/http://lanl.gov/>
    ; rel="memento"; datetime="Mon, 25 Jan 1999 09:05:47 GMT",
  <https://webarchive.loc.gov/all/19990208005037/http://lanl.gov/>
    ; rel="next memento"; datetime="Mon, 08 Feb 1999 00:50:37 GMT",
  <https://webarchive.loc.gov/all/20180305142008/http://lanl.gov/>
    ; rel="last memento"; datetime="Mon, 05 Mar 2018 14:20:08 GMT"
Content-Type: text/html;charset=utf-8
Transfer-Encoding: chunked
Set-Cookie: JSESSIONID=6C40C0CA8C02BF49519DDA6A551632DA; Path=/
```

Fig. 2 The HTTP response headers for a Memento provided by the United States Library of Congress at URI-M https://webarchive.loc.gov/all/19990125090547/http://lanl.gov/. Link headers have been reformatted to ease reading. We have omitted the content of the Memento for brevity

Memento and conveys the capture datetime for this Memento. The Link header contains several relations that help clients find resources to answer other questions about this Memento and its Original Resource. The original relation tells the client that this Memento's Original Resource (URI-R) is http://lanl.gov/. The timemap and timegate relations help clients find this Memento's TimeMap (URI-T) and TimeGate (URI-G), respectively. The HTTP response headers shown in Fig. 2 allow a client to determine that this is a Memento, that the archive captured it on 25 January 1999, at 09:05:47 GMT, that its Original Resource URI-R is http://lanl.gov/, and how to find more Mementos for this resource via TimeGates and TimeMaps. Figure 2 also includes some optional relations. Using these relations, a client can locate the next and previous Mementos relative to this one as well as the first and last Mementos for this Original Resource (URI-R), known to the archive.

TimeMaps provide a full list of all Mementos for an Original Resource, but what if we know the datetime and the Original Resource and want the temporally closest Memento? TimeGates provide this functionality. Figure 3 demonstrates the process of datetime negotiation. Memento-compliant Original Resources make their TimeGate discoverable, and thus, a Memento-aware HTTP client (e.g. a

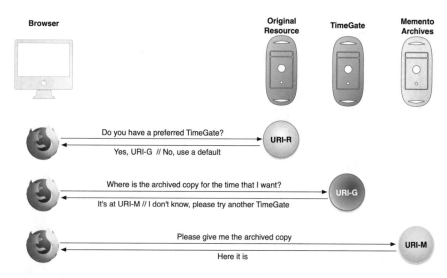

Fig. 3 Datetime negotiation with a Memento TimeGate

browser) first asks the Original Resource for its preferred TimeGate. If the Original Resource does not express a preference, then the client will use a default TimeGate instead. The client then uses the `accept-datetime` request header to supply the desired datetime to the TimeGate. The TimeGate then redirects the client to the Memento (URI-M) that best matches these criteria. Using `accept-datetime` and TimeGates, a Memento client holds the desired datetime steady, allowing the user to seamlessly browse the Web as if it were a date in the past.

2   Architecture of the Memento Protocol

2.1   How Memento Enables Interoperability

The `Link` relations in Memento provide most of its capability. In Fig. 2, the `Link` header provides relations with URIs to other resources related to this Memento. This same method is applied with Original Resources, TimeGates and Mementos to allow software clients to "follow their nose" and find other resources. Figure 4 demonstrates how a client can discover each resource from another via their `Link` headers. From a Memento or TimeGate, a client can find the TimeMap and gain access to the other Mementos for the same Original Resource. From a Memento, a client can find the TimeGate with which to perform datetime negotiation to gain access to other Mementos for the same Original Resource. From a Memento or TimeGate, a client can find the URI-R of the Original Resource, helping them visit the present state of the resource.

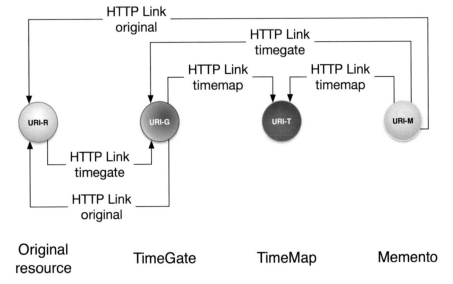

Fig. 4 Workflow of Memento protocol. The arrows show how a client can find additional Memento components through the URIs in Link relations

By using relations the same way, the content of a TimeMap contains links to all other resources. Figure 5 displays an example of a TimeMap in link format (Shelby 2012). The TimeMap informs clients of the Original Resource (URI-R) via the `original` relation. The `self` relation confirms the URI-T of this TimeMap and can optionally provide its date range via `from` and `until` attributes. The `timegate` relation delivers this Memento's corresponding TimeGate URI-G. Each subsequent entry has a relation containing the type `memento`. These entries list each Memento (URI-M) and its Memento-Datetime. The `first` and `last` relations allow a client to easily reach the first and last Mementos, respectively.

2.2 Memento-Compliant Infrastructure and Standardised Access

The Wayback Machine hosted by the Internet Archive is Memento-compliant, but the protocol is also supported across all popular web archiving platforms such as OpenWayback or pywb (Kreymer 2019). More than 20 web archives support Memento,[1] including Arquivo.pt (Melo et al. 2016) and archive.today (Nelson 2013). The Memento Protocol does not require that the URIs listed in a TimeMap

---

[1] http://mementoweb.org/depot/.

```
<http://www.lanl.gov/>; rel="original",
<https://wayback.archive-it.org/all/timemap/link/http://www.lanl.gov/>
  ; rel="self"; type="application/link-format"
  ; from="Fri, 17 Feb 2006 02:53:16 GMT"
  ; until="Tue, 17 Dec 2019 08:38:43 GMT",
<https://wayback.archive-it.org/all/http://www.lanl.gov/>
  ; rel="timegate",
<https://wayback.archive-it.org/all/20060217025316/http://www.lanl.gov/>
  ; rel="first memento"; datetime="Fri, 17 Feb 2006 02:53:16 GMT",
<https://wayback.archive-it.org/all/20060518103556/http://www.lanl.gov/>
  ; rel="memento"; datetime="Thu, 18 May 2006 10:35:56 GMT",
<https://wayback.archive-it.org/all/20060617084403/http://www.lanl.gov/>
  ; rel="memento"; datetime="Sat, 17 Jun 2006 08:44:03 GMT",
<https://wayback.archive-it.org/all/20060617090337/http://www.lanl.gov/>
  ; rel="memento"; datetime="Sat, 17 Jun 2006 09:03:37 GMT",
<https://wayback.archive-it.org/all/20060705231634/http://www.lanl.gov/>
  ; rel="memento"; datetime="Wed, 05 Jul 2006 23:16:34 GMT",
<https://wayback.archive-it.org/all/20060717071357/http://www.lanl.gov/>
  ; rel="memento"; datetime="Mon, 17 Jul 2006 07:13:57 GMT",
<https://wayback.archive-it.org/all/20060717073942/http://www.lanl.gov/>
  ; rel="memento"; datetime="Mon, 17 Jul 2006 07:39:42 GMT",

... truncated for brevity ...

<https://wayback.archive-it.org/all/20191217083843/https://www.lanl.gov/>
  ; rel="last memento"; datetime="Tue, 17 Dec 2019 08:38:43 GMT"
```

Fig. 5 The first 10 lines and last line of a TimeMap provided by Archive-It at URI-T https://wayback.archive-it.org/all/timemap/link/http://www.lanl.gov/. Spaces and line breaks have been inserted for readability

come from the same archive. A client can also produce a combined TimeMap containing the results of a query across multiple archives. For multiple archives supporting the Memento Protocol, a client can request each TimeMap in turn and produce a new TimeMap listing all Mementos across those web archives for a single Original Resource. Similarly, a client can consult TimeGates from multiple archives to simultaneously find the temporally closest Memento for the desired datetime. *Aggregators* provide this functionality across web archives, and they do so by supporting the very concepts of the Memento Protocol. In 2013, AlSum et al. (2014) demonstrated that the overlap between the Internet Archive and other web archives is high. By making use of the content across archives, aggregators ensure that clients can discover content even if one or more web archives is unavailable. A client processes an aggregated TimeMap like any other TimeMap, and a software client performs datetime negotiation with a TimeGate aggregator like with any other TimeGate.

The Prototyping Team in the Research Library at Los Alamos National Laboratory (LANL) developed the first Memento aggregator that allows users to find Mementos from not just a single archive, but across archives. For example, if we want a Memento for http://www.cs.odu.edu from 24 April 2010, a TimeGate aggregator would help us to find the temporally closest Memento across more than 20 Memento-compliant archives. The LANL Memento Aggregator has become a popular resource, receiving roughly a million requests per month (Klein et al. 2019a,b). The TimeTravel service at LANL[2] provides this aggregation capability for the public. LANL also offers additional APIs[3] that provide services built upon this aggregator, such as the Time Travel Reconstruct service that reconstructs a Memento out of content from multiple web archives (Costa et al. 2017). If users want to run their own aggregator, they can instal MemGator (Alam and Nelson 2016), developed by Old Dominion University. Research by Kelly et al. extends aggregators to query both public and private web archives (Kelly et al. 2018), allowing users to seamlessly transition between archives at different levels of access. Without the standardised interfaces offered by the Memento Protocol, such aggregators would need to apply an assortment of hacks specific to each web archive, like those mentioned in Sect. 1.1.

Any system that provides access to versioned resources can support the Memento Protocol. MediaWiki is the platform that supports Wikipedia. The Memento MediaWiki extension (Jones et al. 2014) provides a complete implementation of the Memento Protocol for MediaWiki. We have demonstrated how the Memento Protocol allows a user to temporally navigate across web archives and Wikipedia.[4] We have continually engaged with the MediaWiki community[5] in an effort to add Memento support to Wikipedia,[6] in order to provide this time travel capability could become available to its users and machines alike, unfortunately to no avail to date. Likewise, Memento for Wordpress (Welsh 2019) provides standardised access to different versions of blog posts. Much like the transactional archives provided by tools like SiteStory (Brunelle et al. 2013), these systems are web archives in their own right. When we begin to consider the implications of seamless temporal browsing between web archives and other resource versioning systems, we begin to see the power and capability that Memento delivers for all kinds of research and analysis.

3 Tools That Leverage the Memento Protocol

The interoperability specified by Memento has led to a rich ecosystem of tools to engage with web archives. Prior to Memento, tools were often tied to a specific web archive because the cost was too high to engineer solutions that collected data across archives.

---

[2] http://timetravel.mementoweb.org/.
[3] http://timetravel.mementoweb.org/guide/api/.
[4] https://www.youtube.com/watch?v=WtZHKeFwjzk.
[5] https://phabricator.wikimedia.org/T164654.
[6] https://en.wikipedia.org/wiki/Wikipedia:Requests_for_comment/Memento.

3.1   Browsing the Past Web

The Prototyping Team in the Research Library at LANL developed browser extensions so users could browse the Web as if it were a date in the past. The Memento Time Travel extensions for Chrome[7] or Firefox[8] allow users to set a datetime in the past. From there, they can right-click on any page or link and visit a Memento of the selected resource at their chosen datetime. Figure 6 demonstrates how the extension makes its decisions about URIs. For every URI the browser visits, the extension tries to determine what kind of resource it has encountered: an Original Resource, a TimeGate or a Memento. This knowledge helps the extension determine its next step in terms of datetime negotiation, as depicted in Fig. 3. Kelly et al. (2014) developed Mink, a Google Chrome extension, that does not use datetime negotiation but helps users find other versions of their current URI via TimeMaps. Mink also allows them to save a page they are visiting to multiple web archives. These extensions offload decisions about discovering Mementos to the Memento Protocol infrastructure at web archives. In the past, such tools would have been far more complex, requiring special logic to handle different archives, assuming the tool could find all of the information needed for this kind of exploration.

Developers have improved the existing platforms by adding links to Memento aggregators. Warclight (Ruest et al. 2019) provides an interface for users to explore

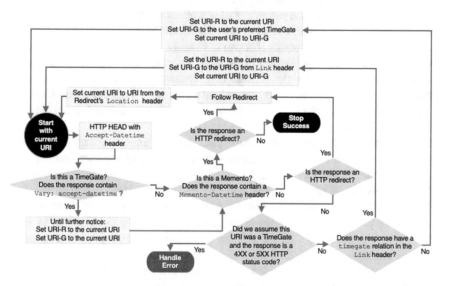

Fig. 6 The algorithm employed by the Memento browser extensions for datetime negotiation

---

[7]http://bit.ly/memento-for-chrome.

[8]https://addons.mozilla.org/en-US/firefox/addon/memento-timetravel/.

WARC files via facets and other search engine features. Because WARC files contain URIs of the Original Resources (URI-Rs), Warclight can query the LANL Memento aggregator to help users find other Mementos for an indexed resource. The New York Art Resources Consortium (NYARC) started a web archiving initiative for online art and art resources, creating 10 collections in the process. NYARC (Duncan 2017) integrates the LANL Time Travel service into their search results. This integration allows users to view the content supplied by NYARC and the surrounding context provided by other web archives. Arquivo.pt links to LANL's Time Travel Reconstruct API (Arquivo.pt 2016), augmenting the holdings of one archive with others. In the past, such improvements providing easy access to a multitude of web archives did not exist.

3.2   Summarising Web Archive Collections

TimeMaps provide us with a roadmap of observations that we can use to summarise and visualise web resources over time. AlNoamany et al. (2016), and later Jones et al. (2018b), incorporated TimeMaps into algorithms that detect off-topic content in web archive collections, allowing users to exclude these Mementos from summarisation efforts. AlSum and Nelson (2014) developed solutions for visualising Memento content across a TimeMap via browser thumbnails (screenshots). Thumbnails must be stored, and the authors' goal was to save disk space by only generating thumbnails when Memento content was significantly different. TMVis (Weigle 2017) is a tool that implements this work. *What Did It Look Like?* (Nwala 2015) uses a Memento aggregator to poll multiple web archives to generate animated thumbnails demonstrating the change of a webpage over time. The consistent interface provided by Memento allowed all of these researchers to consider the TimeMap a building block to an algorithm that applies to any web archive rather than a specific one.

The existing webpage summarisation tools, such as Embed.ly[9] and microlink,[10] misattribute a Memento to the wrong source and fail to separate web archive branding from Memento content, so Jones et al. (2019) created MementoEmbed. MementoEmbed makes use of Memento headers and TimeMaps to find information about Mementos and provides added value over other services. MementoEmbed summaries also link to the LANL Memento Aggregator to provide access to other Mementos for the same Original Resource. Users can aggregate such summaries for social media storytelling in order to summarise entire web archive collections. AlNoamany et al. (2017) provided an algorithm that makes use of TimeMaps for selecting the best Mementos representing a collection so users can then visualise them via this storytelling method. Because of the Memento Protocol, researchers

---

[9]https://embed.ly/.

[10]https://microlink.io/.

can focus on the problems of visualisation and summarisation rather than the problems of integrating many disparate components from different web archives.

3.3   Locating and Dating Content

Researchers have developed tools to help others locate lost content. Klein et al. (2011) developed Synchronicity, a Firefox browser extension, that uses TimeMaps to help users discover missing content. Klein and Nelson (2014) also employed TimeMaps to discover lexical signatures for archived pages in an attempt to locate their content on the live Web. The Tempas system, by Holzmann and Anand (2016), uses Delicious tags to help users find Original Resources and then employs TimeGates to help them discover past versions of that content. SalahEldeen and Nelson (2013a) created Carbon Date, which queries aggregated TimeMaps and social media sources to help users estimate when a web resource first came into existence. To combat link rot and content drift, Robust Links (Klein and Van de Sompel 2015) combines HTML link decoration, JavaScript and Memento aggregator queries to provide long-lasting links to the Original Resource and the Mementos thereof, thus helping readers find the Memento of a referenced web resource that is temporally closest to the time the resource was referenced. Without the Memento Protocol, these tools could not benefit from the coverage supplied by multiple archives.

4   Research Enabled by the Memento Protocol

Web archives offer unparalleled research opportunities with data from the past. Sociologists, such as Curty and Zhang (2011), have conducted longitudinal studies with Mementos that were crawled incidentally by the Internet Archive. Journalists such as Hafner and Palmer (2017) have exposed questionable practices by studying the Mementos of businesses' home pages. Milligan (2019) has noted that web archive data is key to historians studying our contemporary times, allowing them to determine not only what social movements existed, but also how people of our era lived their lives. Such studies require that a researcher painstakingly acquires Mementos from web archives before manual review. A familiar aphorism is that a researcher spends 80–90% of their time acquiring the data needed for their work. The Memento Protocol reduces this time by helping researchers find the Mementos that help support their analysis.

In this section, we highlight work that has applied Memento to different problems. Many of the following studies employed TimeMaps and TimeGates, but some also used tools such as Carbon Date and Memento aggregators that developers had built upon the Memento infrastructure.

4.1 Analysis of Social Media

Central to the social media studies in this section were two capabilities. Some needed to find all Mementos for a captured URI. Others needed to find the temporally closest Memento for a URI at a given datetime across all web archives. Without the Memento Protocol, the researchers would have had to request and process CDX files from multiple web archives, and CDX files are often not available for technical or legal reasons. If these files were available, the transfer, storage, update and analysis of CDX files would then be a new problem that researchers would need to solve before engaging in this work. Alternatively, they could have manually visited the multiple web archives and recorded their results, something that would likely have taken years to complete.

Social media allows users to share links to resources. In some cases, web archives capture a given post, but the resource referenced in the post is no longer available. In other cases, the referenced resource no longer contains the content mentioned in the post. These disconnects were discussed by Klein and Nelson (2011) in their analysis of the TimeMaps of pages tagged by Delicious users. SalahEldeen and Nelson (2012) queried the LANL Memento aggregator to explore the nature of this loss of context concerning the 2011 Egyptian Revolution, an event for which social media played a key role. In the subsequent work (SalahEldeen and Nelson 2013b), the authors highlighted a new issue. If a user creates a social media post about a news event and links to the front page of a news service, then it is likely that a reader at a later date will not see the version of the news service that the user intended. However, if the user creates a post and links to a specific article, then their intention may be more clear. The authors dubbed this new problem *temporal intention*. Thanks to Memento aggregators, they were able to determine if an archive had created a Memento of the referenced resource close to the time of the social media post. They were then able to apply these Mementos in a user study to better understand the context of the post and whether the current linked content still reflected the original poster's intention.

How similar are social media collections about events to web archive collections on the same topic? Nwala et al. (2018a) analysed the text from webpages shared on Twitter, Storify, Reddit and the web archiving platform Archive-It. Their results show that web archive collections about events are very similar to social media collections. With this result, they defended their position that archivists can mine social media collections to bootstrap web archive collections about events. More popular resources tend to be archived more often than less popular ones (Ainsworth et al. 2011); thus, we can use the archived status of a resource as a proxy for its popularity. As part of their evaluation, Nwala et al. queried MemGator to determine if one or more web archives had captured an Original Resource referenced from social media. Without the capability of aggregators, they would not have been able to leverage this metric in their analysis.

Aside from analysing the behaviour of social media users, what can historians learn from social media in a historiographical fashion? Helmond and van der

Vlist (2019) brought MemGator to bear to analyse not only the posts of social media users but also the social media platforms as entities themselves. By utilising Memento, they quantified how well the user documentation and business plans of these platforms are archived. This insight will allow future historians to connect historical events to changes in social media platforms and better understand changes in human behaviour over time.

4.2 Age and Availability of Resources

Memento has also played a pivotal role in helping researchers estimate archiving rates for various types of resources. Ainsworth et al. (2011) investigated how much of the Web was archived and estimated that 35–90% of the existing web resources have at least one Memento. Alkwai et al. estimated the archive coverage of Arabic websites (Alkwai et al. 2015) and later conducted an additional study (Alkwai et al. 2017) to compare the archiving rates of English-, Arabic-, Danish- and Korean-language webpages. Alkwai showed that English has a higher archiving rate than Arabic, which in turn has a higher archiving rate than Danish or Korean. Nwala et al. (2017) established that local news sources have lower archiving rates than non-local sources. Bicho and Gomes (2016) evaluated how well research and development websites were archived, and used this evaluation to construct heuristics and algorithms for proactively identifying and preserving them. Because they used Memento aggregators, each of these studies achieved higher coverage of web history in far less time than if they had developed bespoke cross-archive solutions.

When an event takes place, how many resources that pertain to it can we archive after the fact? Ben-David (2019) analysed web resources that were present during the 2014 Gaza War. While building a web archive for the 2014 event in 2018, she observed that 38.16% of the resources were still available on the Web, 40.63% were inaccessible and 21.21% were redirected or moved. Thus, the Memento infrastructure allowed her to generate the evidence needed to defend the idea that incidental web archiving is insufficient for documenting events. Ben-David's study relied upon Carbon Date to establish which content authors had published during the 2014 Gaza War. Carbon Date relies upon the Memento infrastructure to supply the earliest Memento across multiple web archives. She also gathered Mementos via MemGator for analysis. Each of these tools saved the author time and effort so that she could focus on her research questions rather than the complexity of solving interoperability issues between archives.

Can we build event collections from web archives? Even if resources about events remain on the live Web, Nwala et al. (2018b) detailed how they become more challenging to discover via search engine results as we get farther from the event. Topical focused crawling (Chakrabarti et al. 1999) provides resources whose terms closely match the terms of a desired topic, such as an event, and these crawlers stop when the matching score for new content is too low. Building on the work by Gossen et al. (2017, 2018), Klein et al. (2018) designed a framework to build collections about unexpected events (e.g. shootings) by employing focused crawling of web archives. Focused crawling of web archives is different from focused crawling of the live Web because Mementos have a temporal dimension to consider; thus, the authors' crawler had to score each resource's relevance in terms of similarity to the desired topic and distance from the datetime of the event. The authors considered the canonical Wikipedia article about an event to be a good source of authoritative information for their focused crawls. Because Wikipedia articles are created in response to events and then updated by many contributors thereafter, it takes some time for the article to stabilise into an adequate description of the event. The authors used the article revision corresponding to the datetime of this change point as the source of terms relevant to the event. They also recorded the Original Resource (URI-R) references in this revision as the seeds for their focused crawl. The authors employed Memento TimeGates with these Original Resources (URI-Rs) and the datetime of the event to find candidate Mementos for their event collection. To ensure that they only included resources created after the event, the authors also acquired publication dates from Original Resources (URI-Rs) or HTML metadata. They estimated publication dates with Carbon Date if those methods failed. They found that collections built from the live Web for recent events are more relevant than those built from web archives, but events from the distant past produced more relevant documents using their archive-based method. Without the Memento Protocol, such crawling would be far more costly to implement for a single archive. With the Memento Protocol, Klein et al. were able to create collections from Mementos spanning many web archives.

4.3 Analysing and Addressing Lost Context

Context is key to understanding many documents. Thus, in many cases, merely preserving a single document is insufficient to truly understand the author's intention. Various studies have tried to explore the availability of documents that supply this context.

Because references from scholarly papers provide evidence and justification for arguments, the decay of scholarly references has been of particular concern. Even though there are systems such as LOCKSS (Reich and Rosenthal 2001) for preserving referenced papers, no concerted long-term effort exists for preserving referenced web resources. Sanderson et al. (2011) observed that 45% of the web resource references from papers on arxiv.org still exist but are not archived. Klein et al. (2014) expanded the dataset to include data from Elsevier and PubMed. They observed the rate of decay varied depending on the paper's year of publication, getting worse with the paper's age. Jones et al. (2016) discerned from the same dataset that not only were many referenced resources missing, but, for those references for which the Original Resource still existed on the live Web, 80% had content that had drifted when compared to the time the paper referenced it. The authors demonstrated that the older the publication date of the paper, the greater the number of references that are no longer accessible or have highly drifted from their original content. Zhou et al. (2015) analysed how incidental web archiving misses many of these resources and proposed machine learning techniques to predict which resources might decay faster so that crawlers would archive them sooner. If these studies had queried a single web archive, then the representativeness of their results would have been more easily challenged—however, all employed aggregated TimeMaps and Mementos to get a better view of the archived resources across the world. Memento also provides a solution to the problem identified by the authors. Tools such as the browser extensions or Robust Links can employ aggregated TimeGates to help connect users to an appropriate Memento for a referenced resource (Sanderson and Van de Sompel 2010; Van de Sompel and Davis 2015) and thus restore this context.

Annotations developed via tools such as Hypothes.is provide similar context to documents. If a future researcher has access to the document, but not the annotations, crucial insight is lost. But having access to an annotation but not the annotated resource is probably even worse. Sanderson and Van de Sompel (2010) formulated a theoretical solution and demonstrated how the Memento Protocol can be leveraged both to attach an annotation to the appropriate temporal version of an annotated resource, assuming it was archived, and to find temporal annotations for a version of a resource given a Memento for it. Via the notion of Time Selectors, their insights eventually found their way into the W3C Web Annotation Data Model (Sanderson et al. 2017).

Aturban et al. (2015) analysed the issue of orphaned annotations. By analysing TimeMaps, they determined that 27% of the annotations were no longer available, and 61% were in danger of becoming disconnected from their referenced document. Much like the other lost context studies mentioned above, Aturban's study serves as a call to action to archive annotations and annotated resources so that Sanderson and Van de Sompel's solution can effectively solve this problem.

4.4 Improving Web Archiving

The quality of Mementos can vary depending on a variety of factors. Sometimes webpages are missing images, stylesheets and other embedded resources because the web archive was unable to capture them. Brunelle et al. (2015) developed the metric of *Memento damage* for measuring this notion of archival quality, which compares well with later studies (Kiesel et al. 2018) that employed neural networks for this purpose. They found that 54% of all Mementos were missing at least one embedded resource. Brunelle et al. (2016) were able to identify how much JavaScript contributed to this problem. They later developed a better crawling technique (Brunelle et al. 2017), which captured 15 times more embedded resources than before. Alam et al. (2017) further improved upon this by combining browser technologies and the Memento Aggregator to reconstruct pages from embedded resources spread across multiple web archives.

Missing resources are one thing, but what if the embedded resource in a Memento is the wrong one? Ainsworth et al. (2015) demonstrated that sometimes web archive playback engines choose versions of images from the future or the distant past. The wrong embedded resources can profoundly change the meaning of a page and reproduce a webpage that never existed. They estimated that web archives accurately reproduced only 20% of the Mementos. They introduced the concept of the *composite Memento*, a resource that includes not only the page that the web archive had captured but all embedded resources as well. Aturban et al. (2017) analysed the effectiveness of applying cryptographic hashes to detect when Mementos do not represent the pages from which they were captured. To alleviate issues identified by Ainsworth, Aturban argued that archives should compute such hashes on the composite Memento rather than just the individual resources. They also cited work by Brunelle and Nelson (2013) that indicates that the Mementos listed in TimeMaps are not always the same, affecting the ability to reliably compute these hashes.

Improving aggregators is an active area of research. Early aggregators tried to combine CDX files from different web archives (Sanderson 2012) in order to provide TimeGate responses from the best web archive. As Memento adoption increased, newer aggregators directly queried the TimeGates or TimeMaps from each web archive, and new approaches to optimise these queries emerged. To help aggregators avoid unnecessary queries, several studies tried to predict which web archives to query for a given Original Resource (URI-R). Alam et al. demonstrated that profiling web archives via domain name and language (AlSum et al. 2014) would allow aggregators to route queries more efficiently. Brunelle et al. evaluated the changes in web archive holdings and proposed caching TimeMaps for 15 days (Brunelle and Nelson 2013) to improve response times. Alam et al. (2016a) further demonstrated improvements to query routing via CDX summarisation. Alam et al. (2016b) later demonstrated that queries could be routed based on the results of textual queries sent to the web archive's search engine. Unfortunately, many archives do not provide access to their CDX files nor have search engine capability, so Bornand et al. (2016) trained binary classifiers using data from the LANL Memento Aggregator cache in order to determine whether or not a query should be sent to a given archive. This approach led to a 42% improvement in the overall response times, but Klein et al. (2019b) noted that classifiers need to be retrained regularly to maintain this level of performance.

To analyse these problems and develop solutions, all of these authors queried publicly available TimeMaps and TimeGates. Before the Memento Protocol, this work would have required close collaboration with web archives, screen scraping or manual work to gather the necessary data.

4.5   Temporal Access to Data

Because Memento provides access to previous resource versions via HTTP, the ability to acquire past web resources is independent of the file format of the content. Early on in the effort to formally specify the Memento Protocol, Van de Sompel et al. described and demonstrated (Van de Sompel et al. 2010) its applicability to interact with versions of Linked Data sets. LANL deployed an archive of various versions of DBpedia[11] that provided subject URI access. The associated current versions of those subject URIs in DBpedia pointed at an associated TimeGate exposed by the archive, as per the Memento Protocol. To illustrate Memento's potential, the authors leveraged this infrastructure to automatically plot a time series analysis of the evolving Gross Domestic Product per capita of various countries by obtaining current and past versions of the DBpedia descriptions for each of these countries, merely using Memento's "follow your nose" approach, and extracting the pertinent attribute from each description. In an attempt to provide access to Linked Data sets in a manner that is more sustainable than full-blown SPARQL endpoints and more expressive than dataset dumps or subject URI access, Taelman et al. (2017) suggested Triple Pattern Fragments (TPF) endpoints, which support *?subject ?predicate ?object* query functionality. Vander Sande et al. (2018) argued that the combination of the binary Header Dictionary Triple (HDT)[12] approach to store Linked Data set and TPF to query them offers a sweet spot between functionality and sustainability for Linked Data archives. They refurbished the LANL DBpedia archive using this approach and extended the Linked Data Fragment server software[13] with Memento capabilities, as such providing support for temporal *?subject ?predicate ?object* queries (Van de Sompel and Vander Sande 2016). Since Verborgh et al. (2016) showed that SPARQL queries can be broken down into consecutive TPF queries, in essence, a client can issue temporal SPARQL queries against Linked Data archives modelled in this manner.

Many others have leveraged the Memento Protocol in Linked Data architectures. Coppens et al. (2011) detailed how multiple projects in Belgium disseminate temporal versions of datasets as Linked Open Data and used Memento TimeGates to provide version access. Mannens et al. (2012) provided TimeGates over aggregated Linked Data to provide provenance for news stories. Meinhardt et al. (2015) developed TailR, a system that archives Linked Data resources so that researchers have access to their dataset history via TimeGates and TimeMaps. Neumaier et al. (2017) republished the dataset descriptions of 261 data portals using the standard Linked Data vocabularies such as DCAT[14] and Schema.org[15] and provided

---

[11]http://wikidata.dbpedia.org/.

[12]http://www.w3.org/Submission/HDT/.

[13]https://github.com/LinkedDataFragments/Server.js/.

[14]https://www.w3.org/TR/vocab-dcat-2/.

[15]http://schema.org/.

access to different versions of this data via Memento TimeGates. Van de Vyvere et al. (2019) applied Linked Data Fragments and Memento to create a system that allowed users to explore historical automobile traffic data. Fafalios et al. (2017) semantically annotated Mementos that reside in web archives, for example, connecting entities mentioned in archived webpages to their associated DBpedia URI and as such created enhanced search capabilities. When enriching archived webpages with information from DBpedia, they used the Memento Protocol and the LANL DBpedia archive to obtain DBpedia entity descriptions contemporary of the archived webpage. Conceptually, Sanderson and Van de Sompel (2012) noted that Linked Data descriptions heavily rely on links to external resources, which a client software may need to retrieve. When doing so, most likely, the client requires a description of the linked resource that was the current version at the time the description containing the link was published. In cases where versions of Linked Data sets are maintained, clients can use the Memento Protocol to access temporally matching descriptions of linked resources. Powell et al. (2011) mentioned how one could use the Memento Protocol to analyse the evolution of knowledge graphs over time.

4.6   Other Work Using Memento

Can we use Memento to avoid information? Why would we want to do this? Fans of TV shows and sport may not be able to experience an event as it is broadcast and may watch a recorded version afterwards. Jones et al. (2018a) explored the use of the Memento Protocol to avoid spoilers for TV shows. Fans of television shows update wikis very quickly after an episode has aired. Thus, to avoid spoilers, a fan can just visit the wiki page version that existed immediately prior to the first airing of an episode or event. The authors discovered that wikis, having access to all versions, do a better job at helping fans avoid spoilers than the Internet Archive. For this use case, the authors quantified how temporally closest is not always the best TimeGate heuristic to use when we have access to all revisions of a document because it can lead a user to a Memento captured after the spoiler was revealed. Their results have implications for television shows, sporting events and information security. TimeMaps provided the data necessary to analyse the different behaviours between wikis and web archives. Alternatively, the authors could have requested CDX files from the archive. Even if filtered, these files would have likely contained superfluous information not core to their study (e.g. CDX records not containing wiki page content).

Researchers have applied Memento to analyse web author behaviour. Cocciolo (2015) utilised the Memento Protocol to find the Mementos of prominent American webpages. He discovered that the percentage of text in webpages peaked in 2005 and has been declining ever since. These results confirm Cocciolo's anecdotal observation that webpages have been getting shorter, and this work may lead to further analysis to understand the causes of this behaviour. Hashmi et al. (2019)

performed a longitudinal analysis of the evolution of ad-blocking blacklists by using the Memento Protocol to query the Internet Archive at specific time intervals for advertisement services. They then contrasted this with the Mementos of the blacklists that try to keep up with them.

5 Summary

The Memento Protocol provides client software with an ability to seamlessly navigate between the current Web and the archived Web using the omnipresent HTTP protocol. It separates the concept of an Original Resource from a Memento. An Original Resource exists or used to exist on the Web. A Memento is a capture of that resource at a specific point in time. TimeMaps provide lists of all Mementos for an Original Resource. TimeGates allow a client to request a specific Memento given an Original Resource URI and the desired datetime. With these resources in place, the community has constructed aggregators, allowing for queries across web archives. These components have given rise to a new tool ecosystem for web archives.

Researchers have accessed these tools to conduct studies that otherwise would be too costly, or even impossible to conduct, in terms of time and effort. They have been taken advantage of the Memento Protocol to analyse social media, determine the age and availability of resources, address lost context, improve web archives or obtain temporal access to data.

The Memento Protocol is relatively simple and has its roots in HTTP. What if Memento support existed as a native browser feature rather than as an extension? A user could have some indication that they have reached a Memento rather than a live page. The browser could help them browse the Web of the past via datetime negotiation across all web archives and versioning systems. What if all web archives and versioning systems supported the Memento Protocol? At their fingertips, everyone would truly be able to time travel through the past Web.

References

Ainsworth SG, Alsum A, SalahEldeen H, Weigle MC, Nelson ML (2011) How much of the web is archived? In: ACM/IEEE joint conference on digital libraries, pp 133–136. https://doi.org/10.1145/1998076.1998100

Ainsworth SG, Nelson ML, Van de Sompel H (2015) Only one out of five archived web pages existed as presented. In: ACM conference on hypertext and social media, pp 257–266. https://doi.org/10.1145/2700171.2791044

Alam S, Nelson ML (2016) MemGator – A portable concurrent memento aggregator: cross-platform CLI and server binaries in go. In: ACM/IEEE joint conference on digital libraries, pp 243–244. https://doi.org/10.1145/2910896.2925452

Alam S, Nelson ML, Balakireva LL, Shankar H, Rosenthal DSH (2016a) Web archive profiling through CDX summarization. Int J Digital Libraries 17(3):223–238. https://doi.org/10.1007/s00799-016-0184-4

Alam S, Nelson ML, Van de Sompel H, Rosenthal DSH (2016b) Web archive profiling through fulltext search. In: International conference on theory and practice of digital libraries (TPDL), vol 9819, pp 121–132. https://doi.org/10.1007/978-3-319-43997-6_10

Alam S, Kelly M, Weigle MC, Nelson ML (2017) Client-side reconstruction of composite mementos using ServiceWorker. In: ACM/IEEE joint conference on digital libraries, pp 1–4. https://doi.org/10.1109/JCDL.2017.7991579

Alkwai LM, Nelson ML, Weigle MC (2015) How well are arabic websites archived? In: ACM/IEEE joint conference on digital libraries, pp 223–232. https://doi.org/10.1145/2756406.2756912

Alkwai LM, Nelson ML, Weigle MC (2017) Comparing the archival rate of Arabic, English, Danish, and Korean Language web pages. ACM Trans Inf Syst 36(1):1–34. https://doi.org/10.1145/3041656

AlNoamany Y, Weigle MC, Nelson ML (2016) Detecting off-topic pages within TimeMaps in web archives. Int J Digital Libraries 17(3):203–221. https://doi.org/10.1007/s00799-016-0183-5

AlNoamany Y, Weigle MC, Nelson ML (2017) Generating stories from archived collections. In: ACM conference on web science, pp 309–318. https://doi.org/10.1145/3091478.3091508

AlSum A, Nelson ML (2014) Thumbnail summarization techniques for web archives. In: European conference on information retrieval (ECIR), vol 8416, pp 299–310. https://doi.org/10.1007/978-3-319-06028-6_25

AlSum A, Weigle MC, Nelson ML, Van de Sompel H (2014) Profiling web archive coverage for top-level domain and content language. Int J Digital Libraries 14(3–4):149–166. https://doi.org/10.1007/s00799-014-0118-y

Arquivopt (2016) Arquivo.pt – new version. https://sobre.arquivo.pt/en/arquivo-pt-new-version-2/

Aturban M, Nelson ML, Weigle MC (2015) Quantifying orphaned annotations in hypothes.is. In: International conference on theory and practice of digital libraries (TPDL), vol 9316, pp 15–27. https://doi.org/10.1007/978-3-319-24592-8_2

Aturban M, Nelson ML, Weigle MC (2017) Difficulties of timestamping archived web pages. Technical Report. arXiv:1712.03140. http://arxiv.org/abs/1712.03140

Ben-David A (2019) 2014 not found: a cross-platform approach to retrospective web archiving. Internet Histories 3(3–4):316–342. https://doi.org/10.1080/24701475.2019.1654290

Bicho D, Gomes D (2016) Automatic identification and preservation of R&D websites. Technical report, Arquivo.pt - The Portuguese Web Archive. https://sobre.arquivo.pt/wp-content/uploads/automatic-identification-and-preservation-of-r-d.pdf

Bornand NJ, Balakireva L, Van de Sompel H (2016) Routing memento requests using binary classifiers. In: ACM/IEEE joint conference on digital libraries, pp 63–72. https://doi.org/10.1145/2910896.2910899

Brunelle JF, Nelson ML (2013) An evaluation of caching policies for memento TimeMaps. In: ACM/IEEE joint conference on digital libraries, pp 267–276. https://doi.org/10.1145/2467696.2467717

Brunelle JF, Nelson ML, Balakireva L, Sanderson R, Van de Sompel H (2013) Evaluating the SiteStory transactional web archive with the ApacheBench Tool. In: International conference on theory and practice of digital libraries (TPDL), vol 8092, pp 204–215. https://doi.org/10.1007/978-3-642-40501-3_20

Brunelle JF, Kelly M, SalahEldeen H, Weigle MC, Nelson ML (2015) Not all mementos are created equal: measuring the impact of missing resources. Int J Digital Libraries 16(3–4):283–301. https://doi.org/10.1007/s00799-015-0150-6

Brunelle JF, Kelly M, Weigle MC, Nelson ML (2016) The impact of JavaScript on archivability. Int J Digital Libraries 17(2):95–117. https://doi.org/10.1007/s00799-015-0140-8

Brunelle JF, Weigle MC, Nelson ML (2017) Archival crawlers and JavaScript: discover more stuff but crawl more slowly. In: ACM/IEEE joint conference on digital libraries, pp 1–10. https://doi.org/10.1109/JCDL.2017.7991554

Chakrabarti S, Van den Berg M, Dom B (1999) Focused crawling: a new approach to topic-specific web resource discovery. Comput Netw 31(11–16):1623–1640. https://doi.org/10.1016/S1389-1286(99)00052-3

Cocciolo A (2015) The rise and fall of text on the web: a quantitative study of web archives. Inf Res Int Electron J 20(3):1–11. https://eric.ed.gov/?id=EJ1077827

Coppens S, Mannens E, Deursen DV (2011) Publishing provenance information on the web using the memento datetime content negotiation. In: Linked data on the web workshop, pp 1–10. http://events.linkeddata.org/ldow2011/papers/ldow2011-paper02-coppens.pdf

Costa M, Gomes D, Silva MJ (2017) The evolution of web archiving. Int J Digital Libraries 18(3):191–205. https://doi.org/10.1007/s00799-016-0171-9

Curty RG, Zhang P (2011) Social commerce: looking back and forward. Proc Am Soc Inf Sci Technol 48(1):1–10. https://doi.org/10.1002/meet.2011.14504801096

Duncan S (2017) Web archiving at the New York art resources consortium (NYARC): Collaboration to preserve specialist born-digital art resources. In: Digital humanities. opportunities and risks. connecting libraries and research. https://hal.archives-ouvertes.fr/hal-01636124

Fafalios P, Holzmann H, Kasturia V, Nejdl W (2017) Building and querying semantic layers for web archives. In: ACM/IEEE joint conference on digital libraries, pp 1–10. https://doi.org/10.1109/JCDL.2017.7991555

Fielding RT (2000) REST: Architectural styles and the design of network-based software architectures. Doctoral dissertation, University of California, Irvine. https://www.ics.uci.edu/~fielding/pubs/dissertation/top.htm

Fielding R, Reschke J (2014a) RFC 7230 - hypertext transfer protocol (HTTP/1.1): message syntax and routing. https://tools.ietf.org/html/rfc7230

Fielding R, Reschke J (2014b) RFC 7231 - hypertext transfer protocol (HTTP/1.1): semantics and content. https://tools.ietf.org/html/rfc7231

Fielding R, Reschke J (2014c) RFC 7232 - hypertext transfer protocol (HTTP/1.1): conditional requests. https://tools.ietf.org/html/rfc7232

Fielding R, Reschke J (2014d) RFC 7235 - hypertext transfer protocol (HTTP/1.1): authentication. https://tools.ietf.org/html/rfc7235

Fielding R, Lafon Y, Reschke J (2014a) RFC 7233 - hypertext transfer protocol (HTTP/1.1): range requests. https://tools.ietf.org/html/rfc7233

Fielding R, Nottingham M, Reschke J (2014b) RFC 7234 - hypertext transfer protocol (HTTP/1.1): caching. https://tools.ietf.org/html/rfc7234

Gomes D, Costa M (2014) The importance of web archives for humanities. Int J Human Arts Comput 8(1):106–123. https://doi.org/10.3366/ijhac.2014.0122

Gossen G, Demidova E, Risse T (2017) Extracting event-centric document collections from large-scale web archives. In: International conference on theory and practice of digital libraries (TPDL), vol 10450, pp 116–127. https://doi.org/10.1007/978-3-319-67008-9_10

Gossen G, Risse T, Demidova E (2018) Towards extracting event-centric collections from web archives. Int J Digital Libraries. https://doi.org/10.1007/s00799-018-0258-6

Hafner K, Palmer G (2017) Skin cancers rise, along with questionable treatments. The New York Times. https://www.nytimes.com/2017/11/20/health/dermatology-skin-cancer.html

Hashmi SS, Ikram M, Kaafar MA (2019) A longitudinal analysis of online ad-blocking blacklists. Technical Report. arXiv:1906.00166. https://arxiv.org/abs/1906.00166

Helmond A, van der Vlist FN (2019) Social media and platform historiography: challenges and opportunities. J Media History 22(1):6–34. https://www.tmgonline.nl/articles/434/

Holzmann H, Anand A (2016) Tempas: temporal archive search based on tags. In: International world wide web conference, pp 207–210. https://doi.org/10.1145/2872518.2890555

International Internet Preservation Coalition (2006) The CDX file format. https://iipc.github.io/warc-specifications/specifications/cdx-format/cdx-2006/

International Organization for Standardization (ISO) (2009) 28500: 2009 Information and documentation-WARC file format. International Organization for Standardization

Jones SM, Nelson ML, Shankar H, Van de Sompel H (2014) Bringing web time travel to MediaWiki: an assessment of the memento MediaWiki extension. Technical Report. arXiv:1406.3876. http://arxiv.org/abs/1406.3876

Jones SM, Van de Sompel H, Shankar H, Klein M, Tobin R, Grover C (2016) Scholarly context Adrift: three out of four URI references lead to changed content. PLoS One 11(12):e0167475. https://doi.org/10.1371/journal.pone.0167475

Jones SM, Nelson ML, Van de Sompel H (2018a) Avoiding spoilers: wiki time travel with Sheldon Cooper. Int J Digital Libraries 19(1):77–93. https://doi.org/10.1007/s00799-016-0200-8

Jones SM, Weigle MC, Nelson ML (2018b) The off-topic memento toolkit. In: International conference on digital preservation, pp 1–10. https://doi.org/10.17605/OSF.IO/UBW87

Jones SM, Weigle MC, Nelson ML (2019) Social cards probably provide for better understanding of web archive collections. In: ACM international conference on information and knowledge management, pp 2023–2032. https://doi.org/10.1145/3357384.3358039

Kelly M, Nelson ML, Weigle MC (2014) Mink: integrating the live and archived web viewing experience using web browsers and memento. In: ACM/IEEE joint conference on digital libraries, pp 469–470. https://doi.org/10.1109/JCDL.2014.6970229

Kelly M, Nelson ML, Weigle MC (2018) A framework for aggregating private and public web archives. In: ACM/IEEE joint conference on digital libraries, pp 273–282. https://doi.org/10.1145/3197026.3197045

Kiesel J, Kneist F, Alshomary M, Stein B, Hagen M, Potthast M (2018) Reproducible web corpora: interactive archiving with automatic quality assessment. J Data Inf Qual 10(4):1–25. https://doi.org/10.1145/3239574

Klein M, Nelson ML (2011) Find, new, copy, web, page – tagging for the (re-)discovery of web pages. In: International conference on theory and practice of digital libraries (TPDL), vol 6966, pp 27–39. https://doi.org/10.1007/978-3-642-24469-8_5

Klein M, Nelson ML (2014) Moved but not gone: an evaluation of real-time methods for discovering replacement web pages. Int J Digital Libraries 14(1–2):17–38. https://doi.org/10.1007/s00799-014-0108-0

Klein M, Van de Sompel H (2015) Reference rot in web-based scholarly communication and link decoration as a path to mitigation. https://blogs.lse.ac.uk/impactofsocialsciences/2015/02/05/reference-rot-in-web-based-scholarly-communication/

Klein M, Aly M, Nelson ML (2011) Synchronicity: automatically rediscover missing web pages in real time. In: ACM/IEEE joint conference on digital libraries, p 475. https://doi.org/10.1145/1998076.1998193

Klein M, Van de Sompel H, Sanderson R, Shankar H, Balakireva L, Zhou K, Tobin R (2014) Scholarly context not found: one in five articles suffers from reference rot. PLoS One 9(12):e115253. https://doi.org/10.1371/journal.pone.0115253

Klein M, Balakireva L, Van de Sompel H (2018) Focused crawl of web archives to build event collections. In: ACM conference on web science, pp 333–342. https://doi.org/10.1145/3201064.3201085

Klein M, Balakireva L, Shankar H (2019a) Evaluating memento service optimizations. In: ACM/IEEE joint conference on digital libraries, pp 182–185. https://doi.org/10.1109/JCDL.2019.00034

Klein M, Balakireva L, Shankar H (2019b) Evaluating memento service optimizations. Technical Report. arXiv:1906.00058. https://arxiv.org/abs/1906.00058

Ko L (2019) OpenWayback - IIPC. http://netpreserve.org/web-archiving/openwayback/

Kreymer I (2019) GitHub – webrecorder/pywb – Core Python Web Archiving Toolkit for replay and recording of web archives. https://github.com/webrecorder/pywb

Mannens E, Coppens S, Verborgh R, Hauttekeete L, Van Deursen D, Van de Walle R (2012) Automated trust estimation in developing open news stories: combining memento & provenance. In: IEEE annual computer software and applications conference workshops, pp 122–127. https://doi.org/10.1109/COMPSACW.2012.32

Meinhardt P, Knuth M, Sack H (2015) TailR: a platform for preserving history on the web of data. In: International conference on semantic systems, pp 57–64. https://doi.org/10.1145/2814864. 2814875

Melo F, Viana H, Gomes D, Costa M (2016) Architecture of the Portuguese web archive search system version 2. Technical report, Arquivo.pt - The Portuguese Web Archive. https://sobre. arquivo.pt/wp-content/uploads/architecture-of-the-portuguese-web-archive-search-1.pdf

Milligan I (2019) History in the age of abundance: how the web is transforming historical research. McGill-Queen's University Press, Montreal

Nelson ML (2010) Memento-datetime is not last-modified. https://ws-dl.blogspot.com/2010/11/2010-11-05-memento-datetime-is-not-last.html

Nelson ML (2013) Archive.is supports memento. https://ws-dl.blogspot.com/2013/07/2013-07-09-archiveis-supports-memento.html

Nelson ML, Van de Sompel H (2019) Adding the dimension of time to HTTP. In: SAGE handbook of web history. SAGE Publishing, Philadelphia, pp 189–214

Neumaier S, Umbrich J, Polleres A (2017) Lifting data portals to the web of data. In: Linked data on the web workshop, pp 1–10. http://ceur-ws.org/Vol-1809/article-03.pdf

Nwala AC (2015) What did it look like? https://ws-dl.blogspot.com/2015/01/2015-02-05-what-did-it-look-like.html

Nwala AC, Weigle MC, Ziegler AB, Aizman A, Nelson ML (2017) Local memory project: providing tools to build collections of stories for local events from local sources. In: ACM/IEEE joint conference on digital libraries, pp 1–10. https://doi.org/10.1109/JCDL.2017.7991576

Nwala AC, Weigle MC, Nelson ML (2018a) Bootstrapping web archive collections from social media. In: ACM conference on hypertext and social media, pp 64–72. https://doi.org/10.1145/3209542.3209560

Nwala AC, Weigle MC, Nelson ML (2018b) Scraping SERPs for archival seeds: it matters when you start. In: ACM/IEEE joint conference on digital libraries, pp 263–272. https://doi.org/10.1145/3197026.3197056

Powell JE, Alcazar DA, Hopkins M, McMahon TM, Wu A, Collins L, Olendorf R (2011) Graphs in libraries: a primer. Inf Technol Libraries 30(4):157. https://doi.org/10.6017/ital.v30i4.1867

Reich V, Rosenthal DSH (2001) LOCKSS: a permanent web publishing and access system. D-Lib Mag 7(6). http://dlib.org/dlib/june01/reich/06reich.html

Ruest N, Milligan I, Lin J (2019) Warclight: a rails engine for web archive discovery. In: ACM/IEEE joint conference on digital libraries, pp 442–443. https://doi.org/10.1109/JCDL.2019.00110

SalahEldeen HM, Nelson ML (2012) Losing my revolution: how many resources shared on social media have been lost? In: International conference on theory and practice of digital libraries (TPDL), vol 7489, pp 125–137. https://doi.org/10.1007/978-3-642-33290-6_14

SalahEldeen HM, Nelson ML (2013a) Carbon dating the web: estimating the age of web resources. In: International world wide web conference, pp 1075–1082. https://doi.org/10.1145/2487788. 2488121

SalahEldeen HM, Nelson ML (2013b) Reading the correct history?: Modeling temporal intention in resource sharing. In: ACM/IEEE joint conference on digital libraries, pp 257–266. https://doi.org/10.1145/2467696.2467721

Sanderson R (2012) Global web archive integration with memento. In: ACM/IEEE joint conference on digital libraries, p 379. https://doi.org/10.1145/2232817.2232900

Sanderson R, Van de Sompel H (2010) Making web annotations persistent over time. In: ACM/IEEE joint conference on digital libraries, pp 1–10. https://doi.org/10.1145/1816123. 1816125

Sanderson R, Van de Sompel H (2012) Cool URIs and dynamic data. IEEE Internet Comput 16(4):76–79. https://doi.org/10.1109/MIC.2012.78

Sanderson R, Phillips M, Van de Sompel H (2011) Analyzing the persistence of referenced web resources with memento. Technical Report. arXiv:1105.3459. https://arxiv.org/abs/1105.3459

Sanderson R, Ciccarese P, Young B (2017) Web annotation data model. https://www.w3.org/TR/annotation-model

Shelby Z (2012) RFC 6690 – Constrained RESTful Environments (CoRE) link format. https://tools.ietf.org/html/rfc6690

Taelman R, Verborgh R, Mannens E (2017) Exposing RDF archives using triple pattern fragments. In: Knowledge engineering and knowledge management (EKAW), pp 188–192. https://doi.org/10.1007/978-3-319-58694-6_29

Van de Sompel H, Davis S (2015) From a system of journals to a web of objects. Serials Librarian 68(1–4):51–63. https://doi.org/10.1080/0361526X.2015.1026748

Van de Sompel H, Vander Sande M (2016) DBpedia archive using memento, triple pattern fragments, and HDT. In: CNI spring meeting. https://www.slideshare.net/hvdsomp/dbpedia-archive-using-memento-triple-pattern-fragments-and-hdt

Van de Sompel H, Sanderson R, Nelson ML (2010) An HTTP-based versioning mechanism for linked data. In: Linked data on the web workshop, pp 1–10. http://events.linkeddata.org/ldow2010/papers/ldow2010_paper13.pdf

Van de Sompel H, Nelson M, Sanderson R (2013) RFC 7089 - HTTP framework for time-based access to resource states – memento. https://tools.ietf.org/html/rfc7089

Van de Vyvere B, Colpaert P, Mannens E, Verborgh R (2019) Open traffic lights: a strategy for publishing and preserving traffic lights data. In: International world wide web conference, pp 966–971. https://doi.org/10.1145/3308560.3316520

Vander Sande M, Verborgh R, Hochstenbach P, Van de Sompel H (2018) Toward sustainable publishing and querying of distributed linked data archives. J Doc 74(1):195–222. https://doi.org/10.1108/JD-03-2017-0040

Verborgh R, Vander Sande M, Hartig O, Van Herwegen J, De Vocht L, De Meester B, Haesendonck G, Colpaert P (2016) Triple pattern fragments: a low-cost knowledge graph interface for the Web. J Web Semant 37–38:184–206. https://doi.org/10.1016/j.websem.2016.03.003

Weigle MC (2017) Visualizing webpage changes over time - new NEH digital humanities advancement grant. https://ws-dl.blogspot.com/2017/10/2017-10-16-visualizing-webpage-changes.html

Welsh B (2019) Memento for Wordpress. http://pastpages.github.io/wordpress-memento-plugin/

Zhou K, Grover C, Klein M, Tobin R (2015) No more 404s: predicting referenced link rot in scholarly articles for pro-active archiving. In: ACM/IEEE joint conference on digital libraries, pp 233–236. https://doi.org/10.1145/2756406.2756940

Linking Twitter Archives with Television Archives

Zeynep Pehlivan

Abstract Social media data has already established itself as an important data source for researchers working in a number of different domains. It has also attracted the attention of archiving institutions, many of which have already extended their crawling processes to capture at least some forms of social media data. However, far too little attention has been paid to providing access to this data, which has generally been collected using application programming interfaces (APIs). There is a growing need to contextualize the data gathered from APIs, so that researchers can make informed decisions about how to analyse it and to develop efficient ways of providing access to it. This chapter will discuss one possible means of providing enhanced access: a new interface developed at the Institut national de l'audiovisuel (INA) that links Twitter and television archives to recreate the phenomenon of the "second screen", or more precisely the experience of "social television". The phrase "second screen" describes the increasingly ubiquitous activity of using a second computing device (commonly a mobile phone or tablet) while watching television. If the second device is used to comment on, like or retweet television-related content via social media, this results in the so-called social television. The analysis of this activity, and this data, offers a promising new avenue of research for scholars, especially those based on digital humanities. To the best of our knowledge, the work that will be discussed here is the first attempt at considering how to recreate best the experience of "social television" using archived data.

1 Introduction

Social media has helped to transform people from content readers to content publishers, thereby massively extending the range and number of people whose voices may be captured in web archives. It is an important data source for

Z. Pehlivan (✉)
Institut National de l'Audiovisuel, Bry-sur-Marne, France
e-mail: zpehlivan@ina.fr

© Springer Nature Switzerland AG 2021
D. Gomes et al. (eds.), *The Past Web*,
https://doi.org/10.1007/978-3-030-63291-5_10

researchers in a variety of fields, such as sociology, data science or history. Twitter attracts more attention than any other platform because of its open and public nature, exemplified by its ease of use and ready access to its data. It is also often a place of first response to global news events, a locus of information and misinformation. Consequently, Twitter has become something of a "must archive" source for web archivists. A number of archival institutions have extended their crawling processes to cover social media, and particularly Twitter, but many do not yet make much of this material publicly available.

When the Web is archived, it is generally something approaching a canonical form that is captured, the view that is seen by most users through a PC.[1] Twitter, by contrast, does not really have a canonical form: people can read tweets via an app, through Twitter's own webpages, on another page displaying feeds, etc. This is one of the reasons why application programming interfaces (APIs) are used to archive Twitter data, as explained in this chapter. In contrast to webpage crawlers, the Twitter API also provides a centralized and convenient access point for anyone wishing to collect data. All of this means that when archiving Twitter, the canonical form is considered to be the tweet data itself, stripped of much of its context. For this reason, we need different approaches to re-contextualize Twitter (and indeed other forms of social media) than we do when archiving the Web. There are two main modes of presentation currently being used for archived Twitter data: full-text search and data mining, including aggregations of top hashtags, top emojis, top users or word clouds, etc., and representation of the "second screen", which involves bringing together televisual and Twitter archives to recreate the phenomenon of "social television". It is this latter approach to archiving born-digital data, which is hugely promising from the perspective of digital ethnography, that will be discussed here.

For several years now, the audiovisual media landscape has been expanding beyond a strictly broadcast dimension. The Web has provided new opportunities for airing programmes and for enriching, editorializing or repurposing them. A new ecosystem has thus been framed that creates communities online and enables audience interaction. The affordances of social networks, such as hashtags or mentions, notably increase media exposure and ensure—for better and sometimes for worse—online virality. A "second screen", born from this new ecosystem, involves the use of a computing device (commonly a mobile phone or tablet) to provide an enhanced viewing experience for content on another device, such as a television. The use of a second screen to augment television consumption is now a common practice. Audiences started to interact on social media in connection with programmes or events that mattered to them, and this gave birth to the new phenomenon of "social television". Twitter has played a crucial role in facilitating these interactions. The analysis of "social television", through the combination of social media, web and televisual archives, offers a promising new way for

---

[1]There is, of course, no single view of a webpage, given the different browsers and devices that are commonly used, but the archived Web is most often presented as if seen on a standard PC.

researchers to explore not just the content of born-digital data but the contexts within which it has been used.

A new interface developed by INA (France's National Audiovisual Institute) offers a different kind of access to online archives through the simultaneous presentation of social media and televisual archives. This interface allows researchers in the social sciences to recreate the "social television" experience with archived data. This chapter also discusses the issues that arrive when television and Twitter archives are brought together and studied in this way. The next section introduces in more detail the concept of the "second screen" and social television. Then, the new interface and dataset are presented, and related issues are discussed. Finally, the conclusion gives a brief summary and defines areas for further work.

2   The "Second Screen"

In recent years, the concept of watching television has changed significantly, following the huge growth in web technologies and the prevalence of mobile devices. Together, these have created the popular phenomenon of the "second screen". Although, for a long time, the television ecosystem consisted of a single box with a screen, which was capable of receiving broadcast signals and turning them into pictures and sounds, the concept of the second screen is not particularly new. In the USA in the 1950s, the CBS children's show "Winky Dink and You" (Prichett and Wyckoff 1953), created by Harry Prichett and Ed Wyckoff, was the first interactive television show with a second screen. The show introduced a kit that included a "magic drawing screen", a large piece of plastic stuck to the television screen via static electricity. Audience members could "help" the characters in the programme by drawing on this screen.

Television consumption has often been accompanied by other activities, but their scope and nature have changed over time with the introduction of new technologies. Although the "second screen" lacks an agreed conceptual definition, it refers to a technical device (mostly Internet-enabled) with a screen that is used simultaneously with a television. This device might be a smartphone, a computer or a laptop, but it does not include another TV screen, calculators, books, radios, etc. There is a clear distinction between the "second screen" and using two screens in parallel (e.g. watching television while shopping online) (Strippel 2017). Several studies have identified that the activities on the second screen should be directly related to the television programme (Filho and Santos 2015; Zúñiga et al. 2015). A good example of a content-dependent second screen is HBO's "Game of Thrones" app (Silva et al. 2015) that gives users details (on a device like a smartphone) related to the character appearing on the first—television—screen.

A recent report from Nielsen (2018) demonstrates how digital devices have affected the ways in which we consume and interact with media today. According to this report, 71% of second-screen users deploy their device to look up something

DIGITAL USAGE WHILE WATCHING TV
In what ways have you used your digital device to engage with the TV content you were watching?

DIGITAL USAGE WHILE LISTENING TO AUDIO
In what ways have you used your digital device to engage with the audio content you were listening to?

71%	LOOK UP INFORMATION RELATED TO THE CONTENT	51%
41%	EMAIL/TEXT/MESSAGE ABOUT THE CONTENT	31%
35%	LOOK UP/SHOP FOR A PRODUCT/ SERVICE BEING ADVERTISED	25%
28%	WRITE/READ POSTS ABOUT THE CONTENT ON SOCIAL MEDIA	20%
15%	SWITCH TO DIFFERENT CONTENT AFTER SEEING SOMETHING ONLINE	14%

Fig. 1 From Nielsen Total Audience Report: Q2 2018. Copyright 2018 The Nielsen Company (US), LLC. All Rights Reserved

related to the television content they are watching, while 41% said that they have texted, emailed or messaged someone about that content as shown in Fig. 1.

The combination of the second screen and social media has led to a new phenomenon, "social television". The terms "social television" and "second screen" are often used interchangeably, but they represent two different experiences. While some researchers define social television as a special form of second-screen interaction (Wolk 2015), others (Montpetit and Medard 2012; Bellman et al. 2017; Hu et al. 2014) consider it to be more than a second-screen experience, which allows people to communicate and interact with other audiences, content producers, performers, advertisers, etc., around television content. Among all social media platforms, Twitter plays a special role in relation to social television. Twitter serves as a perfect backchannel for television (Bruns and Burgess 2011; D'heer et al. 2015; Harrington et al. 2012). It does not replace the existing media channels but complements them, providing its users with alternative opportunities to contribute more actively to a wider media sphere (Harrington et al. 2012). According to Albarran et al. (2018), there are three main elements that have contributed to the success of Twitter in the sphere of social television: flexibility, which allows the circulation of information in different formats (image, text or video); the hashtag convention and the visibility that this brings even to users with limited numbers of followers (except for private accounts); and the succinct and convenient nature of tweeting, which supports the expression of opinions in a concise, quick and timely manner.

This interaction is not one sided. Viewers may tweet about a programme, but television producers and advertisers can also encourage audiences to interact by sharing hashtags or tweeting during the programme. Some highly interactive shows, for example, news and current affairs programmes, display these tweets live on air. Thus, "Twitter becomes not only a backchannel but part of the show itself" (Harrington et al. 2012). Discussions related to television programmes regularly feature as "trending topics" on Twitter. Guerrero-Pico (2017) studies how TV fans have made strategic use of Twitter as a tool for activism to launch "Save Our Show" campaigns and highlights a shift towards a collaborative relationship between activist fans and producers in the context of these campaigns. To measure this change in viewing practice, Nielsen and Twitter cooperated to launch the first large-scale survey of social television in 2013. Since January 2016, Twitter television ratings have become "Social Content Ratings", including other platforms like Facebook.

Television sets today are often controlled through an advanced interface connected to the Web. Manufacturers like Samsung, LG and Toshiba have developed their own software to create "smart", web-enabled televisions. Their aim is to draw second-screen activity to the first screen by providing similar options. The most common approach is to have a home screen with a grid of installed apps and widgets for weather, calendars, social media, etc. The social television experience offered here allows users to see their activities from different social media platforms and to interact (e.g. writing a tweet) without needing another device. Most of the work in this field focuses on the development of content-dependent apps. For example, an app called Snapscreen (Lösch et al. 2016) detects both live and recorded television content that is being watched and then offers content-related information and functionality. A tool that recreates the social television experience using archived data offers researchers an invaluable insight into the ways in which social media and television have converged and the behaviour and motivations of the users who engage with the second screen. Capturing Twitter data in isolation allows many forms of analysis, for example, network and linguistic study, but it cannot support different kinds of ethnographic analysis. The experience of the user is missing without the wider context that archives are beginning to provide.

3   A Tool for Researchers

The social television phenomenon has mainly attracted the attention of researchers in the social studies (De Michele et al. 2019; Ceron and Splendore 2019; Delgado et al. 2018; Shokrpour and Darnell 2017; Pfeffel et al. 2016; Gorkovenko and Taylor 2016) but also of those working in different domains, from neuroscience (Seixas et al. 2018) to computer science (Katz et al. 2018). A tool that recreates social television activities using archived data will help social scientists to explore this phenomenon in detail and open up new avenues of research. It allows researchers without any background in programming to handle archived Twitter data, television archives and data statistics in combination, to study the effects of social television (Bruns and Burgess 2011; Katz et al. 2018). In this section, we give a detailed description of the data harvested by INA, present the user interface and explain the issues that have been encountered in developing a new research tool.

3.1 Dataset: Twitter and Television Archives

France's National Audiovisual Institute (INA), founded in 1975, is the world
leading resource for digitized audiovisual content. Its remit is to collect, preserv
and share France's audiovisual heritage. From 1995, the programs of the seve
national Hertzian channels were preserved as part of the "legal deposit of radi
and television", introduced on 20 June 1992, and entrusted to INA. The programme
collected under this remit have gradually been extended to include cable and satelli
channels, the free service known as TNT and regional channels. At the time c
writing, 103 television channels and 66 radio channels are recorded every day. INA
audiovisual collections include more than 40 million records.

Legal deposit in France was extended to cover the public Web in 2006, an
the DLWeb (legal deposit web) team at INA is responsible for the collection an
preservation of French websites related to media and audiovisual content. Twee
have also been archived under legal deposit since 2014. Using Twitter, APIs mor
than 13,000 user timelines and 600 hashtags are archived every day. This collectio
exceeded one million tweets in June 2019, and an average of 300,000 new twee
are added every day. This is the data with which INA has been working, so that
can be made available to researchers in new configurations.

3.2 User Interface

One such configuration is offered by the social television interface that has bee
developed. As shown in Fig. 2, the interface is split into four areas. First, there :
a search facility that allows users to search for a television or radio programm
from the archives by selecting a channel, date, hour and duration. It also contai
a full-text search for tweets archived during the programme. Search keywords ca
be hashtags, mentions related to the programme or a complex query based on meta
data (e.g. hashtags: "cashinvestigation" user_mentions.screen_name: "EliseLucet"
Second, there is a programme area that displays the chosen multimedia in a playe
with "classic" controls (backwards, forwards, volume, etc.). Third, a timeline are
shows the number of tweets per minute during a selected programme. It als
displays a red vertical line that is synchronized with the programme area and ca
be used to rewind or forward-wind the programme. As shown in Fig. 3, differe
keywords can be compared, and significant moments in the show, as reflected i
social media activity, can be detected easily. Finally, a tweets area has two differe
tabs. In the first, activated by default, there is a list of tweets generated by a quer
formulated in the search area. Each tweet is displayed in a Twitter-like layout, wi
date, user's screen name and user's profile image. Retweets and like counts are n
displayed as only the moment of capture is represented. Users can read all of th
tweets using the scroll bar on the left and click on a tweet to move the player to th
moment that it was published during the programme. This scroll bar is only visibl

Fig. 2 Overall view of the user interface

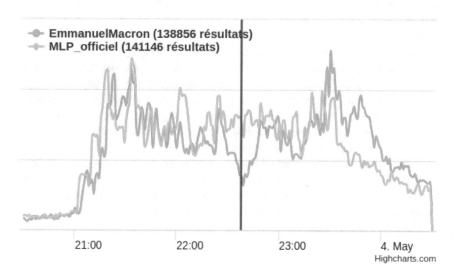

Fig. 3 Timeline for the 3 May 2017 debate for the presidential elections in France showing results for the query "EmmanuelMacron MLP_officiel" that contains official Twitter account screen names for Emmanuel Macron and Marine Le Pen

when the player is turned off. When the player is turned on, the scroll bar disappears and synchronized streaming begins. This gives researchers the opportunity to study social television behaviour in real time using archived data. The second tab, the dashboard, contains statistics for the listed tweets. Different categories are applied to cover different user needs, such as the distribution of tweets/retweets/quotes, languages, geo-localization and top entities (e.g. hashtags, mentions, users, etc.), as shown in Fig. 4. Any other type of aggregation based on Twitter metadata can easily be added to this dashboard. A demonstration video of the tool, which offers a uniquely rich user experience for researchers, can be found at https://youtu.be/XMQF9rQUIyc.

3.3 Challenges

The tool developed by INA allows researchers in the social sciences to analyse the phenomenon of social television, as it plays out on Twitter. It marks the first attempt to visualize audiovisual and Twitter archives in combination, and like any prototype, it has limitations.

The most significant of these lies in the quantity of tweets related to a particular television programme. A regular television show in France, which does not create a particular buzz, generates around 70 tweets (including retweets and quotes) per minute, that is, 1.16 tweets per second. In a case like this, it is easy to display and follow activity and information flows on the player. However, special events both generate more second-screen activity than this and attract more attention from researchers subsequently. This is true of political elections, for example. The debate held on 3 May 2017 during the French presidential elections, between Emmanuel Macron and Marine Le Pen, lasted for 3.5 h and was watched by nearly 16.5 million people. The debate generated more than 3.1 million tweets, that is, 246 tweets per second on average. In this case, it is impossible to generate the synchronization between player and tweets in a human-readable way. As a workaround for this problem, a maximum of 10 tweets per second is displayed in play mode during the synchronization. Users who would like to study such important moments in detail have to pause the player in order to see all published tweets. These challenges of scale and velocity are common to all archives that are concerned with capturing and archiving the Web and social media, and no doubt new approaches and solutions will be found in the future.

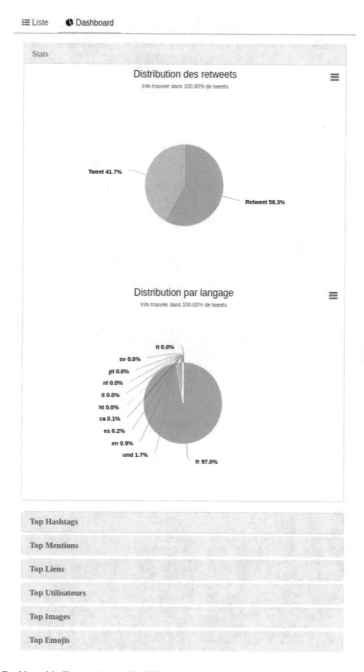

Fig. 4 Dashboard in Tweets Area with different aggregations

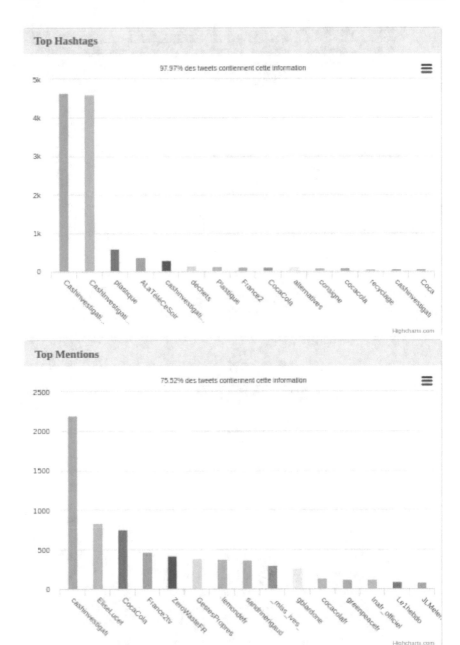

Fig. 4 (continued)

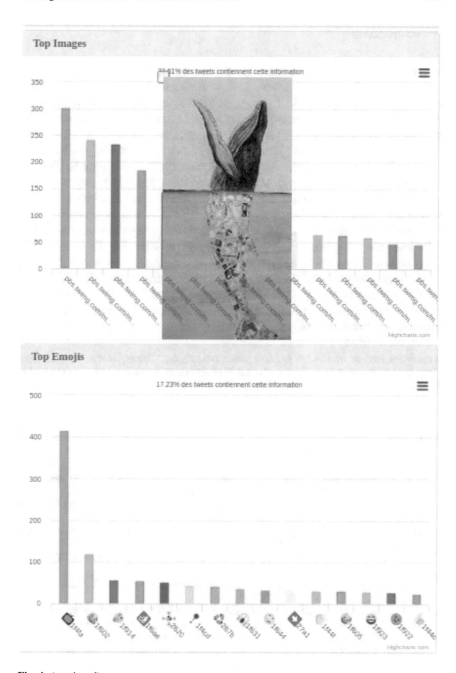

Fig. 4 (continued)

4 Conclusions

This chapter has explored one approach for bringing together televisual and Twitter archives in order to create a new method for analysing archived born-digital data more effectively. The tool developed by INA allows researchers to search multimedia archives simultaneously, to visualize them in a synchronized way and to gain access to contextual statistics like top hashtags, etc. At INA, Twitter archives are created by using Twitter APIs to track accounts and hashtags selected by curators. If a hashtag emerges during a television show, it will only be archived if it is used in association with a tracked account or hashtag. Future work will concentrate on how to visualize this gap, so that researchers know how much data they may be missing; on automatically suggesting hashtags or account names related to particular television shows; and on clustering different keywords, as proposed by Stilo and Velardi (2014), and suggesting new ones to users. For the moment, like many other archives, the focus is on Twitter, but in the future, it is hoped that other social media platforms like Facebook may be added to the dataset. The Web, social media and other forms of media are inextricably linked through the phenomenon of the "second screen", and archives are rising to the challenge of capturing this profoundly networked activity.

Acknowledgements Thanks are due to Thomas Drugeon and Jérôme Thièvre, from the legal deposit team (dlweb) at INA, for their fruitful discussions and inspiration. I am also thankful to Jane Winters for her corrections that greatly improved this chapter.

References

Albarran A, Mierzejewska B, Jung J (2018) Handbook of media management and economics. Routledge, Abingdon

Bellman S, Robinson JA, Wooley B, Varan D (2017) The effects of social TV on television advertising effectiveness. J Mark Commun 23(1):73–91

Bruns A, Burgess JE (2011) #Ausvotes: how Twitter covered the 2010 Australian federal election. Commun Polit Cult 44:37–56

Ceron A, Splendore S (2019) 'Cheap Talk'? Second screening and the irrelevance of TV political debates. Journalism 20(8):1108–1123

De Michele R, Ferretti S, Furini M (2019) On helping broadcasters to promote TV-shows through hashtags. Multimed Tools Appl 78(3):3279–3296

Delgado M, Navarro C, Garcia-Muñoz N, LLuís P, Paz E (2018) TV news and social audience in Europe (EU5): on-screen and twitter strategies. Observatorio (OBS*) 12(4):107–124

D'heer E, Godin F, Evens T, De Neve W, Verdegem P, Van de Walle R (2015) How can Twitter data and viewing rates enrich one another? A conceptual and empirical comparison between viewing rates and Twitter data for TV audience research. In: ICA, proceedings

Filho FC, Santos LA (2015) Second screen and information: history, definition and clues for the future. Comunicação e Sociedade 28:211–227

Gorkovenko K, Taylor N (2016) Politics at home: second screen behaviours and motivations during TV debates. In: Proceedings of the 9th Nordic conference on human-computer interaction, NordiCHI '16. ACM, New York, pp 22:1–22:10

Guerrero-Pico M (2017) #Fringe, audiences and fan labor: twitter activism to save a TV show from cancellation. Int J Commun 11:22

Harrington S, Highfield T, Bruns A (2012) More than a backchannel: twitter and television. In: Noguera JM (ed) Audience interactivity and participation, COST action ISO906 transforming audiences. Transforming Societies, Belgium, pp 13–17

Hu H, Wen Y, Luan H, Chua T, Li X (2014) Toward multiscreen social TV with geolocation-aware social sense. IEEE MultiMedia 21(3):10–19

Katz G, Heap B, Wobcke W, Bain M, Kannangara S (2018) Analysing TV audience engagement via twitter: incremental segment-level opinion mining of second screen tweets. In: PRICAI 2018: trends in artificial intelligence. Lecture notes in computer science. Springer International Publishing, New York, pp 300–308

Lösch S, Willomitzer T, Anderst-Kotsis G (2016) Snapscreen: linking traditional TV and the Internet. In: Proceedings of the 14th international conference on advances in mobile computing and multi media, MoMM '16. ACM, New York, pp 244–249

Montpetit M, Medard M (2012) Social television: enabling technologies and architectures. Proc. IEEE 100(Special Centennial Issue):1395–1399

Nielsen (2018) Juggling act: audiences have more media at their disposal and are using them simultaneously. https://www.nielsen.com/us/en/insights/article/2018/juggling-act-audiences-have-more-media-at-their-disposal-and-are-using-them-simultaneously/

Pfeffel F, Kexel P, Kexel CA, Ratz M (2016) Second screen: user behaviour of spectators while watching football. Athens J Sports 3(2):119–128

Prichett H, Wyckoff E (1953) Winky Dink and You

Seixas SA, Nield GE, Pynta P, Silberstein RB (2018) The neuroscience of social television. Applications of neuroscience: breakthroughs in research and practice, pp 413–426

Shokrpour A, Darnell MJ (2017) How people multitask while watching TV. In: Proceedings of the 2017 ACM international conference on interactive experiences for TV and online video, TVX '17. ACM, New York, pp 11–19

Silva P, Amer Y, Tsikerdanos W, Shedd J, Restrepo I, Murray J (2015) A game of thrones companion: orienting viewers to complex storyworlds via synchronized visualizations. In: Proceedings of the ACM international conference on interactive experiences for TV and online video, TVX '15. ACM, New York, pp 167–172

Stilo G, Velardi P (2014) Temporal semantics: time-varying hashtag sense clustering. In: Knowledge engineering and knowledge management. Lecture Notes in Computer Science. Springer International Publishing, New York, pp 563–578

Strippel C (2017) Praktiken der Second-Screen-Nutzung. Konzeptioneller Rahmen für die Analyse der Parallelnutzung von zwei Bildschirmen. In: Göttlich U, Heinz L, Herbers MR (eds) Ko-Orientierung in der Medienrezeption: Praktiken der Second Screen-Nutzung. Springer Fachmedien Wiesbaden, Wiesbaden, pp 107–136

Wolk A (2015) Over the top: how the internet is (slowly but surely) changing the television industry. CreateSpace Independent Publishing Platform, North Charleston, SC

Zúñiga HGd, Garcia-Perdomo V, McGregor SC (2015) What is second screening? Exploring motivations of second screen use and its effect on online political participation. J Commun 65(5):793–815

Image Analytics in Web Archives

**Eric Müller-Budack, Kader Pustu-Iren, Sebastian Diering,
Matthias Springstein, and Ralph Ewerth**

Abstract The multimedia content published on the World Wide Web is constantly growing and contains valuable information in various domains. The Internet Archive initiative has gathered billions of time-versioned webpages since the mid-1990s, but unfortunately, they are rarely provided with appropriate metadata. This lack of structured data limits the exploration of the archives, and automated solutions are required to enable semantic search. While many approaches exploit the textual content of news in the Internet Archive to detect named entities and their relations, visual information is generally disregarded. In this chapter, we present an approach that leverages deep learning techniques for the identification of public personalities in the images of news articles stored in the Internet Archive. In addition, we elaborate on how this approach can be extended to enable detection of other entity types such as locations or events. The approach complements named entity recognition and linking tools for text and allows researchers and analysts to track the media coverage and relations of persons more precisely. We have analysed more than one million images from news articles in the Internet Archive and demonstrated the feasibility of the approach with two use cases in different domains: politics and entertainment.

E. Müller-Budack · K. Pustu-Iren · M. Springstein
TIB – Leibniz Information Centre for Science and Technology, Hannover, Germany
e-mail: eric.mueller@tib.eu; kader.pustu@tib.eu; matthias.springstein@tib.eu

S. Diering
Leibniz Universität Hannover, Hannover, Germany
e-mail: diering@stud.uni-hannover.de

R. Ewerth (✉)
TIB – Leibniz Information Centre for Science and Technology, Hannover, Germany

L3S Research Center, Leibniz Universität Hannover, Hannover, Germany
e-mail: ralph.ewerth@tib.eu

© Springer Nature Switzerland AG 2021
D. Gomes et al. (eds.), *The Past Web*,
https://doi.org/10.1007/978-3-030-63291-5_11

1 Introduction

The World Wide Web contains billions of webpages and related multimedia content. These webpages include valuable information for many academic and non-academic applications. Therefore, the Internet Archive (www.archive.org) and national (digital) libraries have been capturing (multimedia) webpages with time-stamped snapshots in large-scale archives since the mid-1990s. This serves as a playground for researchers and analysts in different domains such as digital humanities, politics, economics and entertainment. One of the main challenges is to make the available unstructured data, which is rarely enriched with appropriate metadata, accessible and explorable by users. For this reason, it is necessary to develop (semi)-automatic content analysis approaches and systems to extract metadata that can be subsequently used for semantic search and information visualisation in order to provide users with relevant information about a given topic.

In recent years, many tools, such as BabelNet (Navigli and Ponzetto 2012), Dandelion (Brambilla et al. 2017) and FRED (Gangemi et al. 2017), for named entity recognition and disambiguation have been introduced that can be used to generate meta-information from textual web content in order to, e.g., track entities and their relations in web archives. Although these tools already achieve good results, they cannot help us to analyse images. Online news articles are often provided with photos, which potentially show additional entities that might not be mentioned in the text. Furthermore, possible ambiguities could be resolved using the visual content. Thus, visual and textual contents are complementary, and their combination can serve as a basis for a more complete and robust entity recognition. While some approaches aim to find efficient solutions for large-scale datasets in general (Wan et al. 2014; Mühling et al. 2017; Fernández et al. 2017; Mühling et al. 2019), approaches that exploit image or video data in the Internet Archive are rare (Müller-Budack et al. 2018).

In this chapter, we present an approach (illustrated in Fig. 1) that enables researchers and analysts to find and explore the media coverage and relations of persons of interest in the image content of news articles in large-scale web archives such as the Internet Archive for a given domain such as politics, sports and entertainment. We address a variety of problems such as how to automatically define which entities should be considered in such a system and how they can be automatically verified in large web collections such as the Internet Archive. Furthermore, we discuss how developments in other computer vision areas such as geolocation estimation and date estimation can be leveraged to extend such a system to retrieve meta-information for other entity types such as locations, organisations and events.

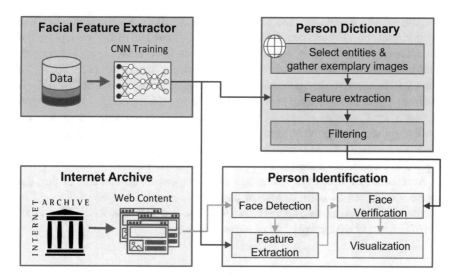

Fig. 1 Workflow of the proposed person identification framework. A convolutional neural network (CNN) is applied to obtain rich feature representations of the faces that are found in the web content and in the exemplary images of persons in a pre-defined dictionary. These feature vectors are compared to verify the presence of the persons in a web image

2 Advances in Computer Vision and Face Recognition

Recent advances in computer vision, especially as a result of the introduction of convolutional neural networks (CNNs) (Krizhevsky et al. 2012) and large-scale training datasets (Deng et al. 2009; Guo et al. 2016), are significant and have opened up many new applications. Impressive results that even exceed human performance in a variety of topics such as object classification (Krizhevsky et al. 2012), face recognition (Taigman et al. 2014) and geolocation estimation (Weyand et al. 2016; Vo et al. 2017; Muller-Budack et al. 2018) have been achieved. However, the underlying CNN models are trained on public benchmark datasets such as ImageNet (Deng et al. 2009) or Microsoft-Celebrity-1M (Guo et al. 2016) for object classification and face recognition, respectively, that only contain a limited number of entities. Thus, the classification output of the CNNs is not suitable for directly predicting a large number of real-world entities in large-scale web archives such as the Internet Archive. In particular, the large and steadily increasing number of persons mentioned in news collection poses a huge challenge for face recognition frameworks. For this reason, face recognition is often treated as a verification task. More specifically, a feature vector that describes the facial characteristics is extracted from an intermediate layer of a neural network rather than the classification output itself. To identify a person depicted in an image, the facial feature vector is compared to vectors of a set of persons covered in a reference dataset. The advantage of this approach is that the reference dataset can be dynamically modified at any time (in terms of covered entities and exemplary images) without the requirement to retrain the underlying CNN model. To increase the performance, research has focused on learning more robust feature representations, for example, by using new loss functions like the contrastive loss (Sun et al. 2014), triplet loss (Schroff et al. 2015) and angular softmax (Liu et al. 2017). To improve robustness against pose variation, some approaches (Masi et al. 2018, 2017, 2016a,b; Yin et al. 2017; Zhu et al. 2016) aim to frontalise the face using 3D head models or synthesise new views of the face to augment the training dataset with all available poses. Alternatively, techniques (Ding and Tao 2017; Yang et al. 2015) that use several image patches around facial landmarks as input for the CNN training are applied to increase the robustness for poses and occlusions.

Another major challenge associated with long-term web archives is that the visual appearance of entities, and in particular persons, changes over time. To overcome these variations, approaches (Best-Rowden and Jain 2018; Wen et al. 2016) that model the ageing of faces were introduced.

3 Person Identification in Archived Web News

In this section, a potential solution for the identification of persons of user interest in images of archived web news is presented. The workflow of the approach is illustrated in Fig. 1. For more technical details, we refer to Müller-Budack et al. (2018).

3.1 Facial Feature Extraction

Convolutional neural networks (CNNs) have shown the best performance for extracting the facial features of each face depicted in an image. CNNs for face recognition are trained on large-scale datasets such as MS-Celeb-1M (Guo et al. 2016) or CASIA-WebFace (Yi et al. 2014) that contain face images and their corresponding identity label. As discussed in Sect. 2, the model is used as a generalised feature extractor to output a compact vector of facial features. In this way, faces that are detected by suitable face detection approaches (Dalal and Triggs 2005; Zhang et al. 2016; Sun et al. 2018; Chi et al. 2019) within a query image can be compared with the facial features of persons in a pre-defined dictionary.

3.2 Definition of a Person Dictionary

In this section, we discuss several possibilities for selecting a set of relevant persons and extracting their corresponding feature vectors for their verification in a web collection of the Internet Archive.

3.2.1 Selection of Relevant Persons

As a first step, it is necessary to define entities of interest that the approach should be able to identify in the archived web news collections. There are several options available to define a dictionary of relevant persons. (1) The person dictionary can be manually defined by the user(s) according to specific needs and goals. (2) Named entity recognition and disambiguation approaches (Rizzo and Troncy 2011; Moro et al. 2014; Van Erp et al. 2013; Kolitsas et al. 2018) can be applied to automatically extract mentions of people from the corresponding textual content. (3) External sources such as the *Wikipedia* encyclopaedia can be leveraged to identify which people are relevant for a general audience. Regardless of which option has been used, the person dictionary can be modified dynamically according to specific user needs. The reference image material is gathered automatically using a web-based approach, as presented in the next section.

3.2.2 Web-Based Retrieval of Sample Images

Since the person dictionary might contain a large number of entities, a manual selection of representative sample images is in general not feasible. Instead, we propose an automatic web-based approach to retrieve exemplary images for each person. Given the names of the selected entities, an image search engine such as Google Images is crawled to find the respective sample images. However, a drawback of this approach is that the collected images do not necessarily always or only depict the queried person but involve some level of noise. This can significantly affect system performance. Thus, several approaches to clean the retrieved sample images are introduced in the next section.

3.2.3 Extraction and Filtering of Feature Vectors

In order to distinguish between images or image regions depicting the target person and those depicting other persons, it is necessary to compare feature vector representations describing the characteristics of all facial regions in the retrieved image material of a specific person. First, a face detection approach is applied to retrieve the facial regions in an image. We have used the *dlib* face detector (King 2009) based on the *histogram of oriented gradients* (HOG) (Dalal and Triggs 2005) and *support vector machines* (SVM). Though not able to detect extreme facial poses, this face detector ensures efficiency in terms of computational speed when it comes to the large-scale image data of news pages gathered by the Internet Archive. For each detected face region, a facial representation is derived using the deep learning approach presented in Sect. 3.1.

The facial representations are leveraged in a data cleansing step to detect image regions in the retrieved exemplary images that depict the queried person. In this regard, we suggest first determining a representative facial feature vector for a specific person using one of the following approaches: (1) a manual selection of one or multiple representative face region(s) within the reference material, (2) calculating the mean of all facial representations in the reference material or (3) applying a clustering approach to calculate the mean of all facial representations within the majority cluster. The manual selection of one or multiple representative face region(s) is the most reliable option since it unambiguously represents the target entities and thus ensures a more robust filtering. However, in contrast to both other unsupervised approaches, it does require human supervision and might not be viable if a large number of entities are considered. The mean of all facial representation relies on the assumption that a majority of facial regions in the retrieved exemplary material already depict the target person. While this is usually the case for popular people, this approach might fail for less popular persons containing more noise in the exemplary material. Thus, a clustering approach seems to be more robust since the facial features within the majority cluster are more likely to represent the queried person. We have applied an agglomerative clustering with a similarity threshold λ_c as stopping criteria. The similarities of all facial representations were calculated using the cosine similarity.

Finally, the representative facial feature vector determined by one of the afore-mentioned approaches is compared to all facial representations in the reference images of the queried person using the cosine similarity. We remove each facial representation with a cosine similarity lower than a threshold λ_c. The evaluation of the proposed approaches for filtering, as well as the choice of threshold λ_c, is discussed in Sect. 3.4. After the filtering step is applied, we choose to calculate the mean of the remaining facial representations since it reduces the number of comparisons for each face found in a web archive to the number of persons in the person dictionary. While a comparison to each remaining facial representation might lead to better results, it is much more computationally expensive.

3.3 Person Identification Pipeline

The components introduced in the previous sections allow an automatic identification of persons in the image data of the Internet Archive. First, a face detector (Dalal and Triggs 2005) is applied to extract face regions in the image content. Based on the CNN described in Sect. 3.1, facial representations for these regions are computed and subsequently compared to the representative feature vectors of each person in the dictionary (Sect. 3.2) to determine the most similar person. Given the similarity value, the identification threshold λ_{id} determines whether the queried entity depicts a person within the dictionary, or an unknown person. Based on the results of person identification, visualisations derived from single and joint occurrences of persons of interest in news articles of the Internet Archive can be created.

Table 1 Results of methods for the cleansing step of the entity dictionary on a subset of 20 politicians

Method	Precision	Recall	F_1
No filtering (Müller-Budack et al. 2018)	0.669	1	0.802
Mean vector (Müller-Budack et al. 2018)	0.993	0.449	0.618
Reference vector (Müller-Budack et al. 2018)	0.977	0.922	0.949
Clustering	0.985	0.912	0.947

3.4 Parameter Selection

For our system, we have used a ResNet architecture (He et al. 2016) with 101 convolutional layers trained on MS-Celeb-1M (Guo et al. 2016) as the feature extractor. Performances on the Labelled Faces in the Wild (LFW) dataset (Huang et al. 2007) were acceptable compared to the much more complex state-of-the-art systems. The benchmark was used to evaluate the cleansing and agglomerative clustering threshold $\lambda_c = 0.757$ to reduce noise in the retrieved reference data (Sect. 3.2.3). A comparison of the proposed option for filtering is shown in Table 1 using a manually annotated dataset containing 1100 facial images covering 20 politicians.

The results demonstrate the best performance with respect to the F_1-score was achieved using manually selected feature vectors for data cleansing. However, results of the agglomerative clustering approach are comparable and were achieved without any supervision. This confirms that this method is a good automatic alternative for person dictionaries containing a large number of entities. The identification threshold is set to $\lambda_{id} = 0.833$, which has achieved 96% accuracy in a cross-fold validation using the same dataset. For a more detailed analysis of the parameters, we refer to Müller-Budack et al. (2018).

4 Exploration of Person Relations in Web Archives

The Internet Archive contains an enormous amount of multimedia data that can be used to reveal dependencies between entities in various fields, as illustrated in Fig. 2. To demonstrate the feasibility of image analytics in web archives, we have selected two popular German news websites welt.de and bild.de. While welt.de addresses political subjects, bild.de has a stronger focus on entertainment news as well as celebrity gossip. The number of images and faces analysed is shown in Table 2. To quantify the relevance of individuals and their relation to other entities, we count how often single entities appear in the selected image data and how often they are portrayed with persons in the dictionary. Exemplary results are shown in Fig. 2 and can be interactively explored in our Web demo.[1]

---

[1] https://github.com/TIB-Visual-Analytics/PIIA.

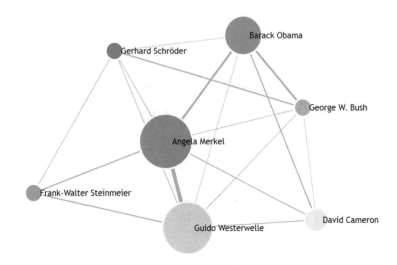

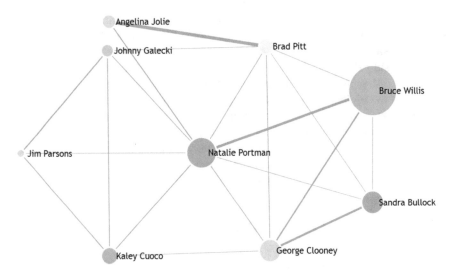

Fig. 2 Graph showing relations among an exemplary set of international politicians (top) and actors (bottom) using the domain welt.de and bild.de, respectively. The size of vertices encodes the occurrence frequency of the entity. The strength of edges denotes the frequency of joint occurrences

Figure 2 (top) visualises relations between well-known heads of states and other politicians in 2013 inferred by our visual analysis system for the German news website welt.de. The graph shows that *Angela Merkel*, the German chancellor, and the former German minister of foreign affairs, *Guido Westerwelle*, appear most frequently in the image data and also share a strong correlation. The most relevant

Table 2 Number of images
and faces in news articles of
the selected domains
published in 2013

Domain	Images	Faces
www.welt.de	648,106	205,386
www.bild.de	566,131	243,343

international politician detected in the news images is *Barack Obama*, with a strong connection to *Angela Merkel*. The connection of *Westerwelle* to *Steinmeier* is due to the transition of power in late 2013. Connections between former and new heads of state of Germany and the USA also exist.

Figure 2 (bottom) visualises connections between different actors in 2013. For example, the graph reveals strong connections between the actors *George Clooney* and *Sandra Bullock*, who both featured in the movie *Gravity*. Moreover, actors from the sitcom *The Big Bang Theory* are connected to each other. A strong connection between *Angelina Jolie* and *Brad Pitt*, a famous acting couple, can also be determined. The actress *Natalie Portman* is connected to all actors in the graph, having the second strongest appearance frequency. We assume that there must be several images published in bild.de, which depict her with colleagues, maybe at a celebrity event like the Academy Awards.

5   Applications and Potential Research Directions

In this chapter, we have presented an approach that is able to automatically identify persons in images of archived web news. This approach is complementary to the existing textual named entity recognition frameworks and can be used in several applications. The meta-information itself is useful for retrieving documents depicting one or multiple entities. This approach also allows an in-depth analysis of the number of occurrences of an entity in web news, which can indicate its popularity. In addition, relations between entities can be explored. In our case study, we analysed news articles from a specific year. One possible research direction is to extend this approach by applying it to specific time spans. This would enable temporal analyses of entity occurrences and relations and can indicate changes and trends in multimodal articles of the Internet Archive. Another important direction is to leverage suitable state-of-the-art computer vision models that would allow the current system to extract meta-information for other entity types such as locations and events. In order to process the large-scale image data in web archives, one major challenge is to develop efficient and scaleable solutions.

Acknowledgements This work is financially supported by the German Research Foundation (DFG: Deutsche Forschungsgemeinschaft, project number: 388420599). This work was partially funded by the European Commission for the ERC Advanced Grant ALEXANDRIA (No. 339233, Wolfgang Nejdl).

References

Best-Rowden L, Jain AK (2018) Longitudinal study of automatic face recognition. Trans Patt An Mach Intell 40(1):148–162

Brambilla M, Ceri S, Della Valle E, Volonterio R, Acero Salazar FX (2017) Extracting emergin knowledge from social media. In: International conference on World Wide Web, IW3C pp 795–804

Chi C, Zhang S, Xing J, Lei Z, Li SZ, Zou X (2019) Selective refinement network for hi performance face detection. In: Proceedings of the AAAI conference on artificial intelligenc vol 33, pp 8231–8238

Dalal N, Triggs B (2005) Histograms of oriented gradients for human detection. In: Conference computer vision and pattern recognition. IEEE, New York, pp 886–893

Deng J, Dong W, Socher R, Li LJ, Li K, Fei-Fei L (2009) ImageNet: a large-scale hierarchic image database. In: Conference on computer vision and pattern recognition. IEEE, New Yor pp 248–255

Ding C, Tao D (2017) Trunk-branch ensemble convolutional neural networks for video-based fa recognition. Trans Patt Anal Mach Intell 40(4):1002–1014

Fernández D, Varas D, Espadaler J, Masuda I, Ferreira J, Woodward A, Rodríguez D, Giró-i Nie X, Carlos Riveiro J, Bou E (2017) ViTS: video tagging system from massive web multime collections. In: Proceedings of the IEEE international conference on computer vision, pp 33 346

Gangemi A, Presutti V, Reforgiato Recupero D, Nuzzolese AG, Draicchio F, Mongiovì M (201 Semantic web machine reading with FRED. Seman Web 8(6):873–893

Guo Y, Zhang L, Hu Y, He X, Gao J (2016) Ms-celeb-1m: A dataset and benchmark for large-sc face recognition. In: European conference on computer vision. Springer, New York, pp 87–1

He K, Zhang X, Ren S, Sun J (2016) Deep residual learning for image recognition. IEEE, Conferen on computer vision and pattern recognition. IEEE, New York, pp 770–778

Huang GB, Ramesh M, Berg T, Learned-Miller E (2007) Labeled faces in the wild: a databa for studying face recognition in unconstrained environments. Tech. Rep. 07-49, University Massachusetts, Amherst

King DE (2009) Dlib-ml: a machine learning toolkit. J Mach Learn Res 10:1755–1758

Kolitsas N, Ganea OE, Hofmann T (2018) End-to-end neural entity linking. Prepri arXiv:180807699

Krizhevsky A, Sutskever I, Hinton GE (2012) ImageNet classification with deep convolution neural networks. In: Advances in neural information processing systems, NIPS, pp 1097–11

Liu W, Wen Y, Yu Z, Li M, Raj B, Song L (2017) SphereFace: deep hypersphere embedding face recognition. In: Conference on computer vision and pattern recognition, vol 1. IEEE, N York

Masi I, Rawls S, Medioni G, Natarajan P (2016a) Pose-aware face recognition in the wild. Conference on computer vision and pattern recognition. IEEE, New York, pp 4838–4846

Masi I, Tran AT, Hassner T, Leksut JT, Medioni G (2016b) Do we really need to collect milli of faces for effective face recognition? In: European conference on computer vision. Spring New York, pp 579–596

Masi I, Hassner T, Tran AT, Medioni G (2017) Rapid synthesis of massive face sets for improv face recognition. In: International conference on automatic face & gesture recognition. IEE New York, pp 604–611

Masi I, Chang FJ, Choi J, Harel S, Kim J, Kim K, Leksut J, Rawls S, Wu Y, Hassner T, et (2018) Learning pose-aware models for pose-invariant face recognition in the wild. Trans P Anal Mach Intell 41(2):271–284

Moro A, Raganato A, Navigli R (2014) Entity linking meets word sense disambiguation: a unif approach. Trans Assoc Comput Linguist 2:231–244

Mühling M, Korfhage N, Müller E, Otto C, Springstein M, Langelage T, Veith U, Ewerth R, Freisleben B (2017) Deep learning for content-based video retrieval in film and television production. Multimed Tools Appl 76(21):22169–22194

Mühling M, Meister M, Korfhage N, Wehling J, Hörth A, Ewerth R, Freisleben B (2019) Content-based video retrieval in historical collections of the German broadcasting archive. Int J Digit Lib 20(2):167–183

Müller-Budack E, Pustu-Iren K, Diering S, Ewerth R (2018) Finding person relations in image data of news collections in the internet archive. In: International conference on theory and practice of digital libraries. Springer, New York, pp 229–240

Muller-Budack E, Pustu-Iren K, Ewerth R (2018) Geolocation estimation of photos using a hierarchical model and scene classification. In: Proceedings of the European Conference on Computer Vision (ECCV), pp 563–579

Navigli R, Ponzetto SP (2012) BabelNet: The automatic construction, evaluation and application of a wide-coverage multilingual semantic network. Artif Intell 193:217–250

Rizzo G, Troncy R (2011) NERD: evaluating named entity recognition tools in the web of data. Workshop on Web Scale Knowledge Extraction

Schroff F, Kalenichenko D, Philbin J (2015) FaceNet: a unified embedding for face recognition and clustering. In: Conference on computer vision and pattern recognition. IEEE, New York, pp 815–823

Sun Y, Wang X, Tang X (2014) Deep learning face representation from predicting 10,000 classes. In: Conference on computer vision and pattern recognition. IEEE, New York, pp 1891–1898

Sun X, Wu P, Hoi SC (2018) Face detection using deep learning: an improved faster R-CNN approach. Neurocomputing 299:42–50

Taigman Y, Yang M, Ranzato M, Wolf L (2014) DeepFace: closing the gap to human-level performance in face verification. In: Conference on computer vision and pattern recognition. IEEE, New York, pp 1701–1708

Van Erp M, Rizzo G, Troncy R (2013) Learning with the web: spotting named entities on the intersection of nerd and machine learning. In: Workshop on making sense of microposts, pp 27–30

Vo N, Jacobs N, Hays J (2017) Revisiting IM2GPSin the deep learning era. In: Proceedings of the IEEE international conference on computer vision, pp 2621–2630

Wan J, Wang D, Hoi SCH, Wu P, Zhu J, Zhang Y, Li J (2014) Deep learning for content-based image retrieval: a comprehensive study. In: Proceedings of the 22nd ACM international conference on multimedia. ACM, New York, pp 157–166

Wen Y, Li Z, Qiao Y (2016) Latent factor guided convolutional neural networks for age-invariant face recognition. In: Conference on computer vision and pattern recognition. IEEE, New York, pp 4893–4901

Weyand T, Kostrikov I, Philbin J (2016) Planet-photo geolocation with convolutional neural networks. In: European conference on computer vision. Springer, New York, pp 37–55

Yang S, Luo P, Loy CC, Tang X (2015) From facial parts responses to face detection: a deep learning approach. In: International conference on computer vision. IEEE, New York, pp 3676–3684

Yi D, Lei Z, Liao S, Li SZ (2014) Learning face representation from scratch. CoRR abs/1411.7923

Yin X, Yu X, Sohn K, Liu X, Chandraker M (2017) Towards large-pose face frontalization in the wild. CoRR abs/1704.06244

Zhang K, Zhang Z, Li Z, Qiao Y (2016) Joint face detection and alignment using multitask cascaded convolutional networks. IEEE Signal Process. Lett. 23(10):1499–1503

Zhu X, Lei Z, Liu X, Shi H, Li SZ (2016) Face alignment across large poses: a 3D solution. In: Conference on computer vision and pattern recognition. IEEE, New York, pp 146–155

Part IV
Researching the Past Web

The past Web is an increasingly important object of study for researchers in the humanities and social sciences. It touches on every aspect of life in the late twentieth and twenty-first centuries and encompasses multiple forms of publication, authors, and viewpoints. Thanks initially to the work of the Internet Archive, the archives of the Web date back almost 25 years, so that patterns and trends may be explored over time and longitudinal case studies may be devised. As theory, method, and practice have developed, often as a collaboration between archivists and academic researchers, groundbreaking qualitative and quantitative analysis has begun to demonstrate the full richness of the archived Web as a primary source. This part presents five examples of research based primarily on the study of the past Web, showcasing the different approaches that can be brought to bear on web archives.

In the chapter "Digital Archaeology in the Web of Links: Reconstructing a Late-1990s Web Sphere", Peter Webster works with data derived from the UK Web Archive—the graph of the links between and within websites—to reconstruct the web sphere of conservative British Christianity. Using hyperlinks to study online networks, and potentially the flow of information and ideas, is an important method for working with web archives, particularly where access restrictions prevent analysis of full content at scale.

Janne Nielsen describes quantitative approaches to the identification and analysis of the Danish national web domain in the chapter "Quantitative Approaches to the Danish Web Archive". The chapter reveals the complexity of the methods required, which can be a challenge for researchers without a computational background, but also the value of engaging with web archives in this way. The exploration of national web domains is an area of enormous interest since so many archiving institutions operate with a national mandate. The research presented here outlines how to get started and how to avoid certain pitfalls.

J. Winters
School of Advanced Study, University of London, London, UK
e-mail: jane.winters@sas.ac.uk

In the chapter "Critical Web Archive Research", Anat Ben-David acknowledges the relative maturity of web archiving and web archive research, certainly compared to work with other forms of born-digital media. But she challenges researchers and archivists not to settle into existing modes of research and practice and take their success for granted. She calls instead for a more critical engagement with web archives, which considers the values, politics, and ideologies of this new primary source by presenting three case studies to provoke reflection.

The chapter "Exploring Online Diasporas: London's French and Latin American Communities in the UK Web Archive" also deals with the values of web archives and considers how more diverse stories can be told through the analysis of the past Web. Saskia Huc-Hepher and Naomi Wells focus on the two special collections that they have developed in partnership with the UK Web Archive team at the British Library, documenting the histories and experiences of the French and Latin American communities in London. They argue for a multilingual approach to web archiving and web archive research.

Finally, in the chapter "Platform and App Histories: Assessing Source Availability in Web Archives and App Repositories", Anne Helmond and Fernando van der Vlist consider how researchers can study apps and platforms which are hard to preserve through existing methods of web harvesting and archiving. They consider the material traces of these objects that remain in web archives and use them to reconstruct important digital histories.

Together, these chapters shine a spotlight on the range and diversity of web archive exploration and offer a range of approaches for others to follow and develop.

Digital Archaeology in the Web of Links: Reconstructing a Late-1990s Web Sphere

Peter Webster

Abstract One unit of analysis within the archived Web is the "web sphere", a body of material from different hosts that is related in some meaningful sense. This chapter outlines a method of reconstructing such a web sphere from the late 1990s, that of conservative British Christians as they interacted with each other and with others in the USA in relation to issues of morality, domestic and international politics, law and the prophetic interpretation of world events. Using an iterative method of interrogation of the graph of links for the archived UK Web, it shows the potential for the reconstruction of what I describe as a "soft" web sphere from what is in effect an archive with a finding aid with only classmarks and no descriptions.

1 Introduction

The attention of contemporary historians is now turning to the 1990s, as we reach a sufficient distance from the period to view it in some sort of perspective. The period from the fall of the Berlin Wall until the 9/11 terrorist attacks—what might be called a "long Nineties"—is beginning to come into focus as one possible analytical unit in world cultural and political history. As a result, historians are increasingly turning to the Internet and the Web as another type of primary source for the study of the period.

This attention is being paid to differing aspects of web history. In their differing ways, both the 2018 special issue of the journal *Internet Histories* on "the Web of the 90s" and the *SAGE Handbook of Web History* (Brügger and Milligan 2019) show the interest in the technical history of the medium itself. My own work on Christian sentiment regarding the early Web and its potential effects is a contribution to what might be called a cultural or affective history of technology (Webster 2018). As academic interest in web history has grown, so has the understanding of the

P. Webster (✉)
Webster Research and Consulting, Chichester, West Sussex, UK
e-mail: peter@websterresearchconsulting.com

© Springer Nature Switzerland AG 2021
D. Gomes et al. (eds.), *The Past Web*,
https://doi.org/10.1007/978-3-030-63291-5_12

archived Web as an object of study. As the work of Niels Brügger has shown, though an archived page replayed in a browser appears seductively similar to its original, scholars must grapple with its fundamental otherness and deal with it on those very distinct terms; there is a need for a philology of the archived Web (Brügger 2018, pp. 23–30). But there is more to the Web than individual objects, and indeed individual sites (though much early work in web history was focussed at this level). What follows is an exercise in understanding a particular "web sphere".

2 "Soft" and "Hard" Web Spheres

Brügger defines a web sphere as "web material ... related to a topic, a theme, an event or a geographic area" (Brügger 2018, pp. 34–5). Here I posit a distinction (at least in degree, if not in kind) between "hard" and "soft" web spheres, defined in terms of the ease with which their boundaries may be drawn, and the rate at which those boundaries move over time. Examples of hard web spheres might be those of organisations that have clear forms of membership or association: the websites of the individual members of the European Parliament, for instance, or of the football clubs in the English Premier League in a given season. Given the clarity with which these particular definitions can be drawn, and the stability of those definitions (5 years for Members of the European Parliament, 1 year for the Premier League), the initial work in isolating a web sphere and its archival traces for study is relatively light.

The study of "soft" web spheres tends to present additional difficulties, since the definition of topics or themes (to continue with Brügger's definition) is more difficult if not expressed in institutional terms. Web spheres defined by a concept or theme without an institutional analogue are by definition more fluid and more subjective, since the definition of "European politics" or "English football" may be contested in ways that "membership of the European Parliament" or "Premier League clubs" may not. This chapter is a case study in the reconstruction of just such a soft web sphere, much of which is lost from the live Web and exists only in the Internet Archive.

3 Conservative Christianity, Politics, Law and Morality: The Problem Defined

Scholars of conservative Christianity have known for many years of various correlations between conservatism in doctrine and particular stances on a number of key political, legal and ethical issues, often questions of personal morality that are in some way regulated by the law. The modern history of British evangelicalism shows periodic rises and falls in the levels of general anxiety about the moral state of the UK, although the particular complex of issues at stake was different at each point (see, for instance, Grimley 2014). In the case of the "long Nineties" in particular, certain issues were prominent, some of which were a continuation of older anxieties. Anglican divisions over sexuality were already visible before exploding in controversy at the 1998 Lambeth Conference, the decennial gathering of the bishops of the worldwide Anglican Communion (Bates 2004); conservative disquiet in the UK was further fuelled by the moves towards recognition of same-sex partnerships in what became the Civil Partnerships Act 2004. Though there was no material change in UK law, public debate continued about the law on abortion and on assisted suicide, in both of which cases there was marked Christian engagement, as there was with the attempt to change the law in relation to therapeutic cloning in 2001. Scholars of right-wing politics in general have also often noted a further correlation between some varieties of conservative Christianity and a generalised sympathy for the politics of the right (Jackson 2010). In the UK, scholars have examined in particular Christian attitudes to the European Union and to concerns about the place of Islam in public life (Smith and Woodhead 2018; Atherstone 2019; Webster 2017).

Less obvious both in the media and in popular consciousness was the engagement of conservative Protestants in particular with issues of biblical interpretation that have cultural consequences: creationism and its place (if any) in science education in schools and in public broadcasting (Numbers 1992, pp. 323–30), and the interpretation of biblical prophecy in relation to current politics, including the Middle East, climate change and the end of the world (Sweetnam 2019). The period from the mid-1990s—the beginning of the web age—was, however, given a particular sharpness—what quizzical journalists dubbed "pre-millennial tension"[1]—by the approach of the year 2000. The projected catastrophe of the Y2K bug was itself a subject of prophetic speculation (McMinn 2001). But there was no shortage of material in world politics to fuel the reflection of Christian Zionists who were already "semiotically aroused" (Clark 2007, pp. 149–255; the phrase is of Landes 2007, p. 4). In Israel, the Oslo Accords of 1993 and 1995 were followed by the assassination of Prime Minister Rabin, the failed talks at Camp David in 2000 and eventually the outbreak of the Second Intifada in 2001. The notion of a "clash of civilisations"—between "the West" and "Islam"—already current in the late 1990s, was brought into new relief by the terrorist attacks of 11 September 2001.

Before the widespread adoption of the Web, conservative Christian anxiety in the UK about issues such as these was often expressed by and through various parachurch organisations—Christian in ethos and leadership but functionally independent of the churches themselves. Some of these had long histories, such as the Society for the Protection of the Unborn Child, set up in reaction to what became the Abortion Act 1967, the decisive legalisation of abortion in most of the UK; some were rather newer. Before the Internet, these organisations tended to communicate

---

[1] 'Have you got pre-millennial tension?', *The Independent*, 29 December 1996, retrieved 16 May 2019 from https://www.independent.co.uk/life-style/pmt-have-you-got-pre-millennial-tension-1316310.html

by means of events and public speaking, video and audio cassette tape distribution, and in a panoply of ephemeral literature; all of these were poorly archived and are now hard to recover. The Web, as it lowered the barriers to entry to public discussion, not only gave existing and newly formed groups alike a novel means of communication but also allowed individuals to add their voices to the chorus.

The archived Web affords an opportunity to address two particular questions that were previously difficult if not impossible to approach. The first of these is the degree to which, though each of these disputes has been observed singly, the same individuals or groups engaged with several or all of them as a package. Was engagement with this particular cluster of issues a function of something more fundamental in theology and practice? Or, alternatively, did conservative British Christians engage with each issue on its own merits, as a singular interest, rather than as part of a wider set of common concerns? The question has not been addressed directly by scholars so far, although the literature when read in the round (and anecdotal experience of the constituency) suggests the former. An examination of the link relationships in the archived Web affords one way of approaching the question. To what degree were the parts of the Web that address each individual issue connected with each other?

Secondly, the same data can also be used to investigate the extent to which the Web allowed an internationalisation of religious interchange. Christians in the UK had for many decades been in dialogue with believers in the USA, but were limited by the cost of travel and of importing print and other material; the well-studied television and radio output of American Christians was largely unavailable in the UK. The Web allowed readers and publishers alike in the UK to access material from other countries that previously would have been difficult if not impossible to obtain. How (if at all) is such an internationalisation to be observed in the link relationships of an Anglo-American conservative Christian web sphere?

How, then, to recover the sound of this chorus of voices, in order to address these two questions? Internet Studies scholars have made creative use of search engine results as a means of identifying soft web spheres on the live Web and of creating archival collections of that content (see, for instance, Ackland and Evans 2017). Such keyword searching, however, presupposes (first) that there are useful keywords to employ, that are distinctive (in the way that "premillennialism" is, but "apocalypse" is not), and stable in meaning over time. It also supposes that one's initial knowledge of the field is sufficient to create such a list in the first place, without omitting terms that are in fact of an importance about which one did not know. Keyword searching also recovers results of the use of particular terms in content from organisations and individuals which might in fact oppose the agenda of those organisations under examination; a useful line of enquiry in its own right, but quite distinct.

The would-be historian of the late 1990s must deal with a more acute problem still—a problem with several layers. First, the vast bulk of content from the period is no longer on the live Web; second, as scholars, we have few, if any, indications of what has been lost—no inventory of the 1990s Web against which to check; third, of the content that was captured by the Internet Archive (more or less the only archive of the Anglophone Web of the period), only a superficial layer is exposed to keyword search, and the bulk may only be retrieved by a search for the URL. Not only do we not know what was never archived, among the content that was archived it is difficult to find what we might want, since there is no means of knowing the URL of a lost resource. To use an analogy from an archival context, there is a finding aid, but one with only classmarks, and no descriptions, or (alternatively) a library catalogue containing only ISBN numbers, when the ISBN registry is lost.

4   The First Stage of the Method: Identifying an Initial List of Domains

Scholars require, then, some means of understanding the archived Web using only the technical data about it that it itself can be made to disclose. In the remainder of this chapter, I outline a method of web sphere reconstruction based not on page content but on the relationships between sites, i.e. the Web of hyperlinks that itself forms part of the archived Web. The method is iterative in nature and involves both the computational interrogation of large datasets and the close examination of individual archived pages, along with the use of printed and other non-digital sources. It builds upon several recent studies, all of which in their different ways explore the available primary sources from outside the Web from which it may be reconstructed, both on small scales (Nanni 2017; Teszelszky 2019) and at the scale of whole national domains (Ben-David 2016; Ben-David 2019). It is an elaboration of two studies of my own in which the particular method was essayed in relation to smaller and less complex web spheres (Webster 2017; Webster 2019).

The first stage was to establish an initial list of the domains of the conservative Christian organisations concerned. This was derived from several sources. The first was the live Web, since many of the campaigning organisations that were active in the late 1990s still exist. As such it was possible to compile the current domains of all those organisations which still existed in 2019. (The assumptions involved in this are examined below.)

The second source was the body of published scholarly work on the subject published during the period under examination. Contemporary historians are well accustomed to relying on the work of scholars in other disciplines carried out in real time. Economists, sociologists and others studying the social phenomena of their own time have left a rich legacy of scholarship that both documents and explains those phenomena. Quite often those discursive insights are accompanied and supported by data, created at the time, which when shared have now become primary sources in their own right. In the case of the religious Web, there is a significant body of pioneering early work by Internet Studies scholars (on the apocalyptic Web see, for instance, Campbell 2004). However, it is now cut adrift from the matters it describes, as the materials it analysed no longer exist. The analogy with economics or sociology thus breaks down; since this research created no research data as such, the work described stands in the same relation to the present as does the embedded observational work of anthropologists, from which data is not usually derived. *Give me that online religion* by the American scholar Brenda E. Brasher was one of the earliest examinations of religious life online (Brasher 2001). It carried the disclaimer that "we know that many of the Websites listed in this book no longer exist. That is the nature of the Web". It referred readers to Brasher's own website for a list of current sites. Nearly 20 years on, that site also no longer exists, and itself was only partially archived.[2] It was possible, then, to derive additional relevant domains from a review of early published scholarship on online religion. Where the scholar gave the domain, the task was straightforward; where they had not, it was possible in some cases to identify the domains using the keyword homepage search in the Internet Archive.

Readers over a certain age will remember a time when publishers rushed to issue printed books that guided surfers to the "best" of the Web. One such book was *God on the Internet* (Kellner 1996), which gave short accounts of several hundred religious sites and their URLs. Some domains were derived from this and other similar publications.

Even at the time they were published, it was clear that such printed accounts would very soon fall out of date, and readers could also turn to sites such as Yahoo, which was listing thousands of religious websites as early as 1996, and the Open Directory Project (dmoz). (On the history of finding things on the Web before the dominance of search engines, see Halavais 2019.) The Internet Archive holds archived versions of these lists from 1996 for Yahoo and 1999 for Dmoz, and these were used to derive further domains of relevance. (An example of the use of historic web directories is Musso and Merletti 2016.) There were also examples of Christians creating directories of websites on a smaller scale, such as the Organization of Christians with Internet Home Pages (ocih.org, created in 1995 in the USA). Archived versions of the OCIH's listing survive from 1999 until 2008, after which the site disappears from view. (The domain passed to Orange County Implant Health, a plastic surgery practice in California.)

The fourth source was data derived from another web archive, the UK Web Archive. I myself was a curator of a special collection in the UK Web Archive on religion, law and the state in contemporary Britain, first as a guest researcher from 2011 and then continuing after I joined the staff of the UK Web Archive in 2012. Using data provided by former colleagues at the British Library, I was able to derive further domains, of three types: those which had been archived and still existed on the live Web; those that had been archived but had subsequently gone from the live

---

[2]The Internet Archive has a single instance of brendabrasher.com but it does not contain the content referred to: https://web.archive.org/web/20010514053625/http://www.brendabrasher.com:80/online_religion.html. Brasher's university pages contained some such listings, but these are only present in the Wayback Machine until 2005, at the URL http://raider.muc.edu/~brashebe/online religion.htm.

Web; and finally those which I had selected but could not at the time be archived because permission from the site owner could be not secured.[3]

From these four sources, then, it was possible to derive an initial list of domains (or, in fact, several lists, concerned with different issues, also categorised by their country of origin). One limitation of this approach is that it tends to foreground those organisations which had troubled to register a domain, or at least a host on a domain, such that content hosted at a location like *prophecy.com* or *prophecy. mywebsite.com* appears in the graph where *mywebsite.com/prophecy* does not. And the evidence of some early listings, both printed and online, suggests that a great many sites in the earliest days did not have their own domains. And, tempting though it may be, we should not assume that the most well-organised or well-funded organisations were the earliest to register domains, since a great many of the most apparently eccentric sites run by individuals had their own domains. In any case, it is clear that this method underestimates the size and density of the conservative Christian Web.

5   The Second Stage: Interrogating the Graph of Links

The second stage was to interrogate web archives themselves, in order both to determine the existence or otherwise of archived versions of these domains and to uncover further relevant domains. The British Library makes available a dataset that serves this purpose, being the UK Host Link Graph. It is derived from the JISC UK Web Domain Dataset, an extraction of the holdings for the *.uk* ccTLD for the period 1996–2013, which forms part of the UK Web Archive's collections. The Host Link Graph records the instance of link relations between .uk hosts and other hosts (both .uk and not). The Link Graph for the period 1996–2010 contains over 2 billion such relationships, expressed in the form:

1997 | host1.co.uk | host2.com | 7.

which declares that in 1997, the Internet Archive found some seven resources (usually pages, but not always) on *host1.co.uk* which contained at least one link to a resource on *host2.com*.

Taking the individual categorised lists of domains, a set of shell scripts were created (one for each list) to extract from the UK Host Link Graph all the edges in the graph that represented either an inbound link to, or an outbound link from, one of the domains on that list. The resulting datasets were then manipulated in turn to extract those domain names that had not previously been identified. These newly discovered domains were then individually assessed and categorised, by means of both the live Web (where applicable) and with archived instances in the Internet Archive. In some cases, a domain was one previously used by an organisation

---

[3]My thanks are due to Nicola Bingham for her assistance in obtaining this data. Some details of the project are available at https://peterwebster.me/2013/01/22/religion-politics-and-law-in-contemporary-britain-a-web-archive/

which later adopted the domain in the initial list; in these cases, the association was recorded and the superseded domain added to the master list. Visual inspection of other previously unknown archived sites revealed numerous webrings, blogrolls and pages of links, from which further domains of relevance were derived and fed back into the master lists.

Using, then, a set of revised scripts, the process was then repeated until no new relevant domains were being revealed by new iterations. Once this point had been reached for each list, the final datasets derived were concatenated to produce a single graph for all the domains under examination, and then duplicate lines were removed. This dataset contained a significant amount of noise—inbound and outbound links with domains that were irrelevant to the study. During each iteration of the process, however, domains that on inspection were classified as irrelevant—for instance, some early general directories of the Web that linked in, or advertising and similar domains to which there were outbound links—had been noted. From these, an additional script was now created, to remove lines that contained those domains from the graph.

By this means it was possible to derive a link graph of the conservative Christian Web in the UK in the earliest days of web archiving. The resulting graph contained two principal types of edge. The first type was outbound links from organisations within the UK ccTLD to related organisations both within that ccTLD and beyond it, and also to churches and other religious organisations, government, civil society organisations and the media. The second type was inbound links to the organisations under examination from other domains within the ccTLD. With this graph, it is possible to begin to analyse the interrelations between campaigning groups on several different issues related to religion, law, politics and ethics in the UK, and their relations with the non-UK Web, and the USA in particular.

6 Summary

This is not the venue for a full rehearsal of that analysis, which I intend to publish at length elsewhere. However, the method outlined here is one by which the boundary of a "soft" web sphere can be drawn by interrogation of a larger link graph. It also demonstrates the kind of multi-source investigation necessary to uncover the archaeology of the early Web. Big data and small, printed sources, the traces of previous web archiving efforts (even when unsuccessful) and echoes in the scholarly record itself: all these come into play when trying to understand an archive without a catalogue.

References

Ackland R, Evans A (2017) Using the web to examine the evolution of the abortion debate in Australia, 2005-2015. In: Brügger N, Schroeder R (eds) The web as history. UCL Press, London, pp 159–189

Atherstone A (2019) Evangelicals and Islam. In: Atherstone A, Jones DC (eds) The Routledge research companion to the history of evangelicalism. Routledge, Abingdon, pp 127–145

Bates S (2004) A church at war: anglicans and homosexuality. I. B. Tauris, London

Ben-David A (2016) What does the web remember of its deleted past? An archival reconstruction of the former Yugoslav top-level domain. New Media Soc 18:1103–1119. https://doi.org/10.1177/1461444816643790

Ben-David A (2019) National web histories at the fringe of the web: Palestine, Kosovo and the quest for online self-determination. In: Brügger N, Laursen D (eds) The historical web and digital humanities: the case of national web domains. Routledge, London, pp 89–109

Brasher BE (2001) Give me that online religion. Jossey-Bass, San Francisco

Brügger N (2018) The archived web: doing history in the digital age. MIT Press, Cambridge, MA

Brügger N, Milligan I (eds) (2019) The SAGE handbook of web history. SAGE, London

Campbell RA (2004) Searching for the apocalypse in cyberspace. In: Dawson LL, Cowan DE (eds) Religion online: finding faith on the internet. Routledge, London, pp 239–253

Clark V (2007) Allies for Armageddon: the rise of Christian Zionism. Yale, New Haven

Grimley M (2014) Anglican evangelicals and anti-permissiveness: the nationwide festival of light, 1971-1983. In: Atherstone A, Maiden J (eds) Evangelicalism and the Church of England in the twentieth century: reform, resistance and renewal. Boydell and Brewer, Woodbridge, pp 183–205

Halavais A (2019) How search shaped and was shaped by the web. In: Brügger N, Milligan I (eds) The SAGE handbook of web history. SAGE, London, pp 242–255

Jackson P (2010) Extremes of faith and nation: British fascism and Christianity. Religion Compass 4:507–527

Kellner MA (1996) God on the internet. IDG Books, Foster City, CA

Landes R (2007) Millenarianism and the dynamics of apocalyptic time. In: Newport KGC, Gribben C (eds) Expecting the end: millennialism in social and historical context. Baylor University Press, Waco, TX, pp 1–23

McMinn L (2001) Y2K, the apocalypse, and evangelical Christianity: the role of eschatological belief in church responses. Sociol Relig 62:205–220

Musso M, Merletti F (2016) This is the future: a reconstruction of the UK business web space (1996–2001). New Media Soc 18:1120–1142

Nanni F (2017) Reconstructing a website's lost past: methodological issues concerning the history of Unibo.it. Digit Hum Q 11. http://www.digitalhumanities.org/dhq/vol/11/2/000292/000292.html

Numbers RL (1992) The creationists: the evolution of scientific creationism. University of California Press, Berkeley, CA

Smith G, Woodhead L (2018) Religion and Brexit: populism and the Church of England. Relig State Soc 46:206–223

Sweetnam M (2019) Evangelicals and the end of the world. In: Atherstone A, Jones DC (eds) The Routledge research companion to the history of evangelicalism. Routledge, Abingdon, pp 178–197

Teszelszky K (2019) Web archaeology in the Netherlands: the selection and harvest of the Dutch web incunables of provider Euronet (1994–2000). Internet Hist 3:180–194. https://doi.org/10.1080/24701475.2019.1603951

Webster P (2017) Religious discourse in the archived web: Rowan Williams, Archbishop of Canterbury, and the sharia law controversy of. In: Brügger N, Schroeder R (eds) 190–203. UCL Press, London, p 2008

Webster P (2018) Technology, ethics and religious language: early Anglophone Christian reactions to "cyberspace". Internet Hist 2:299–314. https://doi.org/10.1080/24701475.2018.1468976

Webster P (2019) Lessons from cross-border religion in the Northern Irish web sphere: understanding the limitations of the ccTLD as a proxy for the national web. In: Brügger N, Milligan I (eds) The historical web and digital humanities: the case of national web domains. Routledge, London, pp 110–123

Quantitative Approaches to the Danish Web Archive

Janne Nielsen

Abstract Large-scale historical studies are important for a comprehensive under-standing of the historical development of the Web, but such large-scale studies pose certain methodological challenges and require a different level of access to web archives from what is often offered, that is, access through the Wayback Machine. The Danish national web archive Netarkivet and the HPC facility DeiC National Cultural Heritage Cluster, both located at the Royal Danish Library in Denmark, have in recent years opened up new ways to access and process materials from the archive, which allow for quantitative analysis of the archived Danish Web. This chapter includes examples of large-scale studies of different aspects of the Danish Web as it has been archived in Netarkivet. It describes several approaches to creating and analysing large corpora using different types of archived sources for different purposes, such as metadata from crawl.logs to undertake measurement studies and text analyses, hyperlinks to conduct link analyses and HTML documents to search for specific elements in the source code, e.g. identifying requests to third parties to study web tracking. This chapter discusses the methodological challenges related to the use of the archived Web as an object of study in quantitative research and the challenges and benefits of applying computational methods in historical web studies. The archived Danish Web will serve as a case study, but the suggested approaches could be replicated using other web archives, and the use cases aim to highlight how access to different kinds of archived web sources and the use of computational methods allow for new types of studies of the past Web.

1 Introduction

Large-scale historical studies of the Web are important for a comprehensive understanding of its development because they can explore vast patterns and reveal

J. Nielsen (✉)
Department of Media and Journalism Studies, Aarhus University, Aarhus, Denmark
e-mail: janne@cc.au.dk

© Springer Nature Switzerland AG 2021
D. Gomes et al. (eds.), *The Past Web*,
https://doi.org/10.1007/978-3-030-63291-5_13

new insights about, for instance, web content and the relationship between web entities. Large-scale quantitative studies pose additional methodological challenges to those encountered in qualitative studies because the amount of data requires different methods and another level of access to web archives than is often offered by web archives, i.e. access through the Wayback Machine. When studying huge amounts of data, for instance, an entire national web domain, we need computational methods to process, sort and clean the plethora of data and to analyse and visualise it, making patterns and trends visible to us.

This chapter will present four different approaches to large-scale studies of the Web of the past, using as a case study the Danish Web from 2006 to 2015, which has been archived in the national Danish web archive Netarkivet.[1] The approaches are part of the project "Probing a Nation's Web Domain—the Historical Development of the Danish Web" (see Brügger et al. 2017; Brügger et al. 2019; Brügger et al. 2020). As very large-scale studies of the historical Web are still relatively few, and we are still in the process of understanding all the implications of working with the archived Web as a source in different types of studies, all the approaches are at present still exploratory. They ask and aim to answer broad research questions as a starting point for discovering patterns that can then be scrutinised subsequently in more focused studies. They also aim to shed light on the potential of different types of archived sources and the different processes involved in preparing them for research use. We need to get to know the material well in order to be able to see what questions can be answered, how and with what limitations.

2 Creating Corpora

An important part of preparing for large-scale analyses of the archived Web is to create one or more corpora for the study. This can be done in different ways depending on the subject of study and the purpose. An issue that should always be addressed, no matter the subject, is how to delimit a corpus, i.e. how to choose and extract the objects that we want to analyse. In our studies, we work with two types of corpora: a "master" corpus from each year called the *yearly corpus* and *derived corpora* based on the yearly corpus but containing different types of data sources. The basic idea behind the yearly corpus is to create a sort of snapshot, which is as close as possible to how the Danish Web would have looked like at a specific point

---

[1] For more about Netarkivet, their harvesting strategies and what is understood as the Danish Web (Brügger et al. 2019; Laursen and Møldrup-Dalum 2017; Schostag and Fønss-Jørgensen 2012). The approaches described here are used in projects that are among the first pilot projects to use the high-performance computer facility the DeiC National Cultural Heritage Cluster situated at the Royal Danish Library and funded by the Danish e-Infrastructure Cooperation (DeiC). The pilot projects allow for close collaboration between researchers and IT developers at the library.

in time (Brügger et al. 2019).[2] To achieve this, we want only one version of each webpage in the corpus. Because most institutional web archiving is based on web crawling, which means that a webpage can be harvested multiple times, we would otherwise get a corpus including several versions of those websites linked to by multiple other sites. This could severely skew our results.[3] The purpose here is to study the historical development of the Danish Web from 2006 to 2015, so we have selected 10 yearly corpora. Each consists of a list of metadata for the resources from between approximately 470,000 and 707,000 domains to be included in the corpus. The yearly corpora are based on crawl log files, which are log files generated during harvests and including a line for each URI that was crawled.[4] Crawl logs hold a lot of metadata, including timestamp, status code, document size, URI, discovery path, referrer, MIME type (file type), etc. (Osborne 2018). These metadata can then be used to create derived corpora, which include the types of sources that we need for a specific study. What is available in a web archive are the objects that together form a website, e.g. HTML documents (including hyperlinks), images, audio and video files, etc.,[5] and metadata about the archived objects. In the following examples, different data sources have been used to map the historical development of different aspects of the Danish Web.[6] The first approach uses metadata to measure numbers and sizes; the second uses full text for text analyses like word frequencies and language; the third uses hyperlinks to analyse patterns in linking; and the fourth uses HTML source code to analyse the presence of tracking technologies. The approaches will be illustrated with a few visualisations of some preliminary results from our studies. The results are not presented or interpreted in any detail here— they will be in other publications—but they are included to demonstrate what types of results can be produced by these approaches.

---

[2]The corpus will never be an exact copy of what was online because the process of archiving influences what is archived (see, for instance, Brügger 2018; Nielsen 2016).

[3]For more on (our) corpus creation, see Brügger et al. (2019).

[4]Not all URIs are necessarily fetched, the crawl.log also contains information about URIs not fetched and why (Osborne 2018).

[5]To the extent that these objects can be archived by the technologies employed.

[6]The identification of corpora is followed by an ETL (extract, transform, load) process, which in the case of Netarkivet is performed by the archive's IT developers, where the data requested are extracted from the relevant web archive files, transformed into a format that can be accessed by researchers, and loaded onto the cluster for subsequent analysis. For a detailed description of an ETL process for a specific project, see Møldrup-Dalum (2018) on the ETL process for the project *Probing a Nation's Web Domain*. It is also important to clean the data and handle issues like deduplication (see Brügger et al. 2019).

3 Approaches

3.1 Measuring Numbers and Sizes

One way to undertake quantitative studies of the development of a national Web, in this case, the Danish Web, is to measure numbers and size(s). A very broad research question about how the Danish Web has developed over 10 years can be operationalised in questions like: How have the number (of objects, file types, status codes, websites, top-level domains used, etc.) and size (of the entire Web, average website, top 100 websites, the average size of specific file types, etc.) developed over time?

To measure this, we can use the metadata in our yearly corpora. We divided the analysis into different parts focusing on, respectively, the number of objects, distinct domains and top-level domains (TLDs), size, MIME types (file types) and status codes. The analysis was exploratory in that we tried to think of as many relevant ways to get information about the corpus as possible, but may not have included everything. How can we get the most comprehensive picture of the development of the Danish Web with regard to measurements? We can, for example, measure the total number and average number of objects per domain, TLD, status code and MIME type, but it is also interesting to study the total and average for the top 100 domains, because we know that web data usually present with a very long tail. So, we tried to think of different ways of exploring the data, which could give us insights into the shape and structure of the Danish Web at different points in time.

The results in Fig. 1 show how the Danish Web (as defined by Netarkivet) has grown both in number and size, and Table 1 shows how much of the Danish Web (based on size) is found in the largest eight top-level domains.

These are just two of many possible ways to study the size and structure of the Danish Web. The calculations and visualisations raise new questions as to how we can interpret and explain the changes that we see in the data over time, thus stimulating further analyses as to how we can understand these historical developments. Questions about the interpretation of data also relate to questions about possible bias or sources of error in the data and methods applied. We need to ask ourselves whether what we see in the results is an actual portrayal of changing characteristics of the Danish Web at different points in time, or whether it is caused by confounding factors, like changes in archiving strategies or crawler settings which do not reflect developments on the live Web but changes in what and how much is archived. We need to critically address the extent to which what we see in the results is genuinely evidence of changing characteristics and what is not.

An example of this can be seen in Fig. 1, which shows a steep decline in the size of the Danish Web in 2012. How can we explain this plunge? Did something change online? Were a lot of websites suddenly taken offline? Did only a few new websites come online? Were all websites suddenly much smaller? Or is it rather a consequence of an outside variable? In this case, our follow-up research and discussion with staff at the archive clarified that new filters used in the archiving

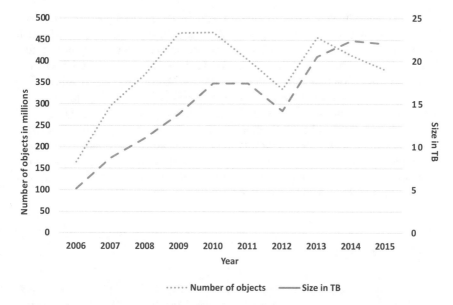

Fig. 1 Size of the Danish Web

Table 1 The percentage of the Danish Web (in size) on the eight largest top-level domains (TLDs)

TLD	2006	2007	2008	2009	2010	2011	2012	2013	2014	2015
.dk	99.81%	84.66%	84.30%	87.16%	88.90%	90.17%	90.87%	91.67%	92.54%	92.40%
.com	0.08%	8.73%	8.64%	7.19%	6.07%	5.68%	5.42%	4.95%	4.37%	4.40%
.org	0.04%	1.23%	1.31%	0.99%	0.81%	0.77%	0.76%	0.70%	0.73%	0.78%
.net	0.05%	1.83%	1.59%	1.35%	1.09%	0.89%	0.82%	0.79%	0.71%	0.69%
.de	0.01%	0.74%	0.80%	0.57%	0.49%	0.38%	0.35%	0.30%	0.31%	0.31%
.nu	0.01%	0.44%	0.42%	0.29%	0.25%	0.26%	0.26%	0.24%	0.22%	0.19%
.eu	NA	0.18%	0.15%	0.19%	0.17%	0.16%	0.14%	0.12%	0.11%	0.14%
.info	0.00%	0.30%	0.26%	0.20%	0.23%	0.20%	0.18%	0.17%	0.15%	0.12%

process were introduced in 2012, which can account for the decline in harvested data (described in Laursen and Møldrup-Dalum 2017). Another example could be seen in previous versions of the figure, which showed an even steeper decline in 2011 compared to this version. We discovered that this decline was caused (at least in part) by an important change in harvesting settings, when the archive chose to respect "do not crawl" directives in robots.txt in the first broad crawl in 2011 (Netarkivet 2011).[7] This meant that a lot of material was not archived, which has likely skewed the results significantly. Therefore, we chose to rerun all the analyses with the second broad crawl in 2011 instead so as not to include this anomaly.

---

[7]For more on robots.txt, see Nielsen (2016) and Rogers (2013).

The examples show that it is important to realise, when working with the archived Web, that smaller or larger changes in archiving strategies and settings happen continually over time, because the harvesting institutions are always trying to refine their methods and improve the quality and coverage of what is archived. Similarly, the percentages shown in Table 2 indicate how the Danish Web was distributed on different TLDs, but it might also attest to strategies in the archiving, for instance, the work being done by curators at different points in time discovering parts of the Danish domain on other TLDs than .dk. Thus, it will not be possible to conduct historical studies of the archived Web without running into issues relating to changes in curating practices and harvesting strategies and settings, for example, what domains and TLDs are included, how many levels of links are followed and the default limits of how much is harvested from each domain, etc.

3.2 Text Analysis

Another way of analysing the development of the Danish Web is to look at the text that has been included on webpages (the so-called body text in HTML documents)[8] and study the properties of the textual content (e.g. language, number of words) or even the content itself (e.g. a semantic analysis of topics). In order to create a text corpus, we need to decide between different ways of extracting the text. One way would be to extract the body text from the selected WARC files, but this would be a somewhat complex extraction process requiring a long compute time (Møldrup-Dalum 2018). Another method is to take advantage of the fact that Netarkivet has already extracted the body text as part of the indexing of the entire archive using Solr, which is used for the archive's full-text search. The method has some limitations in that it relies on the conceptualisation of text in Solr, and therefore, the specific way the text has been generated is not completely within the control of the researchers (Møldrup-Dalum 2018). The HTML markup has also been stripped out to exclude tags from appearing as part of the text,[9] so although the sequence is (mostly) preserved, there is no hierarchical structure in the text and you cannot, for instance, distinguish between headlines and running text. Punctuation is also excluded.

The analysis can be approached in different ways, but it is important to note that this approach for creating a corpus does not allow for all types of analyses because most of the structure has been removed. Thus, analyses focusing on sentences, for example, are not possible. In our project, we focus on word frequencies, languages and specific topics. For example, we examine what languages are used on the Danish

---

[8]The body text is placed in the HTML <body> tag, that is, between <body> and </body> in the HTML source code.

[9]See Cocciolo (2019) for suggestions on ways to remove HTML markup.

Table 2 Top 20 words (with more than two letters) on the Danish Web

	2006	2007	2008	2009	2010	2011	2012	2013	2014	2015
1	til	til	til	til	til	til	til	til	til	til
2	for	the	the	for	the	for	for	for	for	for
3	the	for	for	the	for	the	the	med	med	med
4	med	med	med	med	med	med	med	the	det	det
5	det	det	det	det	det	det	det	det	the	the
6	der	and	2008	der	2010	2011	der	der	der	der
7	2006	der	and	and	der	der	2012	den	den	den
8	den	2007	—†—†—†	har	and	den	den	har	har	har
9	har	—†—†—†	der	den	den	har	har	2013	and	ikke
10	ikke	den	har	2009	har	ikke	ikke	ikke	ikke	and
11	kan	har	den	ikke	ikke	and	kan	and	kan	som
12	and	kan	—†—†—†—†—†—†	kan	kan	fra	and	kan	som	kan
13	som	ikke	ikke	som	som	kan	som	fra	fra	jeg
14	—†—†—†	http	kan	jeg	fra	jeg	fra	som	jeg	fra
15	fra	2006	som	—†—†—†	jeg	som	jeg	2012	2013	2015
16	jeg	som	fra	fra	—†—†—†	dkk	dkk	jeg	2014	alle
17	http	fra	http	2008	2009	2010	2011	her	alle	2014
18	—†—†—†—†—†—†	jeg	jeg	http	dkk	alle	her	alle	mere	eller
19	2005	—†—†—†—†—†—†	dkk	dkk	—†—†—†—†—†—†	pris	mere	kontakt	din	mere
20	eller	www	this	her	you	her	alle	mere	eller	kontakt

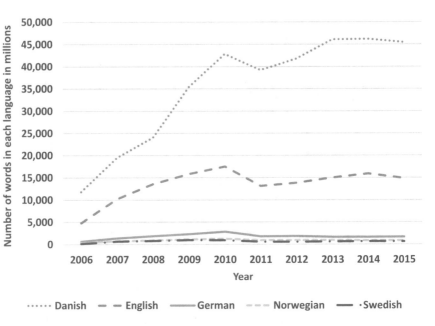

Fig. 2 Top 5 languages on the Danish Web

Web. The preliminary results show—unsurprisingly—that Danish and English are the most used as shown in Fig. 2.

We calculate the number of words and distinct words in Danish and English, respectively, and we find the most used words in both languages and across all languages used.

As seen in Table 2, the preliminary analysis shows that the most used words are essentially the same across all years, and the majority are among the words that are usually considered the most common in Danish. A few of them (for, the, and) are words that are used in both Danish and English, which likely influences their ranking.

We also look at the number of webpages and domains in Danish and English and the average number of words on webpages and domains. In the future, we plan to search for words relating to different topics to see changes over time. Other ways to do content analysis could include much more advanced analysis, like topic modelling or other natural language processing tools.

3.3   Link Analysis

The use of links is a central characteristic of the Web (Brügger 2018; Helmond 2019), and studying link structures, i.e. the way websites link to each other, is an obvious choice for large-scale web studies. Using web archives, we can now study the link structures of the past as well as the development of massive networks online, showing how certain websites cluster together in the web sphere. This is very useful for shedding light on the infrastructures of the Web, the relationships between websites and online power structures. The websites that are often linked to can be understood as central, and they are also likely to be among the most visited websites—although link analysis, like other analyses of archived Web data, in itself does not say anything about the actual use of the Web.

The links can be extracted either from the HTML documents (archived in the WARC files) or from an index if it exists. In our study (see Brügger et al. 2020), we extract the outgoing links from all domains (matching our yearly corpora) in the aforementioned Solr index. The links can then be used for different types of analysis, answering questions like: Which domains have the highest number of outgoing links? What are the number of links to and from different TLDs and ccTLDs (country code top-level domains)? How many links are there to and from different social media websites?

The preliminary results in Fig. 3 show that Danish websites link most frequently to the top-level domains of our neighbouring countries like Germany, the United Kingdom, Sweden and Norway, but there is also a surprising peak in links to Poland, which requires further investigation (Brügger et al. 2020). Looking at links to social media sites in Fig. 4, we see an expected steep increase in links to Facebook and Twitter on the Danish Web in recent years.

While the aforementioned questions can be answered by counting links, others require a network analysis to explore, for example, which nodes are the most central. When conducting network analyses, the websites are represented as nodes (the points in the network), and the links are represented as edges (the relationship between the points). The relationship is directed (one website links to another), and it can go either one way or both ways. Because of the large amounts of data, it is a challenge to undertake network analyses for an entire national web domain which do not result in a network so complex and dense that it is practically illegible—also known as "hairballs" (Joque 2019, 171). A co-link analysis allows us to prune the network, i.e. to remove the less important parts by retaining only the nodes that are linked to by a set number of other nodes in the network. This can result in a more useful view of the most central nodes in the network. We can also "zoom in" on select domains to study the development over time of, for example, the top domains linking to Facebook or MySpace.

3.4 Searching the Source Code

As mentioned above, an HTML document includes the text and hyperlinks of a webpage, but it also contains a lot of other information about the page and its content. A webpage is generated from the source code in this hidden layer of text below what we usually understand as the text of the webpage (Brügger 2018). The

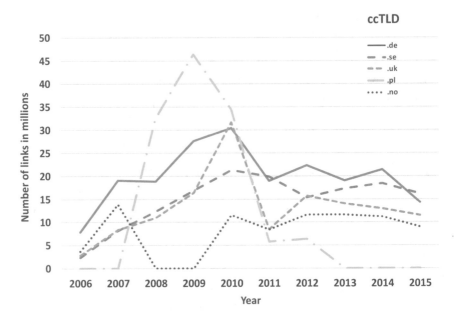

Fig. 3 Links from the Danish Web, which is mostly under the .dk domain, to other ccTLDs (Brügger et al. 2020)

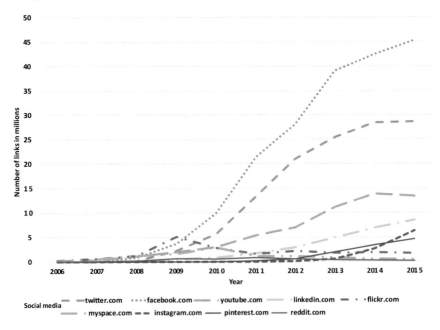

Fig. 4 Links to social media sites (Brügger et al. 2020)

final example I will offer here uses the source code of a webpage to find traces of tracking technologies, i.e. technologies that collect and combine information about users and their online behaviour.[10] These technologies are often invisible to the user, but we can find traces of them in this hidden layer, that is, the HTML document. The source code can be read (and written) by a human being who knows the language it is written in, and it is, obviously, also machine-readable, which allows for computational processing.

Many different types of tracking technologies have been developed in the last 25 years,[11] so a comprehensive study of tracking on the Web would require many different approaches to capture the totality of the data collection taking place. Here I will provide an example, based on Nielsen (2019), of how the development of a specific tracking technology, the web beacon (also known as the web bug, 1×1 pixel and a lot of other nicknames), can be studied historically by using the archived Web. The web beacon is, along with HTTP cookies, one of the "the classical ways to implement third-party tracking" (Ruohonen and Leppänen 2018, 28). Web beacons are very small (1×1 pixel), often invisible, image files embedded in a webpage. Each time an HTTP request to serve the image file is made, information about the user is sent to the server hosting the beacon. If this server is on a different domain from that of the webpage the user is visiting, the domain is called a third party, and this third party obtains information about the user without the user knowing. Not all third-party requests are concerned with tracking, but web beacons are known to be used for this purpose, so a beacon from a third party is most likely some sort of a tracker (see Nielsen 2019).

Our approach uses two sources that have already been mentioned: links from HTML documents and metadata from the Solr index. The links used in this analysis, however, are not the same as those used for the network analysis. Instead of outlinks, we focus on embedded image links with requests to a third party. First, all third-party links to images are extracted from the HTML documents in our yearly corpus (based on the src attribute of <img> tags).[12] Second, the URLs of all images with a height and width of 1×1 pixel are extracted from the Solr index.[13] Third, the URLs of the third-party requests embedded in the HTML and those derived from the metadata on the 1×1 pixel are merged, resulting in a list which reveals the relationship

---

[10]The idea of looking for traces of tracking in materials in web archives is inspired by Helmond (2017), but the approach here is very different. Another interesting study of tracking using web archives is that by Lerner et al. (2016).

[11]See Nielsen (2018) for a short account of the development of tracking technologies over time, including reflections on the relationship between the Web, web archiving and tracking as a practice of recording behaviour on the Web.

[12]In HTML documents, an image is defined by the <img> tag, which includes a src attribute specifying the URL (i.e. the location) of the image, for example, <img src = "image.jpeg"> or, in the case of a third-party link, <img src = "http://example.com/img/image.jpeg">.

[13]Because of the so-called duplication reduction used by Netarkivet (Jacobsen et al. 2007), we must compare each year with all previous years to get all the pictures, but this is too technical to go into here.

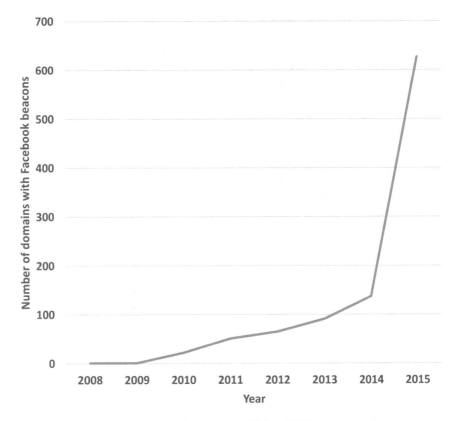

Fig. 5 Number of domains with Facebook beacons (Nielsen 2019)

between domains and third-party domains, i.e. which domains have beacons from which other domains embedded in their website.

The preliminary results from the first analyses show the presence of a lot of different beacons as well as considerable changes over time in which third parties set beacons (Nielsen 2019). If we study the beacons from two of the very big players, Google and Facebook, we see an expected increase in domains with Facebook beacons in Fig. 5 but a surprising peak in Google beacons in 2012 in Fig. 6, which we will need to examine further.

In both cases, the number of domains that include beacons is lower than expected, so we will need to undertake more analysis in order to interpret the results and further test the validity of the approach.

We also plan to compare the list of third parties with a list of known tracker domains to critically assess the results of our initial analysis. This may help us to figure out if all third-party beacons are actually what we would consider to be tracking technology. Here, again, we face the challenge of historical changes because we need to find historical lists with which to compare our data. We also

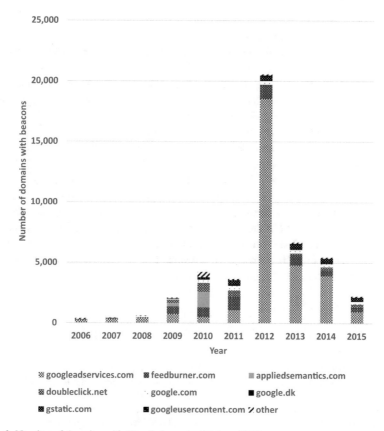

Fig. 6 Number of domains with Google beacons (Nielsen 2019)

have to consider what we might miss if we rely too much on a list, which is very unlikely to be comprehensive. Using source code to study the presence and spread of tracking technologies over time is a challenging endeavour, but the code can be used for other purposes too, for example, tracing developments in web design practices, the use of specific tags and so on.

4   What Comes Next?

The approaches presented here highlight how access to different types of archived web sources and the use of computational methods allow for new types of exploration of the past Web. They are meant to inspire and show the broad range of questions that can be addressed in large-scale studies of the historical Web. They also address important issues of how to create corpora for these types of studies. Although the archived Danish Web serves as the case study here, the suggested approaches could be replicated using other web archives, depending—of course—on the types of access and support offered.[14]

Large-scale studies of the archived Web can focus on many different aspects, and at the time of writing, we are still developing our analyses of the different derived corpora and refining our approaches. We also aim to include additional derived corpora allowing us to study, for example, the development of images, audio and video. We are continually gaining new insights into this uniquely complex and diverse object of study as we examine it from different angles. We find it very fruitful to move between levels, using what Moretti (2000) calls distant and close reading, as the different views offer complementary insights. Another fruitful practice is to combine the different derived corpora and the knowledge obtained in the different analyses. For example, the link graphs can be combined with the beacon analysis to assess the importance (centrality) of different tracker domains depending on the weight of the domains that embed the trackers.[15] Other examples of future research include combining the analysis of languages with the analysis of ccTLDs or analysing the networks of websites that mention a specific topic. And there are still many more aspects that could be explored.

References

Brügger N (2018) The archived web. The MIT Press, Cambridge, MA

Brügger N, Laursen D (2019) Historical studies of national web domains. In: Brügger N, Milligan I (eds) The SAGE handbook of web history. SAGE, London, pp 413–427

Brügger N, Laursen D, Nielsen J (2017) Exploring the domain names of the Danish web. In: Brügger N, Schroeder R (eds) The web as history. UCL Press, London, pp 62–80

Brügger N, Laursen D, Nielsen J (2019) Establishing a corpus of the archived web. In: Brügger N, Laursen D (eds) The historical web and digital humanities. Routledge, Abingdon, pp 124–142

Brügger N, Nielsen J, Laursen D (2020) Big data experiments with the archived web: methodological reflections on studying the development of a nation's web. First Monday 25(3)

Cocciolo A (2019) Quantitative web history methods. In: Brügger N, Milligan I (eds) The SAGE handbook of web history. SAGE, London, pp 153–167

Helmond A (2017) Historical website ecology: analyzing past states of the web using archived source code. In: Brügger N (ed) Web 25: histories from the first 25 years of the world wide web. Peter Lang, New York, pp 139–155

Helmond A (2019) A historiography of the hyperlink: periodizing the web through the changing role of the hyperlink. In: Brügger N, Milligan I (eds) The SAGE handbook of web history. SAGE, London, pp 153–167

Jacobsen G, Fønns-Jørgensen E, Andersen B (2007) Harvesting the Danish internet–the first two years. Retrieved 10 July 2019 from http://netarkivet.dk/wp-content/uploads/CollectingTheDanishInternet_2007.pdf

Joque J (2019) Visualizing historical web data. In: Brügger N, Milligan I (eds) The SAGE handbook of web history. SAGE, London, pp 168–185

---

[14]See Brügger and Laursen (2019) for a brief history of studies on national web domains.

[15]Weight is determined by the number of domains linking to a domain, that is, the more domains link to a domain, the higher the weight.

Laursen D, Møldrup-Dalum P (2017) Looking back, looking forward: 10 years of development to collect, preserve, and access the Danish web. In: Brügger N (ed) Web 25: histories from the first 25 years of the world wide web. Peter Lang, New York, pp 207–227

Lerner A, Kornfeld Simpson A, Kohno T, Roesner F (2016) Internet Jones and the raiders of the lost trackers: an archaeological study of web tracking from 1996 to 2016. In: SEC'16: proceedings of the 25th USENIX conference on security symposium: 997–1013

Møldrup-Dalum P (2018) ETL for dk-web. Royal Danish Library, Aarhus

Moretti F (2000) Conjectures on world literature. New Left Rev 1(Jan/Feb):56–58

Netarkivet (2011) Newsletter August 2011. Netarkivet.Dk. August. http://netarkivet.dk/wp-content/uploads/Newsletter_Netarchive_dk_august2011.pdf

Nielsen J (2016) Using web archives in research. Netlab.Dk. http://www.netlab.dk/wp-content/uploads/2016/10/Nielsen_Using_Web_Archives_in_Research.pdf

Nielsen J (2018) Recording the web. In: Romele A, Terrone E (eds) Towards a philosophy of digital media. Palgrave Macmillan, Cham, pp 51–76

Nielsen J (2019) Experimenting with computational methods for large-scale studies of tracking technologies in web archives. Internet Hist Digit Technol Cult Society 3(3–4):293–315

Osborne A (2018) Logs. Retrieved 6 April 2019 from https://github.com/internetarchive/heritrix3/wiki/Logs

Rogers R (2013) The website as archived object. In: Rodgers R (ed) Digital methods. MIT Press, Cambridge, MA, pp 70–93

Ruohonen J, Leppänen V (2018) Invisible pixels are dead, long live invisible pixels! In: WPES'18: proceedings of the 2018 workshop on privacy in the electronic society. ACM, New York, USA, pp 28–32. https://doi.org/10.1145/3267323.3268950

Schostag S, Fønss-Jørgensen E (2012) Webarchiving: legal deposit of internet in Denmark. A curatorial perspective. Microform Digit Rev 41(3–4):110–120. https://doi.org/10.1515/mir-2012-0018

Critical Web Archive Research

Anat Ben-David

Abstract Following the familiar distinction between software and hardware, this chapter argues that web archives deserve to be treated as a third category—memoryware: specific forms of preservation techniques which involve both software and hardware, but also crawlers, bots, curators, and users. While historically the term memoryware refers to the art of cementing together bits and pieces of sentimental objects to commemorate loved ones, understanding web archives as a complex socio-technical memoryware moves beyond their perception as bits and pieces of the live Web. Instead, understanding web archives as memoryware hints at the premise of the web's exceptionalism in media and communication history and calls for revisiting some of the concepts and best practices in web archiving and web archive research that have consolidated over the years. The chapter, therefore, presents new challenges for web archive research by turning a critical eye on web archiving itself and on the specific types of histories that are constructed with web archives.

1 Introduction

The field of web archiving and web archive research is maturing. A decade ago, most scholarly publications were concerned with questions characterizing the emergence of a new field of research and practice: How to archive the Web? Who is it for? In which ways does web archiving differ from archiving other digital or analog media? (cf. Costa and Silva 2010; Dougherty et al. 2010; Gomes et al. 2011; Niu 2012). Today, there is already a considerable amount of empirical research that no longer asks what web archiving is but instead uses the archived Web for answering various research questions, using a diverse set of methods. In recent years, the number of funded projects, publications, books, and conferences has grown from a handful to

A. Ben-David (✉)
Department of Sociology, Political Science and Communication, The Open University of Israel, Ra'anana, Israel
e-mail: anatbd@openu.ac.il

© Springer Nature Switzerland AG 2021
D. Gomes et al. (eds.), *The Past Web*,
https://doi.org/10.1007/978-3-030-63291-5_14

dozens. The last 2 years, in particular, have seen the publication of monographs and edited volumes on the topic and the establishment of *Internet Histories*, an international journal dedicated to studying the web's past (Brügger 2018; Brügger et al. 2018; Brügger and Laursen 2019; Brügger and Milligan 2018; Goggin and McLelland 2017).

From the theoretical perspective of the social construction of technology, to say that the field of web archiving and web archive research has matured is to point at technological closure and at a growing consensus shared by practitioners and researchers alike (Hård 1994). The professionalization of web archiving is evident in international collaborations and the development of standards. The establishment of international organizations such as the Internet Memory Foundation and the International Internet Preservation Consortium has contributed to the development of standards and best practices (Costa et al. 2017). Heritrix has become the default crawler used by most web archiving institutions (Mohr et al. 2004), the Wayback Machine and "Open Wayback" have become the default devices for replaying archived websites (Maemura et al. 2018), and the WARC file—which just celebrated its tenth birthday—is the standard file format (ISO 2009). In a similar way, there is also a shared awareness among web archivists that the breadth and depth of archival coverage of the Internet Archive differ from that of national web archives (Masanès 2006), that there are temporal inconsistencies in web archiving (Aubry 2010), and that current web archives do not handle duplicates well (Gomes et al. 2006). This consensus is shared by the web archiving research community, which has spent the past years sharing questions, issues, and methods (Schafer et al. 2016; Winters 2017). Recent work on tool development and standardization of methods is also a result of the important collaboration between web archiving institutions and researchers. Research-driven web services such as the Memento API (van de Sompel et al. 2010) and the Archived Unleashed toolkit (Milligan et al. 2019) are indications of this.

Despite the benefits of the ability to share standards, best practices, and knowl-edge across different communities, the maturation of web archiving as a research field, along with the technological closure of web archiving techniques, might also result in "black-boxing" of some of its processes. Since the fundamental questions have already been considered, researchers do not need to rethink the meaning and methods of web archiving every time they engage in a new research project. The problem with black boxing is that these processes gradually become taken for granted (Brügger and Milligan 2019). After the long process resulting in the consolidation of standards, best practices, shared methods, tools, and knowledge about web archiving and web archive research, there is also room for thinking critically about web archives and for rethinking some of their premises.

The purpose of this chapter is therefore to call for a more critical engagement with web archives. Thinking critically about the archived Web does not entail engaging in a righteous debate discerning right from wrong or discussing what ought to be better. Instead, I propose engaging in an epistemic debate and highlight some of the overlooked aspects of web archiving. Instead of asking "What are the best ways to archive the Web?" or "Why are web archives not widely used?", researchers could begin asking questions about the types of knowledge that web archives produce and reproduce, their embedded values and ideologies, their limits, and artifacts and politics.

To make the case for the necessity of critical web archive research, the following sections of this chapter are structured around three case studies that I conducted between 2014 and 2019. Each case study is based on one critical question about web archives and web archive research and is situated in a different geopolitical and temporal context.

2 Is the Wayback Machine a Black Box? Lessons from North Korea

When researchers view a snapshot of an archived website, they consider this snapshot as evidence of the web's past. The snapshot is an indication that this URL—along with its source code, content, and other elements—was part of the live Web at the time of archiving. But do we know enough about the circumstances that led to the archiving of this URL?

One way of addressing this question is to argue that it does not matter, as long as there is an exact time stamp attached to the archived snapshot. Another way is to acknowledge that the circumstances that lead to the archiving of a specific URL (and not another) are important in understanding how web archives might shape historiographical narratives and knowledge. For example, why are certain websites archived more frequently than others? Why, to date, does the Internet Archive have 60,821 snapshots of the website of the White House, compared to 2619 of the website of the Élysée? Who decided to increase the frequency of the archiving of the Olympic games website in the summer of 2016? Why did the frequency of the archiving of Egyptian newspapers not increase during the Arab Spring in 2011?

Asking these questions leads us to understand that, as in any other institutional archive, web archives may be biased and contain significant knowledge gaps. Therefore, one way of studying web archives critically is to try to find answers which account for inconsistencies. North Korea is a case in point.

North Korea might not be the first place that comes to mind when thinking about web archiving. Very little is known about the Internet in this secluded country. The North Korean Web is one of the smallest national webs: in 2016, a DNS leak in one of the country's root servers exposed that there were only 28 websites registered in the .kp domain. Although the DNS leak was treated as "breaking news", the scope of the .kp domain could have already been estimated using the Internet Archive, which had snapshots of most North Korean websites archived from as early as 2010. How did the Internet Archive "know" about the North Korean Web years before the leak?

Researchers make various assumptions about web archives. I, for example, assumed that one of Wayback Machine's crawlers must have captured the North Korean websites incidentally, by following links from other websites. But when we analyzed the sources that contributed snapshots, we found that knowledge about North Korean websites was mostly contributed to the Internet Archive by experts, archivists, and activists, rather than by automation (Ben-David and Amram 2018).

Another epistemic assumption about the Internet Archive is that web archiving is agnostic to geolocation and geopolitics, but through studying North Korean websites in the Internet Archive, we found that this is not the case. While the process of URL contribution is distributed (anyone can save a page to the archive from anywhere in the world), the archiving itself is centralized and based in the United States. Since there is partial access to North Korean websites from the United States, some of those websites could not be archived, even though they were on the Internet Archive's seed list. Put differently, the archivability of websites depends on geopolitics. The effect of geopolitics on web archiving leads us to the second set of critical questions that can be asked about web archives.

3   What Does the Web Remember of Its Deleted Past? Lessons from Yugoslavia

Yugoslavia is a country which was part of the web's history, but no longer exists. In 1989, the Socialist Federal Republic of Yugoslavia (SFRY) joined the Internet after the delegation of its country code Top Level Domain (ccTLD): .yu. Two years later, the country dissolved, and gradually, the countries that were formerly part of the SFRY received their own, new, national domains: Croatia and Slovenia were the first, and North Macedonia was the last. Throughout this time, the .yu domain continued to work—first as the official domain of the FRY and, then, as a historical digital remnant of both the Web and Yugoslavia's part of it (Ben-David 2016).

All these years of war, bloodshed and displacement are a crucial part of human history. These Yugoslav websites also documented a crucial part of the web's history, as it was considered "the first Internet War", involving online reporting and the spread of information warfare (Keenan 2001). But all of the digital remains of this important period are gone, due to unrelated Internet governance policies. In 2010, the .yu domain was removed from the Internet's domain name servers. This means that even if a .yu website is still hosted on a server, it is no longer part of the Internet root, and therefore cannot be found.

Thus, through the lens of the history of the .yu domain, the critical question to be asked about web archiving is: "What does the Web remember of its deleted past?" Of course, the Wayback Machine captured many of the .yu websites in real time. The problem was (and to some extent still is) that user access to web archives assumes that one knows, and subsequently types, a URL, to view its archived snapshots. Four years after the deletion of the .yu domain, it was nearly impossible to use the live Web to find Yugoslav websites. Subsequently, the Yugoslav websites that were archived in real time could not be reached, for all information about their past URLs was removed from the Internet.

Eventually, a list of URLs was found offline, which opened up a gateway to reconstructing a considerable portion of the archived Yugoslav websites in the Internet Archive. Yet, when I visualized the development of the hyperlinked structure of the reconstructed domain over time, I noticed that the domain became significantly interlinked only after the fall of the Milosevic regime, and most significantly after it became the domain of Serbia and Montenegro. That is, the structural evolution of the national domain indicates that sovereignty is inscribed into the politics of Internet governance and subsequently also affects the ability of the Web to remember its past. While the question of sovereignty is less significant for stable, wealthy countries, it seems that national web histories of countries in transition are particularly vulnerable.

The consequences of the inscription of sovereignty in web archives are even more grave for Kosovo, a country that, due to a Russian veto at the UN, does not have a ccTLD (Ben-David 2019a, b). That is, if it was at least possible to develop methods for reconstructing the Yugoslav Web from the Internet Archive through the domain suffix, it is nearly impossible to identify a Kosovar website on the live Web, and that has severe consequences for the preservation of Kosovar web history.

4   What Informs Web Archiving Policies? Lessons from Gaza

The premise of web archiving is that it captures discrete URLs in real time. Since preserving the entire Web is technically impossible and web archiving, in general, is costly, over the years most national web archiving institutions have developed policies that translate their mission to archive the Web into specific technical parameters. These policies often address issues such as the scope of archiving (full domain or special collections?), the boundaries of archiving (everything in the country code top-level domain? websites in a national language hosted elsewhere on the Web?), the frequency of archiving, and so on.

In most cases, this "translation" results in forming "seed lists", or starting points from which web archiving begins. Given the technical complexity of web archiving at scale, it is almost impossible to change these seed lists in real time.

The results, however, are web archives comprised of distinct units: URLs that have been preserved as a result of a given policy and a specific method, at a specific point in time, and for a specific purpose, in order to preserve something that is relevant to a particular country. Are current methods for informing us about web archives sufficient if we are to use the archived Web as a significant source for historical research? What methods can be used to understand the impact of web archiving policies on shaping historiographical narratives, or to critique them?

Recently, my colleagues and I developed a method for building retrospective special collections of URLs around a past issue, or event, across various web platforms and national cultures (Ben-David 2019a, b). Apart from the technical challenges related to archiving the Web in retrospect, which are addressed elsewhere, the method aims to challenge the traditional sources that inform web archives. Most national web archives use seed lists as starting points for domain harvests. However, seed lists are agnostic to the wider context in which URLs are shared and discussed on the Web. With the growing platformization of the Web, information no longer travels across URLs but is rather confined to platform boundaries. Fixed seed lists are also agnostic to dynamic events that may coincide with routine crawls, but were not purposefully captured in real time. A cross-platform approach to web archiving addresses these problems, by incorporating the cultural context that comes along with how websites were distributed across various web platforms and at the same time taking into account cultural differences in URL sharing preferences. The case study we used for building a cross-platform archive was the 2014 war in Gaza.

The war, which lasted 50 days in the summer of 2014 and cost the lives of many Palestinians and Israelis, did not only take place on the ground. On social media, the fighting parties were heavily engaged in information warfare campaigns, and millions of users from around the world were involved in angry debates. News websites were reporting the events, pushing breaking news alerts around the clock, and on Wikipedia, edit wars were taking place about how to properly name and document the unfolding event. However, the majority of online activity relating to the war was not archived.

To reconstruct a cross-platform archive of the war, we used Wikipedia as the authoritative source for identifying the names of the war in 49 languages and used these as keywords for querying and scraping data and URLs from Twitter, YouTube, and Google Search. Using this method, we collected 118,508 unique URIs and relevant metadata, carbon-dated to the period of the military operation, in 49 languages from 5692 domain suffixes. Interestingly, we found significant cultural differences in URL sharing practices across platforms: while there are relatively few references in Arabic on Wikipedia and YouTube, Arabic language speakers mostly took to Twitter to discuss the issue and report the events. By contrast, URLs in Hebrew are mostly published by media outlets, which explains the relatively high proportion of these on Google and YouTube. We also found that some platforms are more prone to link rot than others—especially because of the role URL shortening services play in facilitating link sharing on social media.

These cultural and platform differences are crucial for informing us and thinking about web archives. Current web crawling methods are blind to the rich cultural and temporal dynamics that characterize the Web and are poor in contextual metadata. It would be useful for web archiving institutions to first identify and understand cultural and platform differences, before deciding on how, when, or where to archive the Web. A cross-cultural and cross-platform approach to web archiving also requires web archives to explore beyond their comfort zones. As we have seen with Yugoslavia, North Korea, Kosovo, and Gaza, the standard practice of thinking about web archiving from a national perspective might be a curatorial and institutional solution that stands in stark contrast to the global and networked structure of the open Web.

5 Conclusions

Web archives are the web's memory organs, and as such, they are breathing, dynamic, and constantly evolving. Consequently, web archives entail both a promise and a challenge for historical research. In this chapter, I attempted to take the promise with a pinch of salt, by arguing for the necessity of asking critical questions about web archives as epistemic agents: How is knowledge produced and by whom? What was not or could not have been preserved? What are the sources that inform web history, and how may each source shape a different historiographical narrative? To make the case for these critical questions, I presented examples from contested areas. Arguably, these sites of contestation invite us to think about web archiving critically, for it is at the periphery rather than the center where some of the assumptions we make when archiving the Web and when studying web archives no longer hold.

Critical web archive research may be useful to both researchers and practitioners of web archives: it may encourage them to think more reflexively about web archives as active agents, which have embedded values, biases, and politics, and about how web archiving techniques and policies are canonizing very specific ways of knowing the web's past.

References

Aubry S (2010) Introducing web archives as a new library service: the experience of the National Library of France. Liber Quarterly, Open Access journal of the Association of European Research Libraries, http-persistent

Ben-David A (2016) What does the web remember of its deleted past? An archival reconstruction of the former Yugoslav top-level domain. New Media Soc 18(7):1103–1119

Ben-David A (2019a) National web histories at the fringe of the web: Palestine, Kosovo, and the quest for online self-determination. In: Brügger N, Laursen D (eds) The historical web and digital humanities: the case of national web domains. Routledge, Abingdon, pp 89–109

Ben-David A (2019b) 2014 not found: a cross-platform approach to retrospective web archiving. Internet Hist. https://doi.org/10.1080/24701475.2019.1654290

Ben-David A, Amram A (2018) The internet archive and the socio-technical construction of historical facts. Internet Hist 2(1–2):179–201

Brügger N (2018) The archived web: doing history in the digital age. MIT Press, Cambridge

Brügger N, Goggin G, Milligan I, Schafer V (2018) Internet histories. Routledge

Brügger N, Laursen D (2019) The historical web and digital humanities: the case of national web domains. Routledge

Brügger N, Milligan I (2018) The SAGE handbook of web history. SAGE

Brügger N, Milligan I (2019) Internet histories and computational methods: a "round-doc" discussion. Internet Hist:1–21

Costa M, Gomes D, Silva MJ (2017) The evolution of web archiving. Int J Digit Libr 18(3):191–205

Costa M, Silva MJ (2010) Understanding the information needs of web archive users. In: Proceedings of the 10th international web archiving workshop, 9(16): 6

Dougherty M, Meyer ET, Madsen CM, Van den Heuvel C, Thomas A, Wyatt S (2010) Researcher engagement with web archives: state of the art. Joint Information Systems Committee Report

Goggin G, McLelland M (2017) The Routledge companion to global internet histories. Taylor & Francis

Gomes D, Miranda J, Costa M (2011) A survey on web archiving initiatives. In: International conference on theory and practice of digital libraries. Springer, Berlin, pp 408–420

Gomes D, Santos AL, Silva MJ (2006) Managing duplicates in a web archive. In: Proceedings of the 2006 ACM symposium on applied computing, pp 818–825. ACM

Hård M (1994) Technology as practice: local and global closure processes in diesel-engine design. Soc Stud Sci 24(3):549–585

International Organization for Standardization (ISO) (2009) 28500: 2009 Information and documentation-WARC file format. International Organization for Standardization

Keenan T (2001) Looking like flames and falling like stars: Kosovo, 'the first internet war'. Soc Ident 7(4):539–550

Maemura E, Worby N, Milligan I, Becker C (2018) If these crawls could talk: studying and documenting web archives provenance. J Assoc Inf Sci Technol 69(10):1223–1233

Masanès J (2006) Web archiving: issues and methods. In: Web archiving. Springer, Berlin, pp 1–53

Milligan I, Casemajor N, Fritz S, Lin J, Ruest N, Weber MS, Worby N (2019) Building community and tools for analyzing web archives through datathons

Mohr G, Stack M, Rnitovic I, Avery D, Kimpton M (2004) Introduction to Heritrix. In: 4th international web archiving workshop

Niu J (2012) An overview of web archiving. D-Lib Mag 18(3/4)

Schafer V, Musiani F, Borelli M (2016) Negotiating the web of the past. Fr Media Res

van de Sompel H, Nelson M, Sanderson R, Balakireva L, Ainsworth S, Shankar H (2010) Memento: time travel for the web. Computer science presentations. Retrieved from https://digitalcommons.odu.edu/computerscience_presentations/18

Winters J (2017) Breaking in to the mainstream: demonstrating the value of internet (and web) histories. Internet Hist 1(1–2):173–179

Exploring Online Diasporas: London's French and Latin American Communities in the UK Web Archive

Saskia Huc-Hepher and Naomi Wells

Abstract The aim of the UK Web Archive to collect and preserve the entire UK web domain ensures that it is able to reflect the diversity of voices and communities present on the open Web, including migrant communities who sustain a presence across digital and physical environments. At the same time, patterns of wider social and political exclusion, as well as the use of languages other than English, mean these communities' web presence is often overlooked in more generic and Anglophone web archiving and (re)searching practices.

1 Introduction

In light of the valuable, and potentially neglected, histories of migrant communities recorded in the open Web, this chapter focuses on the analysis of archived web materials included in two special collections developed by the researchers on French and Latin American communities in London. As well as addressing the relationship between these collections and the communities represented, we will draw on examples of archived web materials to illustrate the insights they offer into these communities, into local and national histories and into the wider history of the Web. We will highlight the different types of web objects available for analysis, from individual blogs to collective community sites. Paying specific attention to evolving language and translation strategies over time, we will also address the complex interweaving of different modes of communication and representation, including visual and other media.

S. Huc-Hepher (✉) · N. Wells
School of Humanities, University of Westminster, London, UK

Institute of Modern Languages Research, School of Advanced Study, University of London, London, UK
e-mail: S.V.Huc-Hepher@westminster.ac.uk; naomi.wells@sas.ac.uk

© Springer Nature Switzerland AG 2021
D. Gomes et al. (eds.), *The Past Web*,
https://doi.org/10.1007/978-3-030-63291-5_15

These examples demonstrate the specific skillsets researchers of languages and cultures can bring to web archives research, as well as what can be gained by broadening our traditional objects of analysis. Through the development and analysis of diasporic web collections, the chapter illustrates the vital histories we can excavate from the archived Web, ensuring against the threat of collective amnesia for communities often overlooked in national archives and collections.

The UK Web Archive is aimed at collecting and preserving the entire UK Web (the .uk country code top-level domain), primarily through automated web crawling which can capture the multiplicity of voices and communities present on the open Web. The scale of the Archive, however, means that the wider societal invisibility of specific groups risks being perpetuated by more generic or Anglophone (re)searching or curating practices. Thematic special collections do, however, allow curators and researchers to draw attention to web materials that risk being overlooked, such as those produced by migrant communities who have historically been marginalised from national archives and collections.

This chapter focuses on two such collections: the London French Special Collection (LFSC) curated by Saskia Huc-Hepher primarily between 2012 and 2014 and, following that model, the Latin Americans in London Collection begun in 2018 by Naomi Wells. After introducing the wider context of the "communities" represented in these collections, the researchers analyse specific archived web materials to illustrate what they reveal about these communities and the cultural and sociopolitical contexts in which they operate. At the same time, the analysis provides insight into the wider history of the Web by addressing how members of these communities make strategic and creative uses of the rapidly evolving affordances of the Web. Drawing primarily on qualitative and ethnographic approaches in the fields of applied and sociolinguistics, and with particular attention to multimodality and multilingualism, these examples illustrate ways of engaging with archived Web materials that pay close attention to the linguistic and cultural practices of their creators.

2   Archiving and Representing Communities

The inclusion of "diasporic" collections in a national web archive is an opportunity to disrupt homogenising, monolingual and territorially bounded national narratives and representations, responding also to the UK Web Archive's key mission to "reflect the diversity of lives" in the UK (10 October 2018). It is, however, important to highlight the heterogeneity of the collections themselves, both in terms of reflecting internal differences within these communities and differences between communities. In the case of Latin Americans in London, for example, there are evident differences between those originating from different areas of the continent, not only in terms of nationality but also in terms of class and race. At the same time, the collection is intended to reflect the undeniably powerful sense of collective Latin American identity in London, reflected most clearly by the successful efforts of a coalition of Latin American organisations to have Latin Americans officially recognised as an "ethnic group" by a number of London councils since 2012 (Berg 2019, p. 191). Despite being a relatively recent community and initially lacking visibility in the city, it was in 2013 the fastest growing community in the capital (McIlwaine and Bunge 2016), and this is reflected in the growing attention to the social and political issues facing it in local and national media. Web archives allow us to trace how the community has become increasingly visible and consolidated its presence both online and offline, particularly as it has developed largely in conjunction with the mass uptake of digital technologies and media in recent decades.

The French diasporic presence in London is, in contrast, more fragmented in nature. As previously argued (Huc-Hepher 2015), the very concept of building a French community micro-archive (Brügger 2005) is something of a misnomer, for the "community" seems not to perceive itself as such. While research participants acknowledge that a French community exists, most feel it corresponds to a socio-economic elite with which they do not identify (Huc-Hepher and Drake 2013; Huc-Hepher 2016), based in and around affluent South Kensington (South West London) and home to prestigious French diplomatic, cultural and educational institutions. In this "expat" "community" construct, Frenchness is inextricably entangled with notions of Whiteness (Beaman 2018) and wealth and thus constitutes a homogenous imaginary that disregards the demographic and topological heterogeneity of the contemporary French presence in London, or more accurately *French-speaking* presence. There is consequently a paradox intrinsic to this "presence", being highly visible in the physical urban environment—particularly South Kensington—and representing considerable cultural capital (Kelly 2016) in the "host" imagination yet being invisible as a migrant community per se, both in top-down political conceptions and in bottom-up understandings of belonging to a diasporic collective, as Berthomière's reference to a "French what?" illustrates (2012, p. 2). The French "community" artifice is complicated further by negative associations with "communitarianism" imported in the migrant consciousness from France, where an "imperialism of the universal" reigns (Wolfreys 2018, p. 97), founded on the core values of *égalité* and *fraternité* and resulting in resistance to the community epithet.

It is these implicated collective-identity undercurrents that the curator of the London French Special Collection needed to navigate and which are challenged by the semiotic analysis below. And it is through both curators' cultural, linguistic and ethnographic knowledge of the French and Latin American communities alike that they have been able to contribute positively to the "making of presence" (Sassen 2013, p. 217) in a memory institution of international repute.

3 Researching and Analysing Diasporic Web Materials

3.1 Example 1: Blogs in the London French Special Collection

Alongside the role of the LFSC as a means of enhancing community identity, it constitutes a rich corpus for the purposes of ethnographic research. Taking "a micro-historical approach" (Winters 2017, p. 241) towards this multi-level "diasberspace" enables the researcher to gain immersive and observational knowledge of the community from the fundamentally institutional or corporate to the highly individualised. Indeed, the Bourdieusian model adopted for the original curation exercise (Huc-Hepher 2015) produced a multifaceted dataset comprising web objects of various genres and types, including macro-level London-French cultural, religious, educational and governmental websites, together with meso-level commercial, philanthropic and local media sites. Yet, at the most personal, micro-level of the collection were blogs, which are the focus of this subsection, given the first-person, diary-like insights they provide (Weber 2017).

While readers may question the validity of using web archives to study blogs, given their inbuilt archival affordances, external collections offer multiple advantages. The most obvious and crucial is their safeguarding against obsolescence, particularly important given the recent "cybermigration" of large numbers of blogs to social media platforms (Lobbé 2018b, p. 131) or, in the case of the French in London, "Brexit"-motivated return migration. Second, they preserve socio-culturally meaningful and motivated design choices (Kress 2010) which are lost to updates on the live Web as the technical affordances of the blog develop. Third, they provide evidence of self-editing that can be revealing of otherwise elusive transformations to the blogger's identity. Therefore, by monitoring blogs over time in web archives, as opposed to the integrated micro-archive and taking a fine-grained multimodal approach, changes providing semiotic insights into the migrant experience are made manifest. For instance, by examining modes such as layout, colour, typography and language in archived versions of the aperobloglondon.wordpress.blog.com site, multiple meanings relating to community networks, audience and positioning within the London habitat emerge. These are discussed in detail in Huc-Hepher (2016). However, it is useful to note that since writing that article and consulting additional archived versions, including a more recent incarnation of the URL (aperobloglondon.com), several significant transformations have taken place.

In the snapshot of the blog's landing-page banner archived in 2010 (Fig. 1), we find a rather stereotypical photographic image of London at the time, in which the world-renowned St Paul's Cathedral and the City of London dominate. However, unlike the version previously analysed (Huc-Hepher 2016), the iconic image is disrupted by the superimposition of incongruously large, "hand-drawn" images of alcoholic beverages. These are coherent with the title and purpose of the blog—namely, as a forum to bring together French bloggers living in London for regular "apéros" (aperitifs)—but also offer insights into belonging to a wider community of blogging practice (Wenger 2004) and, as in the later banner captured

Fig. 1 Banner captured on 15 October 2010 and retrieved from https://web.archive.org/web/20101015065548/http://aperobloglondon.wordpress.com/

Fig. 2 Banner included in LFSC and captured on 2 March 2013 and retrieved from https://web.archive.org/web/20130302094706/http://aperobloglondon.com/

in 2013 (Fig. 2), into the incorporation of typically British (according to research participants) eccentricity and humour.

In the 2013 version, the iconic photographic image is replaced by indexical signs which point to the London environment less literally, serving instead to reinforce the message written playfully in rhyming French at the bottom of the banner: "A pied, en vélo, en métro ou en tacot, pourvu qu'on arrive a l'apéro!" [On foot, by bike, by tube or car, as long as we make it to the bar]. The absurdly magnified pint of beer remains, however, in central position. This not only visually underlines the light-hearted tone communicated in the text through a process of intermodal semiosis but demonstrates habituation to London (drinking) customs and embodiment of local characteristics (perceived sense of humour) while serving as a constant in the affirmation of a collective London-French blogging identity through its reappearance in the various incarnations of the blog over time. So, despite the banner no longer featuring in the blog from 2013 onwards, continuity and oneness are maintained through a small logo (Fig. 3), whose semiotic orchestration acts as a nod to the blog's previous identity. In Figs. 2 and 3, the exclusively London-French particularity of the blog is further signalled through the use of the French language. This includes colloquial in-group markers like "tacot" (slang for car) and is more subtly signalled through the font-type itself, which is implicitly embedded in the bloggers' (rhetor and reader) originary culture, recalling the cursive handwriting found in childhood educational settings (Huc-Hepher 2016).

However, perhaps the most telling feature of the successive multimodal reinventions of the aperobloglondon site is its interpersonal function within the network of London-French blogs contained in the LFSC. The same semiotically loaded comic-strip-type imagery, (typically French) cursive writing, (typically English)

Fig. 3 Blog logo first captured as a replacement for the banner on 24 March 2013 and lastly on 12 October 2016, i.e. 4 months after the EU Membership Referendum, retrieved from https://web.archive.org/web/20130324162858/http://aperobloglondon.com/

Fig. 4 Images in the charlottedujour.com blog (captured only 15 times, between 28 June 2015 and 30 November 2016, i.e. 5 months after the EU Membership Referendum) retrieved from https://web.archive.org/web/20160307014101/http://www.charlottedujour.com/blog-charlotte-du-jour/

light-heartedness, French-English translanguaging (Li 2018) and preoccupation with comestible elements of the London habitat are found across multiple blogs. Compare, for instance, the London taxi from the second archived version of the Apéroblog banner with that of the Charlotte du Jour blog illustration in Fig. 4 and the cursive font, humorous wording and mixing of French and English (the speech bubble in French and the laptop text in English), together with the typically "English" large mug of tea/coffee depicted. The same "hand-drawn" and food-centred imagery is found in the Pauline à la Crème anglaise and Londres Calling blogs, as well as the translanguaging at sentence level: "Si si! C'est *British* et c'est délicieux" and "Londres Calling" itself. This blending of French and English language and of cultural referents, such as the allusion to "Pauline with custard" (literally *English* cream) in Fig. 5 or the Marmite, jam sandwiches and Victoria Sponge in Fig. 6, that is, artefactual (Pahl and Rowsell 2011) elements of the host culture expressed through the quintessentially French mode of the graphic novel, known as the "ninth art" in France, and epitomising the prominence of the

Fig. 5 Pauline à la crème anglaise—significantly, her most recent post on the live Web again dates back to 2016. Retrieved from http://paulinealacremefr.blogspot.com/ on 15 June 2019

Fig. 6 Londres Calling blog banner, retrieved from https://www.webarchive.org.uk/wayback/en/archive/20160107232406/http://londrescalling.canalblog.com/

culinary in French—national and regional—culture, is testimony to the common ambivalence of the bloggers' diasporic experience.

As a corpus, therefore, the blogs function both intratextually, as indicators of the bloggers' transnational positioning, straddling French and London cultural and linguistic spaces, and intertextually as semiotic markers of a community of practice. They tap into childhood memories peculiar to this group of blog(ger)s and speak to "insider" community members through multimodal meaning-making that would elude Franco-French and English visitors alike. Significantly, the blogs bear witness to a *London-French* "common-unity" of practice that defies the South Kensington myth, as well as our research participants' rejection of the "community" designation. Equally importantly, their scrutiny within web archives, as opposed to the integrated blog archive, has enabled the monitoring of identity transformation and reproduction over time and defied the inescapable mortality of the blogs. That is, although the Pauline à la crème anglaise blog is available on the live Web, it has not been updated since 2016, and all the others are effectively "dead blogs" (Lobbé 2018a, p. 1), since none are accessible via their original URL. In the case of Apéroblog London, even in its updated aperobloglondon.com website form, it has ceased to exist as the London-French blogger meet-up site it had been since its 2010

Fig. 7 Aperobloglondon in its new Japanese incarnation, first captured on 6 June 2017, retrieved from https://web.archive.org/web/20170606214545/https://www.aperobloglondon.com/

launch and, at some point between October 2016 and June 2017, was reincarnated (Fig. 7) as a commercial food and fashion site in Japanese.

3.2 Example 2: Latin American Community Organisation Websites

One of the distinguishing features of diasporic web materials is the presence of content in multiple languages, reflecting the transnational trajectories of migrant communities and the consequent ability to draw from across a range of linguistic and cultural fields (Li and Zhu 2013, p. 532; Vertovec 2009, p. 7). The complex linguistic repertoires of these communities should not, however, be equated with a confused or chaotic use of language, but rather research in applied and sociolinguistics has illustrated how individuals draw strategically and creatively from their range of linguistic resources for the specific context(s) and task(s) at hand. The strategic nature of these choices is illustrated in the evolving language choices on the websites of cross-Latin American community organisations.

These organisations generally serve the dual function of providing a collective voice for the community, as in the campaign for recognition, and of offering vital Spanish, and to a lesser extent Portuguese, language services for community members. This dual intra- and intercommunity role is reflected in the presence of English, Spanish and in some cases Portuguese on these organisations' websites. Beyond noticing or counting these languages, qualitative research emphasises what can be revealed by looking more closely at the relationships between languages on the page (Androutsopoulos 2006; Sebba 2013). This is illustrated on the website of one of the oldest Latin American organisations in the UK, the Indoamerican Refugee and Migrant Organisation (IRMO).

On the earliest capture of their website (IRMO 10 August 2004), while both Spanish and English are used on the homepage, Spanish is clearly dominant. The main heading, signalled by a larger and uppercase type, is written only in Spanish, as is the description of the organisation's purpose below. Further down the page, we find parallel texts first in Spanish and followed by English, and the website menu also appears with parallel texts, although with the order reversed and English first. Importantly though, we do not find any mixing of languages, but instead the different languages are marked visually as distinct, in the first case through a change in font colour and on the menu with the Spanish italicised. This clear separation of languages is common in written texts, in contrast to the mixing more common in speech, and illustrates the online continuation of the prescriptive language norms associated with writing (Weth and Juffermans 2018, p. 8). The use of italicised Spanish on the menu, despite being the more dominant language on the page, also indicates an awareness of its inescapable role as "other" in the UK context. These visual distinctions between languages illustrate the importance of attention to the visual and graphic elements of multilingual texts (Sebba 2013, p. 102).

While the use of English first in the menu appears to prioritise that language, on the subpages in the archive Spanish remains dominant, with some information provided only in Spanish. This signals that the primary function of the website is to communicate with the Spanish-speaking users of the organisation's services. At the same time, the inconsistent switches between just Spanish and providing parallel language content point to uncertainty concerning appropriate language choices, as is also signalled by shifts between informal and formal registers in both English and Spanish. These inconsistent register and translation choices indicate the emergent nature of this genre of text and the absence of established conventions in these still relatively early years of institutional websites, at least for smaller organisations.

Jumping forward a decade, however, we find in 2014 a more formal description of the organisation in English, as well as a flag icon seemingly linking through to a Spanish-language version of the site (IRMO 22 July 2014).[1] Providing parallel language versions is associated with the now-familiar commercial and institutional practice of "web localisation" (Jiménez-Crespo 2013), whereby companies translate and adapt the content of their websites for distinct audiences or markets. What is interesting though is that this strategy is relatively short-lived, and a year later the

---

[1]The flag used is the Spanish national flag, despite the target audience being those from Latin American. This highlights how the community's strong sense of collective identity is not connected to a single nation or associated national symbols.

link to a Spanish language version has disappeared (IRMO 1 November 2015). In the most recently archived capture of the website, the content on both the homepage and subpages is almost entirely in English (IRMO 17 May 2019).

This switch to content predominantly in English is a trend noticeable across the websites of the primary Latin American community organisations in London. A simplistic explanation might be that this is a community shifting to English over time as it becomes more "integrated". This is, however, to presume that online language practices merely reflect offline practices (Lee 2017, p. 5). In fact, as a rapidly growing community, there continue to be large numbers of new arrivals, and, most importantly, these organisations' main function continues to be to provide services in Spanish (and/or Portuguese) to recent arrivals.

This leaves us with the puzzling situation of organisations whose primary users speak predominantly Spanish and yet with websites almost entirely in English. To understand this strategy, it is vital to remember that online language choices respond to a multiplicity of factors, such as the target audience, the platform and the situated language ecology of the individual or community (Lee 2017, pp. 34–35). While it is not easy to pin down how each factor enters into play, in this case, it is important to consider this specific genre of online text, as well as the wider sociopolitical context of the community. To begin with the genre of public-facing websites of third sector organisations, it is important to note that the point in the archives when we see the shift to English at least partially coincides with the appearance of Twitter and Facebook links, signalling the arrival of Web 2.0. The more interactive affordances of social media undoubtedly provide more effective platforms for direct communications with service users in Spanish, illustrating how language choice intersects with platform and media choice.[2] This reveals how the genre and purpose of public websites have changed, as some of the functions they previously served have been rendered obsolete or shifted to other platforms and media.

At the same time, given technological developments in relation to translation, it remains surprising not to find multiple language versions of these websites. While there is a question of human and financial resource for largely voluntary organisations, it is also vital to think about the purpose of web localisation. In commercial settings, where research on this subject has focused, localisation may appear to be aimed at encouraging closer or more dialogical relationships with customers who speak other languages. However, as Cronin argues, there is an underlying paradox here:

> The dominant ideology of the dialogical implicit in multilingual provision ("speaking the language of the customer") is undercut by the cost imperative to minimize human interaction ("the most expensive resource in the service organization"). [. . .] You can have any language you want . . . so long as it is, preferably, not spoken by a human being. (Cronin 2013, pp. 95–96)

---

[2] As illustrated in research on language use in social media (Tagg 2015), we would also expect to find more examples of language mixing in these more informal and in some cases private communicative spaces.

This is important in relation to a choice not to provide translations for Spanish-speaking service users, particularly when we consider the only information consistently translated on this and similar websites, which are the opening hours and directions to the organisations' physical buildings. This indicates precisely the opposite motivations to those of commercial web localisation efforts, which is that they explicitly prioritise face-to-face communications with their users in a physical location.

This prioritisation of physical community co-presence points to the potential risks of digital substitution and that external funders may see providing Spanish-language information or services online as an inexpensive alternative to sustaining these organisations' physical buildings. This is connected also to the primary social and political issue facing the community in recent years, which is the increasing threat of closure to Latin American community spaces in London (Cock 2011). This illustrates the importance of contextualising online language strategies in relation to the wider sociopolitical context.

Rather than being aimed at service users, the purpose of these predominantly English-language websites is to present a more impersonal and professional image to funders, as signalled by the prominent links to "Donate" on this and similar websites. The use of English, and the absence of language mixing, is likely also connected to the organisation being required to prove its role as a legitimate actor in the public sphere where proficiency in English must be explicitly displayed. At the same time, the use of English signals the strategic deployment of language to establish the community's presence within a predominantly Anglophone public sphere. While there may remain a paradox in delimiting transnational communities within national archival boundaries, ensuring these materials remain visible within the UK Web Archive acknowledges this explicit desire to be recognised as legitimate actors in the UK's public sphere.

4   Conclusions

This chapter has demonstrated the multifarious value of community-specific collections within larger web archives. In particular, close analysis of these web objects reveals more complex motivations and choices than those initially apparent, whether regarding the negation of a collective identity or the strategic use of language in response to wider sociopolitical circumstances. Illustrating the value of working with a defined archival corpus, underlying cultural meanings have emerged through the analysis of the complex semiotic interplay within, between and beyond the different resources. The collections also make visible the multilingual, transnational presence of the communities in ways which blur the boundaries between the physical, the digital and the imagined, as well as disrupting nationally bounded narratives through the purposeful preservation of diasporic web materials within the UK Web Archive.

In relation to the wider applicability of this research, we have illustrated how close attention to multilingualism and multimodality in archived web materials offers web historians and archival researchers an alternative entry point to understanding the history of the Web, while web archives present contemporary (socio)linguists with a vital resource for overcoming an overly synchronic focus on "language in the moment". We have also revealed how diasporic web materials offer insights into distinct, bottom-up, multicultural histories of the Web, which constitute important counternarratives to those of larger, more commercial—often monolingual and Anglophone—entities that have traditionally dominated the literature. In this way, the community collections have given a multilingual voice to comparatively "quiet" communities and thereby ensured that their shared "city has speech" (Sassen 2013, p. 214).

References

Androutsopoulos J (2006) Multilingualism, diaspora, and the internet: codes and identities on German-based diaspora websites. J Socioling 10:520–547. https://doi.org/10.1111/j.1467-9841.2006.00291.x

Beaman J (2018) Are French people white?: towards an understanding of whiteness in Republican France. Identities:1–17. https://doi.org/10.1080/1070289X.2018.1543831

Berg ML (2019) Super-diversity, austerity, and the production of precarity: Latin Americans in London. Crit Soc Policy 39:184–204. https://doi.org/10.1177/0261018318790744

Berthomière W (2012) A French what? À la recherche d'une diaspora française. Premiers éléments d'enquête au sein de l'espace internet. e-Diasporas Atlas:1–16

Brügger N (2005) Archiving websites: general considerations and strategies. The Centre for Internet Research, Aarhus

Cock JC (2011) Latin American commercial spaces and the formation of ethnic publics in London: the case of the Elephant and Castle. In: McIlwaine C (ed) Cross-border migration among Latin Americans: European perspectives and beyond. Palgrave Macmillan US, New York, pp 175–195

Cronin M (2013) Translation in the digital age. Routledge, Abingdon

Huc-Hepher S (2015) Big web data, small focus: an ethnosemiotic approach to culturally themed selective web archiving. Big Data Soc 2. https://doi.org/10.1177/2053951715595823

Huc-Hepher S (2016) The material dynamics of a London-French blog: a multimodal reading of migrant habitus. Modern Lang Open 0. https://doi.org/10.3828/mlo.v0i0.91

Huc-Hepher S, Drake H (2013) From the 16ieme to South Ken? A study of the contemporary French population in London. In: Kelly D, Cornick M (eds) A history of the French in London: liberty, equality, opportunity. Institute of Historical Research, School of Advanced Study, University of London, London, pp 391–430

IRMO (2004) [Indoamerican Refugee and Migrant Organization] (captured 10 August 2004) Homepage. Retrieved from https://web.archive.org/web/20040810033416/http://www.irmo.org.uk:80/

IRMO (2014) [Indoamerican Refugee and Migrant Organization] (captured 22 July 2014) Homepage. Retrieved from https://www.webarchive.org.uk/wayback/archive/20140722213214/http://irmo.org.uk/

IRMO (2015) [Indoamerican Refugee and Migrant Organization] (captured 1 November 2015) Homepage. Retrieved from https://www.webarchive.org.uk/wayback/archive/20151101034931/http://irmo.org.uk/

IRMO (2019) [Indoamerican Refugee and Migrant Organization] (captured 9 January 2019) Homepage. Retrieved from https://web.archive.org/web/20190109101811/http://irmo.org.uk/

Jiménez-Crespo MA (2013) Translation and web localization. Routledge

Kelly DJ (2016) A migrant culture on display: the French migrant and French gastronomy in London (19th to 21st centuries). Modern Languages Open 0. doi: https://doi.org/10.3828/mlo.v0i0.148

Kress G (2010) Multimodality: a social semiotic approach to contemporary communication. Taylor & Francis

Lee C (2017) Multilingualism online. Routledge, London ; New York

Li W (2018) Translanguaging as a practical theory of language. Appl Linguis 39:9–30. https://doi.org/10.1093/applin/amx039

Li W, Zhu H (2013) Translanguaging identities and ideologies: creating transnational space through flexible multilingual practices amongst Chinese university students in the UK. Appl Linguis 34:516–535. https://doi.org/10.1093/applin/amt022

Lobbé Q (2018a) Archives, fragments Web et diasporas: pour une exploration désagrégée de corpus d'archives Web liées aux représentations en ligne des diasporas. Université Paris-Saclay

Lobbé Q (2018b) Where the dead blogs are. a disaggregated exploration of web archives to reveal extinct online collectives. Hamilton, New Zealand, pp. 1–12

McIlwaine, C, Bunge, D (2016) Towards visibility: the Latin American community in London. Queen Mary University of London; Latin American Women's Rights Service; Trust for London, London

Pahl KH, Rowsell J (2011) Artifactual critical literacy: a new perspective for literacy education. Berkel Rev Educ 2. https://doi.org/10.5070/B82110050

Sassen S (2013) Does the city have speech? Publ Cult 25:209–221. https://doi.org/10.1215/08992363-2020557

Sebba M (2013) Multilingualism in written discourse: an approach to the analysis of multilingual texts. Int J Biling 17:97–118. https://doi.org/10.1177/1367006912438301

Tagg C (2015) Language, business and superdiversity: a report on social media across case studies. Working Papers in Translanguaging and Translation: 1–38

UK Web Archive (2018) (captured 10 October 2018) Homepage. Retrieved from https://www.webarchive.org.uk/wayback/archive/20181001033408/https://www.webarchive.org.uk/ukwa/

Vertovec S (2009) Transnationalism. Routledge, London ; New York

Weber MS (2017) The tumultuous history of news on the web. In: Brügger N, Schroeder R (eds) The web as history: using web archives to understand the past and present. University College Press, London, pp 83–100

Wenger E (2004) Knowledge management as a doughnut. Ivey Bus J

Weth C, Juffermans K (2018) The tyranny of writing in language and society. In: Weth C, Juffermans K (eds) The tyranny of writing: ideologies of the written word. Bloomsbury Academic, London, pp 1–18

Winters J (2017) Coda: web archives for humanities research – some reflections. In: Brügger N, Schroeder R (eds) The web as history: using web archives to understand the past and present. University College Press, London, pp 238–247

Wolfreys J (2018) Republic of Islamophobia: the rise of respectable racism in France. Hurst & Company, London

Platform and App Histories: Assessing Source Availability in Web Archives and App Repositories

Anne Helmond and Fernando van der Vlist

Abstract In this chapter, we discuss the research opportunities for historical studies of apps and platforms by focusing on their distinctive characteristics and material traces. We demonstrate the value and explore the utility and breadth of web archives and software repositories for building corpora of archived platform and app sources. Platforms and apps notoriously resist archiving due to their ephemerality and continuous updates. As a consequence, their histories are being overwritten with each update rather than written and preserved. We present a method to assess the availability of archived web sources for social media platforms and apps across the leading web archives and app repositories. Additionally, we conduct a comparative source set availability analysis to establish how, and how well, various source sets are represented across web archives. Our preliminary results indicate that despite the challenges of social media and app archiving, many material traces of platforms and apps are in fact well preserved. We understand these contextual materials as important primary sources through which digital objects such as platforms and apps co-author their own "biographies" with web archives and software repositories.

1 Introduction

Contemporary digital objects, such as digital platforms and mobile apps, pose significant challenges to archiving and research practice. With millions or even billions of monthly active users, some of those platforms and apps are among the most popular products and services around the world (Statista 2017; Statista 2019a, b). Yet, despite their social, economic, and cultural significance, many of their histories are at risk of getting lost. As a result of rapid release cycles that enable developers to

A. Helmond (✉)
University of Amsterdam, Amsterdam, The Netherlands
e-mail: a.helmond@uva.nl

F. van der Vlist
Utrecht University, Utrecht, The Netherlands
e-mail: f.n.vandervlist@uu.nl

© Springer Nature Switzerland AG 2021
D. Gomes et al. (eds.), *The Past Web*,
https://doi.org/10.1007/978-3-030-63291-5_16

develop and deploy their code very quickly, large web platforms such as Facebook and YouTube change continuously, overwriting their material presence with each new deployment. Similarly, the pace of mobile app development and deployment is only growing, with each new software update overwriting the previous version.

In this chapter, we consider how one might write the histories of these new digital objects, despite such challenges. We reflect on the materiality of platforms and apps as specific types of digital objects and outline a method to take inventory of their archived materials for historical studies. As we argue, these archived sources offer various opportunities for historical studies of platforms and apps. That is, the *routine overwriting* of digital objects and their data through continuous incremental software updates constitutes both a core problem and a source of research opportunities for historians—at least, as long as those changes are documented by these digital objects themselves or preserved by web archives. We, therefore, look into the source availability of preserved material traces of platforms and apps.

In the first section, we consider how, from a material perspective, platforms and apps are different from other digital objects such as websites. As a consequence, there are challenges with regard to their archiving and study as well as new opportunities. In the second section, we describe a method of taking inventory of the available materials for writing platform and app histories. The method is not just useful for building corpora of historical platform or app sources but also potentially valuable for determining significant omissions in web archives and for guiding future archiving practices. In the third section, we describe the outcomes of an exploratory case study of the availability of leading platforms and apps today. We conclude with a reflection on the future of platform and app historiography.

2 The Archived Materiality of Platforms and Apps

The early Web mainly consisted of websites and interlinked webpages. As a consequence, the website has become the main unit of archiving as well as the main unit of historical analysis (Brügger 2018). However, in the past decade, we have witnessed the emergence of new types of digital objects, in particular, digital platforms and apps for social media and beyond. But what characterizes these specific digital objects as archived objects, as compared to the website or webpage?

When thinking of how platforms and apps are archived today, we contend that we need to consider their specific materiality. With the term materiality, we refer to the material form of those digital objects themselves as well as the material circumstances of those objects that leave material traces behind, including developer resources and reference documentation, business tools and product pages, and help and support pages (Ankerson 2012; Fuller 2008; Gillespie 2003; Kirschenbaum 2003). Furthermore, developers commonly keep changelogs, release notes, and do versioning. Importantly, rather than secondary sources, which are commonly used for web histories of platforms and apps (Brügger 2015; Poulsen 2018), these materials are primary sources that offer particular research opportunities or that may be supplemented and triangulated for accuracy. These material traces may "tell stories" about the evolving production, preferred usage, and embedded politics of software objects (Gillespie 2003).

We understand these contextual materials as important primary sources through which digital objects such as platforms and apps write, or indeed *overwrite*, their own "biographies", thus building on the emerging genre of media biography, including "software biography", "website biography", and "platform biography" (Burgess and Baym 2020; Natale 2016; Rogers 2017; Pollock and Williams 2008). The dual materiality of platforms and apps, as software objects and as sets of material contextual traces, opens up a productive avenue for historical analysis. Even when a platform or app as such is not archived, we may turn to web archives to look for their contextual material traces instead. These traces "provide a potential entryway to the web cultures, production practices, and symbolic systems informing lost cultural artifacts" (Ankerson 2012: 392). Furthermore, these "textual supplements are perhaps even more potent because they seem to be part of the tool itself" as they document a "self-interpretation" of the software object that we may employ for its history writing (Gillespie 2003).

2.1   Web Archives

The materiality of a web platform manifests as a collection of interrelated web pages that are meaningfully arranged to address different groups of users on different "sides". That is, platforms are programmable infrastructures as well as digital intermediaries that bring together different groups of users (Gillespie 2010; Helmond 2015; de Reuver et al. 2018). For each user group, there are different sets of resources and documentation that describe the operational logics, stakeholder relations, and preferred uses of a platform. For example, social media platforms provide such materials for their various user groups, which include end-users, developers, businesses, advertisers, partners, creators, media and publishers, politicians, investors, and researchers. As we have outlined previously, these different sets of materials are well archived and afford and privilege different types of social media and platform history (Helmond and van der Vlist 2019). To locate historical platform resources and documentation, we may turn toward web archives.

The materiality of apps is different from platforms. While many digital platforms exist principally on the Web and operate tools, products, and services on multiple "sides" to different groups of users, apps are software *bundles* (or packages) that are downloaded directly onto mobile devices from app stores. In contrast to websites and web platforms, mobile apps are not web "native" and instead reside on mobile devices and in app stores, which makes them even more difficult to archive and study. Yet they are entangled with a variety of other web services (Dieter et al. 2019). App stores, arguably, are a "native" environment for apps. For end-users, apps present themselves as contained digital objects that are purchased and downloaded from platform-specific app stores, such as Google Play for Android or the App Store for the iOS operating system. Yet by their design, app stores only provide access to the latest version of an app bundle and not to former versions. With each new software update, a former app version is overwritten—both inside the app store and on the user's mobile device. As a result, neither app stores nor mobile devices keep former versions of apps, which poses challenges for historical app studies.

2.2 App Repositories

To locate former app bundle versions, we may turn to several third-party software repositories, such as Cydia for iOS apps or APKMirror for Android apps.[1] Contrary to traditional institutional archives, these repositories are noninstitutional storage locations for the retrieval of software that were never designed for permanent preservation (Allix et al. 2016). While they may share commonalities with archives, software repositories do not curate collections of "records" for permanent historical preservation and do not necessarily consider their value as evidence or as a source for historical research (Brügger 2018). Additionally, the use of software repositories as app archives raises issues with regard to archive incompleteness and software insecurity. They are incomplete because they rely on users manually uploading app versions; they pose security risks because not all repositories scan package uploads for malicious code injections. When app code is tampered with, this may directly limit or influence historical code-based analyses. And even if we find former app versions in repositories, we still face software emulation challenges with apps as they typically require a complex set of dependencies and will only "run" or operate on specific devices and operating systems of the past (Boss and Broussard 2017; Helmond and van der Vlist 2019; Stevenson and Gehl 2018).

As an alternative or additional strategy, app historians may turn to archived app metadata sources as preserved in web archives that hold "snapshots" of app details pages in app stores or repositories. While apps and app stores both exist primarily on mobile devices, the leading app stores—Google Play and Apple's App Store—also provide web-based graphical user interfaces to their stores. These stores contain a wealth of information about specific apps as well as their relations to other, "similar" apps and the store categories or app collections to which they belong (Dieter et al. 2019). For each app, there is a details page with the app's title, developer, bundle version, screenshots, description, requested app permissions, download statistics, reviews, ratings, and more. Fortunately, these app store details pages are preserved in web archives, which generates opportunities for historical app studies. In short, to locate historical app materials, we may thus either turn to app repositories to retrieve former app versions or to web archives to retrieve contextual information.

---

[1]Cydia, https://cydia-app.com/; APKMirror, https://www.apkmirror.com.

3   Assessing the Availability of Platform and App Sources

To determine whether these materials have been preserved and where they are located, we conducted an exploratory study of the availability of archived sources for platform and app history. Building on previous work (Helmond and van der Vlist 2019), we first detail a method for assessing the availability of archived web sources for platforms and apps in web archives and app repositories.

Making use of market data portals Statista and App Annie, we selected the current top-20 most popular social media platforms and top-10 mobile apps for Android and iOS combined, both based on the current number of active users worldwide (App Annie 2019; Statista 2019a, b). For the first source set of social media platforms, we made an inventory of their most prominent "sides" and created a list of URLs pointing to the location of their principal materials (e.g., twitter.com, developer.twitter.com, business.twitter.com, marketing.twitter.com, investor.twitterinc.com). For the second source set of mobile apps, we created a list of URLs pointing to the app store details pages for each app.[2] These URLs contain the unique bundle identifier of each app, which remains stable even when apps are continuously updated and overwritten. App store links are constructed with these bundle identifiers and thus also remain stable over time.[3] So, although apps are updated continuously, they have a stable bundle identifier and a stable web URL that points to a details page that we may track in archives over time. In addition, we used these unique bundle identifiers to locate these apps in ten prominent third-party software repositories for Android apps.[4]

To assess which web archives actually hold archival records of a particular resource, we employed Memento's Time Travel Service (Van de Sompel et al. 2009).[5] The service functions as a search engine "on top of" the 25 leading

---

[2]Over the past decade, app store URLs changed only once or twice: Google Play (since 2012) was formerly called Android Market (2008–2012), and the domain changed from android.com/market to play.google.com/store; Apple's App Store (since 2008) was formerly called App Store (iTunes Preview) (2012–2019) and before that, Web Apps for iPhone (2008–2012), and its domains changed from apple.com/webapps to itunes.apple.com to apps.apple.com. For our exploratory study, we focused only on the current URLs at the time of writing.

[3]App store URLs are constructed as follows: for Google Play, https://play.google.com/store/apps/details?id=bundle_id; for the App Store, there are three URL formats, https://itunes.apple.com/app/bundle_id, https://itunes.apple.com/us/app/bundle_id, https://itunes.apple.com/us/app/appname/bundle_id.

[4]We included the following app repositories: AndroidAPKsBox.com, AndroidAPKsFree.com, AndroidDrawer, APKMirror, APKMonk, APKPure, APKPure.ai, APKPure.co, Aptoide, and Uptodown.

[5]Time Travel, http://timetravel.mementoweb.org/.

international web archives and may be queried for specific URLs (Memento 2016).[6] For end-users, it offers a graphical user interface (GUI) that may be deployed to manually query and locate a URL across multiple web archives. Additionally, it offers an application programming interface (API) to programmatically request that data. Both methods return a list of web archives that hold one or more Mementos (i.e., time-stamped archived copies of a specific URL). For each Memento, the service returns the first and last Memento available as well as links to all available captures across archives. Time Travel thus provides a simple method to assess the availability of specific archived sources across web archives. To determine the total number of Mementos held or the number of archives holding them, users may follow the "All captures from" link for each web archive and manually count the number of Mementos held.

To scale and automate this process for a large source set of URLs, researchers may use MemGator, an open-source command-line interface utility that is built "on top of" the Memento API and aggregates Mementos.[7] MemGator programmatically requests Memento TimeMaps from a list of web archives that support the Memento protocol (Alam and Nelson 2016). Each TimeMap provides a time-stamped list of all Mementos held in that archive for a given URL (Memento 2015). It also lets researchers customize the list of web archives from which to request TimeMaps. For present purposes, we extended MemGator's list of web archives that natively support the Memento protocol, as specified in "archives.json", with a number of web archives listed in the Time Travel Archive Registry that run Memento proxies (Memento 2015), so as to be as inclusive as possible in our exploratory study. Our custom list included 20 web archives from which to programmatically retrieve data. More specifically, we used MemGator to programmatically retrieve the available platform and app materials from across these 20 web archives and then analyzed the results to assess the availability of sources.[8] In what follows, we describe the results of our exploratory study.

---

[6]As of June 2019, "Time Travel Find" supported the following web archives: archive.today, Archive-It, Arquivo.pt.: the Portuguese web-archive, Bayerische Staatsbibliothek, Bibliotheca Alexandrina Web Archive, DBpedia archive, DBpedia Triple Pattern Fragments archive, Canadian Government Web Archive, Croatian Web Archive, Estonian Web Archive, Icelandic web archive, Internet Archive, Library of Congress Web Archive, NARA Web Archive, National Library of Ireland Web Archive, National Records of Scotland, perma.cc, PRONI Web Archive, Slovenian Web Archive, Stanford Web Archive, UK Government Web Archive, UK Parliament's Web Archive, UK Web Archive, Web Archive Singapore, and WebCite.

[7]MemGator, https://github.com/oduwsdl/MemGator.

[8]All data were collected between May and June 2019.

4   The Availability of Platform and App Sources

We analyzed the source availability of platform and app materials according to three criteria: first, the *volume of availability* or the total number of Mementos held; second, the *depth of availability*, specified as the number of days, months, or years between the first and last Mementos; and third, the *breadth of availability*, referring to the number of web archives holding those Mementos (Helmond and van der Vlist 2019). The first two criteria determine the amount of available material and the possible levels of granularity for historical analysis, while the third criterion enables researchers to triangulate and verify historical sources, such as when certain elements are corrupted or missing.

Table 1 provides a summary of our exploratory study results. We counted the total number of Mementos held across web archives (i.e., volume), determined the time span between the first and last Mementos held (i.e., depth, expressed in number of days), and counted the number of web archives holding those Mementos (i.e., breadth, expressed as a single number up to 20 web archives). Taken together, these three dimensions provide a useful account of source availability and allow researchers to determine the feasibility of certain historical projects or allow archiving practitioners to reconsider their archiving strategy. Based on these counts, we then calculated an availability rank for each platform and app by calculating the number of captures per day (volume divided by depth) and then multiplying that number by breadth.

Table 1 Availability of archived app store page details (Mementos) for each one of the top 10 Android and iOS apps across web archives (accumulated)

App title	Android (Google Play)				iOS (App Store)			
	Volume	Depth	Breadth	Rank	Volume	Depth	Breadth	Rank
Facebook	8198	2637	8	3	390	3389	6	4
WhatsApp messenger	4092	2600	7	4	548	3395	6	2
Facebook messenger	85,222	2638	10	1	99,581	2708	9	1
WeChat	442	2557	5	5	120	3019	4	5
Instagram	13,215	2611	11	2	447	3153	6	3
QQ	38	2551	1	8	16	2547	1	8
Alipay	26	2188	1	9	26	800	1	6
Taobao	31	2147	2	7	50	3168	1	7
WiFi master key	31	1890	3	6	0	0	0	n/a
Baidu	24	2196	1	10	0	0	0	n/a

4.1 Social Media Platforms in Web Archives

As we have analyzed elsewhere, social media platforms have been relatively well archived on all of their "sides" (Helmond and van der Vlist 2019). The five best-archived social media platforms represent an average of 913,440 Mementos, followed by an average of 130,036 for the next 15 platforms (Max = 1,783,855; Min = 3007; Median = 166,412).

As these results suggest, there are many opportunities for historical platform studies about different "sides" and user groups, albeit at different levels of granularity, depending on source availability. In particular, developer and business materials have been well archived and enable researchers to write histories beyond the "front-end" interface for end-users. They may look at platforms' influential roles as development platforms, advertising platforms, content creation platforms, media publishers, and platform companies (Helmond and van der Vlist 2019; Helmond et al. 2019; Nieborg and Helmond 2019). These materials also enable researchers to examine how the technological architectures and economic business models of platforms evolve side by side. In short, platform histories would benefit from considering more than just their end-users and contents and include their multiple user groups to examine how they coevolved with respect to other "sides".

4.2 App Details in Web Archives

Contrary to most popular social media platforms, apps have been less well archived in general, at least when we look at the preservation of their app store details pages in web archives (Table 1). For Android apps, Facebook Messenger is the best-archived app by far, leaving all other apps behind. In fact, other apps have hardly been archived at all. While the four best-archived top Android apps—Facebook Messenger, Instagram, Facebook, and WhatsApp Messenger—represent an average of 27,681 Mementos each, the next six top apps have an average of just 98.6 Mementos (Max = 85,222; Min = 24; Median = 240). For top iOS apps, Facebook Messenger accounts for nearly 99,581 Mementos, while the next nine top apps have an average of just 177.4 Mementos (Max = 99,581; Min = 0; Median = 85). In particular, pages of non-Western apps have been poorly archived, in line with a previously identified imbalance of source availability in archived websites between the United States and other countries (Thelwall and Vaughan 2004).

The archived app materials enable researchers to examine the evolution of individual apps, or app collections and genres. In a previous project, we examined the emergence of secure or encrypted messaging and chat apps on Android and used their descriptions to determine how those apps offered new and different ways of "doing privacy" (e.g., the emergence of new encryption protocols and tradeoffs between security, privacy, and usability). Tracking app descriptions over time thus enabled us to understand how apps or app developers responded to Edward

Snowden's surveillance revelations in June 2013, when digital surveillance became a "matter of concern" on the web and mobile ecosystem (Dieter et al. 2019; van der Vlist 2017). App details pages enable app historians to tell stories about an app's rhetorical positioning (e.g., using taglines, descriptions), production (e.g., using developer names, app versions, changelogs), distribution (e.g., using app collections, relations, pricing models), and reception (e.g., using app downloads, reviews, ratings).

4.3   App Bundles in App Repositories

With regard to the preservation of Android app bundles in third-party software repositories, we found more promising results (Table 2). All of the 10 top apps in our set are relatively well archived based on all three criteria. In terms of volume, the four Facebook-owned top apps—WhatsApp Messenger, Facebook, Instagram, Facebook Messenger—have been stored an average of 3722 times, while the next six, all non-Western, top apps have been stored 297 times on average (Max = 4585; Min = 166; Median = 469). The oldest versions of the apps in our dataset date back to May 2012.

These results suggest that app repositories are promising sources for historical app studies, both to study app bundles themselves and to triangulate app details between app repositories and official app stores. Most importantly, these primary app materials enable researchers to devise historical methods based on "static" app analysis (Dieter et al. 2019). That is, app bundles may be decompiled and analyzed as source code to study requested app permissions, embedded code, and external relationships to other infrastructural web services such as advertising and content delivery networks, for example (Gerlitz et al. 2019). Or, researchers may emulate those app bundles to conduct "dynamic" app analysis and study evolving interface design patterns and the network connections that mobile devices establish on behalf of apps.

Table 2 Availability of top-10 Android apps across app repositories (accumulated)

App title	Android			
	Volume	Depth	Breadth	Rank
Facebook	4585	2584	9	2
WhatsApp messenger	4268	2585	10	1
Facebook messenger	2765	2609	10	4
WeChat	315	2364	10	6
Instagram	3271	2600	10	3
QQ	229	2187	9	9
Alipay	193	1362	8	7
Taobao	258	1844	7	8
WiFi master key	623	1401	8	5
Baidu	166	2242	5	10

5 Conclusions: Platform and App Historiography

In this chapter, we have demonstrated how researchers may use web archives and app repositories to write histories of new digital objects such as platforms and apps, despite their archiving challenges. We have reflected on the materiality of platforms and apps as specific types of digital objects and have outlined a method to make an inventory of their archived materials. Existing archived sources offer many opportunities for historical platform and app studies, and it is our hope that their affordances for research are further explored.

Our exploratory study of source availability for the most popular social media platforms and mobile apps provides important insights into the current state of platform and app archiving, which should be of interest to researchers and historians of web platforms and mobile apps. Furthermore, our assessment of source availability provides relevant starting points and example case studies for different types of platform and app history and may guide future historians in the process of corpus building. Our exploratory study should also be of interest to web and app archiving practitioners. In particular, our source availability assessment method and the preliminary results of our exploratory study may guide or inspire a reconsideration of archiving efforts going forward. Current web archiving strategies or protocols may not capture all of the relevant materials, as in the case of app store details pages which are located deep within app stores. We particularly recommend a more comprehensive archiving strategy that captures the multiple "sides" of popular social media platforms and the app details pages of popular app stores beyond the top apps.

Although we only looked at a small selection of top platforms and apps, we already observed large discrepancies in source availability between both types of digital objects, which inevitably determines and limits the future histories that may be written about and with those apps. Our selection of popular apps is expected to be far better archived than the millions of apps in the "long tail" of app stores. We should note, however, that even with a hundred or fewer Mementos it is, of course, possible to write the histories of platforms and apps. Depending on the historical project, differences in source availability may have implications with regard to volume (e.g., limiting the afforded level of granularity or resolution), depth (e.g., constraining the historical period), and breadth of availability (e.g., limiting the possibilities of triangulation or source verification). Existing services and utilities such as Memento and MemGator offer the opportunity to move beyond the Internet Archive as the primary or even only source of web history. They also enable researchers to triangulate and verify sources and thereby address common issues of archive incompleteness and software insecurity (including corrupt app files).

The ephemerality of digital platforms and mobile apps may be understood as the result of a continuous stream of incremental software updates that overwrite the material presence of a platform or app every time. We may conceive of this process of overwriting as a challenge of material erasure, or as a "native" mode of software history-writing. That is, even though these ephemeral digital objects change continuously, web archives and software repositories, fortunately, capture many of those changes, thereby arresting the ongoing material transformation of platforms and apps at certain time intervals (e.g., with hourly, daily, or monthly captures or "snapshots"). Consequently, we argue that the biographies of platforms and apps are co-written by these digital objects themselves and by web archives and, in the case of apps, also by software repositories. We can employ their different types of primary and contextual sources to "reconstruct" these processes of overwriting at different levels of granularity—from the minute, incremental changes to the longer-term evolution of a platform or app. We can use web archives and repositories to reconstruct what was written on top of other writing and narrate the drama of changes, updates, and versions.

References

Alam S, Nelson ML (2016) MemGator: a portable concurrent memento aggregator: cross-platform CLI and server binaries in Go. In: Proceedings of the 16th ACM/IEEE-CS on Joint Conference on Digital Libraries, pp 243–244. ACM. https://doi.org/10.1145/2910896.2925452

Allix K, Bissyandé TF, Klein J, Le Traon Y (2016) AndroZoo: collecting millions of Android apps for the research community. In: Proceedings of the 13th International Conference on Mining Software Repositories, 468–471. ACM. https://doi.org/10.1145/2901739.2903508

Ankerson MS (2012) Writing web histories with an eye on the analog past. New Media Soc 14(3):384–400. https://doi.org/10.1177/1461444811414834

App Annie (2019, January 16) The state of mobile in 2019. App Annie. Retrieved from: https://www.appannie.com/en/insights/market-data/the-state-of-mobile-2019/

Boss K, Broussard M (2017) Challenges of archiving and preserving born-digital news applications. IFLA J 43(2):150–157. https://doi.org/10.1177/0340035216686355

Brügger N (2015) A brief history of Facebook as a media text: the development of an empty structure. First Monday 20(5). https://doi.org/10.5210/fm.v20i5.5423

Brügger N (2018) The archived web: doing history in the digital age. The MIT Press

Burgess J, Baym NK (2020) Twitter: a biography. NYU Press

de Reuver M, Sørensen C, Basole RC (2018) The digital platform: a research agenda. J Inf Technol 33(2):124–135. https://doi.org/10.1057/s41265-016-0033-3

Dieter M, Gerlitz C, Helmond A, Tkacz N, van der Vlist FN, Weltevrede E (2019) Multi-situated app studies: methods and propositions. Social Media Society 5(2). https://doi.org/10.1177/2056305119846486

Fuller M (2008) Software studies: a lexicon. The MIT Press

Gerlitz G, Helmond A, Nieborg DB, van der Vlist FN (2019) Apps and infrastructures–a research agenda. Computat Cult 7. Retrieved from: http://computationalculture.net/apps-and-infrastructures-a-research-agenda

Gillespie T (2003) The stories digital tools tell. In: Everett A, Caldwell J (eds) New media: theses on convergence media and digital reproduction, pp. 107–126. Routledge

Gillespie T (2010) The politics of 'platforms'. New Media Soc 12(3):347–364. https://doi.org/10.1177/1461444809342738

Helmond A (2015) The platformization of the web: making web data platform ready. Social Media Society 1(2). https://doi.org/10.1177/2056305115603080

Helmond A, Nieborg DB, van der Vlist FN (2019) Facebook's evolution: development of a platform-as-infrastructure. Internet Hist 3(2):123–146. https://doi.org/10.1080/24701475.2019.1593667

Helmond A, van der Vlist FN (2019) Social media and platform historiography: challenges and opportunities. TMG – J Media Hist 22(1):6–34. https://www.tmgonline.nl/articles/434/

Kirschenbaum MG (2003) Virtuality and VRML: software studies after Manovich. Electronic book review. Retrieved from: http://www.electronicbookreview.com/thread/technocapitalism/morememory

Memento (2015, April 23) Time Travel APIs. Memento. Retrieved from: http://timetravel.mementoweb.org/guide/api/

Memento (2016, September 22) About the time travel service. Memento. Retrieved from: http://timetravel.mementoweb.org/about/

Natale S (2016) Unveiling the biographies of media: on the role of narratives, anecdotes, and storytelling in the construction of new Media's histories. Commun Theory 26(4):431–449. https://doi.org/10.1111/comt.12099

Nieborg DB, Helmond A (2019) The political economy of Facebook's platformization in the mobile ecosystem: Facebook messenger as a platform instance. Media Cult Soc 41(2):196–218. https://doi.org/10.1177/0163443718818384

Pollock N, Williams R (2008) Software and organisations: the biography of the enterprise-wide system or how SAP conquered the world. Routledge

Poulsen SV (2018) Becoming a semiotic technology–a historical study of Instagram's tools for making and sharing photos and videos. Internet Hist 2(1–2):121–139. https://doi.org/10.1080/24701475.2018.1459350

Rogers R (2017) Doing web history with the internet archive: screencast documentaries. Internet Hist 1(2):160–172. https://doi.org/10.1080/24701475.2017.1307542

Statista (2017, October 10) Mobile app usage. Statista. Retrieved from: https://www.statista.com/topics/1002/mobile-app-usage/

Statista (2019a, March 28) Social media statistics. Statista. Retrieved from: https://www.statista.com/topics/1164/social-networks/

Statista (2019b, May 27) Global social media ranking 2019. Statista. Retrieved from: https://www.statista.com/statistics/272014/global-social-networks-ranked-by-number-of-users/

Stevenson M, Gehl RW (2018) The afterlife of software. In: Papacharissi Z (ed) A networked self and birth, life, death. Routledge, pp. 190–208

Thelwall M, Vaughan L (2004) A fair history of the web? Examining country balance in the internet archive. Libr Inf Sci Res 26(2):162–176. https://doi.org/10.1016/j.lisr.2003.12.009

Van de Sompel H, Nelson ML, Sanderson R, Balakireva LL, Ainsworth S, Shankar H (2009) Memento: time travel for the web. ArXiv Preprint. ArXiv:0911.1112. Retrieved from: https://arxiv.org/abs/0911.1112

van der Vlist FN (2017) Counter-mapping surveillance: a critical cartography of mass surveillance technology after Snowden. Surveill Soc 15(1):137–157. https://doi.org/10.24908/ss.v15i1.5307

Part V
Web Archives as Infrastructures to Develop Innovative Services

Daniel Gomes

Web archives have an important role to play as societal infrastructures that enable the preservation of memory. Services do not become infrastructures overnight. They evolve iteratively through the development of added-value features and incremental reliability. When Thomas Edison invented the light bulb in the nineteenth century, it was a luxury, an extravagant object. A service for supplying electricity was far from being considered an essential social infrastructure at the time. However, as services become more widely used and reliable, and as new services are built on top of them, they become infrastructures.

Web archives are not able to address the requirements arising from all their possible use cases. However, Internet or electricity service providers have also not addressed all of their users' requirements. Instead, they provide well-defined and robust services that enable the development of solutions by third parties that fulfill diverse usage requirements, by creating new added-value services such as websites or electronic consumer products. When a service is so widely used and stable that most people take it for granted, it becomes an infrastructure. Web archives are crucial services because most information produced by humankind is becoming available exclusively online, and it rapidly disappears from its original source. Web archives are the gatekeepers of the past Web and they must become infrastructures. This part makes the case for web archives as essential research infrastructures for the study of historical information published online and presents several inspiring examples of added-value services built on top of services provided by web archives. It discusses, on the one hand, how web archive services can be used to support innovative practice, and on the other hand, how these innovative services complement existing web archives. The chapter "The Need for Research Infrastructures for the Study of Web Archives" argues that effective infrastructures are needed for the study of archived web material. The chapters "Automatic

D. Gomes
Fundação para a Ciência e a Tecnologia, Lisbon, Portugal
e-mail: daniel.gomes@fccn.pt

Generation of Timelines for Past-Web Events" and "Political Opinions on the Past Web" present two innovative tools developed over web archive services to automatically generate timelines for past events and to analyze opinion articles across time. The chapter "Oldweb.today: Browsing the Past Web with Browsers from the Past" presents a browser emulation tool that reproduces past webpages using past web browsers. This tool is fed by archived web data, and it complements web archives when modern browsers become unable to render past web content correctly. The chapter "Big Data Science Over the Past Web" debates the potential of web archives for big data analytics.

The Need for Research Infrastructures for the Study of Web Archives

Niels Brügger

Abstract Research infrastructures such as buildings, shelves and staff responsible for the collections have always been established to support the research process. With the archived Web, research infrastructures come in new forms, opening up new possibilities, but also new challenges. One of the major challenges is that web archives provide the potential for an almost unlimited number of possible forms of researcher interaction, but not all of them can be supported by those archives, due to a mix of curatorial, technical, legal, economic and organisational constraints. Therefore, a new field of negotiation is open between web archives and research communities.

1 The Need for Research Infrastructures

Research has always relied on some sort of infrastructure, such as instruments and tools, as well as collections of semiotic sources, including written documents, books, film kept in libraries and archives or unique artefacts preserved by museums. This situation prevails with web archives, at least in part, since they mainly collect and preserve the data, but they may (or may not) also provide some of the analytical tools to dig into the collection. Making the collection available for users in itself demands new forms of infrastructure. Shelves and racks have to be replaced by servers, user interfaces and analytical tools.

But in contrast to non-digital media collections where the artefact (book, newspaper, cassette, etc.) can be searched for and then handed over to the researcher, no matter who the researcher is and what the research project is about, with the archived Web the relatively simple activity of "giving access" opens a wide array

N. Brügger (✉)
Aarhus University, Aarhus, Denmark
e-mail: nb@cc.au.dk

© Springer Nature Switzerland AG 2021   217
D. Gomes et al. (eds.), *The Past Web*,
https://doi.org/10.1007/978-3-030-63291-5_17

of possible alternatives. This implies that web archives are pushed to reflect on the extent to which they can cater for very diverse researcher needs.[1]

When talking about research infrastructures, it is also important to be reminded that a research infrastructure is not only a matter of technology and artefacts, as highlighted in the definition given by the European Strategy Forum on Research Infrastructures (ESFRI):

> Research Infrastructures, including the associated human resources, covers major equipment or sets of instruments, in addition to knowledge-containing resources such as collections, archives and data banks. (ESFRI 2011, p. 7)

This chapter will start by identifying some of the specific characteristics of web archives as research infrastructures, before discussing researcher needs, and, finally, debating the extent to which these needs can/should be met by web archives or by research communities. The national Danish web archive Netarkivet will serve as a concrete and illustrative case to highlight what is at stake. It will briefly be outlined how a few other national web archives address researcher requirements.

2   Web Archives as Research Infrastructures

The supplementing of non-digital collections with digital collections has changed the landscape of cultural heritage institutions dramatically, including libraries, museums and archives. Non-digital collections may have been digitised, and born-digital material, including the online Web, may have been collected and preserved. The existence of such collections in digital form has opened new avenues to discovering their content.

However, just because collections comprise digital material does not mean that they are homogeneous.[2] The three phases that characterise the process of building a digital collection—collecting, preserving and making available—vary significantly according to the specific characteristics of the digital material being addressed.

For instance, let us compare a collection of digitised recent newspapers with a collection of archived web material (the following points build on the insights in Brügger (2018), where an extended comparison of digitised newspapers and web archives can be found).[3] First, in a collection of digitised newspapers, there is usually a paper original to go back to in order to make quality checks, but this is not the case with a web archive, since the online version is very likely to have

---

[1] See also Winters (2017a, 2017b) about researchers' (in particular historians') need for web archives and web archives' need to identify researcher requirements.

[2] I have elsewhere used the term "digitality" for the specific ways of being digital (cf. Brügger, 2018, 17–30).

[3] The following mainly applies to web archives based on web crawling. Other ways of collecting the Web include making screenshots or screen movies, or retrieving the material from the producer via an API (cf. Brügger, 2018, 78–84).

changed or even disappeared. This implies that, in contrast to the digitisation of a stable newspaper, the Web that is to be archived is (potentially) in a state of flux and constant updates and changes. A whole website may even change during the process of archiving, for instance, a front page may have changed when other sections of the website are being archived because the web archiving process is not instantaneous.

Second, answering the question of what will be digitised and how with respect to newspapers is mostly straightforward since, in the main, the process of digitisation is not very complex; it is transparent and systematic. In contrast, when it comes to web archiving, answering the "what" and "how" is usually more complex, and the archiving process is less transparent and to some extent unsystematic. Web archiving is based on following hyperlinks, and therefore, it is difficult to know exactly what goes into the archive. In addition, web archiving is based on a great number of configurable settings (e.g. file types to be included/excluded, maximum number of objects to be archived per web domain, timeout, etc.).

Third, for newspapers, what is digitised is the printed version that we have in front of us, but with the Web what is archived is not the webpage as seen in a web browser but rather the HTML file and all the elements of which it may be composed, e.g. images, video, feeds, etc. So whereas a digitised page in a newspaper is a "flat" file, an archived webpage is a cluster of fragments, and that is fragments on two levels: on the one hand, the fragments of which the HTML file is composed, namely, everything between tags in the HTML code, such as a hyperlink identified by the tag <a> or a heading identified by the tag <h>, and on the other hand, the cluster of files and feeds (e.g. images, video, embeds, etc.) that are pulled into the webpage to compose what we see in our web browser. Thus, what goes into the web archive is not what we see in a browser but rather the "invisible" elements from which what is seen in a browser window is composed. Therefore, what a researcher can find in a web archive is best characterised as a bucket of interconnected fragments in the form of HTML files and other file types.

In summary, web archives contribute to a shift from research based on non-digital to digital collections but present significant differences when compared to other digital collections. In particular the third point—the fragmented nature of the web archive—becomes important when discussing web archives as research infrastructures aimed to satisfy researcher needs.

3 Researcher Needs for Web Archive Research Infrastructure

As mentioned before, research infrastructures such as non-digital collections have offered a limited variety of researcher interactions: a researcher might borrow a book or have a document retrieved so that it can be consulted in a reading room. What may not have been clear with these types of interactions is that they were a function of the nature of the collected material: researchers could borrow a book or have a document retrieved because these objects constituted the material entities of the collections. The characteristics of the collected items affected the researchers' interaction with the collection to such an extent that handing over artefacts appeared to be the only natural way of approaching the collection. This natural way of consulting the collection obscured that, in fact, it was the result of a negotiation between the collection-holder and the researcher.

With digital material, this situation changed, because a variety of new forms of interaction became possible. For instance, having more researchers who "borrow" the same item becomes possible because digital copies can easily be produced, and working remotely with the digital material is enabled by computer networks. However, the distinction between the different types of digital material (digitised, born, reborn) also applies when it comes to researcher interaction with the collections. A digitised newspaper is composed of flat files, often one file per page, which limits the possible forms of interaction, in the main, to searching the page by searching metadata such as journal name, date and similar. The text on the page may also have gone through a process of optical character recognition (OCR) which enables the extraction of the written text so that the full-text search may be supported by complementary tools such as digital-library search engines (on OCR, see Cordell 2017; Hill and Hengchen 2019; Milligan 2013). The OCR adds an extra layer of metadata to the scanned file, and other layers may be added, for instance, a layer with the coordinates of the location of individual words on the page (a so-called alto file). It is worth noting that in contrast to web archives, these extra layers of information are added after the process of digitisation, and they were not an integrated part of the paper original.

A web archive offers a large number of possible interactions with its preserved material. First, a web archive holds a large amount of valuable information that has been generated as part of the web archiving process, in particular, what are called seed lists, that is, lists with the names of web domains that the web archiving software was configured to collect, as well as the *crawl log*, that is, an exact record of what the archiving software did during the archiving process. When it comes to the actual content of the archive, there are as many ways of interacting with the material as there are types of tags in the HTML files and types of files in general. In other words, there are a great variety of possible interactions with the many different file formats and their content in the big bucket of a web archive. One researcher may want to study individual webpages that are as close as possible to what they looked like when online in the past; other researchers may want to study hyperlinks, words or images. Thus, potentially, the web archive may offer a broad range of researcher interactions with the material.

All of these potential use forms may not be made available by the collection-holder. They constitute the foundation for negotiations between researcher needs and the available curatorial, technical and economic resources, as well as the legal and organisational restrictions of the web collection-holder (cf. Brügger 2018, pp. 138–139). It is difficult for web archives to meet all types of researcher needs. The archived Web can potentially enable as many forms of interaction as there are researchers and research questions, because the fragments of the archived Web can be taken out of the bucket and combined in so many ways.

The challenge for web archives is that, assuming their relatively limited resources, they must offer some sort of infrastructure to support the potentially endless possibilities of researcher needs enabled by the vast source of information that is the past Web.

4   Meeting Researcher Needs: Web Archives or Research Communities?

When debating what is relevant research infrastructure and how it can be provided, at least the following three points are important to have in mind.

First, actual needs must be identified. Contact with relevant research environments has to be established and maintained over time, and a dialogue has to be initiated which allows researchers to be informed about the possibilities of interacting with the past Web. It is often the case that researchers who are new to the field conceive the archived Web as digitised material and are therefore not aware of its full potential for research.

Second, the web archive should strike a balance between providing general forms of interaction that can be used by most researchers and at the same time allowing for customised and advanced forms of interaction when required. Drawing the line between the general and customised forms of interaction is an ongoing negotiation with the relevant researcher communities. Web archives should provide fine-grained guidance for researchers so that they are informed about general as well as potentially customised access forms. Another relevant point is finding where researchers can have access to the material: only onsite, also online, or having material extracted to researchers' own computer environment outside the web archive.

Third, since web archives are digital, they directly enable the use of digital tools to unlock their potential usage. However, a question arises as to whether analytical tools must be provided by the web archive or by the researchers. On the one hand, web archives can develop their own analytical tools as an integrated part of the services that they provide, such as the Internet Archive's Archive-It web archiving cloud service, or the search, replay and discovery tool SolrWayback, developed by the Royal Library in Denmark (Egense 2018). On the other end, researchers may want to use off-the-shelf tools or develop their own, which is only possible if the material can be extracted from the web archive. Between these two poles, web archives may provide a workspace within the web archive, to which a selection of the web collection can be extracted and where off-the-shelf analytical software can be installed and run.

5   Netarkivet: A Case of Web Archive Research Infrastructure

The national Danish web archive Netarkivet, supplemented with brief overviews of some other national web archives, is useful to illustrate how the previous points have been tackled.

Netarkivet was established in 2005 and it is now hosted by the Royal Danish Library (Laursen and Møldrup-Dalum 2017). Netarkivet is only accessible for researchers through an application procedure. When granted access, researchers can explore the archive either by searching by URL or by using full-text search. Once an archived webpage is identified, it is replayed through the OpenWayback replay software. These general forms of access help researchers because they can view the entire collection remotely online.

Netarkivet also enables the extraction of samples of archived web content from its collection to a computer system hosted in the researcher's institution. This process demands knowledge of the collections, and it is set up based on a series of meetings with researchers where their needs are identified, and the curatorial, technical and resource demands are identified. The result of these meetings is an "ETL description" that defines which data is to be extracted, transformed and loaded. Based on the ETL description, an Extraction Agreement is signed, and the material is extracted and transferred to a secure computer environment at the researcher's institution by a curator on the Netarkivet staff who has IT skills. In case researchers are not able to set up an adequate running environment or if they do not need to consult the material on their own computer, Netarkivet plans to offer running environments inside the web archive, equipped with a "toolbox" of different analytical tools. In either case, the researcher can have the material extracted as files, link lists in the form of a Comma-Separated Values file or in another format agreed with the researchers, even including having the entire sampled set extracted as a new (set of) WARC file(s). The advantages of extracting the material are considerable from the researcher's as well as from the web archive's point of view. The web archive does not have to provide analytical tools and is no longer responsible for keeping the material in a closed environment. On their part, researchers can apply the most adequate analytical tools for answering their research questions and may enrich the extracted material by interacting with it using state-of-the-art replay or analytical software. For instance, a researcher can index the extracted WARC file(s) and access this index through the freely available SolrWayback software, which enables sophisticated search and replay features over the archived material, or use a big data analytical platform such as the Archives Unleashed Toolkit (https://archivesunleashed.org), which generates derived results from archived web data such as a plain-text corpus or a link graph.

Netarkivet's research infrastructure, from collection to forms of access, has developed in a close and long-lasting interplay with relevant research environments, with a view to continually providing relevant research infrastructure elements. Netarkivet was established in 2005, based on a revised legal deposit law, but this revision was preceded by a pilot project focusing on how a national Danish web archive could be established at all, and this pilot project was a collaboration between, on the one hand, the (at that time) two national libraries—the State and University Library in Aarhus and the Royal Library in Copenhagen—and, on the other hand, two Internet researchers (one of whom is the author of this chapter, the other being Niels Ole Finnemann; for a brief cultural history of Netarkivet, see Webster 2017, pp. 177–181). When Netarkivet was established in 2005, it was stipulated in the law that an Editorial Committee with representatives from the researcher communities should be established, with a view to providing input to collection strategies and access forms. Finally, in 2012 the national Danish digital research infrastructure DIGHUMLAB was established. Part of this infrastructure is NetLab, which is a research infrastructure for the study of the archived Web that offers training workshops, IT developer support and researcher support (among others; see netlab.dk). The national library is a partner in DIGHUMLAB. Thus, the close collaboration between the web archive and researchers found yet another home in which to unfold. Since NetLab is a hub for researchers from a great variety of humanities disciplines, a multifaceted feedback loop is in place to ensure the continued relevance of the research infrastructure.

If one looks at the international landscape and how other web archives have accommodated researcher needs, there is a great variety. Most web archives offer URL search and replay with the WaybackMachine or similar; some offer full-text search, like Arquivo.pt. (the Portuguese web-archive); a few offer some sort of API access (again like Arquivo.pt., but the Internet Archive also offers online access to its CDX index, where the content of webpages is indexed); and yet others offer access to prepared open datasets, like the UK Web Archive's "Jisc UK Web Domain Dataset (1996–2013)". When it comes to the accessibility of the research infrastructure, some web archives provide free online access for everyone (e.g. the Internet Archive, Arquivo.pt., the Icelandic Web Archive), others are open for researchers only and must be accessed onsite (e.g. in the Netherlands, France and the UK), and in some cases, the onsite access can be distributed (such as in France, where the web archive can be accessed in regional libraries, and in the UK, where legal deposit libraries provide onsite access). However, in the UK case, two researchers cannot access the same webpage at the same time at the same library, which is reminiscent of earlier times where a print copy could not be accessed by more than one person at the time—and a living example of how the full potential of digital material is not always exploited and historical policies prevail despite the evolution of societies and communication media. Finally, national web collections exist to which there is no access at all (e.g. in Ireland). Interactions between web archives and researchers have taken place in a more systematic form in several countries, including France, the Netherlands, the USA, Canada and the UK (e.g. see Cowls 2017, on the BUDDAH project in the UK).

6 Summary

Because of its digital nature, the archived Web allows for a wide range of researcher forms of interaction. Therefore, establishing a research infrastructure to study the past Web constitutes a challenge. The fragmented nature of the information preserved by a web archive opens a Pandora's box where researchers may want all the potentialities of the research infrastructure to be realised. Web archives will have to balance this desire with the curatorial, technical, legal, economic and organisational reality of the web archive. Thus, the digital nature of the archived Web lies at the heart of the need for ongoing negotiations between research communities and web archive capabilities, with a focus on providing the most relevant forms of access forms, possibilities of extraction and analytical tools. The more popular the web archive gets among researchers, the more fine-grained and customised researchers may want forms of access to be. The more skilled researchers become in terms of using digital methods and tools, the more likely it is that they will demand more sophisticated analytical tools within the web archive or ask to be allowed to extract material to computers outside the web archive. The future will tell us the extent to which researchers as well as web archives will be ready to rise to these great expectations.

References

Brügger N (2018) The archived web: doing history in the digital age. MIT Press, Cambridge, MA

Cordell R (2017) "Q i-jtb the raven": taking dirty OCR seriously. Book Hist 20:188–225. https://doi.org/10.1353/bh.2017.0006

Cowls J (2017) Cultures of the UK web. In: Brügger N, Schroeder R (eds) The web as history. UCL Press, London, pp 220–237

Egense, T. (2018). SolrWayback. https://github.com/netarchivesuite/solrwayback

ESFRI (2011) Strategy report on research infrastructures — roadmap 2010. Publications Office of the European Union, Luxembourg

Hill MJ, Hengchen S (2019) Quantifying the impact of dirty OCR on historical text analysis: eighteenth century collections online as a case study. Digital Scholarship in the Humanities 34(4), 825–843. https://doi.org/10.1093/llc/fqz024

Laursen D, Møldrup-Dalum P (2017) Looking back, looking forward: 10 years of development to collect, preserve, and access the Danish web. In: Brügger N (ed) Web 25: histories from the first 25 years of the world wide web. Peter Lang, New York, pp 207–227

Milligan, I. (2013). Illusionary order: online databases, optical character recognition, and Canadian history, 1997–2010. Can Hist Rev 94(4), 540–569

Webster P (2017) Users, technologies, organisations: towards a cultural history of world web archiving. In: Brügger N (ed) Web 25: histories from the first 25 years of the world wide web. Peter Lang, New York, pp 175–190

Winters J (2017a) Breaking in to the mainstream: demonstrating the value of internet (and web) histories. Internet Hist 1(1–2):173–179

Winters J (2017b) Coda: web archives for humanities research — some reflections. In: Brügger N, Schroeder R (eds) The web as history. UCL Press, London, pp 238–248

Automatic Generation of Timelines for Past-Web Events

Ricardo Campos, Arian Pasquali, Adam Jatowt, Vítor Mangaravite, and Alípio Mário Jorge

Abstract Despite significant advances in web archive infrastructures, the problem of exploring the historical heritage preserved by web archives is yet to be solved. Timeline generation emerges in this context as one possible solution for automatically producing summaries of news over time. Thanks to this, users can gain a better sense of reported news events, entities, stories or topics over time, such as getting a summary of the most important news about a politician, an organisation or a locality. Web archives play an important role here by providing access to a historical set of preserved information. This particular characteristic of web archives makes them an irreplaceable infrastructure and a valuable source of knowledge that contributes to the process of timeline generation. Accordingly, the authors of this chapter developed "Tell me Stories" (http://archive.tellmestories.pt), a news summarisation system, built on top of the infrastructure of Arquivo.pt— the Portuguese web-archive—to automatically generate a timeline summary of a given topic. In this chapter, we begin by providing a brief overview of the most

R. Campos (✉)
LIAAD – INESC TEC, Porto, Portugal

Ci2 – Smart Cities Research Center, Polytechnic Institute of Tomar, Tomar, Portugal
e-mail: ricardo.campos@ipt.pt

A. Pasquali
LIAAD – INESC TEC, Porto, Portugal
e-mail: arrp@inesctec.pt

A. Jatowt
University of Innsbruck, Innsbruck, Austria
e-mail: adam.jatowt@uibk.ac.at

V. Mangaravite
Federal University of Minas Gerais, Belo Horizonte, Minas Gerais, Brazil
e-mail: vima@inesctec.pt

A. M. Jorge
LIAAD – INESC TEC, Porto, Portugal

DCC – FCUP, University of Porto, Porto, Portugal
e-mail: amjorge@fc.up.pt

© Springer Nature Switzerland AG 2021
D. Gomes et al. (eds.), *The Past Web*,
https://doi.org/10.1007/978-3-030-63291-5_18

relevant research conducted on the automatic generation of timelines for past-web events. Next, we describe the architecture and some use cases for "Tell me Stories". Our system demonstrates how web archives can be used as infrastructures to develop innovative services. We conclude this chapter by enumerating open challenges in this field and possible future directions in the general area of temporal summarisation in web archives.

1 Introduction

The growing trend towards publishing and making content available online has raised new challenges for those who want to understand the timeline of a given topic comprising several events. This is partly rooted in an unprecedented number of documents published every day, leading to information overload (Hiltz and Plotnick 2013) and making it hard for readers to quickly understand the unfolding of a topic (Vossen et al. 2015). This exponential increase in the volume of data (also known as big data), the diversity of news and the increasing number of sources (including social media) make it difficult for users to access, manage and memorise information over time without the use of auxiliary tools. Timeline generation systems emerge in this context as an alternative to manually digesting a large volume of data in a short period of time. They can replace human curation and scale to large amounts of data, and users can take advantage of timelines to create their own summaries and understandings of a given topic. In a time when society demands to be constantly connected and informed, such tools may play an important role (McKeown et al. 2005) for a large spectrum of users looking for the most valuable and useful stories within large amounts of information. This may be the case for journalists, policy makers, students or casual readers who need context for a given story or are interested in checking a fact. Imagine how useful it would be to quickly obtain a timeline of news about a candidate for an important public role, or background information to answer questions regarding an unexpected disaster.

While the process of automatically constructing timelines is complex due to text subjectivity, understanding, reasoning and the lack of a formal representation language, extracting stories from multiple documents and developing structured narratives has turned into a feasible task thanks to current advances in natural language processing (NLP). The appearance of new algorithms in the field of information extraction (Niklaus et al. 2018), temporal information (Campos et al. 2014) and multiple document summarisation (Barros et al. 2019) has led to the emergence of new solutions in the context of timeline generation. Despite these advances, the problem of automatically constructing narratives is far from being solved.

One significant indicator of this challenge is the organisation, since 2007, of an increasing number of scientific events that aim to address research issues related to the automatic generation of timelines, such as the Intelligent Narratives Technologies (Magerko and Riedl 2007), the Computational Models of Narrative

(Finlayson et al. 2010) or the Computing News Storylines (Caselli et al. 2015) conferences. Notably, new events, such as the Storytelling workshop (Margaret et al. 2018) or the Narrative Extraction from Text—Text2Story conference (Jorge et al. 2018) continue to be held, showing an increasing interest in this topic in recent years.

Open research questions usually discussed in these venues revolve around text genre detection, cross-document event ordering, multi-document summarisation, interactive visualisation (including timeline generation, flowcharts, videos and image slideshows) and evaluation. The increasing interest in news (Martinez-Alvarez et al. 2016) and social media texts (Alonso et al. 2018) has also raised new questions that have only recently begun to get attention from the research community. Most of these questions are partly rooted in the need to keep an open connection that reads and processes a continuous stream of text articles to automatically identify new, related and duplicate events across different documents while documents are continuously being published over time. Additional challenges came from the fact that a considerable number of these texts are found within large text corpora, which may cause relevant information to be missed and make it difficult for systems to create structured timelines. Moreover, the problems raised by fake news and filter bubbles create additional challenges in the way readers consume news and form their opinion. Fact-checking of news or the provision of contextualised information to the user requires having access to huge amounts of historical data so that coherent summaries (relevant[1] and non-redundant[2]) may be automatically generated from multiple documents.

One way to address this problem is to resort to the summarisation of events, an active topic that has been widely addressed since the 1950s (Luhn 1958). According to McCreadie et al. (2018), it can be framed within four categories:

1. *Multi-document Summarisation* approaches (Barzilay et al. 2002; Mishra and Berberich 2016) aim to offer a concise generated overview of a given event by extracting informative sentences from a set of related documents.
2. Timeline Generation (aka *Timeline Summarisation*) (Alonso et al. 2010; Yan et al. 2011; Ansah et al. 2019) aims to summarise events across time and to put them in an automatically generated timeline. In this case, the temporal dimension plays an important role, and documents are assumed to be time-tagged or to have at least some inherent (possibly ambiguous) temporal information which allows texts to be anchored in a timeline.
3. *Update Summarisation* (Allan et al. 2001; Wang and Li 2010) focuses on producing intermediate summaries to be updated over time as new information emerges, that is, ongoing events are summarised over time as a real-time problem. The rationale is that for some particular events, such as natural disasters, the user's information needs change with time.

---

[1]Summaries should contain textual units that are important to the user.

[2]Summaries should not contain duplicate textual units, that is, overlapping content.

4. *Temporal Summarisation* approaches (McCreadie et al. 2014; Kedzie et al. 2015) focus on extracting text units from streams of news and social media content.

Several approaches have been proposed, but few have used web archives as a source for narrative generation, disregarding the chance of looking for unique historical information over several years. Notice that although archived web information was born digital, it has already disappeared from its original websites.

Web archiving initiatives have emerged over the last few years to address this problem, known as web ephemera (Gomes and Silva 2006). Arquivo.pt., also known as the Portuguese web-archive (Gomes et al. 2013), is a research infrastructure that is at the forefront of these initiatives. It makes available not only a graphical interface to search and access the past Web but also provides APIs that can be used to automatically query indexes and process archived web content.

Having access to archived web documents is useful, but does not answer the requirement to get integrated timelines about past events. Figure 1 depicts the full-text search results for the query "War at Syria" when submitted to the Arquivo.pt. web archive.

For such an information need, it is useful to have a timeline automatically generated from collected archived documents so that users can have a quick temporal overview of a given topic without having to inspect long lists of documents (likely conveying some non-relevant and redundant results). Users could then enrich their knowledge by looking for more details within each of the archived webpages that originated the excerpts presented in a *Snippet* field, that is, a short summary of

Fig. 1 Arquivo.pt. results for the query "War at Syria" submitted on 15 November 2019

the contents of the website that are retrieved in the results, along with the title and the original URL of the webpage. With this motivation in mind, we developed "Tell me Stories",[3] an interactive news summarisation system (http://archive.tellmestories. pt).

Other related works for summarising information from web archives have also been proposed recently. The Dark and Stormy Archive (DSA) framework was proposed (AlNoamany et al. 2017) for automatically extracting summary stories from Archive-It collections to help users to better understand the content of target archival collections. Representative page versions were selected after removing off-topic or near-duplicate pages and were input to a popular storytelling tool called Storify. In another work, focused crawling techniques were applied to extract event-centric collections from web archives (Gossen et al. 2018).

2 Tell me Stories: Timeline Summarisation from Web Archives

"Tell me Stories" is an interactive online news summarisation platform that enables users to explore multiple historical contents and revisit webpages about past events through an automatically generated timeline summary of news articles preserved by Arquivo.pt. Instead of considering the full document's text, it makes use of titles, short informative pieces of texts that have been shown to be valuable sources of data (Piotrkowicz et al. 2017). While the original task of timeline summarisation builds upon generating date-specific summaries for a target query from the full document's text, resorting to titles as an alternative data source is a promising direction. First, dealing with HTML pages requires applying some preprocessing steps, such as cleaning HTML markup and removing boilerplates, as well as removing non-core parts of pages (i.e. adverts, copyright statements and less relevant text), which can be quite an expensive procedure when applied over large-scale and heterogenous collections such as web archives. Second, news titles are, given their nature, quite descriptive, which enables the generation of informative and coherent summaries when compared to summaries generated based on a selection of sentences automatically extracted from the document's full text. This has proven to be a valid assumption in the work of (Tran et al. 2015) who compared their headline-based approach to the summaries produced by document-based methods (Allan et al. 2001).

In "Tell me Stories", we follow this line of research by exploiting the titles of query-related news articles (extracted from the title field) to construct a timeline summary. However, unlike the work of Tran et al. (2015), we begin by selecting relevant time periods (e.g. from 23 May 2015 to 11 April 2016; and from 11 April 2016 to 21 December 2016), before generating the corresponding summary for a

---

[3]Winner of the Arquivo.pt Award 2018 https://arquivo.pt/awards.

Query

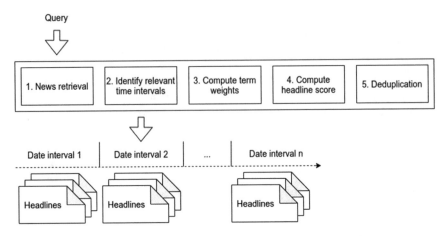

Fig. 2 Tell me Stories pipeline to generate timelines from web archives

particular time span. Furthermore, we make use of web archives as opposed to traditional textual (single view) data sources. While web archives are undoubtedly a valuable source of data, no other work has considered using them as a source for timeline summarisation. In the following sections, we present the steps behind the generation of a timeline for any event when a query is submitted to "Tell me Stories".

2.1 Architecture

Each query submitted to Arquivo.pt. may easily return thousands of results. "Tell me Stories" selects the most relevant non-redundant titles related to the given query. In the context of web archives, we will focus on timeline generation where, given a query (e.g. "War at Syria" or "Brexit"), the system identifies the most important dates (Tran et al. 2013; Campos et al. 2017) and obtains a concise summary for each date (Allan et al. 2001; Tran et al. 2015; Wang and Li 2010; Alonso et al. 2010). We rely on a five-step pipeline depicted in Fig. 2: (1) news retrieval, (2) identifying relevant time intervals, (3) term weighting, (4) computing headline scores and (5) deduplication.

2.1.1 News Retrieval

Given a query posed by the user, the system will fetch matching documents from a collection through search and access APIs, such as the Arquivo.pt. API (https://arquivo.pt/api) or news data sources (e.g. the Signal Media one million news dataset).[4] Notice that documents in our collection (e.g. online news articles) must be time-stamped according to their publication date (i.e. the date when the document was made available online) or to their crawling time (i.e. the date when the document was collected by the web archive).

2.1.2 Identifying Relevant Time Intervals

While traditional search engines focus their actions on acquiring and providing access to the most recent information available online, web archives are designed to be searched across long periods of time, thus yielding long time spans for the returned search results (e.g. years or decades between the oldest and the newest returned document). In this scenario, the frequency of occurrences of the search result set is represented by sparse time series with many periods without any occurrence. Identifying relevant time intervals upon this premise involves a series of steps. Figure 3 describes the computation of the relevant time intervals for the query "War at Syria", from the initial result set (see Fig. 3a) to the final relevant time periods (see Fig. 3d). Figure 3a shows the start of this process, with the plot of the aggregated frequency distributions obtained when issuing a query to the search Arquivo.pt. API. However, the fact that we are addressing long time periods may lead to sparse time series. To tackle this sparsity issue, we begin by dividing the timespan into equal-width intervals/partitions of daily granularity (see Fig. 3b) before transforming the sparse time series into a dense representation (see Fig. 3c). Once we have a dense representation, we identify peaks of occurrences. Based on this, we define the relevant time intervals (see Fig. 3d, where every red line, except for the first and the last, defines the start and end of the adjacent time intervals). The end of each relevant time period is defined by the lowest occurrence before an inflection point takes place. The main goal of this step is to select time intervals that contain at least one peak of atypical frequency of occurrences, thus ensuring that the resulting interval has some event of interest. Figure 3d illustrates the time interval selected for the query "War at Syria". In this case, the system identifies 11 important time intervals (between 2010 and 2018): the red lines represent interval boundaries, while the blue ones highlight the number of news titles aggregated by date.

2.1.3 Computing Term Weights

Next, we determine the importance of each term found in the result set. We begin by determining the vocabulary of the collection by applying common preprocessing steps such as sentence segmentation, tokenisation and stopword removal. Thus,

---

[4]https://research.signal-ai.com/newsir16/signal-dataset.html

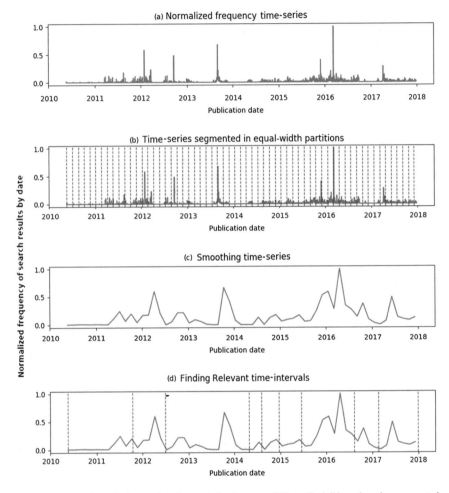

Fig. 3 Computation of relevant time intervals for the query "War at Syria" based on the aggregated frequency distributions of the result set

each vocabulary term receives a score based on five statistical features derived from YAKE!'s algorithm (Campos et al. 2018, 2020):

1. T_{Case}: the number of times a term is capitalised
2. $T_{Position}$: the term position in a headline
3. TF_{Norm}: the normalised frequency of the term within all the titles of the search result set
4. T_{Rel}: term related to context (i.e. to the terms that co-occurs with it, in a window of two terms)
5. $T_{Diversity}$: the number of different titles in the search result set in which a term appears

Each of these features is then heuristically combined into a final score. The smaller the value, the more significant the term(t) will be. Equation 1 explains this process:

$$S(t) = \frac{T_{\text{Rel}} \times T_{\text{Position}}}{T_{\text{Case}} + \frac{TF_{\text{Norm}}}{T_{\text{Rel}}} + \frac{T_{\text{Diversity}}}{T_{\text{Rel}}}} \tag{1}$$

2.1.4 Computing Title Scores

In the fourth step, we determine the most important titles h_i for each time interval. Similar to YAKE!, we take into account the individual $S(t)$ scores of each term of the headline when computing a score. Equation 2 formalises this process:

$$S(h_i) = \frac{\prod\limits_{t \in h_i} S(t)}{1 + \sum\limits_{t \in h_i} S(t)} \tag{2}$$

More details about the rationale of YAKE! features, illustrative examples and the scoring step can be found in YAKE!'s article (Campos et al. 2018, 2020).

2.1.5 Deduplication

Finally, as a means to reduce the amount of duplicated result contents, we aim to understand if two different pieces of text about a given event refer to the same topic. One possibility, as stated by Vossen et al. (2015), is to make use of the temporal aspects of a given event. Anchoring events in time has proved to be of immense value in the context of the live Web. However, it may not be enough within the context of archived web news where multiple mentions of the same event can be repeatedly collected over distinct time periods among the same or different sources, possibly leading to overlapping information. An example of this can be observed when we submitted the query "War at Syria" to the Arquivo.pt. API. The results obtained enable us to conclude that several snapshots[5,6] of the same webpage were collected over different time periods. One possible solution to overcome this problem is to make use of deduplication algorithms, where similar texts are detected and eliminated. In the "Tell me Stories" project, similar news titles are detected based on the Levenshtein similarity measure and a threshold which ignores texts that are more than 80% similar. When comparing a pair of strings of characters, we

---

[5]https://arquivo.pt/wayback/20140515192724/http://www.dinheirovivo.pt/Videos/Detalhe/CIECO348576.html, collected on 15 May 2014.

[6]https://arquivo.pt/wayback/20140516020151/http://www.dinheirovivo.pt/Videos/Detalhe/CIECO348576.html, collected on 16 May 2014.

keep the longer one, assuming it carries more information than the shorter version. This threshold is a parameter and can be fine-tuned for different cases. For each time interval, we then select the top 20 key phrases ordered by their relevance.

2.2 Demonstration

As a proof of concept, we made available a demonstration of "Tell me Stories" (Pasquali et al. 2019), using Arquivo.pt. as a data source. Figure 4 demonstrates the home page where users can submit their queries to produce the respective timeline summarisation and explore pre-loaded topics belonging to the categories of economy, culture and politics.

By submitting a query to the system, the user receives a timeline summary about the topic. This interactive visualisation allows users to navigate back and forth through time periods, enabling the temporal analysis of long-lasting events like wars or international and financial crises. Figure 5 shows this interactive timeline for the query "Guerra na Síria", i.e. "War at Syria". For each selected timeframe (in

Fig. 4 Tell me Stories' home page (http://archive.tellmestories.pt) where users can submit their query or select one from the provided examples

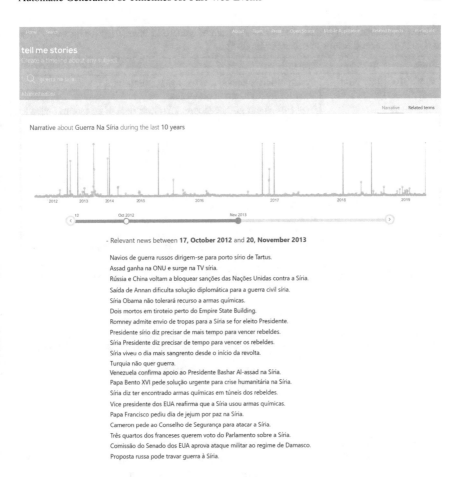

Fig. 5 Result timeline for the query "War at Syria" when submitted to Tell me Stories

green), users are offered the top-20 most relevant titles from that time period.[7] A user interested in getting to know more information about the chosen topic can then click on the corresponding headline to access the preserved webpage.

A more detailed analysis of the results (between the different time periods) can be observed in Table 1.[8] We can observe the most important titles since 2010, when the first popular protests reached the streets and the news. The first titles highlight

---

[7]As a rule of thumb, users are offered time periods from a window of 10 years ago until approximately 1 year before the time of submitting the query, in line with the Arquivo.pt. policy of making available archived content 1 year after publication.

[8]For the sake of clarity, we translated these results to English. A version of "Tell me Stories" over (English) data sources (Bing news search and the signal one million news dataset) is available for demonstration purposes at (http://tellmestories.pt/).

Table 1 Timeline of top-three titles summary (from May 2010 to June 2015) for the query "War at Syria" (query and results translated to English)

From	To	Top titles
May 2010	July 2011	Syrian officials launch tear gas against protesters. Security forces shoot at protesters. *New York Times* journalist with a Pulitzer died of an asthma attack in Syria. ...
Aug 2011	March 2012	Assad promises elections in February in Syria. US withdraws ambassador from Syria for security reasons. NATO says goodbye to Libya and the world turns to Syria. ...
July 2012	March 2013	Russia delivers three war helicopters to Syria. Russian warships head for Syrian port of Tartus. NATO approves a shipment of patriot missiles to Turkey. Bashar Assad reaffirms that he will never leave Syria. ...
July 2013	Nov 2013	Amnesty international defends investigation into possible chemical attack. The United States is waging war with Syria. Putin and Obama on a collision course due to the war in Syria. ...
Apr 2014	June 2015	One hundred thousand civilians fled the Syrian province of Deir Ezzor. Journalist and photographer of the times injured in Syria. ISIS assumes full control of the historic city of Palmyra. ...

the brutal repression and the escalation of violence against civilians and journalists. Moving forward, the user can observe the involvement of other countries in the conflict and the emergence of news regarding the humanitarian crises, including the reference to events where civilians suffered attacks (like the infamous airstrike on and bombing of a maternity unit). In general, the example illustrates how this kind of tool can help users to understand the overall picture of a given topic in a nutshell.

Besides the timeline visualisation, users can explore important related query terms (extracted through the YAKE! keyword extractor) by means of a word cloud. Figure 6 illustrates the word cloud for the query "Guerra na Síria (War at Syria)". By looking at the picture, we can observe multiple related entities and main actors for this story (e.g. "Arábia Saudita (Saudi Arabia)", "Estado Islamico (Islamic State)", "Nações Unidas (United Nations)", "Amnistia Internacional (International Amnisty)", "Cruz Vermelha (Red Cross)", "China", "UK", "USA", "Iran", "Daesh", "Bashar", "Putin", "Obama"). This enables users quickly to familiarise themselves with the related topics at a glance.

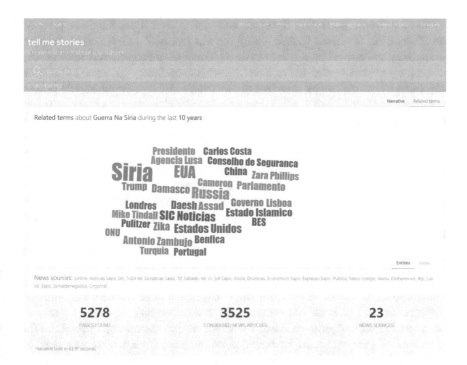

Fig. 6 Related terms for the query "War at Syria"

3 Temporal Summarisation in Web Archives: Open Challenges and Future Work

Constructing coherent summaries based on archives of the past Web raised several challenges that were dealt with when developing "Tell me Stories". In this section, we point out some specific difficulties faced during project development, which might be interesting for those aiming to develop similar solutions.

Unlike traditional Temporal Summarisation (TS), in Temporal Summarisation in Web Archives (TSWA), multiple snapshots of the same webpage may be selected, eventually leading to duplicated content (AlNoamany et al. 2017). Hence, while in TS, the problem is at the level of identifying similar content from different sources, in TSWA the problem is also how to deal with exactly or partially similar versions of the same webpage over time, which leads occasionally to presenting the same titles for different page results. While we were able to reduce this problem, by applying deduplication algorithms, a more elaborated solution could possibly be drawn by applying word embeddings (Kenter and de Rijke 2015).

Another related problem faced when summarising texts from web archive sources concerns the temporal aspects of a given event: related information may be continuously collected over different time periods or a few days after the event occurrence, generating disparate information over time. This was the case on 20 June 2017, when a Canadair airplane was reported[9] to have crashed during firefighting in Portugal by a source in the National Civil Protection Authority. The alleged event was denied hours later.[10] Such contradictory information may be identified by journalists by resorting to tools such as the revisionista.pt.[11] project (Martins and Mourão 2020), which keeps track of the changes made in a given news article. However, contradictory information must not be deleted from web archives because their mission is to preserve web data as faithfully as possible for future analysis. While this neutral behaviour of web archives may be extremely useful in historical terms (for keeping track of the whole story), it creates diffuse information and challenges for applications that try to describe an event automatically. In the case of "Tell me Stories", different versions of the event can be found in different time periods, potentially misleading simple algorithms that are based on peak/burst detection.

Another problem relates to the credibility of the sources, as only a few may have content potentially useful for generating a summary. With regard to this, certain resource types, such as newswire sites, may be selected as prime sources, while others, like blogs or company home pages, could be ignored. Furthermore, the identification of historical web content that documents important events can be improved with algorithms tuned for temporal data processing. Therefore, the relevance of past events to be included or removed from a summary may be measured based on their evaluated long-term impact rather than simply on the popularity they enjoyed at the time.

Issues related to the evolution of terminology, such as changes in word semantics and the dynamics of the expressions used to refer to the same or similar concepts, may also occur. While this may not be a major problem for live web platforms, because only the most recent content is usually provided, it is certainly a challenge for platforms based on web archives, such as "Tell me Stories". This is evident in the case of "Syrian war" and "UK opposition to EU", two events that have acquired different terminology over time, from "Syrian war" to "war refugees" to "migrant crisis" and from "UK opposition to EU" to "Brexit". Another problem has to do with homonyms,[12] because the same word may have different meanings over time, with the documents retrieved by a web archive. This is the case for "Gulf War" as there were actually two different wars, one in 1990 and another one in 2013, and for "George Bush", the father and the son, 41st and 43rd US President, respectively.

We would also like to emphasise how difficult it is to evaluate research in the field of TSWA. The systematic evaluation of automatically generated summaries, such as those generated by "Tell me Stories", is essential for developing and improving

---

[9]https://arquivo.pt/wayback/20170620170425/http://www.publico.pt/

[10]https://arquivo.pt/wayback/20170621181927/https://www.publico.pt/2017/06/21/sociedade/noticia/a-suposta-queda-do-aviao-em-pedrogao-grande-1776377

[11]Second prize of the Arquivo.pt. awards 2019.

[12]Words that look the same but have different meanings.

innovative tools. However, it is a very challenging and time-consuming task, mostly due to human subjectivity in relation to the concept of relevance and lack of research test datasets over web archived collections that could provide comparative baselines. While several approaches have been proposed over the years, the lack of specific annotated corpora has limited the evaluation, requiring researchers to invest a considerable amount of time in building their evaluation datasets. A recent alternative was proposed by Tran et al. (2013) who suggested an approach that links news articles with pre-existing timelines as reference summaries. Most of these works rely on ROUGE, a suite of metrics that have become the de facto standard for the summary evaluation method to compare system-generated timelines against manually constructed summaries. While ROUGE is widely used for quantitative evaluation of computed summaries, it was not initially designed to consider temporal aspects, leading some researchers to suggest extensions better suited to the task of ranking sentences in timelines. In particular, Martschat and Markert (2017) provided an open-source implementation (https://github.com/smartschat/tilse) making available a set of new metrics and a module that allows users to run experiments with their own TS methods and datasets. Despite these advances, TSW still lacks a specific test dataset, and, consequently, adopting evaluations based on shared task datasets (e.g. TREC-TS 2015[13] or SemEval-2015 Task 4[14]) offers opportunities to work with public annotated data on a common ground. Another option is to make use of the datasets[15] proposed by Tran et al. (2013) and Tran et al. (2015), who manually constructed ground-truth timelines by gathering contents edited by professional journalists from a number of news sources. Based on these datasets, we plan to conduct a formal evaluation of "Tell me Stories" in the medium term, by comparing our headline approach with the ground-truth collected contents.

Future work may also involve adapting "Tell me Stories" to be fed by any search engine over archived web collections, thus increasing coverage and the accuracy of the returned search results. Another promising research direction makes use of images over time to visually summarise a topic (Xu et al. 2012). A strong indicator of this is the recent release of the image search API from Arquivo.pt.,[16] which enables keyword-to-image search and access to past-web images. There has also been substantial work in abstractive summarisation (Barros et al., 2019), where instead of selecting the most important sentences from the text to combine them as a summary, users are offered novel sentences automatically constructed through natural language generation techniques. This is a very challenging task that deserves more attention in the future.

---

[13]http://www.trec-ts.org/

[14]http://alt.qcri.org/semeval2015/task4/

[15]http://www.l3s.de/~gtran/timeline/

[16]https://arquivo.pt/api/imagesearch

4 Conclusions

The Web is nowadays considered a reflection of our society, revealing subjects that matter and amplifying major events. It is no surprise, then, that many initiatives have been undertaken to capture and save representative web content and to preserve cultural heritage for future generations. While the usage of web archives is dominated by researchers, digital historians or journalists, the vast data available about our past will soon become increasingly useful for ordinary web users. For this purpose, effective and innovative tools are required, which will seamlessly accommodate the search intentions of users and lower the barrier to exploring web archive data for non-experts who wish to analyse, search and investigate primary sources from the past, rather than relying on results produced by third parties (e.g. reports). Timelines are natural tools for reasoning about evolution, change and progress, and they save much effort in comparing, connecting and meaningfully arranging individual instances of data (e.g. news articles) over time.

In this chapter, we briefly overviewed research conducted on the automatic generation of timelines for past-web events. We demonstrated an example tool, named "Tell me Stories", which operates over Arquivo.pt—the Portuguese web-archive—to automatically generate timelines about topics submitted through user queries. The proposed system uses only news titles, which are concise and informative summaries of news articles. To avoid the issue of noisy data, the redundancy among news reports in certain time periods is maintained to select salient time intervals where key events related to user-submitted queries occurred in the past. We enumerated open challenges in this field and suggested directions for future work in the area of Temporal Summarisation in Web Archives.

Acknowledgements Arian Pasquali and Vítor Mangaravite were financed by National Funds through the Portuguese funding agency, FCT (Fundação para a Ciência e a Tecnologia), within project UIDB/50014/2020. Ricardo Campos and Alípio Jorge were financed by the ERDF (European Regional Development Fund) through the North Portugal Regional Operational Programme (NORTE 2020), under the PORTUGAL 2020, and by National Funds through the Portuguese funding agency, FCT (Fundação para a Ciência e a Tecnologia) within project PTDC/CCI-COM/31857/2017 (NORTE-01-0145-FEDER-03185). This funding fits under the research line of the Text2Story project.

References

Allan J, Gupta R, Khandelwal V (2001) Temporal summaries of new topics. In: SIGIR 2001: Proceedings of the 24th annual international ACM SIGIR conference on research and development in information retrieval, 9–13 September. ACM Press, New Orleans, LA, USA, pp 10–18

AlNoamany Y, Weigle MC, Nelson ML (2017) Generating stories from archived collections. In: Proceedings of the 2017 ACM on web science conference (WebSci'17). ACM Press, New York, NY, USA, pp 309–318

Alonso O, Berberich K, Bedathur S, Weikum G (2010) Time-based exploration of news archives. In: Proceedings of the fourth workshop on human-computer interaction and information retrieval (HCIR), 22 August, New Brunswick, USA, pp 12–15

Alonso O, Kandylas V, Tremblay S-E (2018) How it happened: discovering and archiving the evolution of a story using social signals. In: Proceedings of the 18th ACM/IEEE joint conference on digital libraries, 3–7 June, Fort Worth, USA, pp 193–202

Ansah J, Liu L, Kang W, Kwashie S, Li J, Li J (2019) A graph is worth a thousand words: telling event stories using timeline summarization graphs. In: Proceedings of the World Wide Web Conference (WWW'19), 13–17 May. ACM, San Francisco, USA, pp 2565–2571

Barros C, Lloret E, Saquete E, Navarro-Colorado B (2019) NATSUM: narrative abstractive summarization (A. Jorge, R. Campos, A. Jatowt, & S. Nunes, Eds.). Inf Process Manag 56(5):1775–1793

Barzilay R, Elhadad N, McKeown KR (2002) Inferring strategies for sentence ordering in multidocument news summarization. J Artif Intell Res 17(1):35–55

Campos R, Dias G, Jorge A, Jatowt A (2014) Survey of temporal information retrieval and related applications. ACM Comput Surv 47(2):15

Campos R, Dias G, Jorge A, Nunes C (2017) Identifying top relevant dates for implicit time sensitive queries. Inf Retr J 20(4):363–398

Campos R, Mangaravite V, Pasquali A, Jorge AM, Nunes C, Jatowt A (2018) A text feature based automatic keyword extraction method for single documents. In: Proceedings of the 40th European conference on information retrieval (ECIR'18). Springer, Grenoble, France, pp 684–691

Campos R, Mangaravite V, Pasquali A, Jatowt A, Jorge A, Nunes C, Jatowt A (2020) YAKE! Keyword extraction from single documents using multiple local features. Inform Sci J 509:257–289

Caselli T, Van Erp M, Minard A-L, Finlayson M, Miller B, Atserias J et al (2015) Proceedings of the first workshop on computing news storylines (CNewsStory'15), 31 July. Association for Computational Linguistics, Beijing, China, pp 1–73

Finlayson MA, Whitman R, Winston P (2010) Computational models of narrative: review of a workshop. AI Mag 31(2):97–100

Gomes D, Silva M (2006) Modelling information persistence on the web. Proceedings of the 6th international conference on web engineering (ICWE'06), 11–14 July, California, USA, pp 193–200

Gomes D, Cruz D, Miranda J, Costa M, Fontes S (2013) Search the past with the Portuguese web archive. In: Proceedings of the 22nd international conference on world wide web (WWW'13), 13–17 May, Rio de Janeiro, pp 321–324

Gossen G, Risse T, Demidova E (2018) Towards extracting event-centric collections from web archives. In: International journal on digital libraries. Springer, Cham, pp 1–15

Hiltz SR, Plotnick L (2013) Dealing with information overload when using social media for emergency management: emerging solutions. In: Proceedings of the 10th international ISCRAM conference (ISCRAM'13), May 2013, Baden-Baden, Germany, pp 823–827

Jorge A, Campos R, Jatowt A, Nunes S (2018) Proceedings of the first international workshop on on narrative extraction from text (Text2Story'18@ECIR'18), 26 March. CEUR, Grenoble, France, pp 1–51

Kedzie C, McKeown K, Diaz F (2015) Predicting salient updates for disaster summarization. In: Proceedings of the 53rd annual meeting of the Association for Computational Linguist (ACL'15) and the 7th international joint conference on natural language process (IJCNLP'15), 26–31 July, Beijing, China, pp 1608–1617

Kenter T, de Rijke M (2015) Short text similarity with word embeddings. In: Proceedings of the 24th ACM international on conference on information and knowledge management (CIKM'15), 18–23 October. ACM, Melbourne, Australia, pp 1411–1420

Luhn HP (1958) The automatic creation of literature abstracts. IBM J Res Dev 2(2):159–165

Magerko B, Riedl M (2007) Proceedings of the 1st intelligent narratives technologies, 9–11 November. AAAI, Arlington, USA, pp 1–190

Margaret M, Huang T-H, Ferraro F, Misra I (2018) Proceedings of the storytelling workshop (StoryNLP'18@NAACL'18), 5 July, New Orleans, USA, pp 1–67

Martinez-Alvarez M, Kruschwitz U, Kazai G, Hopfgartner F, Corney D, Campos R, Albakour D (2016) Report on the first international workshop on recent trends in news information retrieval. SIGIR Forum 50(1):58–67

Martins F, Mourão A (2020) Revisionista.PT: uncovering the news cycle using web archives. Proceedings of the 42nd European conference on information retrieval (ECIR'20). Springer, Lisbon, Portugal

Martschat S, Markert K (2017) Improving {ROUGE} for timeline summarization. In: Proceedings of the 15th conference of the European chapter of the Association for Computational Linguistics, 3–7 April. Association for Computational Linguistics, Valencia, Spain, pp 285–290

McCreadie R, Macdonald C, Ounis I (2014) Incremental update summarization: adaptive sentence selection based on prevalence and novelty. In: Proceedings of the 23rd ACM international conference on information and knowledge management (CIKM'14), 3–7 November. ACM Press, Shanghai, China, pp 301–310

McCreadie R, Santos R, Macdonald C, Ounis I (2018) Explicit diversification of event aspects for temporal summarization. ACM Trans Infor Syst 36(3):25

McKeown K, Passonneau RJ, Elson DK, Nenkova A, Hirschberg J (2005) Do summaries help? A task-based evaluation of multi-document summarization. In: Proceedings of the 28th annual international conference on research and development in information retrieval (SIGIR'05), 15–19 August. ACM Press, Salvador da Bahia, Brazil, pp 217–210

Mishra A, Berberich K (2016) Event digest: a holistic view on past events. In: Proceedings of the 39th international conference on research and development in information retrieval (SIGIR'16), 17–21 July. ACM Press, Pisa, Italy, pp 493–502

Niklaus C, Cetto M, Freitas A, Handschuh S (2018) A survey on open information extraction. In: Proceedings of the 27th international conference on computational linguistics, 20–26 August, Santa Fe, USA, pp 3866–3878

Pasquali A, Mangaravite V, Campos R, Jorge A, Jatowt A (2019) Interactive system for automatically generating temporal narratives. In: Proceedings of the 41st European conference on information retrieval (ECIR'19), 14–18 April. Springer, Cologne, Germany

Piotrkowicz A, Dimitrova V, Markert K (2017) Automatic extraction of news values from headline text. In: Proceedings of the student research workshop at the 15th conference of the European chapter of the Association for Computational Linguistics (SRW@EACL'17), 3–7 April. Association for Computational Linguistic, Valencia, Spain, pp 64–74

Tran GB, Alrifai M, Nguyen DQ (2013) Predicting relevant news events for timeline summaries. In: WWW2013: proceedings of the companion publication of the 22nd international conference on world wide web companion, 13–17 May, Rio de Janeiro, Brazil, pp 91–92

Tran G, Alrifai M, Herder E (2015) Timeline summarization from relevant headlines. In: Proceedings of the 37th European conference on information retrieval, 29 March–2 April. Springer, Vienna, Austria, pp 245–256

Vossen P, Caselli T, Kontzopoulou Y (2015) Storylines for structuring massive streams of news. In: Proceedings of the first workshop on computing news storylines (CNewsStory'15@ACL-IJCNLP'15), 31 July. Association for Computational Linguistics, Beijing, China, pp 40–49

Wang D, Li T (2010) Document update summarization using incremental hierarchical clustering. In: Proceedings of the 19th ACM international conference on information and knowledge management (CIKM'10), 26–30 October. ACM Press, Toronto, Canada, pp 279–288

Xu S, Kong L, Zhang Y (2012) A picture paints a thousand words: a method of generating image-text timelines. In: CIKM 2012: proceedings of the 21st ACM international conference on information and knowledge management, 29 October–2 November. ACM Press, Maui, Hawaii, pp 2511–2514

Yan R, Wan X, Otterbacher J, Kong L, Li X, Zhang Y (2011) Evolutionary timeline summarization: a balanced optimization framework via iterative substitution. In: Proceedings of the 34th international ACM SIGIR conference on research and development in information retrieval (SIGIR'11), 24–28 July. ACM Press, Beijing, China, pp 745–754

Political Opinions on the Past Web

Miguel Won

Abstract Political commentary, by so-called pundits, has played an increasingly important role in the editorial choices of news media. Their opinions are disseminated from a privileged position, and they are capable of dictating how the political realm should be introduced into public discussion. Their constant presence shapes public opinion and, if not representative and diverse, can threaten public debate. This work focuses on the opinion articles published by the leading Portuguese national online newspapers. We built an online archive that collects opinion articles published by the leading Portuguese news websites between 2008 and 2016. More than 80,000 articles were collected, approximately 3500 authors were indexed and several search tools were made available over full text, authorship information and key phrases. The Arquivo de Opinião (Archive of Opinion) collection is an innovative online tool, available at http://arquivodeopiniao.pt/en/, that enables the analysis of a corpus of opinion articles that represent a memory of public debate. It offers possibilities for study in several fields, from political science to media studies, as well as for answering questions such as who said what or what was being argued in a particular debate. For example, how was climate change debated in the past? Were today's political leaders concerned with environmental issues? Arquivo de Opinião leverages the public memory required for any healthy and democratic debate.

1 Introduction

The news media are the gatekeepers of "political reality" (McNair 2017), and information dissemination by the news media is constantly shaped by the unavoidable selection of events. The event selection of what "really matters in political affairs" (McNair 2017) is always dependent on editorial choices and is therefore vulnerable

M. Won (✉)
INESC, Lisbon, Portugal
e-mail: miguelwon@tecnico.ulisboa.pt

© Springer Nature Switzerland AG 2021
D. Gomes et al. (eds.), *The Past Web*,
https://doi.org/10.1007/978-3-030-63291-5_19

to biases. Additionally, apart from event selection, the interpretation of facts is not a trivial task because it is often highly dependent on the knowledge of current political dynamics, historical events or political ideologies. Consequently, the awareness of political dynamics is highly subjective and prone to be misinterpreted by the ordinary citizen who is typically not a political expert.

Political commentators, also called pundits, emerge as skilful readers of this complex world, which is highly dynamic and codified with its own rules. They reveal their professional opinion about how particular events could or should be interpreted, guiding those receiving this information to contextualise events in their understanding of the public realm. From this point of view, political commentators can be seen as "deciphers" (Nimmo and Combs 1992) of the complex daily political reality. We can describe political commentators as influencers of public debate due to the unique and relevant role assigned to them by the established mass news media. Thousands of voters read their opinions and are consequently influenced to like or dislike specific policies or political actors. Furthermore, with the massive spread and reach of online news, mainly through social media, these pundits have additionally gained a new level of public attention, as well as proximity to their audience. Their opinions are more than just personal opinions, and news is published about what political position a particular pundit adopts. One clear example in the Portuguese context is the political commentary of Marcelo Rebelo de Sousa, which was aired for several years and during prime time on a Portuguese free-to-air TV channel. His analysis frequently constituted a source of news in the following days, with the central concern being the commentator's opinion about a specific policy. Marcelo Rebelo de Sousa was elected President of the Portuguese Republic in 2016. All political parties are aware of the power of influence by this "punditry world" (Nimmo and Combs 1992). Several of these commentators are themselves professional politicians, sometimes in the exercise of public functions, as former or current party members, or as publicly sympathetic to a political force. For this reason, one may consider many opinions as politically biased and that some "spaces of opinion typically fail to satisfy minimum standards of reason or rational deliberation" (Jacobs and Townsley 2011).

Scrutinising this punditry world is fundamental to understanding the dynamics of public debate today. Given this degree of influence on public opinion, it becomes essential to hold punditry "accountable". Monitoring, archiving and analysing opinion articles published over time can contribute to such accountability. A democratic system needs a balanced and transparent public debate and the creation of a memory for public debate through political commentary. Only by preserving national memory will it be possible to recall past debates, assess the pros and cons of past dilemmas or study previous public debates that gave rise to successful or unsuccessful policies. Political consistency is wanted by voters, and memory of opinions enables them to analyse the historical coherence of political actors. Furthermore, many of these opinion articles are at risk of being lost to the public. Some opinion articles are exclusively published in online format, and their archives are maintained only by the respective publishers (private). Possible closures, bankruptcy or even simply a poor web framework setup can result in the loss of these archived collections for future public consultation.

Arquivo de Opinião (Archive of Opinion) emerges in this context as an online tool that enables access to a memory of born-digital political commentary in the Portuguese news media. It provides a public service that enables any citizen to search, access or browse published opinions issued over time. A preserved memory of this past public debate makes an important contribution to public debate in the present and future. A digital archive with this information structured and indexed results in a higher level of scrutiny and transparency in relation to political commentary.

Due to the high volume of articles published online, a digital archive should not only provide access to opinion articles but also offer user-friendly search tools, such as search engines. The digital format brings added value that is not provided by a physical file. For example, it enables the creation of search tools operating across text, keywords, authors or date of publication. These tools enable the user to search at no cost for specific text within a particular period of time or restricted to a particular author. Arquivo de Opinião offers its users a set of tools that enrich the search and bring an additional layer of exploration for a comprehensive collection of opinion articles. These features can help the typical reader or a researcher from the fields of communication studies or political science to explore in more detail the content of online political commentary in Portugal.

2 Data Collection: Building a Collection of Opinion Articles

Like other infrastructures that preserve past web content such as the Internet Archive,[1] Arquivo.pt. collects and preserves websites mainly registered with the Portuguese domain .pt. Arquivo.pt. preserves the history of websites, which results in the archiving of the same URL at different timestamps. We used Arquivo.pt. APIs[2] to retrieve the URLs of unavailable opinion articles originally published on newspaper websites. The URL search functionality was used to extract all URLs containing regex patterns, such as /opiniao/, slugs of author names and sections. Web scraping was also undertaken. Arquivo.pt. preserves the full website, including its internal links, that is, the links within a specific website linking to an archived URL from the same website. This feature allowed the scraping of the opinion section of each newspaper website from Arquivo.pt.

We collected the opinion section of six daily newspapers, one weekly newspaper and one weekly news magazine. These media sources were selected based on circulation figures and data availability for the period under consideration: 2008–2016. Table 1 shows the news media sources analysed and the corresponding dataset

---

[1] https://archive.org/

[2] https://github.com/arquivo/pwa-technologies/wiki/APIs

Table 1 Sources of opinion articles (original websites and web-archived versions preserved by Arquivo.pt) and the respective number of collected opinion articles

Journal	Sources	Articles	Total
Correio da Manhã	cmjornal.pt	0	
	arquivo.pt	12,595	12,595
Diário de Notícias	dn.pt	0	
	arquivo.pt	12,012	12,012
Expresso	expresso.sapo.pt	5064	
	arquivo.pt	0	5064
Jornal de Negócios	jornaldenegocios.pt	14,746	
	arquivo.pt	0	14,746
Jornal de Notícias	jn.pt	211	
	arquivo.pt	9211	9422
Jornal i	ionline.sapo.pt	2377	
	arquivo.pt	4452	6829
Público	publico.pt	24,903	
	arquivo.pt	0	24,903
Sábado	sabado.pt	0	
	arquivo.pt	2898	2898

size. Two web sources were used for extracting the opinion articles: the live websites of the respective media newspapers and the Arquivo.pt. web archive. As an example, we extracted 211 articles directly from the Jornal de Notícias website and 9211 articles from Arquivo.pt.

This task was helped by the fact that, for most newspaper websites, the old front end has a simple pagination system, with a fixed number of opinion articles per page. This meant that a web scraper could easily be implemented by interactively searching opinion pieces on each page. For example, the archived opinion section of the news magazine "Sábado" from 28 December 2011 can be visited using the following URL: https://arquivo.pt/wayback/20111228012319/ http://www.sabado. pt/Opiniao.aspx?Page=1. This webpage shows the user the 10 most recent opinion articles. We searched for additional opinion articles by iteratively updating the "Page" parameter.

For Expresso, Jornal de Negócios and Público, we collected the opinion articles directly from their websites. Their current websites offer the possibility to go back in time and scrape for relevant pieces published in the chosen period. In the case of Jornal de Notícias and Jornal i, the respective websites make available only a very recent archive of material. For this reason, we considered a blended approach, collecting the most recent opinion articles from their websites and the remainder from Arquivo.pt. For all the remaining newspapers, we scraped the information from the Arquivo.pt. web archive. This web scraping was performed using the

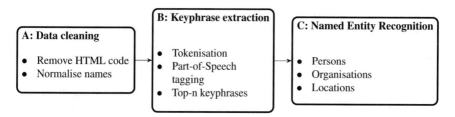

Fig. 1 Pipeline for processing the opinion articles

Python package Scrapy[3]. Since the front-end layout is different for each source, a Scrapy scraper was coded for each website. Each scraper was coded to extract the structured information from the identified URL, in particular the author's name, title, publication date and text body. We restricted data collection to the period between 2008 and 2016, that is, from the year when Arquivo.pt. started regularly to collect data to the most recent available year.

3 Data Processing Pipeline

Every opinion article retrieved was processed through a Natural Language Processing (NLP) pipeline. The main objective was to extract the most relevant key phrases and recognised named entities from each opinion article. This type of information enables data aggregation that provides the user with insightful information about the content of the opinion articles.

Figure 1 details the steps applied to process the collected articles. The pipeline was started with a data-cleaning step, where all possible HTML code wrongly extracted during the web scraping task was removed. This is HTML code that is wrongly present in common fields such as article titles or author names. A second text-cleaning process was executed to remove unwanted expressions used frequently in association with author names, such as "written by". This step resulted in a clean text and author's name. We additionally assumed that, within all media sources, there is a unique name used for each author.

In the second step of the pipeline (key phrase extraction), we extracted the most relevant key phrases for each opinion article following a previously developed method (Won et al. 2019). We first applied standard tokenisation (identify all words within the text with the correct order) to the title and text body using NLTK[4]. This step was followed by a Part-of-Speech (POS) tagging task, where the morphological class (noun, verb, etc.) was automatically assigned to each identified word. The POS classes tagging process was performed with the state-of-art POS tagger, nlpnet

---

[3]https://scrapy.org/

[4]https://www.nltk.org

(Fonseca and Rosa 2013a, b), trained explicitly for Portuguese (European and Brazilian). The POS classes were then used to capture noun phrases, that is, a pattern that matches sequences of nouns that are possibly followed by adjectives and prepositions. Examples are "Serviço Nacional de Saúde" (National Health Service) or "Segurança Social" (Social Security). Finally, for each of these captured noun phrases (candidates for key phrases), a relevance score is measured based on their size, position and frequency. In the end, the top-n candidates were identified as the document relevant key phrases, where n was chosen according to the document size (more details in Won et al. (2019)). This key phrase extraction task was performed with a fully unsupervised process, that is, without the need to train any machine learning (ML) model. This methodology was applied to the full dataset, which resulted in the identification of more than 30,000 unique key phrases.

The third step in the pipeline was the extraction of named entities (Named Entity Recognition). For this step, we applied an ML supervised framework. Equivalent to the POS classes case, the objective was to label each word as belonging to a possible class of entity. Typically, in an NER system, the class is one of Person, Location or Organisation. We, therefore, needed to train an ML model that receives as input the text words and outputs them with the respective class labels. For example, with the sentence "Jim visited New York", the NER system should tag Jim as a name and New York as a location. For the training step, we used the CINTIL dataset (Barreto et al. 2006), which contains approximately 30,000 annotated sentences written in Portuguese, with three types of named entities: person, location and organisation. The trained ML model outputs all words with the respective labels, revealing to which entity it belongs (including a class of no-entity). For this step, we used the state-of-art Stanford Named Entity Recognition (NER) (Finkel et al. 2005) system as our main NER tool.

4   Arquivo de Opinião: Research Tool over Political Opinions

Arquivo de Opinião is a web portal that provides research tools for the analysis of political opinions publicly available at http://arquivodeopiniao.pt/en. The home page offers a graphical user interface to search and explore opinion articles through textual queries. It additionally offers a search engine that supports advanced search options, allowing the user to filter search results by a specific publication date range, author's name and newspaper. Arquivo de Opinião was built with a back end of Django 2.0.3[5] and a MongoDB 3.6.4[6] database. The search results are given by a MongoDB text search feature, which was tuned additionally to use the extracted key phrases as extra weight. For each result, the newspaper, title, author's name and publication date are shown, along with a brief excerpt from the article's text body,

---

[5]https://www.djangoproject.com/
[6]https://www.mongodb.com/

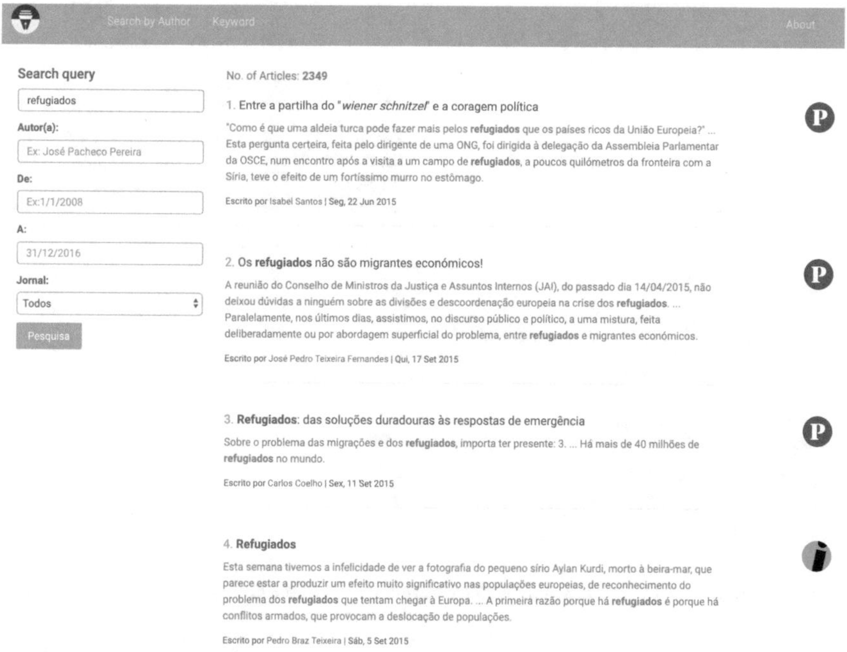

Fig. 2 Full-text search results for the query "refugiados" (refugees)

with the searched text matches in bold. We show in Fig. 2 the webpage generated for the full-text search "refugiados" (refugees).

The second search feature of the Arquivo de Opinião tool focuses on authorship. We generated a dedicated webpage per author, which displays aggregated information extracted from the key phrases and named entities. It contains a feed of the author's opinion articles, the most used entities (person names, locations and organisations) for that particular author and the most frequently used key phrases shown in a word cloud style. As an example, we show in Fig. 3 the webpage for Rui Tavares, a well-known columnist writing for the Público newspaper. We can see that he is a particularly productive author, with 829 articles in 9 years. The most frequent organisation cited is the European Parliament, followed by the European Union. This a good example of the author's main interests, since he is known by the public for having strong opinions about European affairs, is a former European Member of Parliament and has run three times for the European Parliament.

The third search feature of Arquivo de Opinião focuses on the statistical analysis of key phrases. We have indexed more than 30,000 key phrases and counted the frequency of their use in opinion articles. With this analysis feature, the user can search for a particular key phrase. We show key phrase usage over time and by news media source, as well as related key phrases. In Fig. 4 we show an example of the results given by the key phrase "refugiados" (refugees). A trend starting in 2015 is visible, with a very pronounced peak in September 2015. This peak is

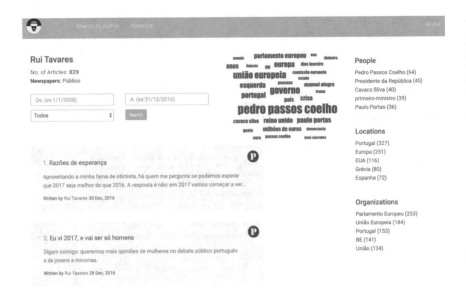

Fig. 3 Term frequency analysis generated for the columnist of the Público newspaper, Rui Tavares

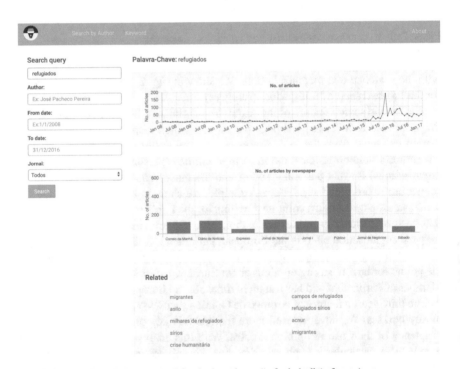

Fig. 4 Statistical analysis generated for the key phrase "refugiados" (refugees)

very likely to be related to the death of Alan Kurdi, a 3-year-old Syrian boy who drowned on 2 September 2015 in the Mediterranean Sea in the course of the Syrian refugee crisis.[7] We can also see that authors from the newspaper Público wrote more than 500 opinion articles with the key phrase "refugiados". The relatedness of other key phrases is shown as similarity measured by the cosine distance between each key phrase word vector (Mikolov et al. 2013a, b). The word vector of a word, also known as word embedding, is a numerical representation of that word. In this representation, words with similar vectors, that is, close distance vectors, have similar semantic meaning. There are several techniques for calculating each word embedding, but one of the most used is Word2vec (Mikolov et al. 2013a, b). It uses a neural network (NN) setup to predict the surrounding context given a particular word.[8] After training the NN with many text examples, each embedding is extracted from the NN internal configuration (the embedding layer) for each word. Since we were interested in the embedding of a full key phrase, we processed all opinion articles and replaced the key phrases found with a single token (e.g. "segurança social" was replaced with "segurança_social"). We then used the gensim Word2Vec module (Řehůřek and Sojka 2010) with the processed opinion articles to extract each key phrase embedding vector. For each key phrase search, we show the related key phrases. In the example shown in Fig. 4, we conclude that the word "refugiados" (refugees) is often associated with the word "migrantes" (migrants). This is probably related to the topic of the Syrian refugee crisis, written about multiple times, and which relates the word "refugees" with "migration", instead of the previous typical relation of the words "refugees" and "war".

5 Conclusions and Future Work

Political commentators play a prominent role in public debate. They have a position of influence and are simultaneously an indicator of public opinion. For this reason, it becomes necessary to create a historical memory of their commentaries. This type of memory is an excellent contribution to a more democratic and transparent debate of ideas. Arquivo de Opinião attempts to fill this gap, by bringing together in a single digital archive the written opinion published by the main online Portuguese newspapers.

Arquivo de Opinião is an online tool that enables the exploration of a fixed corpus of past opinion articles published online between 2008 and 2016. It was built by collecting data from the newspapers' websites and from the web archive Arquivo.pt., which demonstrates how web archives can contribute to the development of innovative projects such as Arquivo de Opinião.

---

[7]https://arquivo.pt/wayback/20150902181001/http://www.publico.pt/mundo/noticia/esta-e-a-fotografia-do-naufragio-da-humanidade-1706669

[8]The other way around is also another possible technique (CBOW).

We are currently working on the next version of Arquivo de Opinião, which will include the period from 2016 to the present and extend the list of news media sources. We will automatically collect all opinion articles at the moment of publication and process the articles through the NLP pipeline described above. This data collection workflow could enable the creation of real-time monitoring tools to detect debate trends and frequently used entities. Users will have access to information about current published opinion articles and be able to select particular key phrases or authors' names for personal notifications.

Online discussions are an important component of public debate. Many of the authors present in Arquivo de Opinião have public online social media accounts, for example, tweets and posts on Twitter and Facebook, respectively. These political publications can enrich a digital archive such as Arquivo de Opinião. For this reason, the next version of Arquivo de Opinião will also include a section dedicated to social media. It will monitor tweets and measure the degree of interaction with them, for example, retweets and likes.

References

Barreto F, Branco A, Ferreira E, Mendes A, Nascimento MF, Nunes F, Silva J (2006) Open resources and tools for the shallow processing of Portuguese: the tagshare project. In: Proceedings of LREC 2006

Finkel JR, Grenager T, Manning C (2005) Incorporating non-local information into information extraction systems by Gibbs sampling. In: Proceedings of the 43rd annual meeting on Association for Computational Linguistics. Association for Computational Linguistics, pp 363–370

Fonseca ER, Rosa JLG (2013a) Mac-morpho revisited: towards robust part-of-speech tagging. In: Proceedings of the 9th Brazilian symposium in information and human language technology

Fonseca ER, Rosa JLG (2013b) A two-step convolutional neural network approach for semantic role labeling. In: The 2013 international joint conference on neural networks (IJCNN). IEEE, San Diego, pp 1–7

Jacobs RN, Townsley E (2011) The space of opinion: media intellectuals and the public sphere. Oxford University Press, Oxford

McNair B (2017) An introduction to political communication. Routledge, New York

Mikolov T, Chen K, Corrado G, Dean J (2013a) Efficient estimation of word representations in vector space. arXiv preprint arXiv:13013781

Mikolov T, Sutskever I, Chen K, Corrado GS, Dean J (2013b) Distributed representations of words and phrases and their compositionality. In: Advances in neural information processing systems, pp 3111–3119

Nimmo DD, Combs JE (1992) The political pundits. Greenwood Publishing Group, Connecticut

Řehůrek R, Sojka P (2010) Software framework for topic modelling with large corpora. In: Proceedings of the LREC 2010 workshop on new challenges for NLP frameworks, ELRA, Valletta, Malta, pp 45–50, http://is.muni.cz/publication/884893/en

Won M, Martins B, Raimundo F (2019) Automatic extraction of relevant keyphrases for the study of issue competition. Tech. rep., EasyChair

Oldweb.today: Browsing the Past Web with Browsers from the Past

Dragan Espenschied and Ilya Kreymer

Abstract Webpages have long stopped being just static "documents". Since the introduction of inline graphics and JavaScript, they have moved towards becoming executable code dependent on specific browsers and feature sets. On the basis of examples from the history of net art and the legacy browser service oldweb.today, this chapter presents the value of preserving browser software along with web archives.

1 The Longevity of Web Archives

Webpages have long stopped being just static "documents". Since the introduction of JavaScript with Netscape version 2 in 1995, webpages have increasingly developed towards becoming executable code that is dependent on the right software environment—the browser—not only to "render" correctly but to "perform" correctly. Only when combined with the right browser from the past will a webpage from the past appear as it used to.

However, so far, the established practice of web archiving is mainly concerned with static resources, such as HTML pages, JPEG images, and so on, which are first captured from the live Web and then stored in a collection to be accessed later.

As for other digital preservation practices, the storage format specifically developed for web archiving, WARC,[1] has been designed to abstract certain complicated

---

[1] WARC is standardised by ISO; the specification can be found on the International Internet Preservation Consortium's GitHub at https://iipc.github.io/warc-specifications/specifications/warc-format/warc-1.1/

D. Espenschied (✉)
Rhizome at the New Museum, New York, USA
e-mail: dragan.espenschied@rhizome.org

I. Kreymer
Lead Developer Webrecorder and oldweb.today, San Francisco, USA

© Springer Nature Switzerland AG 2021
D. Gomes et al. (eds.), *The Past Web*,
https://doi.org/10.1007/978-3-030-63291-5_20

technical and organisational issues to increase a collection's usefulness as far as possible into the future. Microsoft Word documents are often converted to PDF for archival purposes so as not to have to deal with a complicated legacy Office software stack in the future. Similarly, web archiving is not about copying a remote web server, including all of its software such as databases, scripting languages, or any other components that might be involved in producing a live website. The WARC format describes the requests and responses exchanged with web hosts. Essentially, it preserves information at the level of HTTP, the standardised communication protocol that underlies the Web.

When accessing a web archive, a user requests content referenced by URL at a point in time, and a "Wayback Machine" or similar mechanism selects the closest matching resources from a collection's WARC files and sends them to the user's browser. As long as the WARC files are carefully stored and the Wayback Machine[2] works, the archived websites should stay available in perpetuity. However, looking back on more than 25 years of web archiving shows that this is not true. The farther away in the past websites were captured, the higher the likelihood of their looking odd, missing critical elements or behaving differently, even if all resources are still stored in the WARC files. This effect is most obvious with now deprecated browser plug-ins like Flash or discontinued integrations like Microsoft's ActiveX but can also appear in other areas. While this feels like some force of nature is at work and data is "rotting" or "degrading" in the archive, the data is not changing at all—it remains immutable. What is changing is the software on the user's end, since the final stage of assembling and performing an archived webpage is not handled by the Wayback Machine but by the user's browser. Even when considering very recent history, a website captured in 2015 was probably created with Chrome version 42 in mind; in 2020, it might be accessed with Firefox version 72. A lot of things changed in browsers within just 5 years: JavaScript engines were stripped of some functions, autoplay of audio and video was disabled by default, and new options such as blocking social media widgets or adopting "dark mode" became available to users, allowing them to influence how a website looks and behaves. At some point, the sum of changes in browsers over time will inevitably affect how sites captured in the past appear at the time of access. While the above example of two mainstream browsers released 5 years apart already highlights considerable differences, looking at a 2003 website optimised for Internet Explorer 6 in the latest Chrome browser two decades later (see Fig. 1) results in a heavily distorted view: an empty space filled with clouds divides the landscape like a ravine, with a palm tree hovering above. Users have no way of knowing or reasoning that a Java applet[3] is supposed

---

[2]A software system providing archived web resources to users is typically called a "Wayback Machine", after the first of its kind made accessible by the Internet Archive in 2001. In the meantime, additional tools have been created to "replay" web archives, such as the open source fork of the original Wayback Machine, OpenWayback, or new open-source projects like pywb and wabac.js that originated from the Webrecorder project.

[3]Java applets were small, platform-independent programs to be executed in the browser via an embedded Java virtual machine and initially designed for rich interactions beyond the Web's

Fig. 1 Dragan Espenschied, *Bridging The Digital Divide*, 2003, as shown in Google Chrome version 80 on Linux in 2020

to be displayed in this gap. The browser simply ignores the applet without giving any notice in the user interface.

2   Characteristics of Browsers

The history of web browsers is usually told as a story of constant technical progress: in the 1990s, browser back and forward buttons took up half of the typical screen space; they choked on even basic, cranky GIF animations and plastered the screen with popup windows. Thanks to today's browsers we no longer need to download software, instead we can use smooth web applications, stream video, and communicate at lightning speed.[4]

However, the reality is more complex: from a software preservation perspective, not all changes in browser software have made each version "better" than the

---

original idea of interlinked documents. Browsers stopped supporting the plugins required for Java applets to run due to concerns about frequent crashes, slow performance, security problems, legal issues, and the availability of better-performing alternatives like Flash and JavaScript.

[4]The blog posts about the releases of new versions for Google Chrome or Microsoft Edge provide plenty of examples; see https://blog.google/products/chrome/ and https://blogs.windows.com/msedgedev/

previous one—just different. Central elements of a legacy site might be dependent on the capability that legacy browsers used to offer and which were later removed for a variety of reasons. Even if this was done with the best of intentions, archived websites will not be able to perform actions such as spawning a new window with a QuickTime movie playing and therefore might not make much sense at all anymore.

A classic example is the deprecation of the Flash plugin. Even in 2015, Adobe boasted that "More than 500 million devices are addressable today with Flash technology".[5] In 2020, Flash is just a faint memory. Websites based on the plugin display error messages or warnings (see Fig. 2).

Even features that are not usually considered in relation to the "rendering" of content can affect how it is perceived. Many web authors used to put meaningful messages in their pages' source (see Fig. 3), and the "View Source" function introduced with Tim Berners-Lee's first browser used to be heralded as one of the key factors for spreading knowledge about how to create webpages among users.[6] With powerful "developer tools" being offered in today's browsers, their ability just to show the basic HTML source code of a webpage is not getting as much attention from vendors as it used to. Functions for viewing source code are removed from menus or may even display garbled characters.

Ideally, archived websites should be accessed via a software environment that is contemporaneous with their creation. The project oldweb.today with its remote browser framework is offering exactly that.

3 Oldweb.today

On the website https://oldweb.today users can browse the past Web using browsers from the past, instantly and without any previous configuration necessary. The site is hosted by the digital art and culture non-profit Rhizome in New York and was started as an interim experimental software development project by Ilya Kreymer just before he joined Rhizome as an official employee. Rhizome's preservation director Dragan Espenschied designed the site's user interface and the online promotional campaign.

To get going, users have to pick a browser from a list (Fig. 4), provide a URL, and select a point in time (Fig. 5), before hitting the button "Surf the old web!" Users who do not have a clear interest here and just want to enter the past Web quickly can hit the button "I'm feeling random!" to be transported to a curated setting pulled from a list.

---

[5]See Adobe, Statistics, captured on 31 July 2015, https://arquivo.pt/wayback/20150408120146/http://www.adobe.com/products/flashruntimes/statistics.html

[6]One of many possible quotes: "The 'View Source' menu item migrated from Tim Berners-Lee's original browser, to Mosaic, and then on to Netscape navigator and even Microsoft's Internet Explorer. Though no one thinks of HTML as an open-source technology, its openness was absolutely key to the explosive spread of the web". (O'Reilly, 2005)

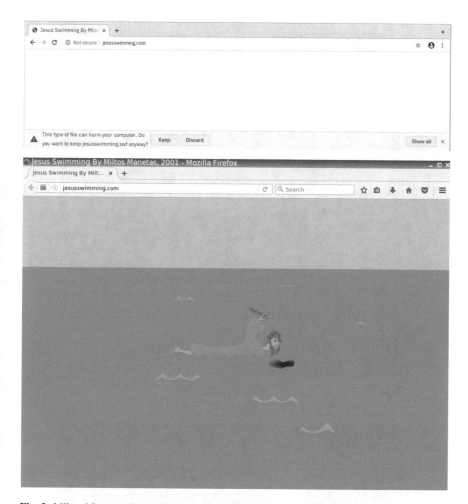

Fig. 2 Miltos Manetas, Jesusswimming.com, 2001, prompts Google Chrome version 80 (top) to display a warning in the user interface. In Mozilla Firefox version 49 with Adobe Flash plugin enabled (bottom) the work is displayed correctly. (Via oldweb.today.)

On the following screen (Fig. 6), oldweb.today establishes a video connection to a "remote browser", a carefully prepared, fully interactive software environment running the selected browser on a cloud computer. That remote browser is tied to a web archive aggregator that locates and pulls the requested materials from publicly available web archives, like the Portuguese web-archive (Arquivo.pt), the UK Web Archive, Rhizome's own web archive, and of course the Internet Archive. Information on all currently connected web archives is listed on the oldweb.today

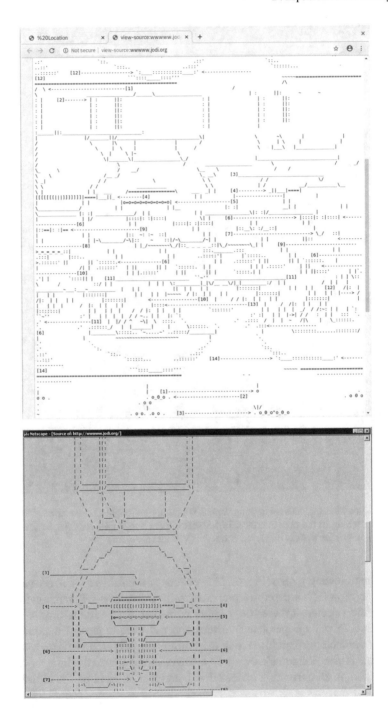

Fig. 3 Source view of JODI, %20Location, 1995, in Google Chrome version 80 (top) shows seemingly random characters. In Netscape Navigator Gold 3.04 for Windows (bottom), the source view of the same piece shows the schematics of an atomic bomb as ASCII graphics. (Via oldweb.today.)

Fig. 4 The expanded browser selector available at oldweb.today

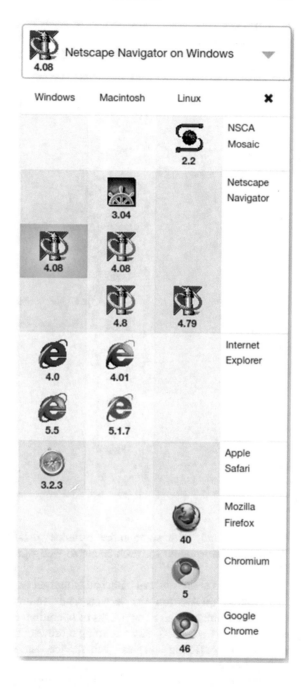

Fig. 5 The date picker on oldweb.today shows a graph of how many mementos of the requested URL are available across all connected public web archives

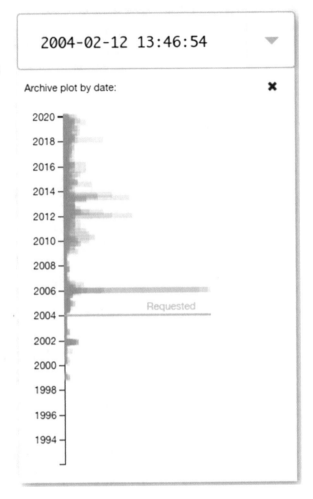

home page, and, with some more technical details, in a GitHub repository.[7] Provenance information for each accessed webpage is displayed on the side (see Fig. 7).

The oldweb.today site was launched with a set of 13 browsers, on 30 November 2015, running on Amazon Web Services, and "went viral" shortly afterwards, seeing over one million users in a few weeks of operation. For every user, a separate copy of a browser is launched. Since running a browser is much more computationally intensive than offering a typical web service, and cloud resources are billed by reserved computing capacity, oldweb.today features a time limit per session and a waiting queue to control the amount of concurrent usage and therefore cost.

---

[7] See https://github.com/webrecorder/public-web-archives

Fig. 6 Oldweb.today providing access to a legacy GeoCities website in Netscape 4.8 for Apple Macintosh

Rhizome promoted the free service with Jan Robert Leegte's net art piece *untitled[scrollbars]*,[8] a webpage created in 2000 that mainly consists of default scrollbars, consciously creating a drastically different look depending on the browser with which it is accessed (see Fig. 8).

In addition to oldweb.today's novelty and accuracy in reproducing what might too easily be dismissed as retro aesthetics, it offers significant digital preservation use cases. For example, the first US website published by Stanford University used the image format X-Bitmap, which was only supported in the Mosaic browser. Other browsers could render the HTML, but not this particular image (See Fig. 9).

Using a framework like oldweb.today effectively makes file format migration work redundant: legacy file formats like images and videos do not have to be transcoded to more current formats, and no intervention has to happen with the materials stored in web archives just so they can stay accessible. Instead, work can focus on a small number of browsers to remain available as running software.

---

[8]In 2010, the artist retitled the piece as *Scrollbar Composition*, http://www.scrollbarcomposition. com/. Discussed here is the version as found in Rhizome's collection.

Fig. 7 Detail of the oldweb.today interface showing some provenance information for different resources and web archives being used to assemble the currently visible page

4 Technical Excourse: Oldweb.today and Remote Browsers

It is possible to keep legacy software available for use in an archival setting (Suchodoletz et al. 2013). This can be confirmed by everyone who ever played a video game for a legacy system like the Nintendo Gameboy on their laptop using an emulator. Emulating early console games is comparatively simple, as the systems themselves had very few moving parts: the hardware of consoles did not change significantly during their time on the market, and the games were delivered on standard media like cartridges and CDs that only needed to be placed into the device to start a game. Console emulators mirror this architecture: a piece of software, the emulator, mimics the console device; an "image file" contains all the data that would be present on a game medium. Browsers are much more complex: they need an operating system that supports window management, Internet connectivity, font rendering, media playback, and much more. Running a legacy browser requires more than just storing an installer file for the software; instead, a complete software environment is needed. Such an environment usually requires expert knowledge to set up, using a general emulator or virtualisation tool.

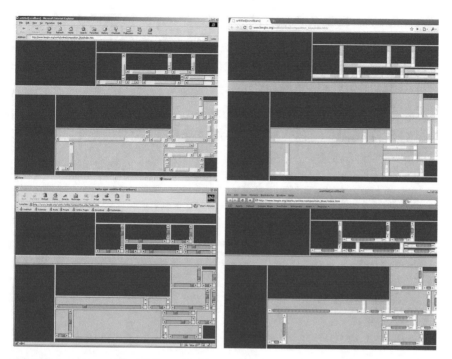

Fig. 8 Jan Robert Leegte, *untitled[scrollbars]*, 2000, accessed via Microsoft Internet Explorer version 4.0 for Windows (top left), Google Chrome version 5 for Linux (top right), Netscape Navigator 4.8 for MacOS 7.5 (bottom left), and Apple Safari version 3.2.3 for Windows (bottom right)

Oldweb.today packages these software environments in such a way that combining a web archive with a suitable browser is as easy as plugging a virtual game cartridge into a Gameboy emulator. This is in general possible because of two foundational features of the Web that have not changed very much: the HTTP protocol and connecting to the Web via a "proxy". Regarding HTTP, even major updates such as encrypted HTTPS or speed-optimised HTTP/2 are just new wrappers around the same data being transmitted. Proxy server settings supported since the first browsers were released are still in use today. Within institutional settings, in particular, it remains common that the browser connects to the outside Internet via an intermediary computer. Hence, a web archival system that allows connection via proxy and can talk in HTTP will be able to serve almost any browser, past, present, and future.

Oldweb.today browsers themselves are running inside Linux containers. Containers are isolated configurations that allow very specific versions of software to be executed on a Linux operating system without clashing with other software that

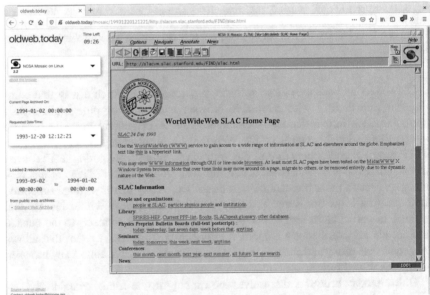

Fig. 9 The 1994 SLAC home page accessed via the Stanford Web Archive's Wayback Machine, with the logo image missing (top). The same resource accessed via oldweb.today using an appropriate contemporaneous browser, Mosaic 2.2, correctly rendering the logo image (bottom)

might need a very different configuration to perform.[9] There are many frameworks freely available to handle containers. Oldweb.today uses Docker because it has been designed to efficiently package, distribute, and run preconfigured software environments and provides sophisticated networking features to connect these environments on demand—and because Docker is extremely popular among web developers and supported by major IT companies such as Google, Amazon, and IBM.

Several historic browsers such as Mosaic and Netscape are able to run directly in Linux containers because Linux versions of them were released in the 1990s. Supporting the much more widely used Windows and MacOS browsers required an extra step to be containerised. Old Macintosh browsers were installed in Linux versions of Basilisk II and SheepShaver,[10] the two free emulators most popular among classic Macintosh enthusiasts. Both of them can run MacOS version 7.5.3, which had been distributed by Apple free of charge, and subsequently provide versions of Netscape and Internet Explorer. A control panel to change the appearance of the operating system's default widgets was used to simulate the look of the later MacOS 8 where appropriate.

For Windows browsers, oldweb.today made use of WINE, an open-source software layer that imitates functions of the Windows operating system on Linux. WINE[11] is very popular among Linux users because it allows them to play Windows games or to use commercially released programs like Photoshop without having to purchase a Windows licence—but it can also run browsers. In the case of oldweb.today, the browsers deployed are several versions of Netscape and Internet Explorer and the Windows version that Apple released of their browser Safari, featuring the famous "brushed metal" design.

The browsers were chosen based on their public availability in archives (such as from the Evolt Browser Archive),[12] their historical significance, and their ability to replay legacy formats in a container setting. A few configurations took quite some effort to figure out, but since they are now packaged and released on the public Docker registry in one container per browser, this process will not have to be repeated. The whole stack is based on either open-source or free-of-charge software. If it can run on Linux, it can be squeezed into a container.

---

[9]Containers are based on core features of the Linux kernel and are used to set up server components on cloud services, distribute Android applications, run development environments, and much more. Organisations like the Open Container Initiative, https://www.opencontainers.org/, aim to create high-level specifications to increase interoperability between different container frameworks.

[10]Basilisk and SheepShaver are two popular open-source emulators of legacy Apple Macintosh platforms originally created by Christian Bauer. The source code is available on GitHub at https://github.com/cebix/macemu

[11]The WINE project provides a compatibility layer enabling Windows software to run on POSIX systems. See https://www.winehq.org/

[12]See https://browsers.evolt.org/

The web archive aggregator to which these remote browsers connect is based on the project "Memento Reconstruct"[13] which Ilya Kreymer previously implemented with the team at Los Alamos National Laboratory (LANL) (Sompel et al. 2009).

5 Using Remote Browsers to Capture Websites

Oldweb.today specifically focuses on historical browsers, bringing a new quality of access to historical materials in public web archives. Web archives of sites created today will soon become historical as well and face similar challenges of being optimised for outdated browsers. How can what we have learned from oldweb.today be fully integrated into common web archiving practice?

Oldweb.today is stewarded by the same team at Rhizome as the integrated web archiving platform Webrecorder.io,[14] which allows users to create a free account and capture web resources interactively by just browsing sites. Oldweb.today and Webrecorder.io are built using the same set of open-source software components; hence, it makes sense to offer users of Webrecorder.io remote browsers for capturing and accessing their own collections. Initially, Webrecorder.io only supported capture and access via whatever browser the user happens to visit the web service with. However, we noticed quickly that, for example, certain websites captured today using Chrome would already not be accessible in another browser such as Firefox. Websites operated by Google, in particular, might use experimental Chrome features like certain image formats, compression algorithms, or JavaScript extensions. On access, a browser other than Chrome would request other data, which would not be part of the collection. And, of course, there are also still plenty of websites on the live Web which are at risk of being abandoned and in need of saving precisely because they use plugins declared obsolete, mainly Flash and Java applets.

Under this premise, in October 2016, the remote browser framework powering oldweb.today was made into a separate component that could be integrated into the Webrecorder.io stack. Contemporary versions of Chrome and Firefox were preconfigured with Flash—and in the case of Firefox, with a Java 6 VM—and offered to users when starting a capture session. That session would be marked as being created with that browser, and, on access, the same configuration would be launched again (Fig. 10).

For example, this integration allows a user running Safari on their native machine to launch a version of Chrome to interactively capture in Webrecorder.io a particular site that contains Flash. Later, when another user running Firefox on their machine

---

[13] See https://github.com/ikreymer/memento-reconstruct

[14] Editor's note: At the time of publication, the web service Webrecorder.io had been renamed to *Conifer* and moved to https://conifer.rhizome.org. A new entity stewarding the software components was created as Webrecorder at https://webrecorder.net. The whole process is explained in a blog post at https://rhizome.org/editorial/2020/jun/11/introducing-conifer/

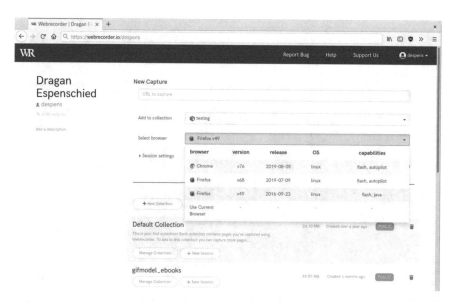

Fig. 10 Before starting a capture session in Webrecorder.io, users can pick from a list of browsers with their special capabilities listed. To not overwhelm users, a small selection is presented for capture: current versions of Chrome and Firefox as well as browsers prepared with plugins. For access, any browser that was used for capture will stay available

accesses the collection, the same version of Chrome will launch remotely and run Flash. This works regardless of what the "local" browser might be (Fig. 11).

6   Looking Back and Looking Ahead

Using a browser released in 1996 cannot bring back resources that were not archived in 1996 but can make accessible resources available from that time in a much more authentic way (Espenschied et al. 2013). It has become more viable to use real browsers to capture content from the live Web for archiving using for instance Browsertrix.[15] As a result, it is hoped that web archives created today will appear more complete when accessed a decade from now, than web archives that have been built using custom crawlers that could never imitate all the features of a full-on browser.

The collecting, storing, and running of browsers will become easier in the future: as browser vendors use tightly structured and standardised release and installation processes, and Linux has become a common target platform, new browser versions could be "containerised" on the day they are released. It might be possible to execute

---

[15]https://github.com/webrecorder/browsertrix

Fig. 11 A copy Dragan Espenschied, Bridging The Digital Divide, 2003, captured and accessed with remote browser Mozilla Firefox version 49 on Linux including the Java plugin, integrated into Webrecorder.io

browsers that are old enough not to require much computing power via emulators delivered in JavaScript, running on a user's local computer rather than in the cloud— a browser itself being the host for one its ancestors, with the possibility of reducing the costs of bandwidth usage and computing. It is likely, however, that a powerful cloud computer would be required to run more recent browsers, making the remote browser concept pretty universal.

Over the past 5 years, remote browsers have demonstrated the possibility and benefits of accessing web archives in an alternative context: through stabilised, emulated browser environments contemporaneous with the archived web content, instead of the traditional "Wayback Machine" style replay. As the Web ages, and once common software like Flash becomes obsolete, running older browser software in emulators may be the only way to correctly view and interact with the old Web.

Preserving browser software is thus as important as preserving the Web itself to ensure future access. The still largely separate discipline of software preservation has to become an integral part of web archiving; not only because historic browsers need to remain available for sentimental purposes but also because the Web itself is transmitting software, not static documents.

References

Espenschied D, Rechert K, von Suchodoletz D, Valizada I, Russler N (2013) Large-scale curation and presentation of CD-ROM Art

O'Reilly T (2005) The open source paradigm shift. In: Wynants M, Cornelis J (eds) How open is the future? Vubpress, Bruxelles, p 102

Sompel H, Nelson M, Sanderson R, Balakireva L, Ainsworth S, Shankar H (2009) Memento: time travel for the web

Suchodoletz Dv, Rechert K, Valizada I, Strauch A (2013) Emulation as an alternative preservation strategy – use-cases, tools and lessons learned. In: Horbach, M. (Hrsg.), INFORMATIK 2013 – Informatik angepasst an Mensch, Organisation und Umwelt. Gesellschaft für Informatik e.V., Bonn (S. 592–606)

Big Data Science Over the Past Web

Miguel Costa and Julien Masanès

Abstract Web archives preserve unique and historically valuable information. They hold a record of past events and memories published by all kinds of people, such as journalists, politicians and ordinary people who have shared their testimony and opinion on multiple subjects. As a result, researchers such as historians and sociologists have used web archives as a source of information to understand the recent past since the early days of the World Wide Web.

The typical way to extract knowledge from a web archive is by using its search functionalities to find and analyse historical content. This can be a slow and superficial process when analysing complex topics, due to the huge amount of data that web archives have been preserving over time. Big data science tools can cope with this order of magnitude, enabling researchers to automatically extract meaningful knowledge from the archived data. This knowledge helps not only to explain the past but also to predict the future through the computational modelling of events and behaviours. Currently, there is an immense landscape of big data tools, machine learning frameworks and deep learning algorithms that significantly increase the scalability and performance of several computational tasks, especially over text, image and audio. Web archives have been taking advantage of this panoply of technologies to provide their users with more powerful tools to explore and exploit historical data. This chapter presents several examples of these tools and gives an overview of their application to support longitudinal studies over web archive collections.

M. Costa (✉)
Vodafone, Lisbon, Portugal
e-mail: miguel.costa2@vodafone.com

J. Masanès
Hanzo Archives, Leeds, UK
e-mail: julien.masanes@acm.org

© Springer Nature Switzerland AG 2021
D. Gomes et al. (eds.), *The Past Web*,
https://doi.org/10.1007/978-3-030-63291-5_21

1 Introduction

Web archives are an extremely valuable source of information to understand the past and leverage knowledge from it. Taken as a whole, they provide a comprehensive picture of our social, cultural, commercial and scientific history. With growing awareness of the importance of web archives, scholars and researchers have been using them to conduct longitudinal studies in different disciplines, such as history, sociology, politics, linguistics, economics, journalism, marketing and computer science (Brügger and Milligan 2018; Dougherty and Meyer 2014; Franklin 2004; Gomes and Costa 2014; Kluver 2007; Starbird and Palen 2012). Despite the obvious potential of web archives, their scholarly and scientific exploration is full of obstacles that hamper their wider use, such as the huge size, fast growth, large heterogeneity and broad scope of the preserved data collections.

The typical way to find information and extract knowledge from a web archive is by using its search functionalities, especially full-text and URL search through graphical user interfaces (GUIs) that also enable viewing and browsing within archived versions of web documents. These functionalities support the main information needs of generic users, such as finding a webpage or collecting information about a topic written in the past (Costa and Silva 2010). They aim to reach the widest range of users and make the content of web archives easily accessible to everyone. Still, these functionalities can hardly fulfil more complex information needs, such as those of researchers who need to understand contexts, relations between actors, the evolution of events or hidden patterns within these aspects. On top of that, the huge amount of data preserved by web archives makes search a slow and superficial process. Users are forced to follow a trial-and-error strategy that requires considerable cognitive effort and decision-making. They interactively submit queries, broadening or narrowing their scope as necessary, and engage in multiple research streams in parallel. In the end, users only analyse a very small subset of the immense amount of content available within a web archive. In the case of researchers, they may also need to track the queries and methodology used to build the corpus of study, which is then published along with the results.

Search engines in general are not good at supporting complex exploration tasks that go beyond expressing information needs with keyword queries (Marchionini 2006; White and Roth 2009). Sometimes users do not even know how to express their information needs with keyword queries, especially when trying to answer open-ended questions within an unfamiliar domain. The very idea of relevance ranking for search results is questionable. Researchers may be unduly influenced by the system if they do not understand the ranking criteria of relevance or which results are filtered (e.g. webpages from the same website domain to promote diversity). Sometimes it is preferable to have a suboptimal ranking algorithm that is understandable, such as ordering search results by date, so that researchers can interpret the results and follow their traditional methodologies. Furthermore, web pages should not be analysed individually without taking into account the topical and temporal contexts provided by their data sources and related pages. Analysing a single webpage independently from its interlinked context is similar to analysing a single sentence without considering the book to which it belongs.

Overall, tools to support knowledge development are lacking when users undertake complex research tasks. The web archiving community still cannot meet the requirements of these advanced users, who in turn find it hard to articulate in advance what they need. Breaking this vicious circle requires creating prototypes and iteratively improving them with tests and studies involving real users committed to solving specific problems. This chapter presents some of the prototypes that have been developed and gives examples of longitudinal studies that they have supported. These examples show the potential uses of web archives and how they can turn into an even more valuable source of information with the help of big data science, which we briefly define as data science[1] applied to big data.[2]

Currently, big data science is a very hot topic in the scientific, industrial and business worlds, mainly because of the results achieved by deep learning algorithms running in extremely fast processors and fed by huge amounts of data. Deep learning continues to break records in most machine learning benchmarks (e.g. in natural language processing and computer vision) and even outperforms humans in some narrow tasks, such as object recognition and video game playing (Goodfellow et al. 2016). These advances are present in breakthrough technologies that help us in our daily life, such as web search engines, recommendation systems and virtual assistants. In the future, these advances will also have a great impact in relevant areas, such as in healthcare (e.g. cancer detection), autonomous driving and real-time language translation. The web archiving community is starting to take advantage of these advances to improve their technology and provide more powerful tools for their users.

The remainder of this chapter is organised as follows. Section 2 presents the big data science frameworks that supported the longitudinal studies described in Sect. 3. These two sections provide an overview of the state of the art of big data science in terms of technology and research conducted over web archives. Section 4 presents GUIs designed to facilitate the exploration and analysis of historical data, as a showcase of the functionalities and data visualisations developed for web archives. Section 5 presents the main conclusions.

2 Frameworks for Big Data Science

Big data is a term used to describe datasets that are so large or complex that traditional systems (e.g. traditional relational SQL databases) are inadequate to deal with them (Chen et al. 2014). Current usage of the term big data also tends to refer to a vast technology landscape developed to handle these datasets efficiently

---

[1]https://en.wikipedia.org/wiki/Data_science.

[2]https://en.wikipedia.org/wiki/Big_data.

throughout the different processing phases (e.g. storage, querying and visualisation). Big data can be characterised by several properties, especially the three Vs: volume, velocity and variety. Volume refers to the amount of data that needs to be processed. Velocity refers to the speed at which the data is generated and processed. Variety refers to the heterogeneity of data, either created by humans or by machines in a structured or an unstructured format. Datasets can be considered as big data if traditional applications cannot process the huge volume of data, with a high variety of sources and formats, in a timely manner, sometimes in real time to maximise their value. Other Vs are also sometimes used to define big data, such as value and veracity.

Big data approaches were initially developed mostly to deal with the fast-growing number of webpages and the specific challenges that their unstructured form posed to traditional data-processing approaches (Chang et al. 2008; Dean and Ghemawat 2004; Ghemawat et al. 2003). Big data approaches are therefore a natural fit for web archives. There has been an increasing number of web archives worldwide, followed by a rapidly increasing volume of preserved data (Costa et al. 2016). Web archives gather all types of digital information, such as image, video, audio and text, from millions of web servers and applications worldwide. This information must be rapidly collected and processed before it vanishes, as it can change up to several times a day (e.g. newspaper websites). Handling the huge heterogeneity of data types, formats and source systems in a timely manner has been a major challenge for the web archiving community.

Data science, also known as data-driven science, is an interdisciplinary field that draws knowledge from other fields like mathematics, statistics, computer science and information science. The methods derived from their theories, techniques, algorithms and computer systems are applied to extract value from data in various forms. Data science helps, for instance, to discover hidden knowledge, obtain predictive and actionable insights, create services that impact people's lives, communicate relevant business stories or build confidence in decisions. Data science, therefore complements big data technology in order to derive value from web archive collections. Notice that big data and data science may have different interpretations and definitions, since they are abstract concepts and sometimes used as marketing buzzwords to sell technology.

Big data science is expected to bring significant benefits in the development of technology for extracting knowledge from web archives and supporting their exploration. The first benefit is providing a scalable and fault-tolerant foundation for processing and analysing very large-scale unstructured data. Big data frameworks, such as Hadoop[3] and Spark,[4] which implement the MapReduce programming model (Dean and Ghemawat 2004), have been widely adopted within industry and academia and are the usual choices to efficiently scale out data processing in the order of magnitude of petabytes.

[3]http://hadoop.apache.org.
[4]http://spark.apache.org.

Warcbase[5] is a framework for processing web archive collections using Hadoop and HBase (Lin et al. 2014, 2017). The latter is a distributed non-relational database based on Google's Bigtable (Chang et al. 2008), which provides an efficient way of storing and accessing archived documents, but only after ingesting them. This ingestion duplicates documents, which is a major drawback in storage space and processing time. Use cases for Warcbase include web mining such as computing the PageRank algorithm (Page et al. 1998) after extracting the web graph of hyperlinks and topic modelling such as learning a Latent Dirichlet Allocation model (Blei et al. 2003) on web collections to uncover hidden topics. Both techniques can be used to get the most important documents and topics within a web collection. The Archives Unleashed Toolkit[6] is the successor of Warcbase and provides a software toolkit that runs on Spark without the overhead of HBase. It can be deployed in a cloud-based environment, enabling researchers to run big data analytics on web archives. Using a cloud platform removes the burden of building a computational infrastructure and setting up the environment to run the toolkit.

ArchiveSpark[7] is a platform developed to facilitate efficient data processing and corpus building from data formats held by web archives. This involves the selection, filtering and aggregation of relevant documents to build corpora that can be enhanced with the extraction of new data and metadata. The frameworks described above (Warcbase, Archives Unleashed and ArchiveSpark) require programming code for processing and analysing the content preserved by web archives. As a starting point for that programming, Python notebooks with source code to conduct common analyses on text and link structure between websites are shared (Deschamps et al. 2019). Their usage may not be immediately attainable by non-computer scientists, but these big data science frameworks accelerate the development of complex applications and analytical tasks.

Regardless of the chosen framework, people interested in conducting large-scale analysis over archived data require automatic access to web archive collections. Several web services via application programming interfaces (APIs) have been provided for that purpose, such as the Internet Archive API,[8] the Arquivo.pt API[9] and the Memento Time Travel API.[10] The last of these interoperates with several web archives and systems that support versioning (e.g. Wikipedia). These APIs provide search functionalities for finding and retrieving data and metadata, which are crucial to feed frameworks for big data science and develop novel applications.

---

[5]http://warcbase.org.

[6]http://archivesunleashed.org.

[7]http://github.com/helgeho/ArchiveSpark.

[8]http://archive.org/services/docs/api.

[9]http://github.com/arquivo/pwa-technologies/wiki/APIs.

[10]http://timetravel.mementoweb.org/guide/api.

3   Longitudinal Studies on Web Archives

The first longitudinal studies over the Web as a research object were conducted to measure its dynamics and content (Fetterly et al. 2004; Ntoulas et al. 2004; Gomes 2007) or to analyse the evolution of websites (Chu et al. 2007; Hackett and Parmanto 2005). Since the Web was too large to be exhaustively processed, subsets were selected and studied instead. Handling the growing size of the Web is still a challenge, and hence, subsets continue to be used.

The online news subset has been the target of many studies, because news articles typically have high editorial quality, are usually easy to date and contain rich information about the main stories and events discussed by society. Several studies conducted on news have aimed to explain past events and predict future ones. A good example is the work of Leskovec et al., which tracked short units of information (e.g. phrases) from news as they spread across the Web and evolved over time (Leskovec et al. 2009). This tracking provided a coherent representation of the news cycle, showing the rise and decline of main topics in the media. Another example is the work of Radinsky and Horvitz (2013), who mined news and the Web to predict future events. For instance, they found a relationship between droughts and storms in Angola that catalyses cholera outbreaks. Anticipating these events may have a huge impact on world populations. Woloszyn and Nejdl proposed a semi-supervised learning approach to automatically separate fake from reliable news domains (Woloszyn and Nejdl 2018).

Web archives are an excellent source for analysing how false information arises and flows over the Web and social media (Kumar and Shah 2018). A related line of research focused on the multiple biases (e.g. data bias, algorithmic bias) present in web content and the ways in which these biases may influence our judgement and behaviour (Baeza-Yates 2018). Weber and Napoli outlined an approach for using web archives to examine changes in the news media industry that occurred with the evolution of the Web (Weber and Napoli 2018). They presented examples of analyses, such as named entity recognition (NER) of locations mentioned in the news stories, to measure the spread of local news, and social network analysis (SNA) to understand the flow of news content between newspaper websites.

Web archives support web graph mining studies and their applications. Examples include analysing link-based spam and its evolution to prevent web spammers from unethically boosting the ranking of their pages in search results (Chung et al. 2009; Erdélyi and Benczúr 2011), as well as detecting and tracking the evolution of online communities with similar interests or behavioural patterns (Aggarwal and Subbian 2014; Fortunato 2010). These studies were supported by sequences of web snapshots crawled over time.

A different type of study uses natural language processing (NLP) techniques to extract knowledge bases from textual content, which are then used for querying and exploration. Hoffart et al. built a large knowledge base in which entities, facts and events are anchored in both time and space (Hoffart et al. 2013). Web archives can be a source for extracting this type of knowledge, which will then be used for temporal analysis and inference. For instance, since the veracity of facts is time-dependent, it would be interesting to identify whether and when they become inaccurate. Fafalios et al. created a semantic layer on top of web archives, which describes semantic information about their textual contents (Fafalios et al. 2018). Entities, events and concepts were automatically extracted from text and may be enhanced with other information from external knowledge bases. There are many knowledge bases with semantic information that can be connected for this purpose, as shown in the Linked Data website.[11] The semantic information generated is compiled in a structured form (RDF format), which enables very complex queries expressed through the SPARQL language. For instance, just one query is necessary to answer the question "What was the year Obama and Trump most talked about each other?" or "Who were the most discussed politicians in the last decade who are still alive?". All processing runs on Spark[12] using the aforementioned ArchiveSpark framework.

Semantically enriching web archives enables their exploration and exploitation in a more advanced way than using the typical search functionalities. The main drawback is that SPARQL is not user-friendly for non-experts in computer science. Further development of GUIs on top of semantic layers, such as the Sparklis view,[13] is required to enable researchers from several areas of knowledge to easily explore web archives.

4 User Interfaces for Exploratory Search in Web Archives

Novel types of Graphical User Interfaces (GUI) are being researched for data analysis and exploration over time, some of which are supported by the technologies described in the previous sections. GUIs are a good showcase for the technologies and data visualisations developed for web archives.

Besides the search box and metadata filters, two types of GUI components tend to be common: n-gram trend viewers and timelines. Regarding the former, Jackson el al. created a GUI to visualise the frequency of terms occurring in an archived document collection over time, similar to Google's Ngram Viewer (Jackson et al. 2016). Trends can be easily glimpsed and compared. The user can then click on the line graph to see a sample of matching results. There are other examples, such as the n-gram chart offered by the British Library's prototype SHINE service,[14] which depicts the number of pages in the collection matching a submitted word or phrase over time. Comparisons can be made by adding multiple words or phrases, as depicted in Fig. 1, where the terms *big data*, *data science* and *web archiving* are compared.

---

[11] http://linkeddata.org.

[12] http://github.com/helgeho/ArchiveSpark2Triples.

[13] http://www.irisa.fr/LIS/ferre/sparklis.

[14] http://www.webarchive.org.uk/shine.

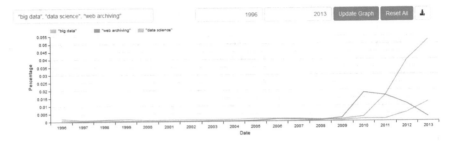

Fig. 1 Trends application provided by the British Library (SHINE prototype) after submitting the "big data", "data science" and "web archiving" queries

Fig. 2 Time Explorer application after searching for "Arab Spring"

A timeline displays a list of events in chronological order as a means of summarising long-term stories. Several techniques are usually used to create these timelines, such as named entity recognition to identify the main actors, locations and temporal expressions, so that events can be temporally and spatially anchored; detection of important temporal intervals to cluster and filter information related to the events and key-phrase extraction or summarisation to annotate the events with the most relevant information. Timelines are usually combined with other functionalities. The Time Explorer, depicted in Fig. 2, combines several components in the same application, designed for analysing how searched topics have evolved over time (Matthews et al. 2010). The core element of the GUI is a timeline, with the main titles extracted from the news, and a frequency graph, with the number of news and entities most frequently associated with a given query (e.g. Arab Spring) displayed over the time axis. The GUI also displays a list of the most representative entities (people and locations) that occur in matching news stories, which can be used to narrow the search. Locations are represented on a world map.

The exploratory search system named Expedition, which is presented in Fig. 3, also provides a GUI with multiple components (Singh et al. 2016). The first is a search box with a suite of ranking models from which the user can choose. They support multiple query intentions, ranging between two dimensions: (1) topical vs.

Fig. 3 Expedition search system: (**A**) search box and ranking model selector, (**B**) search results, (**C**) entity and article type filters, (**D**) timeline where shaded areas represent bursts, (**E**) list of articles saved by the user for corpus creation and (**F**) search trail of user actions

temporal and (2) relevance vs. diversity. Relevance focuses the results on important topics or time periods that match the query, while diversity gives a better overview of results across topics and time periods. The search results can then be filtered by entities and article types and presented in an adaptive layout where the screen real estate of a result is proportional to its rank. A timeline displays the frequency of query matches over time, giving an overview of the important time periods for the query. The time used is a combination of publication dates and temporal references extracted from text. Thus, the time periods with high publication activity or high reference rates are identified. The timeline has shaded areas representing bursts (i.e. a time period with unusual publication of documents), which are labelled to provide the user with more insights. The burst label consists of the headlines of the top three articles published during the burst. The user can interact with the timeline and select a burst to narrow the search to that period. Other types of GUI components were developed to assist with corpus creation. A list of documents saved by the user is displayed, along with a search trail that tracks all the actions of the exploration process.

Other types of GUI exist. For instance, the Zoetrope system enables the exploration of archived data using *lenses* that can be placed on any part of a web page to see all of its previous versions (Adar et al. 2008). These lenses can be filtered by queries and time and combined with other lenses to compare and analyse archived data (e.g. check traffic maps at 6 pm on rainy days). Browser plug-ins that highlight changes between pages, such as the DiffIE Add-on for Internet Explorer, are also of great help for data analysis (Teevan et al. 2009).

Visualisations of large-scale analyses of web archives offer a very succinct summary of research findings. For instance, a mix of graph and text mining was applied to measure the relationship between languages used on the Web.[15] A chord diagram depicts the connectivity between languages used in the webpages by measuring the domains that contain interlanguage links. In the context of the Dutch WebART (Web Archives Retrieval Tools) project, several analyses were conducted that resulted in interesting data visualisations, such as the co-occurrence of query words over time and the geolocation of news origin (Ben-David and Huurdeman 2014; Huurdeman et al. 2013). Other visualisations exist, such as word clouds over time as a way to summarise the content evolution of webpages (Jatowt et al. 2008; Padia et al. 2012).

5 Conclusions

Web archives are a living record of our collective memory, and big data science is essential to fully exploit their potential. Multi-purpose frameworks for scalable data processing and GUIs designed for exploratory search and temporal analysis are presented in this chapter, along with diverse longitudinal studies over historical web data. These topics together provide an overview of the state of the art of big data science in terms of technology and research conducted on web archives. These topics also demonstrate that web archives are gaining popularity among scholars and researchers.

The web archiving community has been developing technologies that help to address innovative research questions that otherwise could not be answered. However, significant efforts are still needed. The lack of specialised tools to support complex exploration tasks over historical data is hampering a wider use of web archives. Big data frameworks can help by scaling out the processing over all data preserved by web archives over time, opening exciting new opportunities beyond those offered by the typical search functionalities. Studies conducted using small web samples can now be conducted over entire web collections to get a more comprehensive and accurate understanding of reality. Data science methodologies, algorithms and platforms extend research possibilities that may lead to novel tools, services and knowledge. Most temporal analyses of web archives continue to focus on text and links of web graphs, but other data types, such as images, will likely be the target of future research thanks to significant advances in deep learning. A straightforward application is the generation of accurate textual descriptions for each object in an image, which can then be used to improve image and full-text search results. Recent breakthroughs in NLP will also likely be adopted by web archive systems in tasks such as language translation, document summarisation and question answering. Big data science is just starting to reshape web archive research and more generally the way we can understand our digital collective memory.

---

[15]https://github.com/norvigaward/2012-naward25.

References

Adar E, Dontcheva M, Fogarty J, Weld DS (2008) Zoetrope: interacting with the ephemeral web. In: Proceedings of the 21st Annual ACM Symposium on User Interface Software and Technology, pp 239–248

Aggarwal C, Subbian K (2014) Evolutionary network analysis: a survey. ACM Comput Surv (CSUR) 47(1):10

Baeza-Yates R (2018) Bias on the web. Commun ACM 61(6):54–61

Ben-David A, Huurdeman H (2014) Web archive search as research: methodological and theoretical implications. Alexandria 25(1–2):93–111

Blei DM, Ng AY, Jordan MI (2003) Latent Dirichlet allocation. J Mach Learn Res 3(Jan):993–1022

Brügger N, Milligan I (2018) The SAGE handbook of web history. SAGE, New York

Chang F, Dean J, Ghemawat S, Hsieh WC, Wallach DA, Burrows M, Chandra T, Fikes A, Gruber RE (2008) Bigtable: a distributed storage system for structured data. ACM Trans Comput Syst (TOCS) 26(2):4

Chen M, Mao S, Liu Y (2014) Big data: a survey. Mob Netw Appl 19(2):171–209

Chu SC, Leung LC, Van Hui Y, Cheung W (2007) Evolution of e-commerce web sites: a conceptual framework and a longitudinal study. Inf Manag 44(2):154–164

Chung Y, Toyoda M, Kitsuregawa M (2009) A study of link farm distribution and evolution using a time series of web snapshots. In: Proceedings of the 5th international workshop on adversarial information retrieval on the web, pp 9–16

Costa M, Silva MJ (2010) Understanding the information needs of web archive users. In: Proceedings of the 10th International Web Archiving Workshop, pp 9–16

Costa M, Gomes D, Silva MJ (2016) The evolution of web archiving. Int J Digit Libr 18, 191–205

Dean J, Ghemawat S (2004) MapReduce: simplified data processing on large clusters. In: Proceedings of the 6th conference on symposium on operating systems design and implementation, vol 6

Deschamps R, Ruest N, Lin J, Fritz S, Milligan I (2019) The archives unleashed notebook: madlibs for jumpstarting scholarly exploration of web archives. In: Proceedings of the 2019 ACM/IEEE joint conference on digital libraries (JCDL), pp 337–338

Dougherty M, Meyer ET (2014) Community, tools, and practices in web archiving: the state-of-the-art in relation to social science and humanities research needs. Assoc Inf Sci Technol 65(11):2195–2209

Erdélyi M, Benczúr AA (2011) Temporal analysis for web spam detection: an overview. In: Proceedings of the 1st international temporal web analytics workshop, pp 17–24

Fafalios P, Holzmann H, Kasturia V, Nejdl W (2018) Building and querying semantic layers for web archives (extended version). Int J Digit Libr 21:149–167

Fetterly D, Manasse M, Najork M, Wiener JL (2004) A large-scale study of the evolution of web pages. Softw Pract Exp 34(2):213–237

Fortunato S (2010) Community detection in graphs. Phys Rep 486(3–5):75–174

Franklin M (2004) Postcolonial politics, the internet, and everyday life: Pacific traversals online. Routledge, London

Ghemawat S, Gobioff H, Leung ST (2003) The Google file system. In: SOSP '03: Proceedings of the nineteenth ACM symposium on operating systems principles, pp 29–43

Gomes D (2007) Web modelling for web warehouse design, University of Lisbon. https://repositorio.ul.pt/bitstream/10451/1589/1/17117_webModellingWebWarehouse.pdf

Gomes D, Costa M (2014) The importance of web archives for humanities. Int J Humanit Arts Comput 8(1):106–123

Goodfellow I, Bengio Y, Courville A (2016) Deep learning. MIT Press, New York. http://www.deeplearningbook.org

Hackett S, Parmanto B (2005) A longitudinal evaluation of accessibility: higher education web sites. Internet Res 15(3):281–294

Hoffart J, Suchanek FM, Berberich K, Weikum G (2013) YAGO2: a spatially and temporally enhanced knowledge base from Wikipedia. Artif Intell 194:28–61

Huurdeman HC, Ben-David A, Sammar T (2013) Sprint methods for web archive research. In: Proceedings of the 5th annual ACM Web Science Conference, pp 182–190

Jackson A, Lin J, Milligan I, Ruest N (2016) Desiderata for exploratory search interfaces to web archives in support of scholarly activities. In: Proceedings 2016 IEEE/ACM joint conference on digital libraries (JCDL), pp 103–106

Jatowt A, Kawai Y, Tanaka K (2008) Visualizing historical content of web pages. In: Proceedings of the 17th international conference on World Wide Web, pp 1221–1222

Kluver R (2007) The Internet and national elections: a comparative study of Web campaigning, vol 2. Taylor & Francis, London

Kumar S, Shah N (2018) False information on web and social media: a survey. arXiv preprint: 180408559

Leskovec J, Backstrom L, Kleinberg J (2009) Meme-tracking and the dynamics of the news cycle. In: Proceedings of the 15th ACM SIGKDD international conference on knowledge discovery and data mining, pp 497–506

Lin J, Gholami M, Rao J (2014) Infrastructure for supporting exploration and discovery in web archives. In: Proceedings of the 23rd international conference on World Wide Web, pp 851–856

Lin J, Milligan I, Wiebe J, Zhou A (2017) Warcbase: scalable analytics infrastructure for exploring web archives. J Comput Cult Herit (JOCCH) 10(4):22

Marchionini G (2006) Exploratory search: from finding to understanding. Commun ACM 49(4):41–46

Matthews M, Tolchinsky P, Blanco R, Atserias J, Mika P, Zaragoza H (2010) Searching through time in the New York Times. In: Proceedings of the 4th workshop on human-computer interaction and information retrieval, pp 41–44

Ntoulas A, Cho J, Olston C (2004) What's new on the web?: the evolution of the web from a search engine perspective. In: Proceedings of the 13th international conference on World Wide Web, pp 1–12

Padia K, AlNoamany Y, Weigle MC (2012) Visualizing digital collections at archive-it. In: Proceedings of the 12th ACM/IEEE-CS joint conference on Digital Libraries, pp 15–18

Page L, Brin S, Motwani R, Winograd T (1998) The PageRank citation ranking: bringing order to the web. Technical report, Stanford Digital Library Technologies Project

Radinsky K, Horvitz E (2013) Mining the web to predict future events. In: Proceedings of the 6th ACM international conference on web search and data mining, pp 255–264

Singh J, Nejdl W, Anand A (2016) Expedition: a time-aware exploratory search system designed for scholars. In: Proceedings of the 39th International ACM SIGIR conference on research and development in information retrieval, pp 1105–1108

Starbird K, Palen L (2012) (How) will the revolution be retweeted?: information diffusion and the 2011 Egyptian uprising. In: Proceedings of the ACM 2012 conference on computer supported cooperative work, pp 7–16

Teevan J, Dumais S, Liebling D, Hughes R (2009) Changing how people view changes on the web. In: Proceedings of the 22nd annual ACM symposium on user interface software and technology, pp 237–246

Weber MS, Napoli PM (2018) Journalism history, web archives, and new methods for understanding the evolution of digital journalism. Digit Journal 6(9):1186–1205

White RW, Roth RA (2009) Exploratory search: beyond the query-response paradigm. Synth Lect Inf Concepts Retr Serv 1(1):1–98

Woloszyn V, Nejdl W (2018) DistrustRank: spotting false news domains. In: Proceedings of the 10th ACM Conference on Web Science, pp 221–228

Part VI
A Look into the Future

The Past Web: A Look into the Future

Julien Masanès, Daniela Major, and Daniel Gomes

Abstract This chapter summarises the book and gives an outlook by highlighting the lessons learned and the resulting dos and don'ts. Authored by Julien Masanès, *Web Archiving* was one of the first books published on the subject of web preservation in 2006. It is time to reflect on the changes that have occurred on the Web and how they have affected the preservation of its content.

1 Evolution of the Web

The Web became the prime medium of access to information in modern societies, and its size and publishing practices have significantly changed, especially due to the widespread use of mobile devices and social networks.

One of the main changes is the regression in the distribution and fragmentation of the Web. During the early days of the Digital Era (1980s–1990s), specific software was required to access information in digital format that was typically not publicly available, or only through a physical carrier (e.g. floppy disk). In the mid-1990s, general-purpose browsers began to be used massively to access an open information space: the Web. In the 2010s, the situation changed quite drastically with the growth of platforms (mainly social media and video platforms) on a more centralised model. A central platform-based Web replaced the navigation-based Web of the 2000s. An increasing amount of information is now exclusively held by social network platforms, where the boundaries between the private and public spheres are blurred.

J. Masanès (✉)
Hanzo Archives, Leeds, UK
e-mail: julienmasanes@acm.org

D. Major
School of Advanced Study, University of London, London, UK

D. Gomes
Fundação para a Ciência e a Tecnologia, Lisbon, Portugal

© Springer Nature Switzerland AG 2021
D. Gomes et al. (eds.), *The Past Web*,
https://doi.org/10.1007/978-3-030-63291-5_22

285

At the same time, social platforms have little concern for long-term preservation, and regulation on the subject is rare, which makes web archiving more challenging.

2 Operation of Web Archives

The first web archive was created in 1996. This timespan of experience has already enabled the development of best practices for operating web archives. The golden rule of web archiving is to perform it on a best-effort basis, according to the resources available and the exploration of the preserved historical data that is required. Preserving the Web is too challenging to aim for perfection. The generation of complementary metadata and documentation contributes to making preserved web content accountable in different usage contexts (e.g. legal proof, institutional heritage, collective memory). The original structure and context of a website should be preserved along with the content. Additionally, the methodology applied to acquire web content must be documented. Archiving the "whole" Web is not attainable, due to resources and time limitations, as well as its de facto infinite generative nature. Thus, web archives must select content to be archived. Broad-scope collections of the Web, such as domain crawls, are important for providing overall views of society's collective memory, and specific-scope collections thoroughly document relevant themes, such as elections or sporting events. These two approaches depend largely on each other: specific collections require broad-scope collections to provide information about the context in which they originated. For instance, a specific collection could target the preservation of the original tweets posted by a controversial politician, while a broad-scope collection would provide complementary information about the overall context in which those tweets originated. Therefore, web archives should engage in creating both broad and thematic collections while defining strong guiding principles for the selection of material to archive, so that preservation policies can be broadly applied.

Another important aspect of web archiving is the variety of media formats which fall within scope and how to preserve them. Preserving audiovisual material collected from the Web is particularly complicated. It is technologically complex and requires significant resources. Still, given the growing importance of videos, web archives must make attempts to archive them. The additional costs of this effort may be reduced by working in a more efficient manner, for instance, by sharing resources and experience, instead of excluding complex data formats from being preserved. It is vital to learn from what has already been done by engaging with practical web archiving. Instead of trying to "reinvent the wheel" all over again, web archivists should build on work that has already been done in order to gain experience and learn how to recognise specific issues.

Modern societies require professionals trained as competent digital preservation specialists. Web archiving is a subcategory of digital preservation, that is, a specialisation of the general skillset required to preserve digital material. In this regard, "web preservation" seems to be a more adequate term than "web archiving" for defining the activities performed by web archives because, by definition, preserving implies maintaining accessibility to the stored content.

Many web archiving initiatives are still subsumed within the scope of traditional data preservation, such as written documents or films. However, classically trained librarians or archivists were not trained to perform web archiving activities. Web archivists need very specific technical skills, especially in web technology and computer science. Web archivists should know about the overall functioning of the Web, such as how the information is transferred between clients and servers, what IP addresses are, and how webpages are constructed or how they change over time. On the other hand, web archivists share the concern of "fighting time" with "traditional" archivists. They must address the question of what time is doing to the preserved artefacts from both a physical and institutional perspective and how to prevent this degradation from happening.

The continuing prevalence of the Web in everyday life turns digital preservation practitioners specialised in web archiving into a "profession of the future". Web archiving requires a specialised set of technical skills, and libraries, traditional archives and web archives must work together to combine their disciplines' methods and specific knowledge in order to preserve web content for future generations.

3   Sustainability of Web Archives

The Web is "self-archiving" to a very small degree. Only a few websites preserve their historical data (e.g. past posts in blogs), and even in these cases, the preservation is partial because their home pages are by definition self-destructive and are not archived. Web archives should be part of Internet infrastructure and adopt adequate models so that they can perform their activities in a sustainable way. However, the organisational models for web archives have not changed much since 2006 and have not proven yet to be greatly successful. One reason for this is that the model applied to preserve digital information has followed traditional methods, which are inadequate because digital artefacts vary radically from non-digital material.

Cultural heritage organisations such as libraries or museums tend mainly to operate within a national scope, which makes sense for historical artefacts supported by physical media, such as books or paintings. These are self-contained objects that can be related to a national context. For web archives, the situation is different because online documents are compound objects spread across a worldwide digital network that does not comply with national geographical borders. For instance, the HTML file of a webpage can be hosted on a website referenced by a national domain (e.g. .fr), while its embedded images, which are crucial for communicating a meaningful message, are hosted on external websites belonging to content delivery networks spread around the world and referenced by general-purpose top-level domains (e.g. .com). Web archive initiatives have usually been embedded in existing national libraries. From a conceptual perspective, web archives are more similar to museums than to libraries, because they preserve unique artefacts when the original server has been updated or turned off. Web archives preserve heterogeneous forms of media, while libraries typically preserve printed documents. On the other hand, web archives share the mission undertaken by traditional libraries because they both preserve artefacts that were publicly available.

We conclude that no pre-existing model of heritage institutions (archives, museums, libraries) can directly accommodate web archiving initiatives. Web archives are a new kind of cultural heritage organisation that must be recognised, with their own identity and responsibilities. They ought to have their own organisational structures, which allow them to develop and apply their own working methods. However, institution-building to preserve new media types takes time. Adopting a transnational organisational model is mandatory to enable effective collaboration between institutions. The Web is worldwide. We need to think globally to be able to preserve it. We need shared transnational infrastructures to support web archiving and enable efficient resource management. The efforts already invested must be efficiently exploited and reused.

It is not the best use of resources to have national teams of web archivists hosted in neighbouring countries struggling independently with universal challenges. Instead, we could have international teams, with members from several countries performing web archiving for larger geopolitical formations, such as international organisations like the European Union or the United Nations. In this model, these teams would select specific information from the content widely available online according to the criteria of the hosting organisation but be technologically supported by shared infrastructures spread across the world. History has shown that the preservation of new media types, such as recorded music or movies, was often initiated by private institutions or individual efforts that independently developed valuable collections and not by the official cultural heritage organisations of the time. With time and increasing penetration of these media in societies, some of these initiatives evolved to become official cultural heritage organisations with their own identity and mission. Thus, at this stage individual efforts are important to widespread web archiving practices.

There are two organisational models for web archives that have proven to be innovative and flexible. One is having non-profit organisations developing collaborative, open-source projects and services to support web archiving. For instance, the Internet Archive developed the open-source Heritrix crawler and operates the Archive-It web archiving cloud service. The other model is hosting a web archive in a governmental institution with a deep understanding of the Internet. Arquivo.pt. is one of the services provided by the Portuguese National Research and Education Network (NREN). NRENs are specialised Internet service providers dedicated to supporting the needs of the research and education communities within a given country. These types of organisations exist all over the world and could collaborate closely with neighbouring countries to physically build cable connections between them while keeping a holistic perspective on the worldwide connected world. Replicating the model of Arquivo.pt. by hosting web archives in NRENs is a promising path to delivering widespread web archiving initiatives efficiently.

Building sustainable business models for web archives has not been straightforward. Profit-oriented organisations have limited scope to act because there is still little awareness about the value of preserving online information and therefore the market is too small to be economically sustainable. Nonetheless, we will discuss four general business models for web archiving. The first model is web archiving on-demand for clients hiring a service to preserve designated information. For instance, a big company such as Coca-Cola hires a web archiving company to preserve its websites, social media and other forms of web presence related to the company. The market for this business model has been very small so far because clients have been limited to a few big companies that became aware of the return on investment from reusing their online outputs or to national libraries that are legally obliged to preserve national heritage in its multiple formats. The second model is intelligence-as-service, to provide results derived from web-archived data for secondary use. However, there is not enough value per unit of data because web data is typically too broad and disorganised to produce results with enough economic value. Marketeers are interested in monitoring trends about price evolution or client feedback on a given product over time. While there is plenty of information online about products, prices and feedback, it is challenging to derive meaningful trends from raw web-archived material. Even so, intelligence-as-service companies with dedicated resources and specialised staff could process large amounts of web-archived content and deliver product trends in a meaningful format for marketeers, such as charts, spreadsheets or structured databases. The third business model is to extract signals from the Web, like the companies that dominate the Internet do (e.g. Google, Amazon or Facebook), and provide some type of "signals-as-service" offering, which may be considered a specific component of intelligence-as-service. Big search engines monitor web data to gather signals that enable the improvement of search results, like incoming links to a particular page, rates of change, levels of text writing and vocabulary, etc. Some data signals require temporal depth. A website focused on a specific subject that has lasted for many years is more likely to be trustworthy than a recently created website that may even be a scam or webspam. Search engines archive web data or at least index it in order to use these ranking features, but preserving web data is not their primary focus. On the other hand, they hold other sources of signals which may offer better value to improve search results, such as traffic logs. In addition, the usage of web-archived content for business models may pose copyright issues as it does not belong to web archives neither to the companies that may wish to make use of web-archived data. It must always be kept in mind that web archives preserve the Web with all of its original issues. The limited number of potential clients and the specificity of their requirements make signals-as-service a challenging business model.

4 The Future of the Past Web

Web archives are a potential source of historical information for temporal big data analytics as they allow for in-depth analysis of past web data. However, web-archived data has been under-explored. Internet giants hold resources to research large web datasets, but most academic institutions do not have access to the same means to gather and process that information. Public infrastructures that provide open access to big web datasets to a wide range of researchers are required. Web archives can contribute to fill this gap between low-value public datasets and privately owned valuable big datasets monopolised by multinational corporations.

Corpora of web data should incorporate temporal perspectives to enable longitudinal analysis and be large enough to express the quality and breadth of the scope of online information. A good example is the SHINE project from the British Library, which allows users to visualise large amounts of data through graphs. However, most existing web datasets are one-shot creations with a limited time scope, such as WebTrec test collections or International Internet Preservation Consortium collaborative collections. Web archives can contribute with web datasets continuously created over time. These represent a unique added-value offer for research. For example, election sites and blogs have more value for research if they have been crawled for several consecutive years. Web archive data can document an interval in space and time and provide unique information about a historical event. Research projects such as BlogForever,[1] Living Knowledge,[2] Living web archives (Liwa),[3] Longitudinal Analytics of Web Archive Data (Lawa),[4] and ARchiving COmmunities MEMories (ARCOMEM)[5] are inspiring examples of research projects that have benefited from web-archive big datasets.

Web archivists generally agree that it is necessary to increase awareness of the importance of web archives within academic and business circles, in order to make the case for the sustainability of their web preservation activities. However, alongside this effort, web archives should invest in lowering barriers to access so that research or commercial results derived from web-archive datasets can be more frequently produced. The first step to achieve this goal is supporting open access to preserved web content. Open-access web content and other forms of media (digital journals and e-books) are in increasing demand from content creators and consumers alike. However, most national web archiving initiatives remain tied to restricted or even closed-access models which diminish the usefulness and visibility of their activities. Web archivists must address the requirements of their audiences when they make decisions about the levels of access to the information that they

[1] http://blogforever.eu/

[2] https://www.livingknowledge.org/

[3] https://arquivo.pt/wayback/20170603224405/http:/www.liwa-project.eu/

[4] https://web.archive.org/web/20140427014650/http://www.arcomem.eu/

[5] https://arquivo.pt/wayback/20170603222054/http://www.lawa-project.eu/

are funded to preserve. Despite the valuable information they contain, web archives remain mostly unexplored due to over-restrictive access politics that close access to information that was born open.

Exploring web archives requires an understanding of the dynamics of the Web and the workflows of a web archive. While most interfaces to web archives are relatively simple, it becomes much harder in open-access archives to enact searches in bulk or to retrieve large amounts of information. One of the reasons web archives are valuable is because of the sheer volume of data. However, there is a gap between those who have the skills to do the gathering and processing, usually computer or data scientists, and those who will use the data for research, such as social scientists or marketeers. It is vital that effective and efficient tools be provided for access, cleaning and processing large amounts of temporal web data to enable wider usage of web archive data.

Both public and private organisations should preserve their own online heritage for business, legal or cultural reasons. However, they tend to be inefficient in keeping their own data. Institutional archiving has a short lifespan, especially when it comes to private companies as they tend to regard their historical data as unprofitable. Ideally, regulations ought to be enacted so that hypertextual documents are preserved in just as serious a manner as printed documents. Until then, the pragmatic short-term solution is to trust in third-party web archiving performed by specialised providers.

5 Final Thoughts

The engagement of new institutions in archiving the Web has been growing. However, their actions are too often limited to discussions on the perimeter of what should be archived. On the other hand, the usage of web archives by researchers has increased, and there are more tools available for doing macro-analysis of temporal web data.

As the Web becomes a tool not only of social communication, but of politics and government, there is an ethical imperative to preserve knowledge for future generations. It is very important to be able to trace the origin of speech and ideas. Obviously, embargo periods need to be taken into account so as to safeguard the privacy of individuals. However, what is published on the Web is part of the public sphere. Web archivists ought to be aware of their ethical duty to archive public content. Indeed, web users in general should be able to archive and access relevant content published on social network platforms (e.g. YouTube, Facebook). Institutions in charge of web preservation should talk to the platform owners to make it easier for everyone to acquire and preserve online public information. Considering that the Web has become the main medium of communication in modern societies, if cultural heritage organisations continue to underestimate the importance of preserving web data, they run the risk of becoming irrelevant. Act now and quickly—the Web is too fragile.

Index

Printed in the United States
by Baker & Taylor Publisher Services